Jackie

ACKNOWLEDGEMENTS

The publishers would like to thank the team at DC Thomson for all their help in compiling this book, particularly Calum Laird and Martin Lindsay.

Endpaper photographs supplied by Rex Features and Corbis (Donny Osmond).

Every effort has been made to acknowledge correctly and contact the source and/or copyright holder of each picture and Sevenoaks Books apologises for any unintentional errors or omissions that will be corrected in future editions of this book.

THIS IS A SEVENOAKS BOOK

First published in Great Britain in 2005 by Sevenoaks
20 Mortimer Street
London W1T 3JW

ISBN-10 1 86200 269 X
ISBN-13 978 1 86200 269 2

Compiled and edited by Lorna Russell
Art Director: Lucy Coley
Design: Barbara Zuñiga
Production: Caroline Alberti

The Best of

Jackie

FOREWORD BY NINA MYSKOW

SEVENOAKS

CONTENTS

Jackie Fashion

Jackie Beauty

On-The-Spot Interviews: Our roving reporters find out what you think

Jackie Teach-Ins

Favourite Features

1
2
3
4

Hello Again

That's how I often started my Ed's Letter each week when I was editor of *Jackie* magazine, a job I held for four years from 1974 to 1978. And I figured that if you're reading this compilation of what was Britain's top-selling teenage magazine, you were probably a *Jackie* reader way back then. So we're just continuing a conversation that started decades ago.

Although I find it hard to believe myself, I worked on *Jackie* for 12 years – I went there straight from St Andrews University in 1966 – so I feel uniquely qualified to guide you through this nostalgic journey back to your adolescence: those years of insecurity, spots, crushes and tears, but also the years when you had carefree fun, your first kiss and loads of laughs. The important years when you were finding out who you were, and where you fitted into the world.

How innocent that all sounds, and how innocent *Jackie* now seems, compared with what's on offer to teenagers today. In *Jackie*'s heyday you were worried about how to kiss: practise on the back of your hand, we advised, as the sadly missed Caron Keating (a faithful *Jackie* reader, I discovered) once reminded me. Now magazines seem to go straight from Barbie dolls to bondage, with no time for that important and precious breathing space between childhood and adulthood.

Jackie was not about sex. It was about romance, but with a healthy does of realism to counter the fantasy. We called it, "A Girl's Best Friend", and that's what we aimed to be. A kind of big sister – without the sibling rivalry! A source of entertainment, pop gossip, solace and fun, a means of acquiring self-esteem; not to mention how to handle the latest hairstyle, wear a maxi-length skirt with panache, and deal, with humour and spirit, with a duff bloke or a best friend who turned out to be your enemy.

Jackie was launched in 1964, and ceased publication in 1993, and the pages shown here, cover the period between 1970 to 1977. Not only are they compulsive reading – once you start, it's hard to stop – they are a unique slice of social history, a fascinating picture of life in those days. As you'll find, pocket money was about £1 a week, our admiration for the royals was unquestioned (the On-The-Spot interviews about the Silver Jubilee, page 140), it was 1975 before women were awarded equal pay, and there were no references at all to single parenthood. It was always Mum and Dad.

On the other hand, the fashion still looks fresh today (we used illustrations rather than photography so that you could really see the clothes), and the quizzes are as addictive as ever. We always made sure it was really hard to cheat and pick the "right" answer. And although the problems on the Cathy and Claire page may seem naïve, in essence the replies are relevant and mostly designed to engender self-respect and independent thinking.

Ah, Cathy and Claire! What a service they provided…we used to get anything up to 400 letters a week, which meant, with a readership ranging from 10 to 16 years old, that there was a complete lack of assistance elsewhere. Knowing what it must take to put pen to paper (no computers) and find a stamp, I reckoned they deserved a fast reply.

Because of the sheer volume of letters I instituted a system of leaflets, covering every possible problem, which could be despatched quickly with a covering letter. However, with such a volume of mail in every department – fashion, beauty and so on – things occasionally went wrong. I got a puzzled letter from a reader which said, "Dear Ed, I wrote to you about my problem bust, which is lopsided. You sent me a knitting pattern for a little woolly hat."

The picture love stories are represented by a Donny Osmond look-alike romance. I can tell you that I still see Donny occasionally, and he's just as gorgeous as ever. Some pop stars have stood the test of time – I'm thrilled to see my interview with Elton John included. And it's quite bizarre to read what Bob Geldof said all those years ago (page 132), way before he married Paula Yates. Incidentally, yes, that is Leslie Ash on page 134. Both she and Bob mis-spelled, I'm ashamed to say!

When *Jackie* ceased publication, many years after I left, I was asked to comment on this national event on TV and radio. As requested I took my four *Jackie* annuals – all I have left – along with me. Never mind the interviews. I had to arm-wrestle them back from every female in her thirties I encountered! They were glued to them, as I hope you will be to this.

Jackie has been a wonderful nostalgic wallow for me, and I hope you enjoy it too. And that it helps you remember the girl you were, and then measure the journey you have been on to become the person you are today. I'm proud to have been part of it, in some small way.

Take care. And have fun – even though we're not around each week to help you!

Love,

The Ed.

YOUR LETTERS PAGE

Sam here. Every letter I print wins a quid, and the best one each week wins TWO.

Want more details?

My address is, Samantha's Page, Jackie, 12 Fetter Lane, Fleet Street, London, E.C.4.

Oh, and please include your three fave features, OK?

All letters must be original.

as conducted by Samantha

I've never been so happy!

Well everyone, my boyfriend has just packed me in. Terrible? 'Course not! In fact marvellous!

Just think, I can get my hair cut and not spend a restless night wondering what his reaction will be. I can buy new shoes, a new dress or coat without saying to myself, "now will he like it?" I can go to a film I want to see for a change.

I don't have to buy as many birthday and Christmas presents and don't have to worry about what my sister's been telling him behind my back and on top of that I'm FREE!

And d' y'know something? I hate the whole idea!

Jackie Fan,
Whitburn, West Lothian.

BED-LAM!

My crazy 19-year-old sis is a nurse. We were on the bus the other day when this dishy conductor comes up and sez, "Hi, there, remember me?"

Sis looked at him then remembered he used to be a patient. At the top of her voice she shouted out, "Oh, you look quite different out of bed."

Did I blush!

Jackie Reader,
Darnall, Sheffield.

NEW LINGO

During a dull English lesson, first thing on Monday morning, a question was put to us. "How would you describe the three witches in Macbeth?" Denise, a girl who has never yet been beaten for phrasing things in unusual ways said,

"Well, they're not quite level, that is, they're a bit off the track, I mean they're a penny short—that is, I mean to say, they weren't quite all there!"

After puzzling this answer out for a few minutes we realised she meant they were slightly demented???!

Sheila Grimshaw,
Manchester, Lancs.

SECOND CHILDHOOD?

The other day, my young sister had a bad nose-bleed, and, Mum being out, Doctor Dad took over.

Not having a clue what to do, we went upstairs to get her Brownie hand-book. Following the instructions, he squeezed the top of her nose, and stood there looking absolutely helpless.

"Why don't you read the next instruction?" I suggested. He read out loud: "Now refer to an adult!"

Lynne Rumney,
Darlington, Co. Durham.

POST HASTE

The other morning just before I trudged off for another boring day at school, ol' spotty-face, the postman arrived and handed me a brown envelope with "ON HER MAJESTY'S SERVICE" printed along the top of it.

"Here y'are ducks, for you. Ah say—wot have you bin up to, now?"

I blinked at him.

"Cor—what *'ave* I done now?" I thought wildly.

Apart from burning mum's rice pudding the other Sunday, or failing my maths test, or not turning up for a date with some creep, I couldn't think what!

Or maybe Prince Charles had finally discovered my hidden beauty and wanted to have dinner with me, or Lord Snowdon had decided that I was the perfect female to photograph! Or maybe . . .

"'Ere—ain't you goin' to open it, ducks?" Spotty-face was still there, wondering what that ever-so-mysterious envelope held.

Quickly I tore open the envelope and out dropped a white envelope, all stamped over with Dutch stamps. I stared, suddenly feeling stupid. It was a letter I had written about two weeks beforehand to join the Cliff Richard fan club, and it had been returned to me because instead of having a 9d stamp on it, I had only stuck a 5d one!

A Manchester United Fan,
Co. Tyrone, Ireland.

SMILER

Have you ever wanted to laugh and couldn't?

I was at the hairdresser's the other week, and while being plastered with Sellotape to keep my hair straight, and getting under the dryer, another customer was having her hair washed.

Suddenly there was a loud shout from one woman, and when everyone turned round she was completely drowned in hair shampoo. The hairdresser had been bumped by someone else and her hand had slipped.

Everyone was laughing but poor little me couldn't, and I was in agony because I could not help smiling and the Sellotape was so stuck to my face that it nearly killed me!

Melanie Lings,
Scunthorpe, Lincolnshire.

PAINED PIN-UPS

I don't suppose you realise what you and your friends are putting us through, by printing all those gorgeous pin-ups. (Not that we don't appreciate them!)

Do you realise that I can't make my bed properly without hitting Leonard Whiting in the face with the bedclothes?

And did you know that I can't draw the curtains without smothering Paul half to death?

And would you believe I have to open the door very slowly unless I want a mad flapping Terence Stamp on my hands?

Leonard Whiting Fan,
New Zealand.

LINE-UP

The other day when I was hanging out the washing, I was looking over my neighbour's garden to see a "Jackie" hanging on the line.

Being nosey I decided to see what it was doing there. The girl next door said that her mother was trying to hide it from her, so that she would tidy up her room before sitting down for an hour reading it, and as her mother was short of hiding-places she decided to put it on the line.

You never know what mothers will think of next do you?

Carolann Duffy,
Glasgow.

Sam's Snippets

If I print a snippet from your letter on my page you'll find a super ceramic ring on its way to you.
Well, what are you waiting for?

I'll challenge you to a game of Russian Roulette or send you my brother's socks . . .

I was busily putting some pan-stick on me knee . . .

And there stood a Clint Eastwood looking Elvis come Engelbert . . .

I reckon I've got a lovelier sister than anyone else ('cept my other brothers and sisters 'cos they've got the same one) . . .

A Redders True Experience . . .

I'm not just writing this to flatter you into sending me a pound, or two or three or four . . .

Last week I felt down in the dumbs . . .

It's not that I'm a vain person, it's just that I like looking at myself . . .

My friend and I were getting ready for a local dance in her bedroom . . .

Have you ever had a 50 m.p.h. bottom slap? . . .

Cover Credits

Photographed at the White Lady Sheiling, Cairngorms. Pink angora dress by Mary Farrin, pink beret and tights by Quant, red welly boots by Russell & Bromley, pink specs by Correna. Ski instructor borrowed from Cairdsport Ski School, Aviemore Centre.

Don't let me catch you with any of those pin heads I've been reading about.

Teenscope

CAPRICORN
(Dec. 22—Jan. 19).
You may easily let small fears and worries dominate your actions but don't get carried away by your imagination. A whole new scene is about to be opened up through a friend but you may have to come out of your shell a bit first. A move to stir up old romances should be squashed.

AQUARIUS
(Jan. 20—Feb. 18).
Most activity seems to be centred round the home this week but this *doesn't* mean no fun. Quite a bit of planning going on and it'll be great as long as you can run the show, but you'll move further and faster if you co-operate with others. Love signs progressing.

PISCES
(Feb. 19—Mar. 20).
Beware of a big build-up of trouble over nothing at all. Try to make your intentions plain at all times and nip any misunderstandings in the bud. Time and energy spent in furthering your career will pay off, and don't be afraid of taking a long-term view here.

ARIES
(Mar. 21—Apr. 19).
Indecision on the part of others mars the week somewhat. A go-it-alone policy will get things moving the way you want. Take the initiative boldly, specially where it affects your social or romantic life. Busy days and you can't win 'em all, but Fri/Sat are definitely yours.

TAURUS
(Apr. 20—May 20).
Could be a long, long week unless you swallow some pride and make friendly noises to you-know-who. Take a fresh look at finances too or the situation could get tricky. Hold a think-in with yourself *then* set about those personal relationships!

GEMINI
(May 21—June 20).
Some good ideas flowing at this time. Treat the week as a springboard for good times later and plan accordingly. An opportunity arises before the weekend to affect the fate of another, but play this carefully. On the whole swinging, with romance better than average.

CANCER
(June 21—July 22).
Your actual love-life could be in for a shaking so concentrate hard and don't rock the boat! One of your pet theories may go for a burton early on and you must be prepared to eat some humble pie ('salright, it's non-fattening!) A good week all-round with a little help on your part.

LEO
(July 23—Aug. 22).
Monday you'll want to join the nearest lonely hearts club but they'll have your resignation come Saturday! A week in which a lot of nice things can happen from the tiniest beginnings so help them along. Fave influences; travel, work. Not so fave; cash, domestic.

VIRGO
(Aug. 23—Sept. 22).
If you can survive some hefty midweek blues all will be well. New friends come more and more into the picture and you may have to increase the pace to keep up. A minor event in your past lovelife takes on a new importance and could lead to renewed interest.

LIBRA
(Sept. 23—Oct. 22).
Indecision is going to get you nowhere fast, so make up your mind and act accordingly. A lot of the recent tension will pass now and you'll see events in a much clearer light. Good time to gear up to a casual lighthearted mood. Stay uncomplicated and choose faces and places to suit.

SCORPIO
(Oct. 23—Nov. 21).
Hey, hey! The girl's in love, though she may not know it yet awhile. Rose-coloured glasses suit you at the moment so wear them triumphantly—it's a good week for lovers. Lesser matters present no problems at all, so you can concentrate on some blissful togetherness!

SAGITTARIUS
(Nov. 22—Dec. 21).
Attempts to influence your actions are more likely to make you dig your heels in and there could be a clash of wills before long. Your heart is unsettled at the moment and a powerful new involvement could begin at the drop of a handbag. A time of some importance futurewise.

Cameo Column

and nobody has seen you go . . .

AT the party, no one would dream what lay behind your gaiety, no one could even suspect your innermost thoughts.

Your dress is beautiful, as indeed you are yourself in it, and your eyes flash, and your lips smile, and your hair swings sideways and then back again.

Enough to break the heart of any boy who saw you.

Any boy?

But there are boys here, too, and somehow there seems to be a distance between you and them.

You're in the scene, and part of the scene, and yet not of it.

How can this be?

When the record stops, there's an interval while someone chooses the next, and you drift across to a corner with two boys and someone gives you some iced squash.

Suddenly the music starts again, and the boys have vanished, and you're alone.

That must be the secret: you're alone.

You're with friends, you know everyone here, so often enough it doesn't show, for most of the time in fact, but just occasionally there's a moment when the truth is revealed, if anyone cares to notice it.

All the boys have their own girls, and none of them has you. All the girls have their own boys, except you: you are the only one alone.

It isn't your fault, particularly. At first, when you were invited, you didn't want to come, but then you thought you couldn't bear, either, just sitting at home alone on New Year's Eve.

So here you are. And you almost think it was a mistake.

But now someone whisks you off in his arms, and again there's the happy smile, the shining eyes, the beautiful swing of your hair.

But all records come to an end, and all dances come to an end, and the clock creeps on, slowly and relentlessly. It's now nearly eleven.

You know well enough what will happen at midnight.

The kisses, between everyone and for everyone, and that'll include you.

But afterwards—everyone will belong to someone, except you.

Will you be able to bear it?

WILL you remember the boy who isn't here, who captured your heart long ago and then dropped it, when he tired of you? Will you remember the kisses and passions of the summer that's so long gone. That golden afternoon of sunlight with him, lying on your back on the grass, that summer, staring up at the drifting sky and clouds, so that you could almost feel the whole world slowly spinning beneath you, and you thought your happiness was unbearable.

And that morning when he came to your home, late coffee and oranges in the garden, sitting together, the quiet talk together of life and love.

And then that bronzed and golden autumn when, in a desolate afternoon, he told you the end had come for both of you.

It wasn't true.

It might have been true for him, it certainly wasn't for you. Not that it made much difference.

Yes, you are remembering, and the dance is over, once more, and you're in a corner of the room, alone, isolated from your friends.

You walk slowly along the wall, out into the hall, collect your coat, and slip quietly out of the front door.

No one has seen you go. No one will notice.

Out into the frosty night.

Closed shops, dark gardens, the deserted square with the statue in the middle.

Walking slowly now along the cold and desolate road, slowly towards the New Year itself, meeting it alone, by yourself, and you wonder if life is really beautiful after all—and if there can be somehow, somewhere, some dream that really doesn't fade and die, and if, one day, to remember this forlorn New Year will not break your heart, as it seems to be doing now.

A Jackie Quiz

WELCOME TO THE SWINGING 70's !

TIME to say goodbye to the 60's and step right into the 70's. How d'you see it? End of something good? Beginning of something greater? Are the 70's going to sort you out—or will you make 'em swing? Try this quiz and find out—you may not like the answers!

1. For making too much noise at that Christmas party you get sent to a desert island. You can only take one thing with you. Which of these couldn't you do without:

a) The disc that holds big memories for you?
b) Make-up?
c) A canoe?
d) A big book to write your memoirs in?

2. In the 70's there'll be more big space achievements for sure. Do you think that space exploration is:

c) Interesting, but it's a shame the moon is so boring-looking?
a) You don't think human beings are meant for space travel?
b) It's a waste of money—but fun to read about those hunky astronauts?
d) It's fascinating. You're longing to know every detail about every planet?

3. Pop world is as dead as old nettles lately—agreed? What would you like to see, popwise, in the 70's?

d) The great groups working harder on good material instead of being content with poor songs?
c) New groups with something really different to offer?
b) You don't agree that pop's in a poor state at the moment?
a) A big come-back for Engelbert, Sandie Shaw, The Searchers?

4. Which of these things would you wish for the boy you love, in the 70's?

a) That he'll find real happiness—even if it isn't with you?
c) That he'll get engaged to you?
d) That he gets what he wants out of life?
b) That he'll make a stack of money so you both have a good time?

5. What do you think's best value for 6d?

d) Jackie?
b) An ice lolly?
c) Saving stamp?
a) A peep through a telescope?

6. Of these things, which do you wish for most?

c) Long life, lots of friends?
b) Short life, loads of laughs?
d) Someone you can really love?
a) Someone who'll really love you?

7. As far as entertainment's concerned do you hope in the 70's for:

a) More really good romantic films on cinema and TV?
b) More discos and clubs for dancing and meeting people?
c) Something new in entertainment—that no-one's ever thought of before?
d) A wider choice of things to do?

8. If there's a spider on your ceiling above the bed just when you're climbing in, do you:

c) Stay up an extra half hour and hope it goes?
d) Leave it there?
b) Swat it down?
a) Scream for help?

9. If you've looked forward fanatically for days or weeks for the Big Event, when it actually comes do you often find:

c) It's not nearly so much fun as you'd hoped?
a) It's fun, but looking back at it seems even better?
d) It's great, as good as you thought?
b) You always try not to look forward to things too much?

10. Which of these do you think is the most important quality for a girl friend to have:

c) Someone who'll give you new ideas, plans?
b) Someone that'll keep you company when you don't have a boyfriend?
a) Someone you can share secrets with?
d) Someone who respects you too much to pinch your make-up or your latest boyfriend?

Answers

MOSTLY A's

So far you haven't looked ahead beyond tomorrow breakfast time, so you're certainly not looking ahead to the 70's. Perhaps you don't want to. Maybe you prefer to look back—to good times, nice memories, sweet dreams.

The future doesn't interest you much because you're content with a cosy world of yesterday's dreams. You won't swing into the 70's because for you 60's, 70's or 80's are all alike, just a good time for wishing and hoping and dreaming.

MOSTLY B's

So far you haven't looked towards the 70's much. You're very much wrapped up with what's happening here and now. You don't care much about looking back and you're not gone on looking at the future either!

Now's the time you cherish and you'll take the 70's in your stride.

All right, you think the present is all that counts, but be careful not to hurt people's feelings, particularly boys', when you refuse to look ahead . . . or behind you. They may think you're a good time girl with no real feelings.

MOSTLY C's

You look ahead so much . . . and so much. You hope for good things all the time; right now you're probably hoping for really exciting things to happen to you in the 70's. We hope so too, but we think you often pin too much hope on things you're looking forward to. You'll have fun ahead of you in the 70's but try not to rush at them too madly.

Remember you have to make good times for yourself. You can't just wait around for them to happen by magic.

MOSTLY D's

Yes, you'll swing into the 70's and good luck to you. You have just the right blend of respect for the past, hope for the future and enjoyment of the present.

This is because you don't hang around waiting for other folks to make your entertainment for you. You go right out and get what you want out of life because you know you only get old and grey waiting for other people to make life great for you!

be a beautiful dreamer. . .

be a beautiful dreamer. . .

HOW you look in the morning depends a lot on what you did last thing the night before. So face the world each a.m. with confidence, the Jackie way.

1 We know! You can hardly wait to hit the pillows—but ten minutes won't shorten your beauty sleep too much, and you can get a surprising amount of beautifying done in that time! So, kick off your shoes, set the stop-watch and begin the count-down! Time . . . ten minutes to bed-time!

2 Pickled onions and cheese sandwiches are definitely OUT for late-night snacks, but take a minute to pour yourself a glass of hot milk (non-fat, if you're slimming) and drink it. It's easily digested, soothes you ready for sleep and gives you a good start for tomorrow, too.

3 Now lift off your fake lashes and store them away—then remove all that eye goo, completely! Rimmel eye make-up remover pads at 2s 5d are good value and so is Eyes Off by Quant. Or Maws new cleansing lotion, in a pretty plastic container, can conveniently be used for removing eye make-up as well as skin make-up—costs 9s 9d.

4 Now there's no eye-colour to smudge and streak, cleanse your skin. Spend two minutes on this, because you need a double-cleanse to get deep into the pores. If you use cleansing milk, cleanse once, hold a warm flannel to your face, then cleanse a second time.

If you use rinse-off cream cleanser, repeat after rinsing first with cool, then with warm water. Use PHisoHex if your skin has been playing up.

5 Next on the list, two minutes to clean teeth really thoroughly. While you're in the bathroom with a good light and a decent mirror, give your face a keen look for signs of approaching spots, and dab on some medicated lotion to do its work overnight.

6 One minute brushing your hair will remove every last trace of your day's hair spray, it'll flock off surface dust and spread the natural oils, too.

Have your head hanging down, this improves circulation at the scalp while you brush, and the dust falls straight out, too. Use a clean brush at least every 3 days!

If you've got a style that needs no setting, just slip on a band or a head-scarf, so your hair can't tangle too much. Wearing a headband helps keep your hair parted the way you want it, incidentally, or can push a fringe down and stop it flattening itself upright while you sleep.

Otherwise, pop in a few soft rollers, and spray with cologne or hair spray to set while you snooze.

7 Now sixty-seconds' worth of beauty treatment for your CLOTHES. If you intend wearing them tomorrow or not, shake them, hang them up while warm from your bod, and the creases drop out like magic.

Don't crush them in a narrow wardrobe, tho'—leave them hanging from the outside of the 'drobe, or a picture rail, all night.

Open those windows—fresh air's good for skin and deep sleep! If you want a quick start tomorrow, put skin tonic and cotton wool by your bed, then you can wake up your skin as soon as you open your eyes, all ready for new make-up. Finally—zoom into bed, the count-down's over!

YOUR COUNTRY NEEDS YOU [but does your boss?]

ARE you getting the most out of your life? That's what we want to know.

This quiz is cleverly disguised as a fun-thing, but in actual fact, it's designed to find out what your basic personality is, to help you sort out what's possible—and what's got to be kept strictly for day-dreaming!

Then, if you feel you're really missing out on the Fun in Life, we'll give you a hint or two how to go about changing things for the better.

So you see, a lot of time and thought has gone into this so . . . DON'T DARE CHEAT!!!

Imagine that you have been given a piece of work to do, and told you have a month in which to finish it. Be honest! Which of these sounds more like you?

a) Get down to it right away and have it finished 3 weeks ahead.
b) Mean to get down to it right away, but put it off till the last week.
c) Spend two weeks on research and two weeks doing the work.
d) Think about it quite a bit, but cram all the work into the last day.
e) Worry about it, and do it two or three times over before you're satisfied.
f) Forget all about it until the day after the work was due.

Do you think your best quality, job-wise, is:

a) A good worker.
b) Ambitious.
c) Clever.
d) Imaginative.
e) Get on well with people.
f) Lively personality.

What would your reaction be, if a complete stranger stopped you in the street and offered you a job modelling for his photographic agency?

a) "No thanks, I'd make a terrible model."
b) "It's tempting, but it'd be too risky to give up my present job."
c) "Prove you're on the level or I'll call the police."
d) "I'd love to try it, but only part-time not as a regular job."
e) "This is the chance of my life!"
f) "Wonderful! But I want a contract to sign, please!"

If you're already working, or are studying towards a definite type of work, why did you choose that line in particular?

a) Someone you respect recommended it to you.
b) It's what you've always wanted.
c) You've just somehow drifted into it.
d) It's a start, though not what you really want.
e) You feel you can't possibly earn a living any other way.
f) It's the best-paying job you can get, till something with even more money turns up.

If you AREN'T already working, and have no idea what you will do in a few years' or months' time, how do you aim to choose a job?

a) Get advice from your careers advisor at school.
b) Make the best of the opportunities that come along when you're ready.
c) Probably take the same sort of work as every other girl in your class and neighbourhood.
d) Read advertisements and trek round the agencies.
e) No idea. Wait till the time comes.
f) Get to know important people who might put a good job your way.

How d'you feel about romance-versus-a-career?

a) You hope for romance, naturally, but you've got to earn a living mean-time.
b) Getting the right kind of job will help romance, because you'll meet interesting people who are your own type.
c) You'd rather have love, but jobs seem easier to get than boyfriends.
d) You'd like to get your career settled first, then think about serious romance.
e) If you could get married tomorrow and not have to bother with a career, you would.
f) Romance is important, but having fun in an exciting job would be better than getting tied down to a serious boyfriend too early.

What's the thing that's most often mentioned in your school reports?

a) Can't seem to find much to praise except your good attendance and neatness.
b) Hardworking, reliable member of class.
c) You get pretty good marks, on the whole.
d) Good marks, but some of the teachers have it in for you and seem to try to take you down a peg with remarks like "doesn't know as much as she thinks"!
e) Terrible marks, but good on the arts and crafts side.
f) Should talk less and work harder!

Let's imagine you live in a very small town, and the only job that's open to you is in Bloggs' factory, where they make tiny chrome screws by the million. Not exactly a thrilling prospect, but would you comfort yourself with the thought . . .

a) At least all the other girls are in the same boat.
b) If you work hard enough, you can knock up good wages.
c) You don't HAVE to do it for the rest of your life.
d) Maybe there'll be a chance to get into the research, advertising or administration side, away from actually making the screws!
e) You'll be working with all your friends from school.
f) You aren't stuck in an all-girl show, and there is plenty of male talent in the factory.

Suppose you are walking home in a quiet street, without any other passers-by, and you see two men with masks on rush out of a small bank, carrying what's obviously the contents of the safe, and brandishing guns. What would you do?

a) Hope they haven't seen you, and stay quiet.
b) Make a note of the car number they drive off in, and phone the police immediately they have left.
c) Head into the bank the minute they have disappeared.
d) Memorise all the details you can about the men's physical appearance, make and number of car, direction it was heading in, then phone police from the bank.
e) Scream.
f) Throw your handbag at them, scream, and be sure to tell your story to the papers and TV men who arrive soon after?

If you were lucky and happened on exactly the right job, what would be the best thing it could do for you?

a) Pay well, and be interesting.
b) Give you a chance to do something different.
c) Be a bit of a challenge and something you could be proud of doing.
d) Lead you to a real top-girl status job.
e) Be fun, and involve travelling and meeting "in" people.
f) Give you all you've ever dreamed of—fame, a four-figure salary, exotic living, all earned by your natural talents without boring routine work.

Now add up your scores! To fit perfectly into any group, you should have scored 5 or more under that heading. If you scored fairly evenly among two or more headings, for example, 3 As, 2 Bs, 2 Cs, 2 Ds, read section G instead.

A—You have a quiet, steady sort of temperament, and you approach getting a job sensibly and seriously. You will do extremely well in work where your attention to detail and sense of responsibility will be appreciated; in nursing, teaching, (particularly teaching in primary schools or nursery schools) or in a library.

If you don't fancy taking long training, but would like working in a shop, for example, try to work for one of the big chain stores where they offer the chance of promotion to manageress.

You are rather reserved and shy, but should try to develop your character by taking on more responsibility.

You can make yourself a more interesting person by developing hobbies and creative interests, joining clubs or evening classes.

B—You are practical and fairly ambitious, but at the same time you need something to push you into being a little bit more adventurous.

If you haven't had much encouragement at home, you may be inclined to take up the first job that comes along.

Any experience is good, but don't stay at a job that bores you, for more than six months. With the right kind of talent, you could make a good journalist, receptionist, police-woman, home economist or demonstrator (not the flag-waving sort!)

If you find that your present job isn't very enlivening, maybe your interest in a sport or hobby will lead you into other ideas. Try to exploit your natural talent and self-confidence.

C—You may feel that you are a "no-person" without any special qualities, but actually you have a very good head, and though you wouldn't be very happy in a job with a lot of responsibility, you certainly shouldn't be satisfied doing the most boring work available.

You will probably be happiest working in a large organisation, on a fairly settled basis. You could consider working for the G.P.O., perhaps as a telephonist, doing office work for one of the big national firms, or for the Gas or Electricity Boards, British Rail or something similar.

Office work would seem to be your best bet, but there is a wide variety, and you should certainly try to improve your chance of getting an interesting job by having something extra to offer—learning short-hand, for instance, or how to work some kind of office machinery.

If you are prepared to spend some time training, computers would be a very good field for you to make a start in. You'll always work best as one of a small team, remember, and take advantage of working for a firm with a social side to it.

D—You are independent, strong-minded and have very firm ideas. It's quite likely that you'll already have come up against parental opposition, but you're quite able to take care of yourself!

Your disadvantage is that you are rather impulsive, and may rush into jobs without preparing properly, first. If it's not too late, don't leave school in too much of a rush!

If you've already left, don't fall into the trap of turning down jobs because they are too routine for you, and refusing to take training because you are in too much of a hurry to start working.

You would work well on your own, in such jobs as social work, physiotherapist, scientific research (maybe for a large firm or government department), teaching (in secondary schools), horticulture, dentistry, or on a local newspaper.

E—You dream of an exciting career, but you are a little too quiet and shy to push yourself forward and grab your opportunities.

Your best chance of getting an interesting job is to take some training for a creative career, in something like hair-dressing, beauty culture, art or dancing, then although your work will be fairly repetitive and routine, you will be working with more interesting people and you'll enjoy it a lot more.

You're not quite pushy enough to make a career as a dancer or singer, for instance, but you would be very successful teaching music or dancing.

If you can't spare time to take the necessary courses, and have to work at a fairly boring routine job, you should get the best-paying job you can. Then set yourself to developing your talent as a side-line in the evenings, for your own amusement.

Working in advertising or publicity, or as a receptionist, for example in a model agency or somewhere you will brush against glamour without actually doing glamorous work yourself, will be best.

F—You are rather an impulsive, exotic sort of character! If you've got real talent, you can make it under your own steam as a model, pop singer, actress or in any other exciting, creative career, so the first thing is to find out what talent you've got, and make full use of it.

You tend to rush off alone, but this is when you really need expert advice, so go to someone who really knows—an agency, talent-spotter, even a careers' teacher, and listen to their advice. If they give you the dispiriting news that you haven't really got outstanding talent, though, rather than make yourself miserable (and broke) by pressing on alone, you'd be well advised to train for a secondary career, while not forgetting your original ambition. When you have developed more, you may find you're able to do something about your real aim in life. Use any ability you have—if you can drive, you might work for a mini-cab company. If you can-type, look for work behind the scenes in television, airports, and so forth where at least the atmosphere is full of excitement and bustle!

G—You've got to sort your ideas out a bit before you can find the kind of work that will develop your character, fill your purse and leave you contented at the end of the day, instead of bored and frustrated!

You must make a choice, too. Either settle for a good pay packet, though the work is fairly routine, or be prepared to take less money for more interesting work. Don't forget, it's never too late to change your mind and go in for some training or other, for a specialised job. Grants are sometimes available, too.

To give you ideas, there is a very good series of books about all kinds of careers, in the Careers series put out by H.M. Stationery Office.

You can browse through the lot, free, in any public library, and buy any that seem particularly helpful by ordering them through your bookseller. Your local Youth Employment Officer should also be helpful if you make it clear that you are really keen to get to grips with a good job, and prepared to put something into it by way of effort and perhaps training.

Read the ads. in your local paper and national evening papers, and don't be put off applying for a job even if you don't quite come up to the standard they ask for. If you're prepared to work and learn, your doggedness and enthusiasm will get you there in the end!

8 AIDS TO A HOLIDAY ROMANCE

The one thing every girl wants, whether she's going to Blackpool or the Bahamas, is a holiday romance. But it isn't that easy to catch your man when the beach is packed with beauties. You've got to pay attention to every detail to stand out in a crowd. Here are the points to watch. And don't just forget them when you come back off holiday. Good grooming matters all year round!

TAKE away her figure and her looks and what has she got?" you may sourly ask—answer is, THAT SMILE. You may not be able to acquire beautiful shape and looks in 30 seconds, but the smile can be yours, and that's a start! Instant recipe: super-clean teeth, fresh breath, and a relaxed, natural smile. The first two ingredients are easy with Maclean's toothpaste (spearmint or standard flavour) and Amplex mouth capsules; the smile comes easy if you DON'T practise it, but let it come naturally! If you've got bad breath, it may be due to either bad teeth or poor health, so see your dentist first, and if he can't help, see your doctor. A spray or phial of Gold Spot (8/6 or 3/1) will get rid of any odours temporarily.

TENSION is ugly—and tension is what you get sitting cramped up over your work all day. So try to fit in some muscle-loosening activity a couple of times a week. Could be judo, karate, dancing, tennis, swimming, cycling, walking or fencing! Or do a few limbering-up exercises after work, to help you relax and get you that model girl poise!

This one's good for getting the cramp out of your spine: Stand with feet apart, and flop forward from the waist. Gently swing your body and arms from one side to the other, consciously trying to relax. Then slowly stand up straight, and do a few gentle, slow knee-bends, to help relax legs and thighs. Finally, kick each leg, and shake each arm vigorously (one at a time) and you're through!

A GIRL with her eye on the talent won't mind how long she spends putting the final touches to her clothes, and checking the most minute details of grooming. An hour a week will do the same job for you—means you'll never have droopy hems, buttons missing, fastenings broken, or coats that need a good brushing. A boy probably won't notice if you've done all your mending but he'll say "yuck" if he spots something you've missed, so it's a good investment to take care of the details! And it's a good idea not to buy gear that's obviously going to need loads of upkeep, if you know you aren't the type to bother. Rows of teensy buttons, for example, are asking for trouble! Carry a sachet of stain remover in your handbag for emergency use, and a spare pair of tights, if there's room.

DAMPNESS is a big confidence-ruiner. Clever girls know they'll suffer from nervous tension on holiday—bound to! So they make a point of looking for the magic words "anti-perspirant" on their chosen under-arm deodorant—and treat feet to a spray too, to be on the safe side. Good brands to choose are, Odorono's Dri-Mist, Femfresh Underarm Spray perfumed with Fougere, Cool Charm, and Mum, now in new perfumes. Don't forget a feminine deodorant too—Femfresh do one to match the underarm one, and Freshette and FDS are also very good.

If your face tends to perspire, use a skin tonic under your make-up, and carry Face Savers to mop up grease.

YOU don't quite match up to perfection without false beautifiers? That's okay, so long as you can pop on lashes, nails, wigs, etc. with expert ease. Most males don't care how a girl gets to be beautiful, as long as the aids she uses aren't noticeable. So don't brag about your false wig, fiddle with false nails or eyelashes—or anything else! Newest lashes on the scene are long spindly Bambi lashes from Outdoor Girl—guaranteed to make anyone look a little-girl-lost! They're 12 black or brown.

HOLIDAY girls can't afford unlucky days, off days, or any other kind of day on which they're less than 100%! Don't waste chances! Make sure you've got a health routine—plenty of sleep, fresh air, energy-giving food and no stodge, plus plenty of water and milk to drink. Then you'll be bright-eyed and full of go, whatever happens. Nagging little pains making you bad-tempered and grouchy? Try taking more exercise the week beforehand, this loosens up muscles and helps you relax more. Use a safe pain-killer like Anadin for head-aches, etc..

THE top three in any boy's list are charm, sincerity and warmth. So, even if you were born with a face like the back of a number 9 bus, you can still end up with a dish of a holiday romance! Shyness is the thing to beat, it makes the nicest girl seem dull, cold and stand-offish. Remember, every time you try to lose your shyness, it makes it a little bit easier next time! If you aren't a natural "mixer," don't force yourself to go in for clubs and social activities that are a nightmare—concentrate on developing your personality by taking part in things that really interest you, for their own sake. Losing shyness will follow naturally.

DON'T forget, a good walk makes the best of your figure—and models painstakingly LEARN the most attractive kind of walk. But any girl can get the knack of moving gracefully at a P.T. club, dancing lessons or at home with a full-length mirror. Walk all in one flowing movement, not jerking along like a puppet on strings. DON'T practise with books on your head—this tends to make you stiff. DO limber up first, and get a friend to tell you where you're going wron

DRESSES for MEN!

For MEN?!!! I hear you gasp! Certainly for men! And especially for the man YOU want to look your best for.

You can wear clothes that get the envy of the other girls but here's a little selection that will catch the eye, attention and anything else you fancy (!) of all the blokes!!

Switch on your most seductive look and go all out for the kill. Excellent man-bait is a long crushed-velvet maxi draped daringly over yer bod.

It's a bit pricey but the effect it's liable to create makes it well worth every penny.

Make: Medusa. Price: **£12 19s 6d.** Fabric: Crushed velvet. Colours: Black, plum, purple, brown. Sizes: 10-14.

Footnote—Ravel shoes. Style: Hi Brows. Price: **89s 11d.** Colours: Black patent, cognac, loganberry, navy. Sizes: 3-8.

You too can be a sexy siren! Passionate purple—that's the colour to get 'em going!

Focal point in this man-catchin' midi is the slit front to show you at your dynamic best.

Make: Etam. Style No.: 82/304. Price: **89s 11d.** Fabric: Tricel. Colours: Purple burgundy. Sizes: 1-2-3.

Tapestry shoulder bag from Elliotts. Style: Gapace. Price: **£5 11s.** Colours: Black only.

Tights from British Home Stores. Style: Nu-Way. Price: **7s 11d.** Colours: Black, white, buttermilk, smoke, mahogany, navy, burgundy, seville (orangey shade), lavender, olive slate blue.

Dolcis suede shoes are called Gideon. Price: **99s 11d.** Colours: Purple or plum suede. Sizes: 3-8.

Go on, 'ave 'im on his knees to you! That shouldn't be too difficult in this irresistibly different ankle-length dress with its super slashed sleeves.

It comes from Bus Stop. Style No.: 9724. Price: **£7 10s.** Fabric: Crepe. Colours: Lilac/cream, black/red. Sizes: 8-14.

Shoes by Ravel. Style: Viva. Price: **99s 11d.** Colours: Black, brown, bordo. Sizes: 3-8.

Beaded choker from an assortment at Bus Stop. Price: **28s.**

Stockists of Medusa dress are Topaz, New Brighton Square, Brighton, as well as Medusa, 1A Elystan Place, Chelsea, London, S.W.3. Mail Order from this address also (4s p. & p.)

Bus Stop dress and choker from all branches, Kensington, Croydon, Birmingham, Nottingham, Manchester, Glasgow, or by post from Bus Stop, 3 Kensington Church Street, London, W.8. (3s 6d p. & p.)

Etam dress from all branches. More inquiries to Susan Shanks & Partners, 22 Long Acre, London, W.C.2.

Tapestry bag from Elliott "Caterpillar" shops. Extra info from Pauline Watkins, 3 Bott Mews, London, W.2.

Ravel shoes from branches and by post from Ravel Mail Order, 103 New Bond Street, London, W.1. Post and packing is 3s 6d—also free catalogue on request.

Dolcis shoes from main branches. By post from Dolcis Mail Order, 350 Oxford Street, London, W.1. (3s 6d p. & p.)

Back To Cool

This is the time when most vacations are finished and it's back to school, college or work for everyone. (Boo, hoo!)
It's also time to say a fond farewell to hot sunny days and get ready for the cool to come.

Nobody fancies going back to school only to slog over a desk all day—but how's this for a cool uniform? It's in a class by itself.

Midi waistcoat by Littlewoods Style No.: BR 181. Price: 99s 11d. Fabric: Fibro wool. Colours: Green, burgandy, purple harlequin check. Sizes: 10-16.

Sweater and trousers by Alan Rodin.

Sweater Style No.: 823. Price: Approx 59s 11d. Fabric: 100% Acrylic. Colours: Wine, beige. Sizes: Small, medium, large.

Trousers Style No.: 1400. Price: Approx. 5 gns. Fabric: 100% Acrylic. Colours: Wine, airforce, purple, pink, rust, brown, grape. Sizes: Small, medium, large.

Clumpy platform-sole shoes with metal trim by Ravel. Style: Splash 4426. Price: 69s 11d. Colours: Black, bordo. Sizes: 3-8

If you didn't quite pass your exams with flying colours—try wearing them instead!

Top marks go to this super striped cardigan with the terrific matching scarf and pull-on hat set.

Cardigan by Erica Budd. Style No.: EB574. Price: Approx. £5 9s 11d. Fabric: Orlon. Large assortment of colourways. Medium size only.

Scarf and hat by Erica Budd. Style No.: EB716. Price: Approx. 69s 6d. Fabric and colours as cardigan.

Fabulous uncut cord trousers from Biba (no mail order). Price: £5 19s 6d. Colours: Pale blue, dark blue, black, gold, blood, brown.

Smooth leather shoes by Ravel with thick, thick, thick rubber soles. Style: Flaneuse 4509. Price: 99s 11d. Colours: Black, bordo. Sizes: 3-8.

Naturally, you're not looking forward one bit to cool days coming up again but this little lot surrounding you would definitely make you change your mind.

All by Shar Cleod.

Midi cardigan Style No.: 20/39. Price: Approx. £9 19s 6d. Fabric: Wool tweed. Colours: Black, Kenya red, green, purple, gold, brown. Sizes: 34-38 bust.

Long sleeved polo sweater style No.: 20/189. Price: Approx. 62s 6d. Fabric and colours same as cardigan. Sizes: Girls, medium, large.

Trousers Style No.: 20/188. Price: Approx. £4 19s 6d. Fabric and colours same as before. Sizes: 10-14.

Scarf and beret Style No.: 20/21. Price: Approx. 59s 6d. Fabric: Shetland wool. Colours: Red, black, navy, lilac, amber, white, magenta, green, natural, Kenya red, purple.

Super softie shoes with criss-cross thonging on vamp, by Ravel. Style: Slogan 3972. Price: 79s 11d. Colours: Olive, bordo, black. Sizes: 3-8.

Harlequin waistcoat from major branches of Littlewoods, or by post from Littlewoods, 204-211 Oxford St., London, W.1. 2s 6d for post and pack.

Alan Rodin sweater from Impact, McDonald's, Buchanan St., Glasgow; All branches of Snob and Chic boutiques; "Honey and Spice" Dept., Northovers, Reigate.

Trousers from Fenwicks, Northumberland St., Newcastle-on-Tyne, Impact, McDonalds, Buchanan St., Glasgow.

More from Alan Rodin, 62 Margaret St., London, W.1.

Erica Budd cardigan from Avanne, Rose St., Edinburgh; Ricky, Station Road, Beaconsfield, Bucks.

Hat and scarf from Griffin and Spalding, Long Row, Nottingham; Girl, Oxford St., London, W.1.

More from Erica Budd, 9 Little Portland St., London, W.1.

All Ravel shoes available from branches or by post from Sandra Sussman, Ravel Shoes, 103 New Bond St., London, W.1. Don't forget your 3s 6d for post and pack. Ask Sandra for her free Ravel catalogue at the same time.

Shar Cleod cardigan from Copeland's, Glasgow; Pacesetters, Edinburgh; Fenwicks, Bond St., London, W.1.

Polo neck sweater from James Stewart, Manchester; Brown Muff, Bradford; Rackhams, Birmingham; Irvine Sellars branches; Mugwump, Durham.

Trousers from Seniors, Rochdale; Pacesetters, Edinburgh; Copelands, Glasgow; Brown Muff, Bradford.

Scarf and beret from Anon, West Byfleet; Pacesetters, Edinburgh; Marshalls, Leeds; John Lewis, Oxford St., London, W.1.

All Shar Cleod garments available by post from Mr McTavish's Wise Woollies, P.O. Box 5, Atherstone, Warwicks, plus 5s for p. & p.

KNICKERBOCKER GLORY...

We've had almost every other shape of trousers imaginable—skintight trews, cigarette slacks, wide and narrow bellbottoms etc. etc... and now it's time for the daddy-of-'em-all—KNICKERBOCKERS—to step back into fashion.

Dash about, gad-aboutfit for the girl who wants to be noticed—and definitely will be!

A real go-getter from the top of her French cotton cloche to the tips of her fringed suede boots.

Taking it from the top. From a selection of pull-on hats by the Stitch Place. Prices: 32s 6d for wool, 37s 6d for cotton, 55s for Lurex. Colours: White, black, rose, pale blue, aqua, pale pink, gold, citrus green, royal blue, forest green, steel grey. Made to customer's orders. Special colours done if required.

Striped sweater by Erica Budd. Style No.: EB573. Price: 75s approx. Fabric: Orlon. Colours: Raspberry/mint/cream, navy/mint/wine, wine/blue/pink. Sizes: medium.

Thonged and fringed belt by Salisbury. Price: 39s 11d. Fabric: Hide. Colours: Red, brown, navy, black, white. Sizes: 28-30 inch waist. From branches of Salisbury.

Knickerbockers by Sharcleod. Style No.: 20/71. Price: approx. £4 5s. Fabric: Shetland wool. Colours: Kenya red, navy, moorish blue, amber, white, lilac, natural, red, black, magenta, green. Sizes: 10-14.

Fringed boots from main branches of Dolcis. Style: Texas. Price: £8 19s. Fabric: Suede. Colours: Brown, camel. Sizes: 3-8.

Yum-yum knickerbocker suit with keyhole tie neck has softly gathered cuffs to match the knicks. Great with boots, or shoes and matching knee socks.

Make: Miss Impact. Style No.: BB3044 the dress and BB8005 the pants. Price: £8 approx. (£5 for the dress alone, £3 for the pants.) Fabric: Unbonded moss crepe. Colours: Green, black, brown, purple, mulberry. Sizes: 10-14.

White knee-high socks by Ballito. 30 denier. Price: 5s. Colours: Dusky rose, cocoa brown, lilac, black, white, pastel blue, sunshine yellow, apple green, french navy, pale face (creamy beige), exotic red.

White calf-length wet-look boots by Lilley and Skinner. Style: Bounty. Price: 9 gns. Black also. Sizes: 3-8. From main branches of Lilley and Skinner.

The only decent type of knickers to be seen without a skirt! Natty knicker-bocker suit with sporty golf check trouser design repeated on yoke of slim-fit sweater.

Make: Erica Budd. Style No.: EB740 the pants and EB751 the sweater. Price: Approx. 89s 6d the pants, 69s 6d the sweater. Fabric: Orlon. Colours: Maroon/white, brown/white, pink/white. Sizes: 10-14.

Boots by Dolcis. Style: Parmoss. Price: £10 19s. Colours: Black, brown, leather, purple, plum suede. Sizes: 3-8. Main branches of Dolcis.

Knit hat from a selection at the Stitch Place.

Stockists

Miss Impact suit from all Miss Janet branches. More information from Miss Impact, 50 Mortimer St., London, W.1.

Erica Budd sweater from Girl, Oxford St., London, W.1; Chic boutique, 96 High St., Bromley, Kent and 67 North St., Guildford, Surrey.
Extra details from Erica Budd, 9 Little Portland St., London, W.1.

Sharcleod knickerbockers from Pacesetters, 25 Rose St., Edinburgh; Brown Muff, Bradford; Seniors, Rochdale, Kent; Girl, Oxford St, London, W.1. Mail Order from Mr McTavish's Wise Woollies, P.O. Box 5, Atherstone, Warwicks.

Erica Budd suit from Debenham & Freebody, Wigmore St., London, W.1; Brown Muff, 26 Market St., Bradford, Yorkshire. For more provincial stockists, write to Erica Budd, 9 Little Portland St., London, W.1.

Dolcis boots by Mail Order from Dolcis, 350 Oxford St., London, W.1. Extra 3s 6d for post and pack.

Lilley & Skinner boots from Lilley & Skinner, 360 Oxford St., London, W.1. and branches. Mail Order 3s 6d extra.

Pull-on hats from the Stitch Place Mail Order, 87 Regent St., London, W.1. plus 1s 6d p. & p.

STAR DATING CHART

Here it is . . . a dating system that gives you an advance warning of what to expect! How's it work? Simple. Find out the boy's zodiac sign, from those at the top of the page. Check yours, from those at the side. Where the two cross, that's what dating him will mean for you!

HIS SIGN →
YOUR SIGN ↓

	CAPRICORN (Dec. 22–Jan. 19).	AQUARIUS (Jan. 20–Feb. 18).	PISCES (Feb. 19–March 20).	ARIES (March 21–April 19).	TA (Ap
CAPRICORN	TWO OF A PAIR CAN BE BORING DEADLY DULL WHEN YOU SHARE THE CAPRICORN BIRTHSIGN	YOU'LL FIGHT. —BETTER LEAN TO HIS WAY OF THINKING.	HE'S A BIT EASY-GOING, BUT HE'LL DO ANYTHING FOR YOU.	HOT STUFF! ALL KISSES AND MAKING-UP.	MI A S MU HE
AQUARIUS	HE'S SERIOUS, AND FLATTERING —BUT IS THAT ENOUGH?	THIS WILL FIZZ FOR A WHILE. DON'T BANK ON IT.	HE'S NICE—BUT HE COULD CLING ON LONGER THAN YOU WANT.	YOU WANT YOUR WAY, HE WANTS HIS. IT WILL BE FIREWORKS, BUT YOU MIGHT GET BURNED.	HE FO ID CO YO
PISCES	DON'T LET HIM PUSH YOU AROUND, THEN IT'LL BE FINE.	IF YOU LIKE HIM, OKAY, BUT REMEMBER THAT THIS BOY COULD HURT YOU EVENTUALLY.	YOU GET ON ALMOST TOO WELL. YOU'LL BE HAPPY—BUT MAYBE YOU'LL DREAM OF A REAL ROMANCE!	HE DOESN'T MEAN ALL HE SAYS.	A C
ARIES	YOU MIGHT FIND HIM A BIT TOO SENSIBLE AT TIMES.	CAREFULLY DOES IT!	HE NEEDS ENCOURAGING.	FIRE-WORKS	HE FU A E SH SO TH
TAURUS	HE'S GOT AMBITION—DON'T STAND IN HIS WAY.	HIS TALK IS WILDER THAN HE IS.	YOU'RE PERFECT FOR EACH OTHER! YOU'LL NEED TO GIVE HIM A LITTLE PUSH IN THE RIGHT DIRECTION EVERY NOW AND THEN, BUT DON'T NAG! HE LOVES FOR GOOD AND ALL!	A BIT TOO PRIMITIVE?	GO AR FIN GO FR
GEMINI	HE ATTRACTS YOU PHYSICALLY. BUT THERE'D BETTER BE MORE TO IT THAN THAT. LONG-TERM	FUN—NOT TO BE TAKEN TOO SERIOUSLY.	CUTE, ISN'T HE?	ROWING MEANS HE LOVES YOU!	
CANCER	TAKE YOUR TIME, WHERE'S THE HURRY?	DON'T PLAN TOO FAR AHEAD. THIS BOY LIKES HIS FREEDOM, DON'T MAKE HIM FEEL TIED.	HE'S SHY. TALK TO HIM.	A BOY TO SWEEP YOU RIGHT OFF TEN LITTLE TOES! COULD BE WONDERFUL—BUT DON'T LISTEN TO WHAT JEALOUS GIRL-FRIENDS TELL YOU. TRUST THIS ONE WITH YOUR HEART.	
LEO	IF YOU BOSS HIM AROUND, HE'LL VAMOOSE.	YOU'LL NEVER FORGET HIM—A ROMANCE THAT FIZZES ALL THE WAY, FIGHTS AN' ALL.	HE KNOWS HOW TO PLEASE!	DON'T FIGHT TOO OFTEN.	K
VIRGO	YOU'LL GET ON WELL RIGHT FROM THE START.	LET HIM SET THE PACE, AND BE READY WHEN HE CALLS!	MAYBE YOU'RE TAKING HIM FOR GRANTED. TREAT HIM UNKINDLY, YOU MIGHT LOSE HIM.	DON'T BE A FUSS-POT WHEN HE'S AROUND.	VE RE
LIBRA	DON'T FORGET, HE'S GOT AMBITION.	YOU MIGHT FIND OUT THE HARD WAY THAT YOU'RE NOT AS IMPORTANT TO HIM AS YOU THOUGHT.	WHAT A SWEETIE. BUT BE CAREFUL—MEAN WHAT YOU SAY.	THIS COULD CLICK. IT RATHER DEPENDS ON YOU—SO GENTLY.	HE DE ON
[SCORPIO]	WHIRLWIND ROMANCE! ANYTHING GOES WHERE YOU TWO ARE CONCERNED —COULD BE YOU'LL HAVE TO FIGHT OPPOSITION, BUT WITH LUV LIKE THIS, ANYTHING'S POSSIBLE. BE TRUE!	YOU'RE TOO MUCH FOR HIM!	BETTER WEAR YOUR ASBESTOS VEST, DUCKY. THIS ROMANCE WILL WARM THINGS UP!	POOR LAD, HE WON'T KNOW WHAT HIT HIM!	A ST
SAGITTARIUS	YOU'VE GOT HIM PUZZLED!	LOVE'S YOUNG DREAM! EVER SO ROMANTIC, YOU WON'T COME DOWN TO EARTH FOR QUITE A WHILE, SO BETTER MAKE SURE YOUR FLYING GEAR IS IN GOOD ORDER FIRST!	YOU FEEL PROTECTIVE TOWARDS HIM.	TAKE CARE. THIS COULD LAND YOU IN DEEP WATER. HE MEANS JUST WHAT HE SAYS!	GIV W BE WR OFF QU

–May 20).	GEMINI (May 21–June 20).	CANCER (June 21–July 22).	LEO (July 23–Aug. 22).	VIRGO (Aug. 23–Sept. 22).	LIBRA (Sept. 23–Oct. 22).	SCORPIO (Oct. 23–Nov. 21).	SAGITTARIUS (Nov. 22–Dec. 21).
. BIT OF -IN-THE- UT A OF GOLD.	IT'S A LOVE-HATE RELATIONSHIP, AND IT WILL BRING YOU PLENTY OF TROUBLE.	HE WON'T WANT TO SHARE YOU WITH YOUR OLD BUDDIES.	LEO'S LOVING —BUT A BIT BOSSY. CAN YOU KNUCKLE UNDER?	HE COULD BE A BIT MEAN.	NICE GOING!		HAPPY-GO-LUCKY DATING.
OO DULL OU. HIS ARE VERY ENTIONAL, AREN'T.	FUN WHILE IT LASTS! HE CERTAINLY CAN BE AMUSING.	GET TO KNOW HIM.	A BIT UNUSUAL.	TALK LESS!		DON'T HURT HIS FEELINGS	YOU'RE LUCKY— HANG ON TO HIM. LOTS OF GIRLS ENVY YOU YOUR CHANCE.
DD SOLID EN!	YOU WON'T UNDERSTAND HIM, BUT THAT WON'T STOP YOU HAVING FUN!	HE'S A PLANNER.		A BIT PENNY-PINCHING?	LIBRA MEANS MORE'N HE SAYS	CAREFUL WHAT YOU SAY ABOUT THE PAST.	HE LIKES LOTSA GIRLS . . .
REAT IT HE'S ASILY ED BY OF THE YOU SAY.	HE'S TOO QUICK FOR YOU! BETTER RUN TO KEEP UP!	APPEAL TO THE INNER MAN —HE'S FOND OF HIS TUM.	LEO LOVES HIMSELF ALMOST AS MUCH AS YOU.	DON'T LAUGH AT HIS AMBITIONS.	YOU BOTH LIKE A GOOD TIME, BUT FOOTING THE BILL MIGHT BE UNPLEASANT FOR YOU LATER.	SLOW AND EASY DOES IT.	
FRIENDS ARD TO SO STAY S.	DON'T ASSUME YOU KNOW THIS BOY WELL, EVER. COULD BE A HEART-BREAKER.	DANGER HERE IS, TAKING EACH OTHER FOR GRANTED.	GOOD LOOKS AREN'T EVERYTHING.	BETTER THE MORE YOU KNOW HIM.	YOU MIGHT NEED TO PUT IN SOME PRACTICE WALKING HOME!	LUCKY THE DAY YOU MET THIS ONE.	DON'T LISTEN FOR WEDDING BELLS FOR AGES!
IF HIS MUM LIKES YOU, YOU'RE IN!	YOU'RE GREAT AS A TEAM— UNLESS YOU BOTH CHEAT!	HE LIKES A STEADY GIRL-FRIEND TO BE STEADY.	WILL YOU LET HIM BE THE BOSS?		GREAT FOR GOING PLACES.	VERY ROMANTIC, SPECIALLY IF HE'S GETTING OVER SOMEONE ELSE.	DANGER—YOU THINK YOU'VE GOT HIM WHERE YOU WANT HIM. BUT COULD BE YOU IN THE TRAP.
A GOOD FILL-IN.	HE'LL BE AMUSING, BUT DON'T TRUST TOO MUCH TOO SOON.	YOUNG LOVE DOESN'T ALWAYS LAST—BUT IT'S WONDERFUL.	ALWAYS RELIABLE.	YES, BUT WILL IT LAST?	LOOK ON IT AS GOOD EXPERIENCE, IF NOTHING ELSE!	THIS CAN BE GREAT, OR IT CAN MEAN HEART-BREAK. YOU KNOW HOW TO HURT	LUCKY OLD YOU! THIS BOY CAN'T RESIST A SWEET-TALKING FEMALE. HOPE IT'S YOU!
	A DRIFTER, DRIFTING YOUR WAY?	DON'T BET ON IT . . . YET.	LET HIM BE THE BOSS, YOU TAKE THE CREDIT.	HIS FUSSY WAYS MEAN HE CARES.	HE'S QUITE A CHARMER, ISN'T HE? LET HIM KNOW HE'S NOT THE ONLY FISH!	YOU'LL NEVER REALLY KNOW WHAT HE'S THINKING.	HE'S VERY HAPPY-GO-LUCKY, AND A DETERMINED GIRL COULD LAND HIM EASILY—BUT IS IT YOU?
.E.	A BIT OF A TEASE!		HE'S A BIT CASUAL.	DON'T SETTLE FOR THIS ROMANCE UNTIL YOU'VE SHOPPED AROUND, IN A NICE WAY!	HE'S TOO NICE TO LET YOU DOWN WITHOUT GOOD REASON.	IF YOU WANT THIS BOY, YOU'VE GOT TO BE A LOT MORE ADVENTUROUS, AND LESS CHOOSY.	A VERY NICE WAY TO SPEND A FEW FUN-PACKED WEEKS!
	YOU MIGHT FIND HIM HARD TO LOSE.		LEO WILL MOVE AROUND BEFORE HE SETTLES	GET OFF WITH HIM BY TAKING AN INTEREST IN SOMETHING HE'S NUTS ABOUT.	HE CAN BE RATHER OFF HAND TO START WITH, BUT KEEP ON WITH THE OLD CHARM!	BE VERY CAREFUL—IF YOU TREAT HIM BADLY, YOU'LL REGRET IT.	ALL GOOD CLEAN FUN—AND SOMEONE YOUR MUM WILL APPROVE OF!
W ER.	NOBODY WINS, IF YOU TWO FIGHT.	COULD BE A YEA-AND-NAY ROMANCE, THIS ONE.	YOU'RE NOT THE SORT TO LET ANYONE SHOVE YOU AROUND . . . HE LIKES TO BE BOSS.	YOU'LL NEVER FIGURE HIM OUT.	YOU MAY THINK YOU'RE THE SMARTIE-PANTS, BUT THIS CHAP HAS GOT IT ALL WORKED OUT.	IT STARTS CASUALLY— COULD END THE SAME WAY.	TWO OF A KIND . . . DON'T ALWAYS MAKE A GOOD PAIRING.
M A O E YOU IM A BIT	HE LIKES YOUR GAY SPIRIT AND EASY-GOING WAYS BUT HE'S OUT FOR SUMMAT ELSE IN A STEADY	HE'S GOT STRONG IDEAS THAT MAYBE DON'T TALLY WITH YOURS.	IF HE'S GETTING OVER SOMEBODY ELSE, YOU COULD HOOK HIM, EASY.	YOU RUB EACH OTHER UP THE WRONG WAY, AND IF YOU'RE GOING TO MAKE IT STICK, SOMEONE'S GOTTA GIVE!	DATING HIM BECAUSE OF HIS REPUTATION? COULD BE DANGEROUS!	HE'S A BIT OF A GAMBLER. YOU'D BETTER BE LUCKY!	YOU'LL PROBABLY HAVE SEVERAL GOES AT DATING EACH OTHER BEFORE YOU REALLY DECIDE!

THIS IS IT! HE TAKES YOU RIGHT OUT OF YOURSELF! THIS IS LOVE LIKE IT WAS MEANT T'BE! YOU'LL GIVE UP ANYTHING FOR THE HAPPY-EVER-AFTER STUFF.

HE'S THE LOVING KIND OF BOY YOU'VE BEEN LOOKING FOR! COULD BE PERFECT DATING, AND EVEN IF IT ONLY LASTS A LITTLE WHILE, THIS IS THE ONE YOU'LL ALWAYS REMEMBER.

HANG ON TO THIS ONE! THIS COULD BE IT! HE MAY SEEM SELF-CONFIDENT, BUT ALWAYS REMEMBER HE'LL DEPEND ON YOUR SUPPORT AND LOVIN' ADMIRATION.

THIS IS THE BOY FOR YOU —BUT BE PREPARED FOR A LONG WAIT. HE WON'T WANT TO SETTLE DOWN TOO YOUNG, SO DON'T SCARE HIM OFF. HE'S WELL WORTH WAITING FOR!

MAYBE AT FIRST YOU WON'T FIND HIM TERRIBLY EXCITING, BUT IT COULD TURN OUT TO BE THE BIG ROMANCE OF YOUR LIFE, SO DON'T WRITE HIM OFF . . . GIVE HIM TIME!

YOU MIGHT ...E TO DO THE ...SING TO START ...H. BUT WHEN HE ...S THE MESSAGE, ...OM! THAT'S JUST ...AY IT'LL FEEL . . . HIM INTERESTED, ...O HE'S YOURS ...FOR KEEPS!

MAYBE YOU FEEL ORDINARY TO YOURSELF, BUT REMEMBER THAT TO THIS BOY, YOU'RE TERRIFIC! DON'T SELL YOURSELF SHORT, THIS COULD BE A BIG ROMANCE IF YOU'LL LET IT.

MAYBE YOU DON'T KNOW IT YET, BUT YOU'RE HIS IDEA OF THE PERFECT GIRL FRIEND! HE DOESN'T ALWAYS LET ON HOW HE FEELS STRAIGHT AWAY, BUT GIVE THE LAD TIME!

Dust Down Your Dating Ideas...

SPRING-CLEANING has sprung on' us again, and while you're at it this year, why not turn out your ideas about dating. Dust them off and see if they're worth keeping—or best turfed out with all the other junk that's cluttering the place up.

Then you'll be all set for a fresh start with some lively new talent—and a problem-free summer of romances!

First of all, let's see if we can throw out completely some junk you may have been hoarding—like that dusty old idea that you just aren't a 'success' unless you've got a boyfriend all to yourself!

That was O K in the days when you weren't let loose anyway until you were 16 or 17, and then all the girls had to rush out and grab up boyfriends as fast as they could. These days, girls-only schools are on the wane, thank goodness, and even if you don't meet boys during school hours, it's the accepted thing for girls and boys to go around together from quite an early age.

So it's daft to think there's something wrong with you if you don't go in for solo dating yet! There's loads of time—plenty of opportunity, too, if you keep knocking around with the crowd. In fact, most girls find it's a bit too restricting to tie up with a steady too early—gives the family all the wrong ideas.

Also, you may find you're letting yourself in for a lot of trouble. A steady boy may think he's got the right to lay down rules—if you've several boyfriends, they wouldn't dare!

HARD TO GET

Next for the dustbin—the notion that boyfriends are hard to get. Dating is as natural as swimming or dancing, and just as easy . . . once you forget about it. It's when you concentrate hard on it, and think about it too much, that you find it difficult!

Just like swimming, too, throwing yourself in at the deep end is NOT the answer, you're just as likely to sink as swim! So, if you haven't really started dating yet, don't ask one of your pals to fix you up with a date—or get yourself invited to one of those awful parties where everyone separates into couples from the word go.

You're bound to find yourself with the worst boy there, it's one of the rules of the game!

Instead, just relax and enjoy yourself with friends you really like, and don't worry if they're all girls at the mo! Sooner or later, boyfriends will appear on the scene as if by magic. They really like to do their own hunting, you know, and what gets them interested is a relaxed, natural sort of girl who seems as if she has good time whoever she's with

TIME AND PLACE

Well, that's cleared a bit of space. Now to have a look at some of the other junk. What about all those formal patterns of behaviour girls were supposed to stick to on dates?

Turning up never too early, never too late, but just right, for instance. That's fine if you happen to have picked a lad who is punctual. But if he's not, waiting around for him to have the goodness to turn up will screw you into knots of tension, embarrassment and anger that are practically guaranteed to ruin the entire evening.

It's different, of course, if he does it on purpose to madden you or because he's so conceited he likes to see a girl running round in circles after him. Who needs that kind of date anyway?

But these days, things are pretty informal, he probably has a lot to do (specially if he's at work, or studying hard) and traffic can be another good reason for being late.

It's better and more modern to make different arrangements now. Like being at a club, coffee bar, disco-joint or what-have-you in the early part of the evening—where the first to arrive can enjoy themselves till the other turns up, then go on somewhere else.

HOW MUCH?

And how about who-pays-for-dates? This has got to be pretty elastic in 1970, if it's going to go smoothly. Admittedly, some boys still like to feel that when they take a girl out, they do the paying. If he's like that, O K—but don't get grouchy when he's broke and your dates have a way of being the healthy, out-door walking kind!

Boys seem to think it's fair for a girl to pay her share these days, specially if she's earning more than he is anyway—but they are a wee bit coy about the actual taking of coins in public! What they really like is for a girl to "pay her way" by inviting him for a meal now and then, or getting tickets for a show off her own bat, or maybe supplying the transport occasionally.

If you don't drive yourself, loan of a brother's or dad's car might be in order, if your boyfriend is a reliable driver . . . but check with the owner first!

Introducing the boy back home is another ploy that has got pretty dusty through the years! Of course, if you're shy about talking about your friends to your family, then suddenly announce you have a boyfriend and blush with embarrassment, you're bound to whip up the interest! Then they're going to insist on casting the parental eye over the poor lad—you'll have to march him in and it will be very uncomfortable for everyone concerned.

It's much better to be frank right from the start, tell your folks about the boys who are included in the crowd you roam around with, then they won't make such an issue of your first solo date and neither will you! Also, if you start the habit of having friends call by for you, they may even have met the boy casually, and no big introductions are necessary.

PLAY IT STRAIGHT

Finally, there are a few goodies among your hoard of ideas that never really go out of date, and are well worth keeping. It's always worthwhile being honest and sincere, you get into far fewer tangles! So avoid trouble by not cheating; whether it's double-dating on the sly, saying things you don't mean or giving a false reason for not turning up for a date!

Another thing, it's not particularly smart to act as if dating means nothing to you—putting on a cool act, not saying thank-you or letting him know if you had a good time. These are still as off-putting to a boy, especially one who's new to dating himself. But this is only plain manners and courtesy anyway.

Today, the whole idea of dating is to keep it casual and friendly, so that a girl can meet as many boys as possible, without getting too deeply involved, and when she finally makes her choice, she's more likely to make a good lasting relationship. But there's no need to go to the other extreme and indulge in a lot of scalp-hunting, just for the sake of being the girl with most dates!

In other words, when you're spring-cleaning your ideas about dating, don't throw out the romance along with all the other junk!

THE JACKIE TEACH-IN

For new readers, this is where our Special Correspondent tells you about things of burning interest, like . . . Well, read on and you'll find out.

the truth about the secret shoe fillers

CULTS are the in thing at the moment. So if you want to be in you'll have to think seriously about joining one. If you don't, you run the risk of being ostracised and that might be a bit painful as ostriches are notoriously bad tempered. Especially at this time of year.

You don't have to worry too much about what sort of cult to join, the important thing is to belong. There's the Hippie cult, the cult of non-violence, the skinhead pro-violence cult, flat earthers (those people who insist the world is flat and don't realise it's really pretty square), religious cults, anti-religious cults and Moira Gritburgle, of 36 Dustbin Alley, Grimsby, to name but several.

Or you could go for something entirely new, like Mary Murple, of Maidstone. Not that Mary is new, she's so old she's fraying at the edges. But the cult she started, *that* was new. And highly successful.

Mary started the devastating Refusal cult which swept the country like a gorse fire in a drought. It was a secret cult and all members refused everything. They even refused to admit they belonged to it. According to Mary, the success of her cult was proved when she called a mammoth sit-in of members on Ilkley Moor. Not one person turned up! This meant that every man, woman and child in the British Isles must have belonged to the cult at that time and possibly a few dogs and cats as well. True to the spirit of the cult, they had all Refused to attend. So the membership of the Refusal cult at that time was approximately 53,000,000 (or 53,000,001 if you included Moira Gritburgle, of 36 Dustbin Alley, Grimsby). If Mary could find a way of collecting membership fees she'd be rich. But, of course, every member would refuse to pay. It's a problem she's still working on.

It's probably not a good idea to join a cult like the Thugs. For one thing it's a long way to cult headquarters in India and for another, creeping round at night and strangling people with lengths of cord may not be your idea of fun.

Then there's the kinky Shoe Filling cult. This started harmlessly enough in Norwich. Sybil Knutt, a terribly polite girl, had been to a party. The sight of strawberry jelly always had the effect of making her stomach feel as if it was turning inside out (an X-ray later proved that it actually was) and at this particular party there seemed to be nothing but strawberry jelly.

Rather than eat it, Sybil filled her handbag with the stuff. Next day she went to the pictures and discovered to her horror that she had forgotten to empty her handbag. As the girl in the next seat had taken off her shoes Sybil furtively deposited the jelly in them. It seemed a good way of getting rid of unwanted jelly and after that she always did it. People all over Norwich found their shoes full of strawberry jelly. The cult had started.

Now there are branches of the cult in all major towns. If you find your shoes full of jelly, and there's absolutely no reason why you shouldn't, you can tell which branch the secret filler belongs to by the flavour. Strawberry, of course, is Norwich. Orange is London. Raspberry is Cardiff. Lemon is Manchester. Edinburgh members are working on a haggis flavoured jelly and an offshoot of the Cult in Leeds actually prefers custard.

But perhaps, in spite of all this stuff, you don't want to join a cult at all, even an exciting one like the Secret Shoe fillers. Well, all right. It could be that you're too busy battling against the worst cult of them all—the fanatical Anti You cult.

This cult has members everywhere and their sole aim seems to be to make life difficult for you. The bus conductor who rings the bell just as you burst breathlessly round the corner only seconds late—he's a member. So is the girl who snatches the dress you were after at the Boutique sale. And the man who cunningly sliced a little splinter out of the desk for you to catch your new tights on. And the lady in the shop who smirks and says "Sorry, dear, you're too late. We're closed."

Some members even seem to be mind readers. How do they know what you're after, for example, when you walk into that big department store? They must know ('Look out, here she comes, hide the Misty Pink lipsticks and size 34 dresses') because they won't have the lipstick you're after or that fab dress in your size. All you can do is hope that one day they'll get tired of the cult and stop picking on you.

As for Miss Moira Gritburgle, of 36 Dustbin Alley, Grimsby, who wrote to complain that she's never been mentioned in a Teach-In—are you happy now?

Around the Boutiques with Sam

THEY'VE GOT A "TOP OF THE POPS" DOUBLE . . .

"UP The Junction" — a boutique in Clapham, London, S.W.11, that is—has the craziest group of girls looking after it in the whole of South-West London.

There's Jackie, who used to be girl-Friday to photographer Stephen Coe. "Remember the ad. for 'I'm Backing Britain'," she grinned, "with a pair of braces holding up a pair of Union Jack trousers that were slipping—well, that was his.

"I used to do just about everything there. Get the models, make his coffee, organise his clothes, even used to model for him myself. All sorts of things, really.

"I've been at 'Up The Junction' eighteen months, now, and I really think it's great. The normal customers are fantastic. Only some are grotty!"

The boutique, since it opened in June, 1968, has always stocked masses of trousers in all shapes and sizes, although, as Michele, who's French—and looks it!—said, "We're stocking a lot of long dresses now, and they're selling well, for every-day wear."

Michele's been in this country nine years, and with the boutique for just one. Quite recently, she went along to Top of the Pops with Angela, one of the other girls, and managed to win the Best Dressed Girl Competition!

Michele wore a very fitted red suede jacket with fringes to the floor, and matching red trousers for the "Top of the Pops" show. They were handmade for her. She hasn't been back, but she watches it every Thursday. Now her main problem is that a lot of the customers peer at her and say, "Didn't we see you on 'Top of the Pops' and poor Michele is so shy, she never quite knows how to answer!

She lives with her mum, and on her days off, just listens to records. "I'm blues mad. I put the record player on, and start dancing. We do that in the shop, too. If we get bored or fed-up, we put the radio or record player on and dance.

"Quite often you get a crowd of people outside, just standing watching. One time we were a bit bored, so we got masses of tinfoil, cut it out into flower shapes, and pinned them all over the ceiling and the windows of the shop. It looked fantastic!"

"I'd like to be a dancer like one of Pan's People, or something," says Michele, "I wanted to be a model, too, but I'm too short." She's just over five foot.

Angela was born in Greece, speaks fluent Greek, Spanish and German and last year spent half the year working her way round France, Spain, Germany and Geneva. This year, she's off to Germany and from there, she said, "Who knows? I'm going with another girl and we hope to get to South Africa and America.

"Allan, the owner of 'Up the Junction', is pretty good. He usually takes me back when I decide I've got homesick for this country again. Well, you can do it when you're young, can't you? I'd love to travel all the time, even although I've got a boyfriend I'm pretty stuck on at the moment."

She went along to 'Top of the Pops' wearing a gipsy-style outfit, and she too won Best-Dressed Girl. She says she got the surprise of her life!

Like Michele, customers tend to say they've seen her on the box, but Angela doesn't mind.

She's crazy about swimming—has certificates for it and swims summer and winter—but when she's not travelling, working in the boutique, listening to Led Zeppelin, going to parties or swimming, she loves (wait for it!)—housework!

"Anything. Making beds. Dusting. The lot. It's fantastic. But I hate cooking! Can't stand it!"

So with Michele looking French all over the place, Angela careering round the world, and Jackie hoping to join friends in Thailand later this year, poor ol' Marian, who's more or less the boss, seems a bit left out!

She used to manage a boutique in the King's Road, but got really bored with it and's been with "Up the Junction" for several months.

"We get a lot of regular customers now. They tend to buy from us most of the time, and they'll come in quite often just to look through the stock. But they don't want to spend a lot of money—or very few do—on clothes. I think we've got the best selection of clothes in Clapham Junction. We've got a lot of things that the Kings Road has, and also Oxford Street.

"Allan does most of the buying, but if we see anything we like from a traveller who comes in we buy a few to try out. And the girls are a good bunch when it comes down to problems with customers."

So there you are, next time you're up the junction, take a look in the orange-painted boutique for four of the maddest, most helpful girls around!

You never know, you might find you'll join in the dancing too!

L to R: Michele, Angela, Marian and Jackie

A reader's true experience

I have to get out now

IF I look up now I'll see him—eyes firmly fixed on the television screen; the cup of coffee I made ten minutes ago between his feet on the floor. He'll have kicked off his shoes to reveal the inevitable stretch nylon socks.

If only, just once, he'd swing me into his arms and whisper, "Let's elope. There's a train leaving for Gretna Green in half an hour", or even, "Jill, you're beautiful and I love you". But he won't, and I know it, so perhaps it'd be better to stop pretending.

He's a solid person. Tall and dependable and honest. But he'll never give me the moon—not even if I ask for it. He'd simply say it was a waste of time and where would I keep a moon anyway? Because that's the way he is—down-to-earth, not a streak of the rebel in him.

Would it cost him so much to say something more than, "You look fine, now we'd better go or we'll miss the big film" every time I ask if he likes my hair or my clothes? If only just once he'd whisper something that would knock me out! Even if it were rubbish or completely untrue, at least it would sound as if he cared.

He can be so gentle when something, like a stray kitten we found in the park, is hurt or lost. But when it comes to being gentle with me he dries up somehow.

I know how his mind works and every date's predictable. We go to the cinema; to the club; play tennis in the summer; skate in the winter. He spends his three weeks' holiday with his married brother in Bournemouth. He buys me records for my birthday and something gift-wrapped out of the chemist's at Christmas. He talks to Dad about the Union situation for miners, but never attempts to explain it to me.

We've been going around for over a year now, and I'm beginning to think it's becoming a habit. I've never seen him do anything he didn't think about first; or even say anything he hadn't almost planned in advance. Even when he asked me to meet his parents, it was a set speech. He might almost have had it written down on his shirt cuff!

I want someone who'll be a sort of Romeo to my Juliet. Who'd fight battles for me; kill dragons and bring home their heads; risk life and limb for me—or even just kiss me in public once in a while to show me he cares.

A single red rose would be wonderful but he's never even bought me violets. So I don't suppose he'd think of that. I wouldn't care if he'd pinched a chrysanthemum from somebody's garden to give to me—it would mean he'd been thinking about me.

It's almost funny—we haven't even got an 'our song'. And most people have.

I'd love to be 'courted'. Perhaps that's a bit out now and we can't be silly and young and laugh at nothing forever. But we don't seem to do it at all.

Bob's so realistic and practical. He doesn't see any sense in walking a couple of miles if he misses the last bus—but just once, it'd be fantastic if he were so absorbed in kissing me goodnight, he didn't notice when it chuntered down the hill past us.

He wouldn't hurt me for the world, I know that, too. But I'm only going on 17. We just don't seem to behave or look in love like other young couples. He takes life so seriously, and he's too conscientious—I keep feeling we're missing something.

It'd be fun to decide on the spur of the moment to go somewhere different for a change. It'd be great to hold each other close under a tree while the rain poured down—instead of making for the nearest bus shelter. And I wouldn't laugh, honest, if he got down on one knee, and swore undying love for me.

But it won't ever happen. He won't ever change. In a way I suppose I do love him—there must be something more than habit there.

Maybe it's my fault. Perhaps I wouldn't respond properly to the big romantic line, but how can I know if I never get the chance?

He even takes it for granted we'll get married—he's altogether too 'cosy' sitting there in his parents' front room with the Saturday night telly blaring in the corner and the dog lying asleep on the hearth rug.

He doesn't even guess I'm going to get out now—make the big break and start looking around for some of those silly creams.

I-TIDDLEY-TIE-DYE

Have you got yourself any of the latest in cheapie gear for trendy chicks yet? Well, there's no excuse if you don't —'cos tie-dye stuff's all over the place and one of the great things about it is it has hardly any effect on your budget.

Have a boggle at this great fun dress! This is your chance to be completely original 'cos no two tie-dyes are alike.

Make: Miss Impact. Style No.: A3224. Price: Approx. £2 10s. Fabric: Cotton jersey. Colours: Red, lilac, yellow, blue. Sizes: 10-14.

Crepe choker from Biba, 124-126 Kensington High Street, London, W.8. Price: 13s. Colours: Purple, black, brown, pink, blue.

Dolcis white leather sandals are called Vine and cost 59s 11d in sizes 3-8. Available by Mail Order from Dolcis, 350 Oxford Street, London, W.1. and all branches. Cost of post and packing is 3s 6d.

Tiddley tie-dye T-shirt with contrast stitching on short sleeves and neck is by Chester Martin.

Price: 30s. Fabric: Cotton. Colours: Red, yellow, blue, green, purple, black. Sizes: Small, medium, large.

Trousers by Alan Rodin. Style No.: 6220. Price: Approx. £4 19s 6d. Fabric: Cotton gaberdine. Colours: Brown, black, red, lilac, kingfisher, blue. Sizes: 10-16.

Biba belt with either cloud or butterfly fastening. Price: £3 15s 6d. Fabric: Suede or leather with snakeskin motif. Colours: Purple, black, brown, pink, blue.

Long, lean tie-dyed maxi like a second skin comes from Miss Impact.

Style No.: A2114. Price: £3 12s 6d. Fabric: Cotton Jersey. Colours: Red, lilac, yellow, blue. Sizes: 10-14.

Tie-dyed scarf from Biba. Price: 2 gns. Fabric: Crepe. Green only.

Stockists of Miss Impact dresses include Stop the Shop, Kings Road, London, S.W.3. (and mail order); Marments, 11-17 Queen Street, Glasgow; Miss Janet, 71 Church Street, Liverpool and 45 Corporation Street, Birmingham.

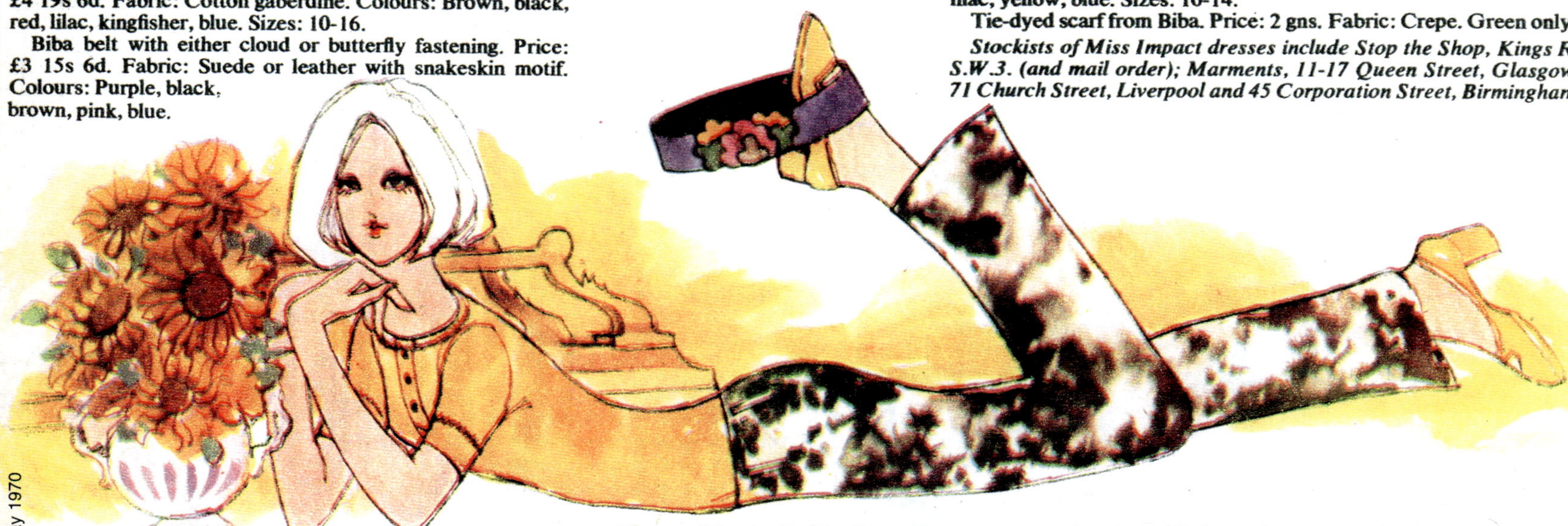

Chester Martin T-shirt from Emmerton and Lambert, Chelsea Antique Market, Kings Road, London, S.W.3; Jigsaw, 16 Duke St., Brighton; Moss, 47-49 Castle Arcade, Cardiff.

By post from Chester Martin, 39 De Vere Gardens, London, W.8.

Alan Rodin trousers from all branches of Peter Robinson; Impact, McDonalds, Queen Street, Glasgow.

More info from Alan Rodin, Margaret Street, London, W.1.

HOW TO TIP THE SCALES IN YOUR FAVOUR . . .

A JACKIE BEAUTY QUIZ

SLIMMING isn't easy, and there's a lot more to it than just not eating so much! Quite a lot of people find it absolutely impossible to slim—but before you get too depressed about that little statement, consider this: there are all sorts of reasons WHY people find it hard to slim. If you understand the reason, you're half-way to the solution . . . and a nice slim figure.

Here's how to find out what's keeping you in the fatties' brigade.

1. Everyone has certain chores that have to be done. Do you:
- a) Fit them in when you can, but always have a nagging feeling there are things undone?
- b) Do them regularly on certain nights, because otherwise your mum kicks up a fuss?
- c) Let them pile up until you've just got to tackle the chores because you've nothing left to wear and the bedroom's a mess?
- d) Potter about meaning to do your chores but find you start reading a mag. instead?

2. Which of these sounds most like you?
- a) You enjoy eating, and look forward to food a great deal.
- b) You try to clear your plate at every meal, as a compliment to whoever cooked it.

- c) Meals don't interest you, but you love "bitty" eating, snacks between meals, and the kind of main meal that's made up of lots of bits and pieces.
- d) You can limit yourself to a small meal, but if there are sweets or biscuits in the house you can't rest till they're gone.

3. Is your main reason for wanting to slim:
- a) So that you can buy more attractive clothes?
- b) To attract more boys?

- c) To be more popular with everyone?
- d) No particular reason, just a feeling things would be better if you were slim?

4. Are you easily depressed?
- a) Only when you fail at things through no fault of your own.
- b) Yes, you feel your parents are against you and they are stronger than you are.

- c) Yes, nothing you ever do seems to turn out right, and you don't feel popular, and you feel like this quite a lot of the time.
- d) Sometimes, because you don't seem able to handle your own problems, but this feeling doesn't last long.

5. When you begin a new diet, do you think!

- a) This time I'll make it work?
- b) It would probably work if only I didn't have to eat the meals Mum cooked for me?
- c) It probably won't work, but it's worth a try?
- d) I'll give it a couple of weeks, anyway, and see what happens?

6. The supermarket has over-charged you, and rather than open the till again, they offer you a choice—which do you take?
- a) A shilling off an exotic foodstuff.
- b) A 1s credit note
- c) 1s worth of slimming foods.
- d) 1s worth of chocolate.

7. Think back to the last time you tried to slim. Is your reason for failing to keep it up:
- a) You eat out too much, where you can't choose your own meals?
- b) Shortage of money, or your mother's insisting that you pack it in?
- c) You felt too miserable to keep it up?
- d) You couldn't resist a particular dish and having broken your diet, never went back to it?

Now see which letter you picked most often, then see where you went wrong!

MOSTLY A's . . . . You are probably a gay, lively kind of person with a busy social scene. Diets don't fit too well into your life, and you will find it much easier to slim if you do it by concentrating on exercising more, rather than by eating less.

A regular visit to a health club, or an interest like an active sport, dancing or walking, will do the trick. When you need to slim drastically, remember that alcohol is far more fattening than food, and it isn't the peanuts and crisps at parties that put on the weight as much as what you take with them!

MOSTLY B's . . . You've probably got rather domineering parents, who think they are doing their best for you, and they like to see you looking plump rather than thin, just as people always admire fat babies more than scrawny ones!

You've got into the habit of eating everything that's put in front of you, as the easiest way out of an argument. Maybe you try to slim by not eating EXCEPT at home, but this is terrible for your health and probably one reason you can't stick at diets.

If you are very overweight, speak to your doctor and get him to talk sense to your mother. Otherwise, you'll just have to toughen up and start leaving potatoes and piecrust at the side of your plate. It's your mum or your figure, remember!

MOSTLY C's . . . You eat as a comfort. There may be good reasons why you feel lonely, boring or unsuccessful, or it could all be in your mind. Stop worrying about your figure and lack of friends, and find out the things that you really enjoy doing, regardless of whether they will make friends for you or not.

Once you stop worrying about being popular, you will find it easier to make friends, and once you have a busy life it will be much, much easier to forget about food, and slim. So start by doing something new, something interesting. And make it today!

MOSTLY D's . . . Afraid the painful truth is you are just too weak-willed to deny yourself anything! The best thing for you to do would be to join a group of other would-be slimmers, because people like you find strength in numbers.

You can start a club just by asking around among your friends, or you could join an organised one run by the local authorities, or a nationally-advertised brand of slimming foods.

You'll find that once you are actually losing weight regularly it is much easier to stick with the diet, and eventually you will get out of the silly habit of over-eating and will be able to keep slim, which is as important as getting slim!

NINA'S CHOC CAKE

Our Nina's been raving on for ages about how fantastic this cake is, so to shut her up we're letting you into the secret too!

4 oz. luxury margarine, 6 oz. castor sugar, 6 oz. plain flour, 2 eggs, ½ cup milk, 2 teaspoonfuls baking powder, 1½-2 tablespoonfuls cocoa.

Place all ingredients in mixing bowl—beat together for 3 mins. Place in 2 greased sandwich tins (7 in.) and bake for 25-30 mins. at 375 deg. F.,—Regulo 5.

When cool, sandwich together with raspberry jam. Top with whipped cream, melted choc or chocolate icing.

a Jackie Quiz

are you easy to get on with ?

DOES Mum gripe at you for being 'difficult', do friends find you moody, do boy friends give you up because you are hard to please, or do you get into sulks for no reason at all?

This quiz doesn't pull any punches, it deals fair and square and tells you just how you rate—and what to do, if you're getting to be a bit of a so-and-so, before you lose too many friends!

Think you can stand the challenge? Go on—there might be a nice surprise in store!

1. You want an exact shade of pink in a sweater; the shop assistant assures you she can get it, and orders one for you. When you go to collect it, it is completely different from the snippet of cloth you left with her. The sweater costs 89s 11d, and the girl says as you ordered it, you must pay. Would you:

A. Take the sweater and wear it with something else.
B. Refuse to pay and ask to see the manager.
C. Say you will call back tomorrow with the cash for the sweater, but never go in the shop again.
D. Feel terribly upset, and shout at the assistant.
E. Say if she can change it for a better match you will pay, otherwise you don't want a sweater at all.

2. Imagine that you get home and find your mum has done up your bedroom for you as a surprise—and you hate it!

D. You burst into tears, and accuse her of invading your privacy.
B. You tell her, she could have saved herself the bother, as you prefer it the way it was, dirt and all.
C. You say you like it, but a few days later ask if she'll mind you buying new curtains and painting over the wallpaper in a colour you prefer.
A. You'd thank her for her trouble, and say nothing about hating it.
E. You say she's made a wonderful difference, and it's all beautifully clean—but ask if you can buy a few bits and pieces to make it more your style.

3. Two films on in town, and you and your boyfriend differ about which to see! What d'you think would happen, in a case like this?

D. You make a big issue out of it and say he will forgo his choice if he really loves you. If he still won't see "your" film, you go home alone, in tears.
C. You'd go to see "his" film, but make it clear throughout that you aren't enjoying it.
B. You'd go to "your" film, or none at all.
E. You go to see "his" film—and go to see "yours" with a girlfriend, another night.
A. You'd go to see "his" film—he's paying.

4. You are going to set up house with three other girls, and you agree to make a few rules that everyone must stick to. Which of these rules do you think would make it easier for everyone to get along together without rowing?

D. No poaching other girls' boyfriends.
C. Don't borrow other people's things.
A. Share everything—bills and chores included.
B. Everyone choose a certain chore and stick to it.
E. The one who makes the mess cleans it up.

5. There is no particular rule in your home about what time you have to be in; last week you went out and got in at 11.15 and nothing was said. This week, you got in at 11.10 and Mum flew off the handle! What would you think?

E. You think she's probably tired, and decide to let it drop—but check what time to be in before you're out late in future.
A. She'll have forgotten about it by next week, so why worry?
C. You say OK, you will be in by 10.30 next week—but don't mean to.
B. You tell her if she wants you in earlier, she ought to make it clear before you go out, so really it's her fault.
D. You say all the other girls your age are allowed out after midnight, and nobody says anything to them about it.

6. Your friend says you can borrow her tranny any time you like. You ask, a few weeks later, if you can have it to take on a rather boring car journey the family is making, and she ums and ahs and says it will be difficult that particular week-end. Your reaction?

D. "I thought you were my best friend! I'd lend you *anything* of mine!"
C. You grin and say it doesn't matter—but resolve that next time she wants to borrow something of yours, she won't get it, so there!
B. "Now look, you *said* I could have it, so what's the problem, don't you trust me with your precious tranny, or something?"
E. You'd think that maybe her folks have forbidden her to lend it or something, so you don't press her for her reason but say, maybe some other time.
A. "It doesn't matter, it was just a thought . . ."

7. Be honest! Do you have "moods"?

A. Sometimes, but you try to make it up to people afterwards.
E. About the same as everyone else has, you think!
B. Not without good reason.
C. No—but other people are sometimes very trying.
D. Yes, they just sweep over you for days at a time.

8. You loaned your pal something new, that you like a lot—new gear, or something like that. It comes back with a small, damaged place that would be fairly un-noticeable to someone who didn't inspect it carefully. What would you do?

D. Say nothing to *her*, but maybe accidentally, tell friends all about it.
A. Forget it.
E. Have the damage cleaned or repaired, and say nothing unless it costs a bomb, in which case mention it to her casually.
B. Point it out to her at once, so she has the chance to offer to put it right.
C. Say nothing, but never lend her anything again.

9. Think about the rows you have, if any. Are they:

B. Because your opinions clash directly with someone else's, mostly about big issues or important personal things.
D. Big fireworks over nothing very much—except that they seem vital, at the time!
A. Mostly your own fault, you think.
E. Mostly when you can't get your own way, to be honest!
C. You don't have many, but they build up over a long time until the storm breaks.

Answers

MOSTLY A's—*You try to be easy to please—too hard. You let people walk all over you, and then wonder why they have a low opinion of you! Maybe your parents are a bit strict, and you have found the easiest thing is to go along with the rules they make, but you're old enough to make your own rules now, and one of them should be, to learn to stand on your two feet when necessary!*

If you ticked A for questions 1, 2 and 8, you may not have thought of it this way, but you aren't giving people the chance to do the decent thing. If you have a gripe, try to air your point of view in a reasonable manner. Bottling it all up will only give you ulcers! **Your surprise:** *people can be a lot nicer, more understanding, and helpful than you are giving them credit for at present!*

MOSTLY B's—*You don't know if you are difficult or not, because you don't even think about it. You have a strong personality, and your own very determined views, and you don't shrink at being unpleasant or very frank if you feel it is justified. What you don't realise is, that to other people, their views, though opposite to yours, can seem just as important, and equally well justified! You really have a lot to learn about getting along with other people! It isn't a sign of weak character, sometimes to give ground in an argument—on the contrary, it's a sign of maturity.*

If you ticked B for questions 2, 3 and 6, you don't really stop to consider other people's feelings very much. There is often an equally good, but far less hurtful way of resolving the situation. For example, read 2E, 3E and 6E. **Your surprise:** *you sometimes get the feeling that people admire, but don't LIKE you. If you try to be a little easier to get along with a lot more people will like you better—and it's nice to be liked!*

MOSTLY C's—*You think you are very easy to get along with, but actually you are extremely difficult, because you have a habit of saying one thing and meaning something different. Rather than be unpleasant, you evade the issue—but this doesn't solve problems. Also, it means that people don't know how you will react, and they may think you are being moody or difficult, when if you had explained your feelings in the first place, trouble would not have arisen!*

If you ticked C for questions 3, 6 and 8, you are building up a reputation for yourself for being unfair or mean, and this will lose you friends of both sexes very quickly indeed. **Your surprise:** *Life need not be anywhere near as complicated as you are making it! Don't make mountains out of molehills, but look for the simplest way out of your problems.*

MOSTLY D's—*If you're very young (under 14), these are just "growing pains", but if you don't learn to think before you act, and control your emotions, you could end up miserable and neurotic! There's really no sense in making yourself unhappy over things you can't change—life is often unfair, but it's best to accept the situation and learn to live with it, for a time at any rate!*

If you ticked D for questions 3, 5 and 8, these are all situations where it is difficult to say what is "fair" or "unfair" and by getting emotional about it you are just making the problem worse, not better. Read some of the other answers to those particular questions—A gives a point of view that you may not agree with, but it will give you something to think about, and E is, we think, a more reasonable, practical solution than yours. **Your surprise:** *Your worst enemy is not Life, or The Unfairness Of Parents—but yourself. Beat that, and things will be much happier for you!*

MOSTLY E's—*You probably have your difficult days the same as everyone else, but on the average, you're a reasonable, sensible human being who finds it more easy to get along with others rather than constantly to quarrel and bicker. People wouldn't be able to say you are difficult to get along with—but they might find your habit of being always right a bit annoying, and you might appear a bit smug at times, specially if you've hit on the E answer 8 or 9 times! OR—nasty thought—could you just be a crafty quizzer who picks the right answer on paper, but not in real life? Anyway, even that is a good start because it shows you know what SHOULD be done, even if it's hard to live up to!* **Your surprise:** *If you GENUINELY ticked all those E answers, you are very popular, even though you may not always think so. But if you cheated, your friends must wonder if it's worth the effort, sometimes!*

THIS IS IT!

THE JACKIE ZODIAC RING

We're giving away

FREE

NEXT WEEK

bright and silvery
fits any finger
contains your lucky birthsign—and all the others, too.

And to match our Zodiac mood, the On-The-Spot Interview question next week is "How Do You Measure Up To Your Horoscope Characteristics?"

Here are just three of next week's other attractions—

Robert Wagner Pin-Up Diary
Great Georgie Best pic for your bedroom
& a howl of a Teach-In—How To Get The Most Out Of Your Jackie

Plus, of course, the next exciting instalment of "The Man In Black" and more amorous adventures of Ann Foster, the girl who gets mixed up with "Your Friendly Neighbourhood Ghost."

21 WAYS TO MAKE HIM NOTICE YOU

YOU'VE got your little gimlet eye on this likely-looking bod—but as far as he's concerned, you don't even exist! It's about time the poor lad knew what he was missing, so do him a big favour and get yourself noticed! How? Well, work your way through this lot . . .

THE SUBTLE APPROACH, FIRST

1. Get wise to his favourite haunts, and just be there, ever so casually.

2. At the club, don't strive to win games or push yourself forward if it's not your usual routine, (lots of boys are scared of pushy girls), but lose games with a good - humoured laugh, stick around and help clear up the debris afterwards, he'll cotton on.

3. A nice sincere smile and a friendly 'hallo'—WITHOUT obviously angling for more talk will relax him, make him think he must know you!

4. Don't cling to a girl - friend for courage, it'll put him off. Being on your own, with a slightly lost look (but not hidden at the back of the crowd!) encourages him to get things started.

5. Find a nice, unmanageable, preferably large, dog and take it for walks where you'll meet your other dumb friend, and leave the rest to nature!

6. At a crowded social do, wear something that makes you stand out. A plain, clear colour is often better from the eye-catching point of view than patterns. Or an all-white trouser-suit. Or a mini, when the rest have gone maxi (specially if you've good legs).

7. Perfume. Lots of girls don't bother. Make yours always the same, and he will recognise you before he sees you. But make it a subtle one, nothing overpowering!

THE DIRECT INVITATION, BUT NICELY . . .

8. Ask him the time (but hide your watch, or let it run down!)

9. Request change for the phone, the bus, the juke box.

10. Ask him the way somewhere, if you're suitably dense he may even take you himself!

11. Carry a large (empty) parcel everywhere. Ask him to hold it while you get your purse out of your bag . . .

12. . . . and if necessary leave the parcel behind, beside him! Have your address on it!

13. In the coffee bar, ask him to pass you the sugar, the salt, the tomato sauce, the mustard, more sugar, and the menu. As you've only ordered orangeade, that should get him interested!

14. On a bus or train? Ask him the best stop to get off for the swimming baths (or whatever).

IF ALL ELSE FAILS—

15. Look the other way and walk right into him.

16. Drip the cornet you are licking all over his sleeve . . . then you have to clean it off, don't you!

17. Offer him a sweet, or a chip!

18. Ask him if he will sponsor you for a charity walk, and make sure you get his address to collect what he owes, later.

19. Pretend you think he's a friend of someone you know, and chatter away nonstop before you 'discover' he isn't.

20. 'Faint' in front of him.

21. Ask him for a date!

WHAT, you've honestly worked your way through all 21 red-hot notions and he still hasn't noticed you? Are you sure he's still breathing? Maybe you should call the fire brigade, or an ambulance, or summat . . . or try your fatal charms on another bloke. Good luck!

So Far Sew Good

PATCH IT UP!

Revitalise tired gear with contrasting patches—any fabric will do. Remember, if you're fitting an elbow or pocket patch, to hem it before fixing, to give a neat unfrayed edge.

If it's a tricky shape like a shoulder section, it's much better to stick it in place with fabric glues, or with "Bondina Fusible Fleece"—an iron-on adhesive layer between patch and fabric.

FOLLOW SUIT

Following the fellas has its problems—you never can tell where they'll lead you! So get yourself geared up ready for the action and wear something suitable for tracking 'em down!

Suit yourself how you go about it, but this bolero and midi suit is DEFINITELY the best way!

Make: Travers Tempos. Style No.: 7037. Price: Approx £6. Fabric: Wool. Colours: Brown, turquoise, lilac, green. Sizes: 10-16.

For stockists write to Travers Tempos, 9 Little Portland Street, London W.1.

Knee high wet-look boots with laced-up vamps from all branches of Freeman, Hardy Willis.

Style: Attack, Price: £5 19s. Colour: Black or brown. Sizes: 3-8.

Freeman, Hardy Willis enquiries to Sunningdale Road, Leicester.

Follow him to the ends of the earth? You won't have to, luv. When he spots this topper of a trouser suit he'll about turn and head straight in your direction!

Make: Littlewoods. Style No.: 810/5 Price: Approx £6 10s. Fabric: Knitted Vonnel. Colours: Green/white, coffee/white. Sizes: 10-14.

From all branches of Littlewoods, 204-211 Oxford Street, London W.1., plus 3s 6d p & p.

True-Form low heeled shoes with gilt are called Venice. Price: 69s 11d. Fabric: Leather. Colours: Black wet-look, brown or red rub-off leather. Sizes: 3-8. From all main branches.

True-Form enquiries to Caroline Jackson, P.R. Dept., Lilley and Skinner, 206 Pentonville Road, Kings Cross, London W.1.

Moc-croc and suede shoes from main branches of Freeman, Hardy Willis. Style: Elite. Price: 69s 11d. Colours, Black, brown, red, Sizes: 3-8.

Stockists of Alan Rodin shirt include Fenwicks, Newcastle; Hammonds, Hull; County Clothes, Cheltenham; Fenwicks, New Bond Street, London W.1.

More from Alan Rodin, 62 Margaret Street, London W.1.

You always get your man! Even if you've been tailing him for weeks! Catch his eye in a knock-out smash suit cut on figure-flattening lines with two tiny triangle pockets.

Make: C & A. Style No.: 0950/62/32/2658. Price: Approx £3. Fabric: Neospun courtelle. Colours: Black, navy, moonstone, red, tropic, grey. Sizes: 10-16. From all branches of C & A.

High neck shirt with yoke stitching by Alan Rodin. Style No.: 330. Price: Approx £4 14s 6d. Fabric: Polyester/Cotton. Colours: Plum/beige, black/beige, brown/beige, green/beige. Sizes: 10-14.

Up-tights by Winfield. Price: 4s 9d. Fabric: 20 denier crepe nylon. Colours: Black, lime, tangerine, light blue, cream, pearl grey, French grey, petal pink, white, three shades of tan. One size. From most Woolworth stores.

SNAKES & LADDERS

You should throw a six to start this little game—but we'll let you off with a three!
Three great snake outfits to see you at the top of the fashion ladder.

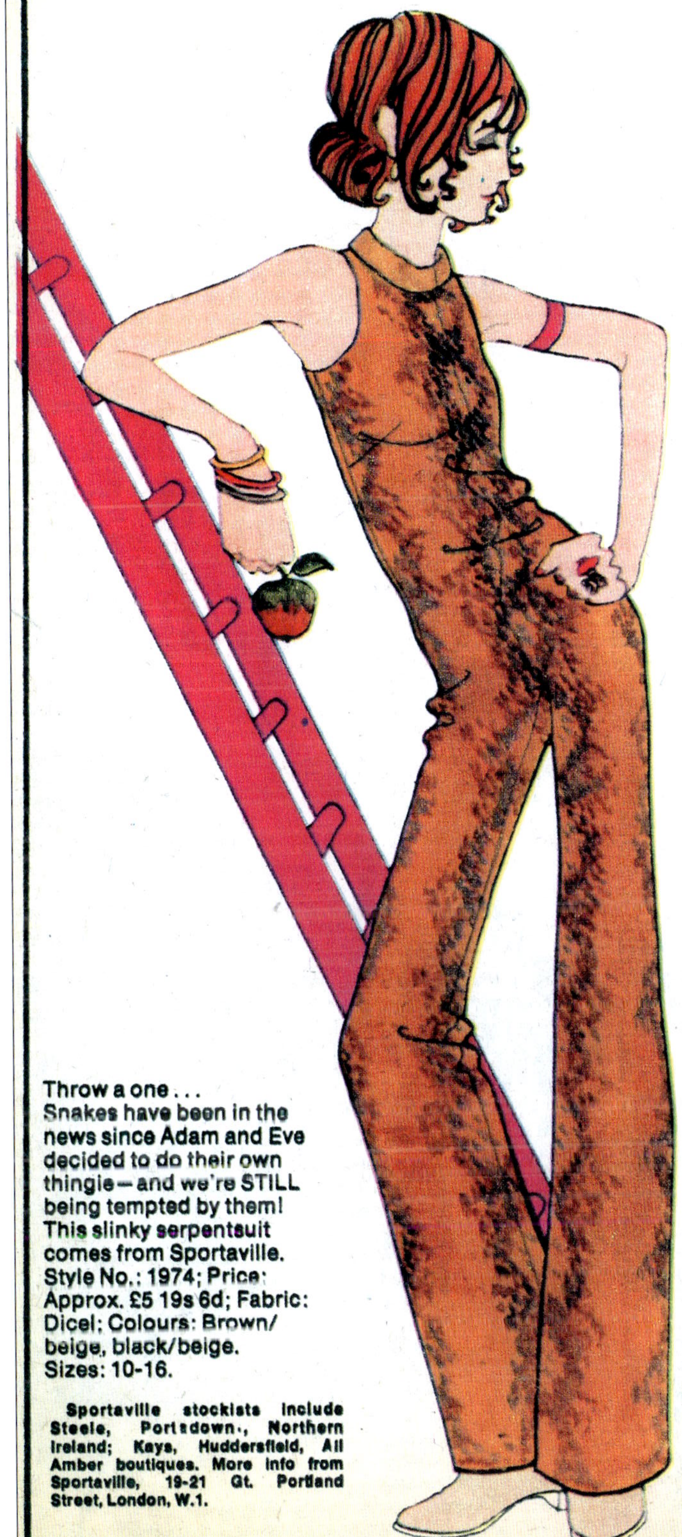

Throw a one . . .
Snakes have been in the news since Adam and Eve decided to do their own thingie—and we're STILL being tempted by them! This slinky serpentsuit comes from Sportaville. Style No.: 1974; Price: Approx. £5 19s 6d; Fabric: Dicel; Colours: Brown/beige, black/beige. Sizes: 10-16.

Sportaville stockists include Steele, Portadown., Northern Ireland; Kays, Huddersfield, All Amber boutiques. More info from Sportaville, 19-21 Gt. Portland Street, London, W.1.

Throw a two . . .
Super snake print top, with ruched sleeves and elasticated waist, comes alive with grey and red check plus-fours.
Step up the ladder with fake snake boots by True Form.
Called: Hugger; Price: 69s 11d; Colours: Mock snake-skin, black or white wet look. Sizes: 3-8.
Alan Rodin top Style No.: 391; Price: Approx. 99s 6d; Fabric: Acetate; Colours: Pink, turquoise, grey, brown; Sizes: 10-16.
Trousers by Travers Tempos. Style No.: SL 29; Price: Approx. 95s; Fabric: Wool; Colours: As illustrated; Sizes: 10-16.

Alan Rodin top from Guys and Dolls, 2007 Oxford Street, London, W.1., Impact, McDonalds, Glasgow. Further stockists from Alan Rodin, 62 Margaret Street, London, W.1.
Travers trousers from Brown and Thomas, Dublin; Arana, Colchester, and all Amber boutiques. More from Travers Tempos, 9 Little Portland Street, London, W.1.
Fake Snakeskin boots from all branches of True Form.

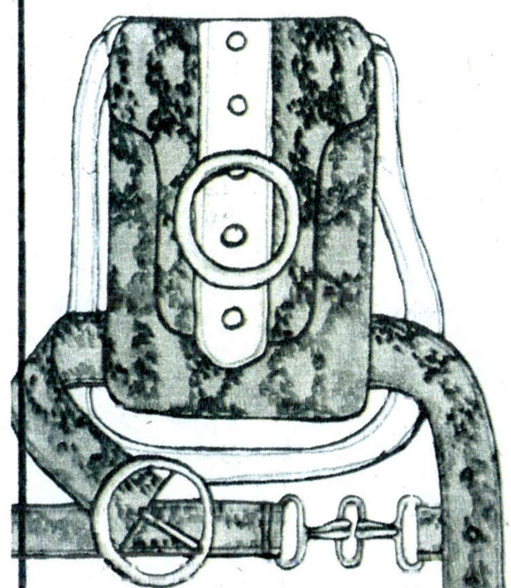

Snakeskin bag from Salisbury. Style No. 961201/1; Price: £5 10s 0d; Fabric: Mock python; Colours: Black/white.
Coil a snake round your middle. Narrow synthetic python belt. Style No.: 29/618; Price: 29s 11d. Wide belt with buckle. Style No.: 29/605; Price: 39s 11d. Write to us for your nearest Salisbury branch.

Throw a three . . .
This dress is a runaway winner in any game. Attractive detail stitching gives way to a super easy swing skirt.
Make: Dolly Dolly; Style No.: 2032; Price: Approx. 5 gns.; Fabric: Acetate jersey; Colours: Pink, grey, blue, green, brown; Sizes: 1-3.

For stockists of Dolly Dolly dress, write to, Dolly Dolly, 5-11 Riding-house St., London, W.1.

A Jackie Quiz

Are You In Four-Leafed Clover?

Black cats mean anything to you? Have you a lucky rabbit's foot to take into exams? Or do you sit back and wait for events to take their natural course? Well, do the quiz and find out—oh, and by the way, . . . good luck!

1. What would give you the best chance of a win at roulette?
a. a bet on black
b. a bet on your lucky number.
c. a bet on a lucky system.

2. Meeting the right guy is a matter of—
a. skill.
b. luck.
c. fate.

3. You enter the "Lucky Lady" toothpaste competition but you've got to send a slogan. Pick one of these.
c. 'Brushwyte' makes teeth sparkle.
a. Morning and night I use 'Brushwyte'.
b. Brush white with 'Brushwyte'.

4. The phone rings and they tell you you've won a free lesson at the local dancing academy. This is
a. a trick.
c. lucky!
b. business.

5. Let's assume that black cats are unluckier than white ones. But it's true—
a. only if you see them.
b. only if they cross your path.
c. only if they cross your path by moonlight.

6. Your friend's eaten nearly a whole quarter of Lucky Hearts (gree-dy!) but she's offering you one of the last three left in the bag. Take one while you have the chance!
b. Flirty!
c. True love.
a. Kiss and tell.

7. It's best to be born—
a. rich.
b. beautiful.
c. lucky.

8. Here's some-one selling raffle tickets but you can't really afford one. Do you—
a. refuse.
b. buy one.
c. buy one and pick a special number.

Answers

MOSTLY A's Luck doesn't enter into your reckoning at all, you are much too cool, calculating and level-headed to leave things to chance. You're likely to have quite a sensible head with money and save up successfully for the things you really want. Your love-life is likely to be uncomplicated if a bit unexciting and predictable.

You probably plan things well in advance and have the temperament to carry them through. Things just don't happen by chance in your scene and it could mean long visits to dullsville.

MOSTLY B's You seem to be pretty well adjusted and though you might deny taking much heed of luck it does play a part in your makeup. While sensible in most things you sometimes let wild hopes push logic into the background.

Romance-wise you have a pretty firm hand on events and your lovelife will usually go your way, though you occasionally lead with your heart and get hurt. You have the ideal formula for life—calm reasoning, with, just that bit of trusting to luck which sometimes pays off.

MOSTLY C's Luck and superstition plays a very important part in your life. You are likely to be no great shakes with finances and budgeting and are consequently quite often short of cash. Kind and generous, you are sometimes badly let down through misplaced trust.

Love affairs are likely to be pretty tempestuous, but you are not likely to be unhappy for long. Chances of a happy marriage are excellent, though it will largely be a case of luck!

SEW FAR SO GOOD

GO VEST YOUNG WOMAN—AND DYE!

DYING to tell you about our latest craze, tie-dying! All the swingers are wearing tee shirts and vests again this summer, but if you want yours to look a bit different like the one in the illustration, for instance, here's how to go about it.

Gather up the area where you want the pattern, and bind it securely with string or tape. The nicest results come from binding a centre circle (as in the picture), or trying for horizontal or vertical stripes—take pot luck and just squash the whole thing up if you like, though! It's sure to turn out original!

Now dip the whole thing in water, then pop it into a large saucepan or bucket containing boiling dye. Check the dye packet for instructions, of course, and boil for the required time. Couldn't be simpler, could it?! And all for the price of a packet of dye!

You can even be a bit more enterprising, and try other colours on top once the first colour's dry.

Tie the string in a different place for really wild colour-harmonies!

On-The-Spot Interviews

What would you vote the worst number one in 1969/70

Joe Ryan, Leinster Square, Dublin.
"Two Little Boys" by Rolf Harris. It's the most ickey song I've ever heard . . . a real "hand me my stick of rock and skipping rope" type of thing! Anyway, my yucky brother loves it—so that's enough reason for me NOT to . . .!

Dessy Rust, Cherry Road, Wisbech, Cambs.
I never liked "Bridge Over Troubled Waters" really. I know it was probably a very good number, but I found it mournful and depressing. I like happy hits.

Susan Tomkins, Brookfields Road, Oldbury.
"Wandering Star" by Lee Marvin. It sounded like my grandfather with laryngitis.

Alistair Biddle, Poplar Avenue, Bearwood, Birmingham.
"Give Peace A Chance." Not only was it a dirge itself, but it started off a whole queue of equally draggy records of the same type.

Antionette Overson, Fleet Road, Holbeach, Lincs.
Little kids seem to be making all the number one hits these days. I'm sure they must have been the only ones buying "Wandering Star," and the worst of them all—"Two Little Boys." It was awful.

Wendy Scott, Torridon Avenue, Glasgow.
"Wandering Star" would get my vote. I can't stand Lee Marvin's voice.

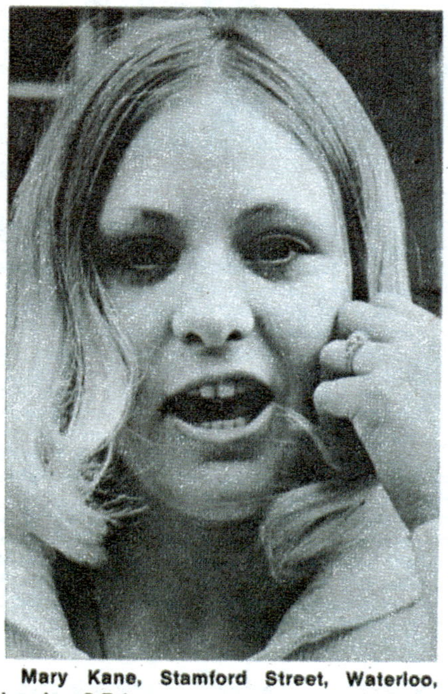

Mary Kane, Stamford Street, Waterloo, London, S.E.1.
"Back Home" the England World Cup team's song. It only got there because of the World Cup, not because it's a good song. I didn't like it, anyway!

Sylvia Morton, Elgin Road, Dublin.
That drippy song: "Je t'aime Moi Non Plus" by Jane Birkin and that Serge bloke. All I can say is, that if that's supposed to be a SEXY song—then I know why I'm called "Sexless Sylvia" . . .!

Alison Cox, Kelynmead Road, Birmingham, 33.
I think it's a toss-up between "All Kinds of Everything" by Dana and the awful Lulu song that won the Eurovision contest in 1969. They're both so sweet, they make me feel ill.

P. Jarvis, Hollingbury, Brighton.
"Ruby Don't Take Your Love To Town!" I thought it was a right rotten miserable old record!

Jenny Kent, Wisbeck, Cambs.
"All Kinds of Everything" by Dana. All the songs that are entered for *that* competition are pretty bad, but they always seem to be able to pick the worst out as winner.

Jill Lesley, Lindsay Road, Dublin.
That record "Sugar, Sugar" by The Archies—I think it's a howl, 'cos my brother's in a group and according to him, he does a beautiful impersonation of the disc!! So everytime I hear the Archies singing it, I just picture my brother with his hair hanging in his eyes doing his "Elvis Bit," and I just can't stop laughing!

Pat Kennedy, Florence Road, New Cross, London.
"Two Little Boys." Rolf Harris shouldn't sing—he's got a terrible voice. How it got number one I'll never know!

A Jackie Teach-In

HOW TO BE POPULAR

THE only way to be sure you're the most popular girl around is to be the only girl around.

To achieve this state of affairs, you've either got to live somewhere in the wilds where there's a shortage of girls, or arrange to have the entire female population of your neighbourhood kidnapped by slave traders and sold off to a short-sighted sheik.

Are you willing to go to that much trouble or will you settle for being just *one* of the popular girls around? You will? Good.

Right, then. What is a popular girl? She's likeable and easy to get along with. She's a good listener, which means that she not only doesn't interrupt when somebody's talking, but she doesn't yawn and fall asleep, either.

She doesn't greet her friends with remarks like *"Hi, ratface!"* or *"I do love your new coat—it reminds me of the one Farmer Stringbritches put on his scarecrow"* or even *"If I felt as bad as you look I'd be dead."* She finds it easier to make friends than enemies. In fact, she's very much like you, isn't she? She's also very much like Drusilla Wretch, of Wolverhampton.

Drusilla was pleasant and easy to get along with. She was also easy to get along without, which is what most people did. Where did Drusilla slip up (apart from on a banana in Blackpool on the 14th July last year)?

For readers who collect question marks, here is a free gift from Jackie—? Take care of it.

Drusilla tried to be too popular. She rescued cats from trees, helped old ladies onto buses and baby sat for Mr and Mrs Groggis regularly every week.

And yet nobody really liked her. The cats didn't like being rescued from trees; they were all quite capable of getting down by themselves.

The old ladies were generally trying to get *off* the buses she helped them on and Mr and Mrs Groggis didn't want to go out every week.

Not only that, but Egbert Groggis, their son, didn't appreciate having nursery stories read to him while sitting on Drusilla's knee. This may have been due to the fact that he was 45. Or perhaps Drusilla had bony knees, it's hard to say. Especially with a mouthful of porridge. You try saying *"bony knees"* with a mouthful of porridge and you'll see just how hard it is.

Anyway, the thing is not to work on the popularity thing too hard. It's the little things that count, like remembering to say "thank you" after a party to the host or hostess instead of just wandering out with the best looking boy and muttering "I've been to livelier funerals."

When some weedy grot of a boy asks you to dance, don't screech with laughter and make him wish he'd stayed at home under the bed—*dance* with him.

You may have trouble getting rid of him after that, but we've all got problems, haven't we? Maybe you could adopt him as a mascot or something and keep him on the mantelpiece at home.

When you're out with a boy on his scooter and it starts to rain and your hairstyle is ruined and mascara runs down your cheeks like prison bars, don't snarl in his ear about how you wish you were still going out with your last boy who owned a mini. *Think* it if you like, but don't *say* it.

The popular girl is also someone everybody likes to see. This means that she's not only gay and cheerful but also that she doesn't look like something Farmer Stringbritches has just dug out of his turnip field.

In other words (and there are plenty of other words, like "susurrus" and "parergon") she looks after her appearance, too.

Of course, a lot depends on whether you just want to be generally popular or popular with one group.

Eulalia Crone, of Cardiff, was extremely popular with the lads of the local Rugby team.

She never missed one of their matches and was always yelling support. But perhaps the thing that really made her popular was the way she shared the shower room with them after every match. Everybody else hated her, but those lads loved her.

It's safer, though, to be popular with everybody. So off you go—get out there and Be Popular.

You may have a little trouble getting started if you're so unpopular at the moment that no one will even speak to you but keep trying. Don't give up. If it doesn't work now it might later. When you're 85 you may be voted the most popular old lady in town. Well, it's something, *isn't it?!*

A Jackie Quiz

Could you get an A-level on boys?

SO far as we know there are no academic exams on the subject of Boys, but it's probably only a question of time! Meanwhile we'll have our own exam paper on this fascinating and thrilling topic.

Those passing at 'A' level will not actually get a diploma, but they'll always have that comforting thought of that 'A' rating up their sleeve whenever the subject is fellas!

1. If your boy goes on about a "big home attraction" is he likely to mean—
- a) Tele?
- b) United v. City?
- c) A cute little dolly-next-door?

2. You've noticed that guy around once or twice and he interests you. How do you get things moving in your direction?
- a) Let him see you are interested, in subtle little ways.
- b) Ignore him.
- c) Make it obvious you are interested, and blow the subtle bit.

3. He can't and won't dance—but you love dancing. What's to do?
- a) Enrol him in a 'beginners only' dance class.
- b) Persuade him with your subtle charm to go dancing and teach him yourself.
- c) Abandon dancing and grudgingly take up something else.

4. Which phrase is likely to get a reluctant boy home for the first time?
- a) My mum wants to meet you.
- b) My dad wants to meet you.
- c) My parents want to meet you.

6. He's very tall, and now you're about to kiss goodnight for the first time. It could be embarrassing. What's best—
- a) Cleverly see that you are standing on the step when it's kissing time?
- b) Completely ignore any difference in height and let love find a way?
- c) Laughingly forestall any embarrassment with a joke?

5. If he is proud of a new snap tackle he's invented would you steer the conversation towards—
- a) Rugby?
- b) Fishing?
- c) Stock car racing?

7. He's a member of the local gang and you want him to break out of it. The best way is—
- a) Ridicule them and pour scorn on them every chance you get?
- b) Crowd them out?
- c) Ultimatum—he must pack them up or never see you again?

8. He's mad keen, wants to see you every night. You go for him, too, but is this smart?
- a) No. He might become bored if you see too much of each other.
- b) No. See him every night, but make it for only a few minutes some times.
- c) Yes! Yes! Yes!

9. He prides himself on his table-tennis, but you know you are much better than he is. Do you—
- a) Win every time easily?
- b) Not play him?
- c) Work it so he just beats you every time?

MOSTLY A's You do not qualify for an 'A' level pass, with all these A's, but you do earn an 'O' level with your answers. This shows a fair knowledge of the subject and indicates that with a little more perseverance an 'A' level rating is possible. A prolonged study of the topic in which the student maintains regular interest will ensure a high rate of passes in the future. A good effort.

MOSTLY B's Congratulations, you are an obviously knowledgeable student and you get an 'A' level pass, with honours. You show a remarkably keen interest and expert appraisal of this wide-ranging subject which could lead to great achievement later in life, when student days are over. Further study might see even more honours and it is worth remembering that some of the most successful marriages are brought about by degrees. Full marks!

MOSTLY C's You have failed to pass the exam and show little knowledge of the subject, though by entering you have indicated that a pass would be of interest to you. We recommend that you spend more time on this subject with practical experience and less home-work. Lectures may take the place of home work but carry on with your studies and you will find yourself improving, and with an effort, you might pass next time. Keep at it!

stripe up the band

And it's your turn to call the tune. So strike a high note in time with the pick of the spring range pops.

Keep up the beat with a pair of foot-stompers from Ravel. Mudguard style, to give your toes room to tap in time, high vamp with metal detail and low clumpy heel. To match is a concertina-style bag with double pouch and adaptable strap. The attractive brass buckle and strap is purely ornamental, concealing an easy clip fastening.
Shoes Style No.: 2019 "Smash Hit"; Price: 79s 11d; Colours: Green/black, brown/black, brown/green; Sizes: 3-7.
Bag Style No.: 2019; Price: 49s; Colours: Green/black, brown/black.

If you're playing "The Field," (a well-known oldie!) you can pluck a few strings and fiddle yourself any date in this unbeatable duo. Conducted along classical lines turned to pop with easy-flare pants.
Style No.: S1; Price: 6½ gns. for the dress 4½ gns. the trousers; Fabric: Arnel and Linnel; Colours: White with navy/pink stripe, turquoise/brown, pink/brown; Sizes: 1, 2, 3; Make: Gillian Richard.

Look sharp even if you feel flat 'cos by now you know the score and can really afford to blow your own trumpet in this jazzy little number.

Bands of beige and navy tune in to a self-coloured navy skirt with a perky hip pocket.

Harmonising along is this bazzazy Bellino striped scarf, style No.: 4392; Price: 16s 6d; Colours: Assorted; Fabric: Tricel.

Dress Style No.: 3081; Price: £4 19s 11d; Colours: Navy, peach, turquoise and beige; Fabric: Neospun jersey; Sizes: 10-16; Make: Dorothy Perkins.

No need to lose your tempo 'cos he doesn't come in on time.

He'll regret missing his cue when he sees you in this little masterpiece.

Cut-away shoulders and two cute pockets in super tones and all going for a song.

It's cymbally (groan) smashing!

Price: 59s 11d; Colours: Navy/white, lilac/violet, pink/violet, turquoise/white; Sizes: 1, 2; Make: Etam.

Gillian Richard outfit available from Sidney Smith Mail Order, 38 Kings Road, London, S.W.3., enclosing 5s postage and packing. Further inquiries to Gillian Richard, 106 Gt. Portland St., London, W.1.
Dorothy Perkins dress from all main branches. Info from Mary West, Flat 8, 89 Gt. Portland St., London, W.1.
Etam inquiries to Susan Shanks and Partners Publicity, 22 Long Acre, London, W.C.2.
Ravel shoes obtainable by post from: P.R. Dept., Sandra Sussman, 103 New Bond St., London, W.1. including 3s 6d p. & p.

P.S. If you want a pair of boots like the bandsman's, try the Scots Guards at Caterham, Surrey. You'll have to sign on for 22 years to get 'em free.

MUCHOS GAUCHOS

Buenos Dias, Señorita! (That's yer Spanish for "Hi babe! What's your groove?")

Here are some newer-than-new knicks wot look as if they've just been whipped off a passing bandito!

Reason they're called GAUCHOS is because of their resemblance to the trousers worn by Mexican ranch-hands.

Looking as if they've stepped straight from the rancho El Cause-a-Chaos stride these groovy gaucho pants with matching tops in sizzling stripes. Both by Bus Stop. Sweater price: 55s. Fabric: Bouclé. Colour as illustrated. Medium size. Gauchos price: 85s. Fabric: Bonded jersey. All colours. Sizes: 8-14.

Boots by Bata Style No.: 709 9051. Price: 7 gns. Fabric: Calico. Colours: Beige, turquoise, purple. Sizes: 3-8. Indian silk scarf from a selection at Second Skin. Price, 29s 6d.

Gauchos may take a bit of nerve to wear, at first, but if you've got the cheek(s!) this is for you! (ooo-oo!). You COULD say it's a Juan-piece!! (groan). One-piece gaucho suit by Dollyrocker Style No. 2088. Price: Approx. £7 15s. Fabric: Wool. Colours: Brown, burgundy. Sizes: 10-16.

Fringey boots by Elliott. Style: Marta. Price: (wait for it) £20 19s (gasp!!!). Fabric: Suede. Colours: Blue, purple, brown, beige, maroon, yellow. Sizes: 4-8.

Leather choker from a selection at Second Skin. Price: 12s 6d. Colours: Green prune, coffee, beige, blue and other mixed colourways.

This outfit is just about enough to make a Mexican hat dance! 'S just too much, isn't it?! Careful, though, this kind of clobber is apt to attract the decidedly dishonourable intentions of every gringo around! Grr-eat!!

Suit by Dollyrocker. Gauchos Style No.: 2082. Price: Approx. £6 5s. Fabric: Panne Velvet. Colours: Grey, black, red. Sizes: 10-14. Waistcoat is part of a Dollyrocker kinderbocker suit. Details from us.

Embroidered top by Bus Stop. Style No.: 9868. Price: £6 10s. Fabric: Crepe. Colours: Purple, red, blue, rust Sizes: 8-14.

Side-lacing shoes from Lilley and Skinner main branches. Style: Troy. Price: 99s 11d. Colours: Black only. Sizes: 3-8.

Knee-high socks from British Home Stores. Style No.: 3400. Price: 3s 11d. Fabric: 40 denier micro mesh. Colours: Black, white, grey, navy, scarlet, seville, olive, lavender. All stores.

Bus Stop suit from all branches. By post from Bus Stop, 3 Kensington Church Street, London, W.8. 3s 6d p & p. Bata boots by post from Bata International, 151 Oxford Street, London, W.1. Post and packing—3s 6d. Second Skin items from Second Skin, 220 Kensington High Street, London, W.8. 2s p & p.

Dollyrocker one-piece from Renée Shaw of Sutton and Brighton; Rivetts, King's Lynn; Frasers, Glasgow. Dollyrocker info from Jean Moriarty, 21 Cavendish Place, London W.1. Elliott boots from branches. More gen from Pauline Watkins, 3 Bott Mews, London W.2.

Dollyrocker velvet gauchos from Miss Selfridge; Chelsea Girl; Renée Shaw branches—Sutton and Brighton; Owen Owen branches. Bus Stop top from branches. By post from Bus Stop, 3 Kensington Church Street, London, W.1. Lilley and Skinner shoes from main branches. Mail Order available from 360 Oxford Street, London, W.8. 3s 6d p & p.

On-The-Spot Interviews

What's your favourite T.V. or radio programme and why?

Keith Brown, High Road, London, N.12.
I like "Callan" because it's so human and down to earth. I think it's one of the few feasible spy-type programmes. You'd never see him driving a car with machine guns out of the headlights and knives in the hub caps!

Caroline Mirkam, Wolesley Street, Dublin, 8.
Well, my favourite of all time is "Coronation Street"—but it's cost me quite a few dates! You see, if any bloke asked me out on a Monday or a Wednesday, by the time I watched "Coronation Street", it'd be half-eight before I could meet them, and as that's kinda late to go anywhere, by the time they've asked me WHY I can't meet them till that late, I find it easier to just say "No!"

Dorothy McHugh, Ansty Road, Coventry.
"Cinema" because I like seeing trailers, they're usually better than the whole film! And Michael Parkinson who introduces it, is very funny.

Helen Adair, Severne Road, Acocks Green, Birmingham.
Jimmy Young's show on radio! He's so awful. He has me curled up and rolling around on the floor when he's giving his recipe for the day. And it's even funnier when my mother tries to make the stuff and can't remember whether Jim said add a teaspoon of salt or a tablespoon of sugar.

Jenny Williams, North Gray Road, Bexley, Kent.
I like Roskp's show on Saturday lunch times. He has a fantastic personality and I really love his American accent. He plays some pretty good records too!

Linda Sneddon, Baldovan Crescent, Glasgow.
My favourite is Tony Blackburn. I listen every morning. His jokes are corny but you have to laugh at them.

Alison Smithers, Russell Road, Wimbledon, London, S.W.19.
"Top of the Pops" is my favourite TV programme. They have such good music on there. I think Tony Blackburn's the best D.J., and I like his smile! I watch it every week, even if there's a good film on the other channel that my parents want to see. I always get my own way with that programme!

Eirian Rees-Jones, Darley Road, Whalley Range, Manchester.
I'm really sad! They've taken "I'm sorry I'll read that again" off the radio. It was a half-hour of larking about, but it was quick and witty—and very, very funny. I used to listen to it every weekend—and sometimes to the repeats during the week as well.

William Armstrong, Garth Twelve, Killingworth Township, Northumberland.
Steptoe and Son was The Greatest! I never stopped laughing.

Maggie Fletcher, Bath Avenue, Dublin, 4.
"Ironside" because it keeps the whole family happy—my mum fancies Robert T. Ironside himself, my dad fancies the girl in it, Officer Whitfield, and me, I go for that he-man Ed Brown! So how's *that* for family entertainment.

Lorna Hill, St. Pauls Street, Brighton.
"Department S" or ANYTHING with Peter Wyngarde in!

Penny Humphreys, Bryanston Road, Solihull.
The Magic Roundabout on telly. My mother and I sit glued to it laughing at Dougal and Florence and the others. But my 7-year-old sister thinks the programme is childish!

Carole Benton, Fidle Street, Boston, Lincs.
Disco 2 is pretty good. It gives you a chance to see a lot of underground groups that wouldn't stand a chance of getting on Top of the Pops because they don't make singles.

Hillary Walton, Melrose Avenue, Dublin, 3.
For me, it's "Doctor in the House." Watching all those fellows flitting around, it gives us girls a great insight into the devious, cunning, male mind—invaluable information 'cos you can trick them at their own game!

Derek Plant, Swanshurst Lane, Birmingham, 13.
Kenny Everett's [redacted] show. I like the records, but the bits he does in between them are worth waiting for too. Most disc jockeys drive you mad when they start to talk!

Sharon Clarkson, Gunthorpe, Peterborong.
What about Monty Python's Flying Circus? It's the maddest TV programme I've ever seen. I can't wait for it to come back.

SHOW A LEG!

Midis are difficult to wear—if you're not careful, your legs can look really awful. But never fear, remember it's not what you wear, but the way that you wear it . . .

LEGS TOO THIN Heavy, medium-heeled shoes, ankle straps, maybe? Skirt mid-calf.

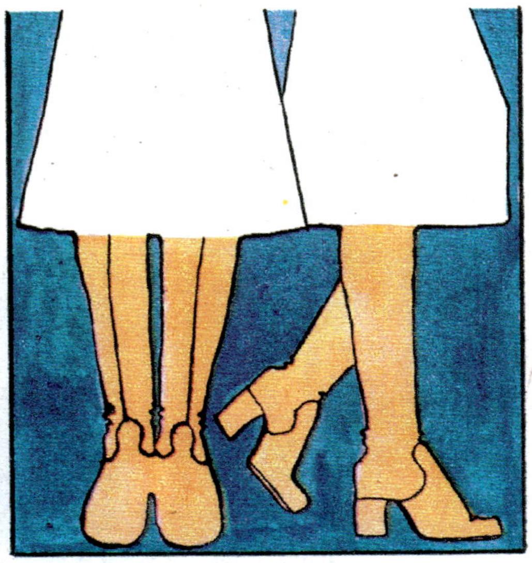

LEGS TOO FAT Keep to high-heeled boots. Skirt 2" below knee.

LEGS TOO CURVY Shoes with low heels (high heels throw you forward, make big calves curvier). Skirt 3-4" below knee.

LEGS TOO SHORT Wedges and platform soles for you. Heel as high as you like—Skirt *just* below the knee.

SOLID, HEAVY LEGS Shoes with medium heels and medium high fronts. Avoid 'little' shoes. Skirt *just* below knee.

PERFECT Wear anything. You're the only girl who can wear longer skirts and Grecian sandals.

FACE FACTS

EVERY feature on your face gives away something about your personality. So learn how to discover more about your friends—and find out a bit about yourself, too!

THE EYES are the first thing you notice. They set the key: large eyes, a dreamer or idealist; narrowness, a perceptive, practical character; close together, self-centred or introspective; expressive, an emotional character; eyes that flicker about continually, and that avoid looking directly at another person, indicate a light-weight personality, possibly full of ideas, but without staying-power. Got the eye-dea?

Look next at THE EYEBROWS, to see if these underline the characteristics you noticed in the eyes, or amend them. The thicker the brows, the stronger the personality. A marked curve in the centre indicates wilfulness and determination to have their own way. Wispy brows that are very wide apart and shallow show a child-like trust in others.

THE LIPS reveal the emotional side of the character. Wide, full lips are sensual. Narrow lips indicate a firm character not much influenced by emotions. The width indicates generosity—a narrow, pursed mouth with small round lips shows primness and narrowness of outlook. Look, too, at the space between the upper lip and the nose—where this is small and deeply indented, it indicates a quick reaction in emotional situations—a long or smooth area shows calmness and forethought.

Now study THE NOSE. Small, neat bones are feminine attributes, broad, large bones are masculine ones. Therefore, a large nose in a girl shows a good measure of the "masculine" virtues of practical commonsense, determination, and firmness of character—a dominant personality. A small nose in a man, on the other hand, shows the 'feminine' virtues of creativity, delicacy and tact, and a persuasive personality. The bridge of the nose indicates arrogance and pride—the smaller the bump, the more easy-going the personality.

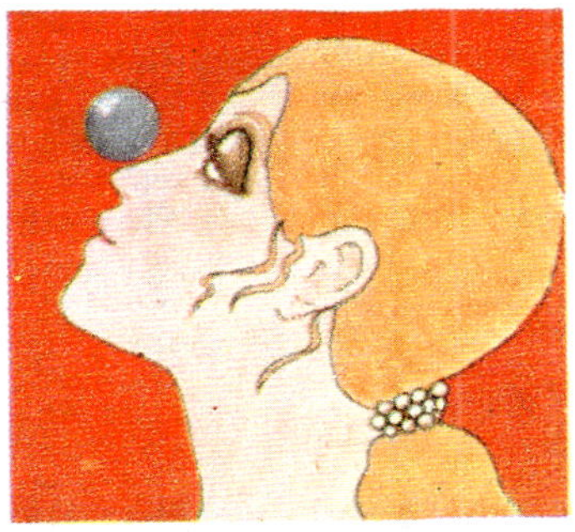

THE FOREHEAD should be considered in shape, rather than its size. A narrow forehead shows that the main influence on the character is emotion rather than the intellect. On the other hand, a high forehead shows intelligence, and deep, though not necessarily decisive, thought. Marked bumps on the forehead are the sign of an egotist, and a forehead that easily crumples into deep creases indicates a fluid, changeable personality. Tiny lines that appear early, over each eyebrow, show wit.

When you study THE CHIN, don't be too hasty. It's true that lack of chin can mean a weak character, but the shape is more important than the amount! A firm, small and well-shaped chin indicates determination and logic. A large, loose sort of chin that melts into the jaw shows indecisiveness and self-indulgence.

Dimples and clefts in the chin are important. Small round indentations are marks of charm, deep straight clefts show a forceful personality, and a small downward curving line just under the lower lip shows a rather ruthless streak.

THE EARS indicate the balance between the intellect and the emotions. The nearer the eyes they

come, the more store is set by ideas. Small, flat ears are a sign of an aggressive personality. Large ears usually belong to a calm but confident person. Fleshy lobes to the ears indicate sensuality.

Now that you've studied all the various features, remember that when the SAME characteristic is repeated in different features, this means that the virtue or failing plays an important part in the character. If DIFFERENT characteristics are shown in the various features, this indicates a many-sided personality.

You should consider the face as a whole. If any particular features stand out, pay close attention to their characteristics. Look, too, at the lines on a person's face bearing in mind the age of the subject. A face that lines comparatively easily may indicate an experienced personality, but the direction of the lines is the most important thing about them.

When the lines running from the corner of the mouth and nose, and from the eyes, tend to curve up, the whole character has a friendly, sunny aspect. Narrow, down-ward shaped lines indicate a gloomier approach, and possibly lack of self confidence, or doubt. Good humour is shown by a network of fine lines at the corners of the eyes, and mean-ness by tiny lines etched along the upper lip.

Obviously, these lines will be easier to see in older people. When you're studying young faces which haven't properly formed yet, always remember the most important thing is not the characteristics the person has inherited, but what they're making themselves, that really counts!

Cameo Column

The most precious gift of all

YOU'VE been to the pictures together.

He was attentive, but not more than usual; kind, and friendly, but not more than usual. At one moment in the film, when you were very anxious at a moment of drama, he took your hand, quietly, and you squeezed his, tightly, not with any passion, or even really with any awareness that it was *his* hand you were holding.

And then, when the moment passed, you let go, and he made no protest.

Though you were often tense: the film was a story of wailing at sundown, mourning for kings, weeping of widows, and the young lovers crushed and twisted in the dust.

The film came to an end, and you relaxed again; the lights came up for the interval, and he bought you an ice cream.

Took off your corduroy coat, and aware, wistfully, of your silky red blouse. The gold light falling upon you.

You talked, but not about anything important.

You looked round, recognised a schoolgirl friend a few rows away, waved.

Then the second film began, less interesting, something of an anti-climax, and you decided to leave before the end.

So out into the cold, with ice and snow lingering in narrow gabled streets, looking up at starlit attics in dark houses.

You had supper together.

In your usual restaurant, at least usual enough for you to like going there, from time to time.

You weren't to know the thoughts in his mind, you weren't to know, in fact, that somehow tonight you were looking quite beautiful. You caught sight of yourself, sideways, in venetian glass.

At any time you're attractive, with your long dark hair, happy smile, vivacious laugh, beautiful mouth.

But tonight there was more than that: the sparkle in your eyes, the gaiety in your voice.

No wonder his heart belongs to you.

When you left, you found you'd missed the last bus home. Not that it mattered: it was only two or three miles, it was—and still is—a lovely night, with the stars shining, and a sharp frost on roads and paths.

And pale moonlight, so pure that it seems even to freeze the water on which it has fallen.

But you're warm, and happy.

And in love?

That's a thought that hadn't occurred to you, really.

But it must have occurred to him, and perhaps had done long ago.

You are both standing now on a slope down from the crest of a hill, standing alone together, at midnight.

The city has disappeared far behind you, and although you're on the main road, it's deserted.

Far ahead, almost out of sight, dark shapes of buildings, and a twinkling light here and there, against the breathless curtain of night. And at your side a wooden fence, and the long deserted waste of winter fields, scattering of trees. On the opposite side of the road, a wood, with bare inter-laced branches of darkness.

You stand quite still, hand resting, ungloved, on the wooden railing, looking into his eyes, that seem like shadows or like mirrors.

Serious, suddenly.

And he, in his turn anxious, awaiting your reply.

He has told you that he loves you.

He has offered you the gift of his heart.

He can offer you no greater gift.

And in a few moments, you must answer, and at this instant you don't know what you're going to say. You turn towards him, suddenly, impetuously, hair blowing gently in the dark wind, and then hesitate, again, yet again.

Look up into his eyes, and sigh.

And then, in a happiness that suddenly overwhelms you, and which you didn't in the least expect, so intense is it, you speak.

Cathy and Claire Page

If there's anything worrying you which you can't work out for yourself, why not drop us a line? Address it to Cathy & Claire, at Jackie, 12 Fetter Lane, Fleet Street, London, E.C.4.

DEAR CATHY & CLAIRE—I have liked this boy for ages, and he knows it, but he never attempts to ask me out or anything—in fact he completely ignores me, and smiles and speaks to my friend. Why? She doesn't even like him, yet I do, and I just can't get him. Please give me some advice. My friend and I are 15, and he is 17.

The whole thing is given away by one sentence "She doesn't even like him." She doesn't like him so she doesn't go out of her way to make him notice her or anything, and *that's* what attracts him. He knows you'd fall over backwards if he as much as looked at you, but your friend is aloof, casual, and that interests him.

Take a leaf out of her book and play more hard to get. Be seen around with other boys and *don't* chase him. That may do the trick, but be prepared for disappointment, luv. Could be that he just doesn't fancy you as much as you fancy him.

DEAR CATHY & CLAIRE—I have a sister who is 16, and a lot less attractive than I am. I'm not being big-headed, but I'm only 14 and I've been dating for a whole year, but it was only last week that my sister got her *first* date.

But that's not the problem. You see, Mum and Dad don't approve of him, and asked me to explain, that it isn't right to get serious over your first boyfriend, which is exactly what *she's* doing.

When I tackled her about it, her reaction was that I was trying to take him away from her! Her new boyfriend doesn't know we're sisters and he asked me out, but of course I refused. I don't like him anyway.

But how can I explain that her first boyfriend ever is no good and will only cause her a lot of hurt? Before she met him, I used to try and get her off with a lot of other boys, by going out in foursomes, but none of them asked to see her again. What can I do? She is going out with this one soon. I know what he's like, but how can I tell her?

You can't. That's the only answer, and don't let Mum and Dad involve you in this. Your sister'll find out in her own good time that Boyfriend Number 1 isn't all he seems. But if you interfere, you're going to cause ructions all round. She's old enough to make her own decisions, and it sounds as if she's a bit shy and unsure of herself, so what she needs is a bit of the old morale-boosting.

You seem to be pushing her a bit hard to fit in with *your* set, and let's face it, the couple of years *does* make a difference. Well, you don't think like your sister, do you? And that works both ways.

But there's no point in taking all her confidence away by saying she's picked a loser in this boy. You had to make *your* mistakes, and she'll need to do the same. Best thing is to waterproof your shoulder and have it at the ready if it all goes wrong, but until then, play it cool and don't offer advice until she asks for it. She's probably dead chuffed she's got a boyfriend at last—show a bit of sisterly love and leave her to work things out on her own.

DEAR CATHY & CLAIRE—I know you'll probably think I'm being stupid and I feel an absolute TWIT myself, writing to you about this, but I've got the most sickly smile you ever saw.

And my face is liked a bashed turnip when I laugh, so I just don't know what to do. I've tried going around poker-faced, but everyone keeps saying "Don't worry, it'll never happen," so I gave that up. I know a smile is the best way a girl can attract boys and when I smile they run—in the wrong direction! Please help. I've tried practising a smile, but it even puts *me* off to see it.

Don't practise smiling. First of all, make sure your mouth looks as attractive as possible by having nice bright teeth, and super shiny lips. Then *forget it*. Nearly everyone thinks their own smile looks sick, but we've never seen anyone, no matter how plain, looking worse when they smile—as long as they have a good mouth to start off with. No one wants to look at dull, gungy teeth so make sure your pearlies are always shining. That's all there is to it!

DEAR CATHY & CLAIRE—I'm 16 and every time I have a boyfriend I find I don't like him after the first couple of weeks. I find it's always me who has to break it up, or I'll be stuck with him forever.

It's getting to the stage now where I say to myself "It's not worth me having any boyfriends because I won't like him if I do get one."

It would be better if a boy was to chuck me, but it never seems to work that way. I definitely don't want to get serious yet, this is usually another reason why I always have to finish it. Please help.

You're 16. You don't want to get serious about any boy just yet. The way we see it is . . . what's the problem? Your attitude sounds pretty sensible to us, ducks. And don't go getting chewed up over the fact that you've been giving your boyfriends the old heave after only a couple of weeks.

Maybe you don't know what you're looking for in a relationship right now. But, believe us, you'll know once you find it. Better by far to be the kind of girl who has enough confidence in herself to walk away from a boy when it's clear the bells aren't ringing and never will, than to be so insecure that you'll hang on grimly in the mistaken belief that any feller is better than none.

DEAR CATHY & CLAIRE—I'm 14, and mum has just told me and my older brother that she's going to have a baby.

Honestly, I can hardly believe it. I just don't know what to think. People'll say, "Fancy them carrying on like that at their age!" My brother says it's because I'm jealous of the attention Mum'll give to the baby, but it's not that. I think I'll like helping to look after it. I'm just so embarrassed.

We sympathise—you've had an awful shock. But look at it this way. Your mum and dad still love each other—surprised? You're just beginning to think that you'll get married and have children, and you're wanting to show too, how different you are from your parents. So you can hardly believe that they've got feelings like yourself. But if they have, it's not a bad thing, is it?

Hope it's a lovely bouncing thing when it comes!

DEAR CATHY & CLAIRE—I share a flat with a couple of other girls and just recently we've had the chance to get a really super place. Trouble is, it's a bit more than we can afford but there'd be room for a fourth girl to share. We just can't agree who it should be.

A lot of the people we work with are looking for flats, but this doesn't seem fair to me. What d'you suggest?

Depends on why you don't think it's fair. You could set up a resentment thing with the other girls at work who aren't chosen, and that could cause complications—but it shouldn't if you all work in different places. Safest answer is to advertise for a fourth girl to share (remember to say in the ad. how much you want in rent, etc.), and see who turns up.

Failing that, there's a lot of flat-finding agencies who'll provide you with a suitable sharer.

DEAR CATHY & CLAIRE—I am 15 and recently started a job as a sales assistant in a large store. But it's not all that I thought it would be, the people are dead snobby and the work just bores me to tears. What's more, my father won't let me leave and says I was lucky to get such a cushy job. But he just doesn't know what it's like.

We have a big family, and I hand over all my pay and only get 7s 6d pocket money, and I hardly ever get any clothes. I think if I'm helping to keep the family, I should at least enjoy my work. My mother sympathises, but she just won't *do* anything.

I would love to work in a boutique in town, but my father thinks that if I leave this job, I'll never be able to settle down and find a job that suits me. But my heart's not in it. What can I do? Don't say talk it over with him, because I've tried that, but it gets him so angry, I just shut up.

I hope you understand. It's horrible having no money and hating your job, and not being able to do anything about it.

Yes, we understand. You're in a nasty situation and right now things look a lot blacker than they probably *are*. Sounds as if Dad's got a touch of the Victorianas. If he really *won't* listen to you—and you could always have another try at talking, couldn't you—shutting up's likely to just add fuel to those flames. Seems to us, too, that perhaps you're not making absolutely the best you could out of the job—there must be *something* about it that interests you, or why did you go there in the first place?

Unfortunately, until you're 18, Dad's got quite a say in what you do and where, so unless you can talk him round, looks as if you'll have to make the best of it.

SUMMER TEARS

I SIT in the sun on the beach and watch people. The Great British Public on holiday. Some of them smile at me and I grimace back.

Can't they see my heart's broken? Isn't it obvious that, as [illegible] tan oil into my arms, I'm crying far away inside? I don't like the world, right at this moment, and there isn't any point in it grinning at me.

I've been here in sunny Bournemouth for a week—and it feels like centuries.

Back at the caravan, Mum'll be making coffee. Dad, lying in a deck chair with his shirt off and a handkerchief over his eyes. All great, jolly fun, and "Let's-go-to-Bingo-tonight, dear." They deserve their holiday, I suppose, but dragging me along isn't the brightest thing they've ever done.

I'm 16. Old enough to have a boyfriend. So why not old enough to stay at home—or go to France with Tim?

Tall, slim and 20. Money in his pocket, a smile that warms you right down to your toes; driving his sports car and flashing around in the mysteries of advertising—which is what he does for a living.

Mum and Dad quite liked him when they met him first. Although Mum kept straightening her hair and looking embarrassed that somebody half Dad's age should be earning twice what he'll ever make.

But when I told them I wanted to go to Nice for a fortnight with Tim, the roof came off.

"Too young."

"Not that we don't trust you, dear."

"If I hear another word about it . . ."

And finally, "No. You're coming to Bournemouth, and that's the end of it."

All the arguments about, of course they could trust me, I wouldn't do anything stupid, promise; Tim's sister and her boyfriend'll be there; it's only for a couple of weeks; and the ultimate explosions, "Oh, you're so old fashioned!" didn't do any good at all. I don't think I ever really thought they would.

But trying to tell Tim—that was when the tears started. He just looked, and laughed. "You must be joking! You're a big girl now, aren't you?" That's what really hurt.

"Well, if you're going to let your parents rule your life . . ." The sports car door slamming as he got into it, the engine revving into life—and Tim disappearing.

Tim's father was the director of a company while mine was simply a carpenter. Tim didn't know any more than all the people milling about the beach do. There was a world between us, and he hadn't realised it.

To be honest, neither had I—not in the beginning. Tim was just Tim, someone I loved and thought loved me.

So I sit in the sun and the tears come, dripping down under the dark glasses and splashing on my legs.

What do you do when you fall in love with someone who's so completely different? Who doesn't understand things like saving your wages and respecting your parents? Who's never had to go on holiday with anyone he doesn't want to, and who'd think a fortnight in Bournemouth was the most boring thing in the universe?

The only thing you can do is sit and cry, now and again, and pretend to yourself that maybe you'll see him when you get back; maybe it'll all be the way it was before.

I rub at the tears with the back of my hand. Maybe next year, when I'm older . . . Maybe the way it's all happened is the way it was meant. I don't know. Perhaps I should've fought a bit harder, but there wouldn't've been any point.

When we get back home, I suppose I'll see Tim again—you can't avoid someone like him in a town our size forever. It's stupid, but I'll feel embarrassed—speaking to him, asking how Nice was—because I went to Bournemouth with Mum and Dad, and that's ordinary.

The sun has dried the wet patches on my legs. But, after all, they were only summer tears.

Face To Face With *DAVID BOWIE*

The secret of my lost year....

What interests do you have outside music?
People. Architecture. And painting—I used to be a commercial artist six years ago. I spent just one year at it.

What's the best advice you've ever received?
To try to make each moment of one's life one of the happiest, and if it's not, try to find out why. I was told that by a Tibetan friend of mine, Chimi Youngdon Rimpoche.

Why was his advice so important?
Because I'd reached a crucial point in my life. I was a terribly earnest Buddhist at that time, within a month of becoming a Buddhist monk. I had stayed in their monastry and was going through all their exams, and yet I had this feeling that it wasn't right for me.

Are you still a Buddhist?
No, though a lot of the basic ideas are still with me. But I don't believe it's suitable for the West in its Eastern format.

What attracted you to Buddhism in the first place?
I was very interested in Tibet while I was still at school, and wrote a thesis on it. That made me interested in the country, and I started reading about its history and its religion.

I suppose I would still like to go there, but it's been impossible to get into the country since the Communists took over.

How did you get it all out of your system?
I suddenly realised how close it all was: another month and my head would have been shaved—so I decided that as I wasn't happy, I would get right away from it all. I vanished completely for a year. No-one knew where I was.

Actually, I had joined the Lindsay Kemp Mime Company. I spent a year with them and learned from Lindsay that people are much more important to me than ideas.

Have you continued this interest in theatre?
With a couple of other people, I started an Arts Laboratory down in Beckenham which is still thriving. It meets at a pub down there. We have about 600 people attached to it now—all pursuing their own ideas: art, poetry, music, mime, writing.

We've done a marvellous puppet show with 7ft high puppets, and I'm trying to get them a TV series at the moment.

Are you superstitious?
I never whistle in theatre dressing rooms, because that's something you're told not to do as soon as you start in the theatre—but that's more of a habit. I'm not superstitious about it or anything else.

Who has influenced you most?
My brother, Terry. He's seven years older than I am—I'm 22 now, he's 29. He was very keen on jazz when I was at a very impressionable age, and that led me into it.

I idolised John Coltrane and Eric Dolphy, and learned to play the clarinet and tenor saxaphone when I was 12. When I first came into the business six years ago it was as a jazz musician.

Terry was very Bohemian and introduced me to the writers that meant a lot to him—like Jack Kerouac and Allen Ginsberg. And all this led me into songwriting.

Do you write your own material still?
I've always written all my own songs. I've had 137 published so far and my latest L.P. is all my own. I also did another one years ago when I was the first singer to record an L.P. before doing a single.

My stage act consists entirely of my own material, apart from one or two songs that I like very much—"Port of Amsterdam" by Jacques Brel and "Buzz the Fuzz" by Biff Rose.

Do your fans expect this when they come to see you?
I think most of them are a bit astonished, but they sit and listen. I'm always getting really nice letters from people saying they like what I do.

What has been your most embarrassing moment?
When I was singing with a group called The Buzz four or five years ago. I forgot the words to three songs in a row. That was dreadful.

Have you been surprised by fan reaction?
I stand bemused by it all. I would never have believed in a million years that people would scream at me. I'm really incredulous.

The first night it happened to me was at Perth—as I was singing a number called "Wild Eyed Boy From Free Cloud." I suddenly heard three or four screams from a corner of the theatre!

Now I'm always getting presents, gonky things with big eyes, and funny little love letters.

What is your most treasured possession?
There's no one possession that I couldn't part with quite easily. I've never attached too much importance to material things.

Do you expect to stay in pop music for a long time?
I don't know. I never plan ahead, and I'm very fickle. I'm always changing my mind about things. If I thought another media would mean more to me, I would move into it.

I never expected "Space Oddity" to be the success it was, and it's all rather overwhelmed me. I couldn't tell you what I'll be doing this time next year, but I'm quite happy at the moment.

Beauty Queries

Dear Beauty Ed,
I have quite nice nails, and manicure them regularly, but whenever I wear nail varnish it tends to chip and flake off quickly. Is there any way of applying the stuff that will help to make it more long lasting?

Before putting on varnish, wipe over your nails with some nail polish remover to take off any remaining grease or dirt, then you can apply a basecoat which does help to strengthen the nails, and fix the polish. Max Factor do one for 28p.

Use two coats of the colour you choose, then—most important for you—use Top Coat, by Max Factor. Same price as the base coat, it seals your varnish and makes it much more resistant to chipping during messy chores.

Nice new varnishes out now from Max Factor are their Californian Nail Tints, in creme or frost, 32p. Colours include, Champagne, Dusky Beige Frost, Pale Lilac Frost, Petal Frost, and Sugar Frost—all nice delicate shades for spring!

Dear Beauty Ed,
I'm going to a special dance soon, and my long straight hair would look much better in a different style. I haven't worn it up before, so I'd like a specially simple style that won't collapse half-way through the evening!
Could you give me an idea to try out?

How about something like this style in the picture. First condition your hair by using a gentle shampoo like Polyherb, (Plus, Rainsoft, or Normal, depending on your hair type) then Polycare Instant Conditioner.

Set all the hair, except the nape of the neck tendrils, plus side ones if you want them, on large rollers. The remaining strands, set on small pin-curlers.

When dry, brush through, sweep into a pony tail, then wind the hair round the band and secure with fine pins. Wind the tendrils round your fingers to give the ringlet effect.

You may need a light spray of Poly Spray Silk, or your favourite hairspray, just to keep it tidy.

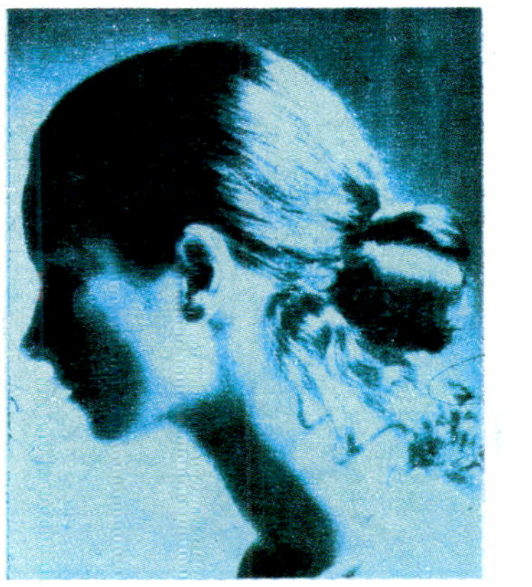

On-The-Spot Interviews

What d'you think you'll be doing in 10 years' time?

Ann Travers, Cromwell Road, London, S.W.7.
Travelling round the world. That's what I'm doing right now and I should still be doing it in 10 years. I'm from Boston, in the States, and so far I've been to England and the Continent. I just move on when I feel like it.

Lynda Chard, Welsord Avenue, Gosforth, Newcastle-upon-Tyne.
In 10 years' time I hope to be married to Georgie Fame!

Sandra Loft, Church Road, Northfield, Birmingham 31.
Taking my kids to school and telling them schooldays were the happiest days of my life. I've always been a liar.

Susie Nelligan, Wellington Road, Dublin 4.
Oooooh! I'll be absolutely ancient by then—27! (Heck, pass my walking stick) And all I can say is that if I haven't hooked a bloke by that time, I'll either join the Foreign Legion or jump in the nearest, deepest river . . .!

Jenny Clarke, Eton Avenue, London, N.W.3.
I don't know what I'll be doing but I hope I'll be a top dress designer—maybe in Paris or Rome.

Caroline Rafferty, Marlborough Roads, Dublin 4.
Well, I'm not getting married, that's for sure—with seven brothers would you blame me . . .? So, to get my revenge, I'd like to be a Supervisor in charge of about 500 men—and boy would I make them skip through the hoop . . .!

Alan Sargeant, Tyseley, Birmingham.
I'll be living on my island with a beautiful girl and a yacht and six horses. I've saved up £20 so far!

Harriet Aldrich, Barr Beacon, Aldrich, Staffs.
I'd like to make my way as a writer. I've had one or two things printed so far. I hope someone marries me though, just in case I don't make any money out of it!

Susan Dadson, Willmot Road, Dartford, Kent.
I reckon I should be married by then. I'd love to be living in the country, looking after my family, rather than going out to work.

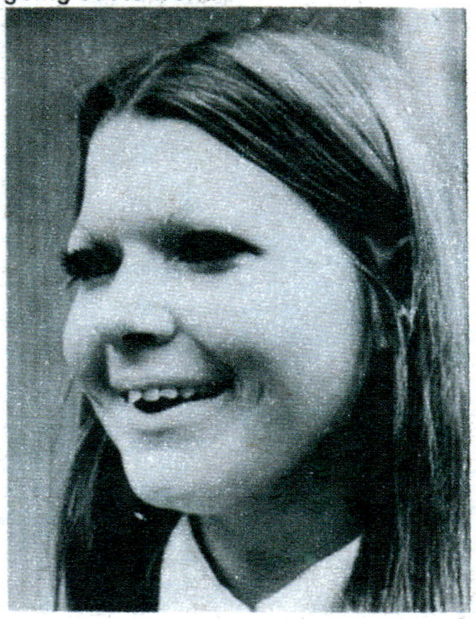

Dan Bliss, Fox Hollies Lane, Solihull, Warricks.
Living on the moon, I hope!

Celia Hawley, Mt. Ararat Road, Richmond, Surrey.
I'd like to work on perfecting a real cure for cancer, but if they do that before I get there, then perhaps I'll just be trying to cure the common cold!

Ted Whitewood, Avenue Road, London, N.8.
I hate to sound gloomy, but I honestly think we may all be fighting a war by then. I HOPE not . . . but it is a possibility.

Jill Rodgers, Usk Ave., Jarrow, Co. Durham.
In 10 years' time, I'll probably be looking forward to my old-age pension!

Maureen Clarke, Raddlebarn Road, Bournville, Birmingham.
Worrying about my first wrinkles, and complaining about the younger generation.

IT'S THE PAPER PATCHWORK PAGE

Our special orange Patchwork page of a few weeks ago was so popular (we're glad to say!) that we decided to feature another special page, this time all about paper!

We unearthed all sorts of amazing facts about paper, things to do with it, things not to do with it, things made from it — well, read on for yourselves and see!

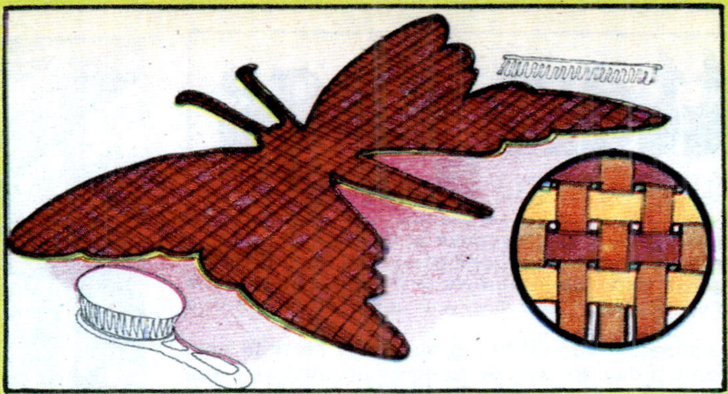

GET IT TAPED!

Sellotape, of course, is a paper product, too and here's a super way to brighten up your bedroom with a butterfly dressing table mat, made from, would you believe, Sellotape's "Brilliant Tape."

To weave the mat:

1. Cut a sheet of white cardboard large enough for your mat.
2. Now cover a sheet of white paper, (big enough to cover your mat), with strips of Brilliant Tape in assorted colours, carefully laying each strip right up next to each other.
3. When you've stuck down all the tape, cut the lengths of tape out with scissors — so that you end up with lots of strips of Brilliant Tape backed with white paper.
4. Take half the strips and lay them onto a table top — next to each other in a regular pattern of colours.
5. Now take the remaining strips and weave them in an "over and under" pattern, one at a time, through the other strips.
6. When you've woven all the threads carefully, lift them and stick them onto the cardboard with glue. When dry, cut out into a butterfly shape (it'll help if you draw the shape on the underside of the cardboard and use this as a guide to cutting) — and there you are! A shimmering, glimmering, sparkling butterfly!

Help!

"War On Waste" is important! It's the national campaign to re-cycle and save all sorts of things you would normally throw away — such as used stamps, silver paper, old coins, paper and bottles. Believe it or not, all these things can be re-cycled and used to help people who haven't got anything to wear, or enough to eat, or . . . get the message?

For example — just one book of trading stamps can buy 75p worth of vital supplies — so you can see how important the cause is.

And you can help!

It's easiest if you can get together with a group of friends and organise collections — you'll be amazed at how quickly your "rubbish" mounts up!

Furthermore, for every collector, there's a super free badge, like the one shown here. All you need do is form a school group, or in fact any group — and let the society know who you are and how many badges you'll need.

Write to "War On Waste," 467 Caledonian Road, London N7 9BE for details of badges and for a poster giving information about where to send your contributions.

But please DON'T send anything straight to the society, as there are different addresses for each separate item.

Note Paper

All together now — aah! What more can we say about this absolutely gorgeous range of Betsey Clark stationery from Hallmark, available in most stationery shops now?

The notepaper and notelets shown here cost 45p and 30p per box respectively, and are part of a large range of Betsey Clark paper-type goodies, including posters, wall hangers and even badges!

The theme of the range is friendship — so take the hint — be a friend to someone (even if it's only to yourself!) and buy something beautiful today.

Calling all animal lovers!

Next time you go out to buy tissues, have a look at the 'Kleenex' range — and find out how to help what must be everyone's favourite charity — the RSPCA.

All packs of Kleenex Tissues For Men (which are great for girls too!) are offering a beautiful silver-coloured medallion, commemorating the 150th anniversary of the RSPCA, for only 75p.

At the same time, you can collect the tear-off 20p vouchers on the packs and for every voucher you return to Kleenex, they'll forward 20p to the RSPCA. Isn't that super?

In addition to that, at no extra cost, free gratis and for nothing! — each pack features a card giving helpful hints on one of a range of six popular pets.

So go on — spoil yourself with a box of super-sized tissues, and help a very worthwhile charity at the same time!

Table Topping

Fancy a quick change of furniture in your room? Then this little coffee table is easy to make, looks stunning and — shall we let you into a secret?

It's made from sweet papers!

Just take a piece of chipboard, the size you want, and cover it with sweet wrappers — the coloured silver paper kind — smoothed out carefully till they're flat. Glue them all down carefully to make a colourful collage, spray with varnish for a lasting finish, and sit the chipboard on a few Coke cans. Very cheap, very easy, and very nice!

MEET THE DISHY DUSTMAN!

No, he's not a new pop star — or a male model — but a dustman! Really!

Dishy David Robb, of Dunfermline, Scotland, is 6 foot tall, has dark brown hair and green eyes — and is definitely not our idea of the average dustman!

David won the unlikely title of "Refuse Collector Of The Year" recently, for his knowledge of all the aspects of his job — including the re-cycling of paper.

We couldn't resist printing David's photo to show that even dustbin emptying has its good points!

Love Is . . .

. . . A party! Why not get together with your friends and have a "Love Is" party? Great fun for you, and no work afterwards for poor Mum, as there's no washing up to do!

You see, Cross Paperware have brought out a new range of paper cups and plates, all decorated with the super "Love Is" cartoon we know so well.

Each item in the set portrays a different drawing and message, for example, the little party dishes say "Love Is . . . Needing One Another" (sob, sniff!)

The range consists of sets of plates, cups, placemats, serviettes, coasters and dishes, all at 22p per set, and invitation cards at 30p per set. All are available now at large stationery stores.

All you need now is a boyfriend!

Hangabout!

It doesn't matter what age you are — mobiles are great fun for everyone!

The super Owl and Lion, shown here, are just two of a great range of "Hangabout" paper mobiles by McDermott and Chant.

They're printed in full colour on both sides of the board, so that they can career round in any direction when the wind blows. They're easy to assemble, cheap, and can be hung from ceilings, light fittings, doors or anywhere else you fancy!

They make really original decorations and for 50p, are available from most large stationers or gift shops.

Your Letters Page

We're in a bit of an uproar this week. The Ed's decided it's time to play musical chairs — in other words all the desks are being moved.

I'm writing to you from my exalted seat — on my wastepaper bin!

All around me is chaos and confusion and people keep shouting at me cos I'm so little they don't see me and they keep falling over me . . .

Fear not though, if I can manage to write to you through all this muddle, I'm sure you can return the compliment.

Write to me: Sam at Jackie, 12 Fetter Lane, Fleet Street, London EC4A 1BL.

You could win yourself £1.00 or if you're extra clever a choice of a Mary Quant Overnighter, a Pifco Go-Girl Hairdryer, a £4.00 record voucher or £4.00 in cash.

All letters must be original — and remember to tell me your full name and address — and your 3 favourite features in Jackie.

Oh and don't forget to add a PS at the foot of your letter telling me your three favourite features in Jackie.

See you.

EXAMINATION BLUES

I've recently completed both my C.S.E. and G.C.E. examinations, and I feel really exhausted.

All my friends feel just like me, and I'm sure other 'Jackie' readers who have been taking exams are the same.

I don't feel as if I've done very well in any of my exams, I got so worked up over them, I just couldn't think.

I personally think that exams should be abolished, and that subject teachers should give each pupil a grade, taking into consideration their work over the years and the pupil's own personal conduct. This way, I'm sure pupils would work much harder.

An example of the tension some of us experienced was shown, while I was sitting my maths C.S.E.

One of the girls actually passed out, falling on to the floor, and cutting her head.

The doctor who examined her at the hospital said it was caused through tension.

I for one think exams are stupid and I wish they had never been invented.

Linda Hemmings,
Essex.

This week's winner has chosen a PIFCO GO-GIRL HAIRDRYER.
(What do other readers feel about this? – Sam)

THE DREADED SCHOOL REPORT

Have you ever stopped to think what your school report **really** means? — I've worked out a few meanings which go to show that sometimes you're not as bad as you think — but sometimes you're worse!

Good — Well, she's not **bad** . . .
Quite good — It's past midnight and I can't think of anything more original!
Fair — Who is the girl anyway?
Shows quiet interest — Suspect paralysis of the vocal organs.
Shows lively interest — Asks awkward questions.
Sound, but lacks originality — Her essays bore me to distraction!
Tries hard — But really hasn't a clue.
More application needed — Bone idle.
Has an original approach to the subject — Shows signs of becoming either a crank or a psychopath.
Must learn her work thoroughly — Only scraped up 27% in the exam out of pity.
Helpful — She always tells me when I repeat myself!

Kay Seddon,
Yorks.

(Shows originality – You're worth a pound! – Sam)

GIRLS WILL BE GIRLS!

Hope you don't mind a boy writing, but I want to make a point that my mates and I feel strongly about.

I met a great girl in the local youth club one night, and eventually plucked up enough courage to ask her out. And she accepted. I was over the moon.

Imagine my horror when she turned up for our date plastered in make-up and wearing horrible false eye-lashes!

I almost didn't recognise her! What attracted me in the first place were her natural looks and healthy complexion.

Perhaps Jackie readers could explain why girls spoil their faces with artificial aids?

Keith Martin,
Penre-Bach,
Cards.

(Well girls – what have we to say about that? – Sam)

PAIN AT THE THOUGHT

Have you ever thought what pain we'd suffer if we did everything we said?

For instance we "cry our eyes out," "laugh our heads off," "work our fingers to the bone," "break our hearts" and "tickle each other to death!"

Dawn Farrell,
Stratford.

(We killed ourselves laughing, but we'll still manage to send you a pound! – Sam)

THE WOMBLES

At our high school there is a class representing the Wombles.

They go out to different places in Hawick collecting litter. They do this every week and the total time spent collecting litter is 80 minutes each week.

They are also being sponsored at 2p a time and for this, people try to guess the weight they think the class will collect in so many hours by a certain date.

They have decided the money will go to the Katherine Elliot Centre for handicapped people. And it's all thanks to the Wombles.

A Donny Fan,
Hawick.

SIGNS . . .

When we were going into a low-ceilinged restaurant I noticed on one of the beams near the door a sign saying: DUCK OR GROUSE!

Claire Abbott,
Kent.

HI THERE, GUYS AND GALS . . .

I am sure there are other girls who agree with me about D.J.'s who cut off half the singles just to let someone have their name read out or tell a corny joke (no names mentioned!)

The only time we school girls are able to listen to the radio is in the mornings, (I am not complaining about Noel Edmonds though), and between 12.30 and 1.30 where only a small amount of time is taken up by records.

And after school it's time for the romantic messages and more corny jokes. I'm sure I am not alone in thinking more records should be played instead of all this talking!

Jane Cole,
Milton Keynes.

WOE, IS ME!

As I'm skinny, small and plain,
I thought I'd write to Fetter Lane,
To tell you Sam how sad I am,
And ask you to make my day.
By sending me a Mary Quant Overnighter,
So I can make my face much, much nicer!

A Rod Stewart Fan,
Berks.

(Afraid you've only got a pound – hope it'll be enough to go round! – Sam)

ATTENTION ALL KNITTERS!

I read the other day, that if you can't afford wool to knit for Oxfam, but would like to help they will send you a pattern and wool free.

I didn't know this and I think there are probably quite a lot of readers who would like to knit for Oxfam.

If you are interested in doing so, write to this address:

Oxfam House, 274 Banbury Road, Oxford.

Jan,
Co. Durham.

EMBARRASSMENT IS . . .

. . . Going over on your ankle while walking past a long bus queue, and seeing everyone in knots, laughing at you.

. . . Trying on a halter neck dress in a crowded, communal changing room, and discovering everyone except you seems particularly well-endowed!

. . . Going to a disco and discovering that the ultra-violet lighting is making your white bra show up, and your freckles look green.

. . . Getting up to dance a slow record with a gorgeous guy you've been ogling all night, only to find that he is smaller than you. (Funny how it seems the record is never going to end!)

Bowie Fan,
Belfast.

THE ED'S LETTER

Now's the time of year when everyone starts thinking about holidays... in fact it's all this lot in here ever seem to think about. And it's got worse since we started our super new summer serial "Under Summer Skies" (you'll find it on page 14) All they talk about now is Greece, Greeks sun, sea and sand. I don't know, maybe if I hire a Greek waiter to hand round a bucket and spade to each of them it'll keep them quiet.... honestly, the things I do for peace...

love, The Ed

COVER PATTERN

Hope you like the super camisole top and skirt pictured on the cover this week. If you do, then you'll be glad to know that with the help of a Simplicity Pattern (50p) you can make it for yourself in no time at all!

It's cheap too, for instance a size 12 takes only 3⅜ yards for the skirt, ⅞ yd for the top, plus ⅞ yd. of embroidered eyelet edging (3 ins wide) for the lovely frilled waist!

And don't worry if you're smaller or larger than that, it comes in sizes 8-16, with the choice of a shorter top should you want to be a bit more daring.

So if you want to keep your cool, get yourself into this cotton camisole from Simplicity. The style number to look out for is 6382.

TEEN SCOPE

LEO. (July 22-Aug 21).
A row with relatives soon sorts itself out and as a result you'll be invited out somewhere new. Go along — a great meeting could result. If you don't have a steady, don't panic — you'll be glad you're on your own at a certain party you're invited to. Workwise, don't let someone supposedly smarter put you down — you may only be going on that good old Leo instinct, but you're right.

VIRGO. (Aug 22-Sept 21).
Someone else's mistake lets you succeed where they failed, but don't start boasting about it or you'll be right back where you started. There's a man in your life, but he's not THE man, so keep things light and don't let him get possessive. You can help a brother or sister who's got problems, but don't expect thanks for it. Something you buy on impulse brings you luck.

LIBRA. (Sept 22-Oct 22).
You're dreaming of love, yet still love passes you by. However you're due for a break — and a break will come early this week so keep your eyes open. You'll have an interesting chat with someone you don't know well and you'll get some new angles on life. At the weekend there's a success to be celebrated, so dance the night away!

SCORPIO. (Oct 23-Nov 21).
Give yourself a treat — get your hair cut and styled a new way — someone very interesting will notice. There are changes afoot and you may not like them, they're not worse, just different, so try to accept them and don't mope for what was. Any chance of you fixing up a party? It would give everyone a boost.

SAGITTARIUS. (Nov 22-Dec 20).
You don't care where you stand, as long as it's out in front, but if someone else has the star part now, don't fuss. A money problem needs sorted out and the sooner you do it the better. You may hear tales that make you suspect a friend's motives, but keep quiet for the moment. All will be revealed very soon.

CAPRICORN. (Dec 21-Jan 19).
It's no good hoping the guys will dig you if you're not too keen on yourself — so stand in front of the mirror and make up your mind to beat whatever it is that's spoiling your looks. Some new gear could do a lot to beat your blues. Plenty of socialising later, but don't cling too tight to new friends — they'll be around a while.

AQUARIUS. (Jan 20-Feb 18).
It's yo-yo time for you. You'll change your mind about tricky problems a dozen times, and your views on the guy on your mind will be just as changeable! With luck, he'll find your moods challenging and stick around, but don't push him too far. A mix-up in daily life is best faced and sorted out quickly — you'll get on better afterwards.

PISCES. (Feb 19-Mar 20).
If there's one thing you don't want right now, it's steadiness and security — excitement is what you're after. You could find it with a new boy you're introduced to but don't expect him to be faithful, it's possible he's after excitement and change too. News from a friend makes you happy.

ARIES. (March 21- April 20).
You should know by now exactly how you feel about your boy, but if you want to fool around for fun, don't worry: he's well hooked and won't run away. There's a job ahead for you that means using your Arian charm on people — you'll enjoy doing it, but don't squander any cash rewards till you've had a look at your money matters — they need help!

TAURUS. (April 21-May 20).
Feeling friendless and frustrated? Talk things over at home — someone understands you better than you think. An old flame may turn up out of the blue but don't expect romance to blossom again as a result. Things will be strictly on a friendship basis this time.

GEMINI. (May 21-June 20).
A dull period's ending, and suddenly you've lots to do! In affairs of the heart you may be feeling a bit rebellious, and this should make for some interesting arguments with your fella! You won't be feeling particularly generous, but will want to spend some cash on yourself — looks like an unexpected windfall will enable you to do just that.

CANCER. (June 21-July 21).
The sun's shining for you again, but your boy may not have noticed this — so make him! You'll be extra busy this week, both at work and play. There's lots of socialising in the air this week. Pay a visit to a friend — if you can fit it into your busy schedule!

AS I WRITE THIS LETTER...

A LOVE letter to your boyfriend doesn't only show how much you love him, it can also reveal a lot about the secrets of your personality. You'll find that in our love letter there's a choice of sentences. As you read through it, tick the ones that you'd write yourself. Then turn the page upside down to find out what he can read between the lines!

Dear John

Since you went away last Friday —

(a.) I've been ever so good sitting in watching the box every night.

(b.) I've been thinking about you all the time.

(c.) I've been wondering how you're getting on and what life is like up there.

I suppose it's too early to get a letter from you yet, but —

(c.) Do write and tell me about yourself.

(b.) I can't tell you how agonising it is not knowing whether you miss me as much as I miss you.

(a.) I'll bash you over the head with a rolling pin if you don't write to me soon.

We had a wonderful time on our last date at the disco - Mum was furious about me getting home so late but —

(c.) I managed to calm her down in the end.

(a.) It was OK, 'cos I told her I'd called in to see my dotty old aunt on the way back — and she can keep *anyone* talking for hours.

(b.) Don't worry, I'd go through a million rows and upsets for the sake of being with you, John.

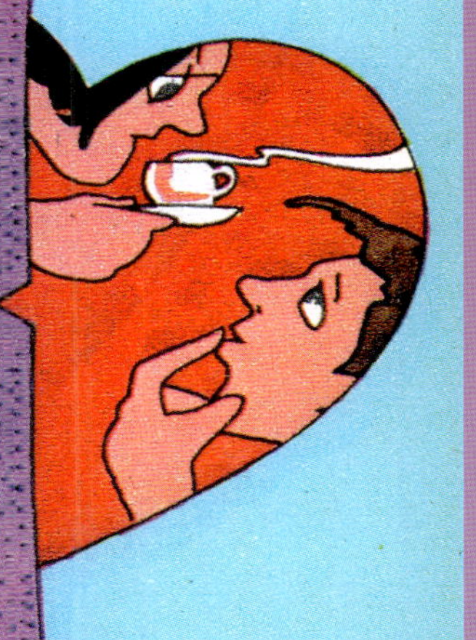

I hope you won't mind meeting my mum when you come back because it would make things easier for me —

(a.) She's a nice old girl, really — promise she won't bite you!

(b.) As soon as she realises how wonderful you are I know she'll be pleased about us, because you make me so happy.

(c.) She always likes to meet my friends, so maybe you could come to tea.

I'm writing this letter up in my room where I'm supposed to be swotting for a history exam. It's driving me mad, and besides —

(b.) I can't concentrate on anything since you've been away — I keep going over all our wonderful times together in my mind.

(c.) I felt like a break, so it was an ideal opportunity to get down to writing to you.

(a.) I find you much more interesting than boring old Gladstone and his horrible Ballot Act.

I looked up where you are on the map and it seems an awfully long way away. I feel very lonely and —

(c.) I miss all our long conversations, because I can't talk to anyone else the way we talk together.

(a.) I'm going bonkers without you — I only hope you're as miserable as I am, that's all!

(b.) Since you've been away, the days pass so slowly, I'm only living for the moment when I'll see you again.

It's strange, but I've never met anyone like you before —

(a.) I mean, all the other people I meet are nice and sane and reasonable, and they don't make my knees quake and my hair stand on end like you do!

(b.) I never dreamt I would meet anyone like you; I've never felt like this before — dear John, it's as if fate just drew us together.

(c.) I've never got on with anyone so well, and I've never ever been able to confide in a boy like I can with you.

I wish I knew what you are doing at this moment, what you are thinking, John: —

(c.) I hope you don't mind me writing to you in this way, 'specially as we haven't known each other long.

(b.) I'm so mixed up, so happy because I love you, and so unhappy because we're apart — all I want in the world is to be in your arms again.

(a.) I'm just longing to see your funny lop-sided grin again, and to find out if you're still wearing that baggy, raggy old sweater your mum knitted for you!

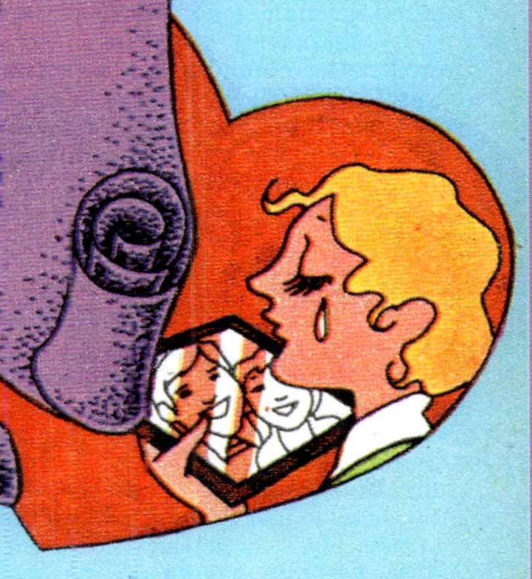

Please write to me soon —

(b.) I count the minutes, the hours and the days until we meet again. I don't know how I'm going to manage for the coming weeks. So think about me, my darling, and never forget that I love you.

(a.) I can't wait to see you — don't be surprised if you come back to find your name written in huge red letters all over the town — with me skipping down the high street singing at the top of my voice like a mad woman!

(c.) I hope you'll still want to see me when you come home, John. Two months seems such a long time, and so many things can happen, but whatever happens, let's always be friends.

Love from

Mary xxx

Count your score, mainly (a) (b) or (c) and turn the page upside down to read the conclusions.

CONCLUSIONS

Mostly (a) — The boy who reads your letter will most likely congratulate himself on finding such a fun girl, with a witty and zany line in love.

Although you feel deeply about love, romantic sentiment is not your scene. You tend to hide your real feelings by making a joke of them and even if you feel hurt sometimes, you'll try not to show it.

As slushy romance doesn't appeal to you, the moony, intense boy will leave you cold — you need an extrovert, manly type of boy. You are good at platonic relationships, too — you can be a good companion, a zany sister and a loving girlfriend all in one. What boy could ask for more?

Mostly (b) — The boy who reads your letter will get the message loud and clear. You let rip with your feelings, you spill out all your emotions, you fall headlong into romance dizzily and with no inhibitions.

You just *have* to be madly in love all the time. You have a magic sort of appeal — you are the kind of girl who can command instant romance and attraction, but you tend to be rather possessive, easily hurt and jealous when the first glorious flush wears off.

Either you need a constant, endless supply of handsome fascinating boys around you, or you need to steady up a bit, and go a bit deeper into relationships. Lack of shyness is a wonderful thing, but make sure your love for the boy is real, and not just an excuse for another romantic flight into dreamland.

Mostly (c) — You have a very loving nature, and your feelings for boys and love are sincere and deep. The boy who reads your letter will realise that you are a very gentle, feminine girl, but he will have to read between the lines to realise how much you really love him.

You are obviously extremely sensitive and aware; you take life and love seriously, and in the final judgement you are the girl capable of the greatest love.

It might take a boy a while to realise this, and some may be put off by what they think is a cool manner, so perhaps it would be worth trying to let your feelings go a bit more. You may end up getting hurt and feeling foolish sometimes, but then it's worth the risk when you could gain so much from friendship and love with the right person.

MY VERY OWN DONNY OSMOND

H-HELLO. I'M JULIE EVANS...
YEH. SHE LIVES NEXT DOOR AND WE'RE MATES SO YOU'LL SEE ME ROUND HERE QUITE OFTEN, STEVE.
As he looked at me with those big, dark eyes I felt suddenly very shy. It was just as if Donny was standing in front of me . . .
I felt so silly and stupid, I just wanted to run away.
IT—IT'S LATE. COMING IN FOR COFFEE, CAROL?
ER—NO, THANKS. I'LL HAVE TO GO HOME IN A MINUTE ANYWAY.
But she didn't go home. She kept him talking another half hour.
WHAT'S UP WITH ME? WHY DON'T I GET OUT THERE AND CHAT HIM UP TOO? COS I KNOW IT'S PROBABLY HOPELESS, THAT'S WHY. NOW CAROL'S GOT HER MITTS ON HIM, SHE'S NOT LIKELY TO LET GO. AND WHEN SHE DECIDES SHE WANTS A BLOKE, SHE USUALLY GETS HIM.
I couldn't stop thinking about Steve over the next few weeks, but I fell apart with shyness every time I saw him, so I reckoned he just thought I was a stupid little kid . . .
HI, JULIE. WE'VE BROUGHT OUR NEW ALBUMS ROUND. LET'S HAVE A RECORD SESSION IN YOUR ROOM.
ER—'FRAID I CAN'T JUST NOW. I'M ON MY WAY OUT TO THE DENTIST'S.
WONDER WHY THEY'RE SO MATEY ALL OF A SUDDEN? THEY'VE NEVER BOTHERED BEFORE...
Then the penny dropped.
HI! YOU'RE NEW HERE, AREN'T YOU?
WE'VE SEEN YOU AROUND.
HOW'D YOU LIKE TO COME DOWN THE DISCO WITH US ONE NIGHT? WE COULD SHOW YOU AROUND.
I...ER...WELL...
I SUPPOSE WORD WAS BOUND TO GET AROUND THAT DONNY'S TWIN WAS IN TOWN. THAT LET'S ME RIGHT OUT, COS WITH ALL THESE GIRLS OUT TO GET HIM, I DON'T STAND MUCH OF A CHANCE...
The more they hung around Steve, the more I avoided him. Then, one day . . .
HI, JULIE. YOU COME OUT OF HIDING, THEN?
I...ER...DUNNO WHAT YOU MEAN...
HERE AM I LIVING RIGHT NEXT DOOR TO THE NICEST BIRD IN TOWN, AND ALL I EVER SEE IS A FLEETING GLIMPSE AS SHE DIVES INDOORS EACH EVENING. HAVEN'T YOU NOTICED ME HANGING ROUND WAITING FOR A CHANCE TO DAZZLE YOU WITH ME SPARKLING CHAT?
I—WELL, YOU ALWAYS SEEMED TO BE TALKING TO OTHER GIRLS, AND...
THOSE GIGGLING TWITS AREN'T MY TYPE. QUIET, DREAMY BLONDES ARE MORE MY SCENE. SO—IF YOU'RE NOT DOING ANYTHING—EM—HOW ABOUT GOING FOR A WALK WITH ME...?
A—A WALK? YOU? M-ME...? YES—YES, I'D LIKE THAT.
I felt like a burbling idiot, but he didn't seem to notice. Just smiled and said, "C'mon then . . ."
We left the crowds behind and made for the woods.
BETTER GIVE ME YOUR HAND...IT'S A BIT SLIPPY JUST HERE.
YEH. I KNOW. I USED TO COME HERE AS A KID. I ALWAYS USED TO THINK THESE STONES WERE A BRIDGE TO A MAGIC KINGDOM...
YOU WERE RIGHT. THAT'S EXACTLY WHAT THEY ARE.
WHAT'S MORE, I'M THE RULER OF THE KINGDOM AND I PUT SPELLS ON UNSUSPECTING MAIDENS. I DON'T SET THEM FREE UNTIL THEY PAY ME A RANSOM.
HARD LUCK. I LEFT MY BAG OF GOLD AT HOME ON THE SIDEBOARD.
WHO SAID ANYTHING ABOUT GOLD...? AND I DON'T THINK I'LL SET YOU FREE—EVER.
My throat went dry and my heart was going like a steam-hammer as he kissed me. It seemed to grab him the same way . . .
After that, Steve and I started going out together. I'd never been so happy. Until one evening . . .
OH, HELLO, CAROL. HAVEN'T SEEN YOU FOR AGES. THOUGHT YOU WERE AVOIDING ME.
JULIE, YOUR MUM SAID YOU WERE OUT AND—OH, STEVE...HELLO. I—I DIDN'T KNOW YOU TWO WERE GOING OUT TOGETHER.
BUT YOU DID, CAROL. I TOLD YOU...

But she didn't pay any attention. Just started being all nasty.
WELL, STEVE, HOW DOES IT FEEL TO BE A STAND-IN FOR JULIE'S DREAM BOY?
EH? WHAT YOU ON ABOUT...?
CAROL, PLEASE. WHAT'RE YOU TRYING TO DO...?
OH, DIDN'T YOU KNOW, STEVE? LOOK AT THIS THEN. JULIE'S INSANE ABOUT DONNY OSMOND—AND SEEING AS YOU'RE A DEAD RINGER FOR HIM, YOU'RE BOUND TO BE A HIT WITH HER!
OH, I GET IT. SAME OLD STORY.
CAROL! STOP IT! SHUT UP!
Having done the dirty, she suddenly split.
WELL, SEE YOU, FOLKS! HAVE FUN.
TAKE NO NOTICE OF HER, STEVE. SURE I LIKE DONNY BUT...
I CAN SEE YOU DO. MAKES ME FEEL JUST GREAT THAT A BIRD ONLY FANCIES ME COS I LOOK LIKE SOMEONE ELSE! BUT DON'T FEEL BAD! IT HAPPENS TO ME ALL THE TIME. BIRDS THINK I'M LIKE DONNY OSMOND. THEN, WHEN I TURN OUT TO BE LIKE ME, THEY DON'T WANT TO KNOW. BUT I THOUGHT YOU WERE DIFFERENT, JULIE. SILLY ME, HUH?
OH, STEVE. I AM DIFFERENT! I DO LIKE YOU COS YOU'RE YOU. CAN'T YOU SEE CAROL'S JUST BEING HORRIBLE? SHE'S AFTER YOU HERSELF. SHE WANTS TO BREAK US UP...
WELL, SORRY TO SHATTER YOU AND YOUR FRIEND'S ILLUSIONS OF ME, DOLL, BUT I'M ABOUT TO TURN YOU BOTH OFF! Y'SEE I'VE BEEN TOLD I NEED THESE FROM NOW ON—PICKED 'EM UP THIS MORNING.
BET I DON'T LOOK LIKE HIM IN THESE, EH?
NO, YOU DON'T. BUT I KEEP TELLING YOU—
THEN I'M NO USE TO YOU ANY MORE, AM I, JULIE? 'BYE. SEE YOU AROUND.
STEVE...WAIT...
But he didn't. And though we both hung around our gardens the next few days, he wouldn't speak to me.
COULD KILL CAROL! HOW COULD SHE BE SO CREEPY? OH, STEVE, HOW CAN I SHOW YOU I'M STILL NUTS ABOUT YOU...?
Then I'd a brainwave . . .
SORRY ABOUT THIS, DONNY. BUT WHEN IT COMES TO LOVE YOU HAVE TO USE DRASTIC MEASURES.
WHAT...?
MESSAGE FOR YOU!
IF I THOUGHT YOU REALLY MEANT THAT, JULIE...
COME ON OVER AND I'LL PROVE I MEAN IT, YOU DAFT THING.
I ONLY LIKE DONNY NOW 'COS HE REMINDS ME OF YOU NOT THE OTHER WAY ROUND
JULIE
I—I—RECKON YOU MUST DO, TO MESS UP AN EXPENSIVE POSTER LIKE THIS—QUITE A SACRIFICE FOR AN OSMOND FAN. BUT—HEY, DON'T SMASH THE RECORDS AS WELL!
I'M NOT. I'M PUTTING ONE ON...
I'M STILL A DONNY FAN. HIS SINGING PUTS ME IN JUST THE RIGHT MOOD—FOR BEING WITH YOU...
I kinda went for those specs, too. And now he just looks like himself I bet I'll STILL have problems with all those other girls hanging around . . . but then—what can you expect if you're going out with your very own Donny Osmond . . .?
THE END

A JACKIE QUIZ

Are You As Beautiful As You'd Like To Be?

ONCE upon a time, being beautiful meant having a set sort of good looks, with a particular shape of nose, measurements that fitted the fashionable pattern, hair and eyes of a certain shade. But not any more! Anything goes if you've the know-how to make the very best of the face and shape you happen to have been born with. So you can't blame ol' Mother Nature any more if you aren't getting second glances! It's up to every girl to make the best of herself, and if you aren't as beautiful as you'd like to be . . . maybe it's your own fault!

Before you reach for your shotgun to come gunning for us — reach for a pen, and do our quiz, instead.

1. We'll jump in at the deep end, and set you a really stiff one, for starters. A girl can't help it if she's born with a blotchy skin, but we say she can make her complexion LOOK soft and ivory-tinted if she uses . . .

(a) heavy beige make-up from throat to forehead?

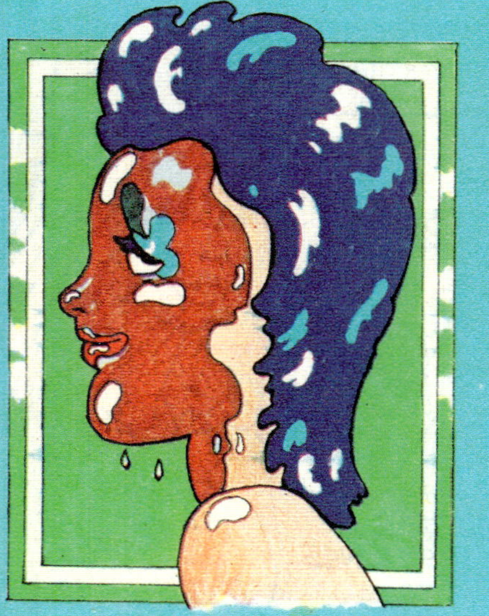

(b) no make-up at all until the spots clear?
(c) concealing spot cream on the spots, but light liquid make-up elsewhere?
(d) light liquid make-up all over?

2. Best idea for a girl who has a large, bulbous nose, is . . .

(a) plastic surgery?
(b) dramatic eye and lip colours to draw attention away from her nose?

(c) a swept-back hair-style?
(d) brown shading at the sides of the nose?
(e) brown shading at the tip of the nose?

3. If you have vivid blue eyes, which colour of eye make-up should you never use?

(a) blue; (b) green; (c) mauve; (d) brown; (e) grey; (f) pink; (g) yellow.

BONUS POINT: why?

4. If your hair is quite long, and only two days after you give it a shampoo, it seems greasy, yet the tips are splitting, dry and brittle, the cause is most likely to be . . .

(a) you are using the wrong shampoo?
(b) you have been colour-treating, perming or bleaching your hair too often?
(c) you don't brush your hair enough?
(d) you use the wrong sort of comb on your hair?
(e) your diet is at fault?
(f) you have grown your hair too long?

BONUS POINT: what should you do about it?

5. When you are applying eye make-up, which of these methods is best?

(a) work on one eye first, go through each stage, and only when you are finished should you turn to the second eye?
(b) work on both eyes together, one stage at a time. It doesn't matter which eye you start with?

(c) if you are right-handed, do the left eye first, (left-handed, do the right eye first,) working stage by stage?
(d) if you are right-handed, do the right eye first, working stage by stage?

6. When you are plucking your eyebrows, the correct idea is to . . .

(a) remove ONLY the hairs that grow outside the natural brow-line?
(b) remove as many hairs as necessary to make a completely even brow-line all the way along?
(c) remove hairs to create a brow-line that is thicker at the inner side, and thinner at the outer side?
(d) create a brow-line that flatters the particular shape of your own face, which may be quite unlike the way your brows naturally grow?

7. If you are very limited on money, is it best to buy . . .

(a) a lot of cosmetics, cleansers, etc., from cheap, budget ranges?
(b) very good cosmetics from expensive ranges, making do with only one colour for lips, eye make-up, etc?
(c) good quality skin-care and hair-care products, from middle-range and expensive products, and cheaper products for eye and lip make-up?
(d) giant economy bottles of everything, big lipsticks, palette eye make-up, etc?

BONUS POINT: if you know which of these is a really FALSE economy.

8. Facial hair can be removed by several methods. If you have quite a noticeable dark "moustache," are you best-advised to . . .

(a) use a ladies' razor?
(b) choose a depilatory cream?
(c) bleach the hair?
(d) have an expert use electrolysis to remove it permanently?
(e) buy a home-use electrolysis gadget?
(f) wait until you are older?

BONUS POINT: three of these are actually BAD. If you can pick the right three, you'll score!

9. If you develop an allergy (most likely in the form of an irritating rash, or sometimes a patch of flaky skin that won't go away), should you . . .

(a) see a doctor right away?
(b) stop using make-up?
(c) use a medicated ointment on the rash or flaky skin, but continue with your normal make-up?
(d) change to a hypo-allergenic or non-perfumed make-up range, as it may be the perfume that is upsetting your skin?

BONUS POINT: make-up needn't be the cause of the allergy. A point for each other possible cause you can think of.

10. It's not what you wear, but the way that you wear it! These days many girls successfully break all the fashion rules. But if you are plump, it pays to obey some of the rules some of the time! Which of these are true for the plump girl?

(a) avoid stripes that go across your figure.
(b) light colours make you look fatter, dark ones are slimming.
(c) large patterns are more slimming than small ones.
(d) flares are slenderising, gathers and pleats are fattening.
(e) wide belts are better on a big waist than narrow ones.
(f) V-necklines are slimming.

BONUS POINT: if you can tell which of these is absolutely taboo for the plump girl.

ANSWERS

1. (c) scores 1 point. All the others are wrong — from a beauty point of view. (a) will actually encourage more spots, (b) will help the spots heal but will be so depressing, and a sad face can't be a pretty one! And (d) will take the spots slightly longer to heal, without really covering them up.

2. (c) scores 2 points, because it is simple and surprisingly effective, and can be used all of the time, even in school. (d) scores 1 point, because it is definitely slenderising for this shape of nose. None of the others scores — plastic surgery isn't the answer, because we reckon you don't have the kind of money that could buy this transformation! The other two ideas would actually make her nose more noticeable.

3. None of them need be avoided! Sorry to try and trick you, but you get 1 point if you guessed right, plus a bonus point if you realise that you don't choose eye make-up solely by the shade of your eyes, but also according to hair colour, skin type, what clothes you are wearing and the effect you hope to create.

4. Surprisingly, C scores the point here. All the others may POSSIBLY be to blame for this condition, but the most common is lack of thorough brushing. Brushing spreads the natural oils evenly down the hair shaft, so that you don't get a build-up of grease at the scalp end, where the oils come from, and oil starvation down at the tips. You get an extra point if you realise there are THREE things to be done, for instant success — trim a fraction off the tips, use a shampoo that mends split-ends and start brushing regularly! If you only guessed two of these, no point.

5. C. is correct, and you'll find, if you try it, that the left eye is actually slightly more tricky to make-up. So if you start with this, it is easier to make the right eye to match at each stage, than the other way about. Saves time in the long run!

6. D is correct — score 1 point.

7. A scores 2 points for the best all-round advice. B scores NOTHING. C scores 1 point, because it is not bad advice, but will work out slightly more expensive. D is very bad advice, and you only get 1 point if you picked this as the false economy, for a bonus!

8. D scores 2 points. B and C get a single point if you chose either of these, which are moderately successful and quite safe. LOSE a POINT for either A or E which can be dangerous. You get a bonus point if you realise the "bad" answers are A, E, and F. "Wait till you are older" means adding unnecessary misery to a perfectly ordinary beauty problem!

9. A scores 2 points, D scores 1 point. You get a bonus point for each correct one if you realise that make-up may not be the cause, other reasons for an allergy patch developing could be: using a razor or depilatory cream underarm and applying anti-perspirant immediately; food or drink; nervous reaction to strain or worry; using soap or other chemicals you have become allergic to; any medical treatment you may be taking for some other health trouble, may occasionally be the cause of an allergy.

10. Score 1 point each for realising that the following are still true:- A), B), D) and F). Score a bonus point if you know that C) and E) are both taboo for plump people. Large patterns are NOT more slimming than smaller ones, and a narrow belt is definitely MORE slimming.

JOURNEY INTO THE UNKNOWN

Come with us on a strange journey into the unknown, travelling along untrodden paths to mysterious lands. You won't find a casket of gold at the end of your journey, but you WILL discover the secrets of your personality. So take a deep breath and set off remembering you can only choose one of the four paths in front of you.

1. Embarking on this strange and dangerous journey, are you escaping from:—
(a) the cruelty of a wicked step-mother?
(b) the heartbreak of a false lover?
(c) the vendetta of an evil syndicate?
(d) the hounding of the press after exclusives on your private life?

2. Setting out into the dark unknown do you feel:—
(a) proud and beautiful?
(b) tragic, but strangely calm?
(c) lost and bewildered?
(d) tensed with excitement?

3. Shortly after starting your journey you come to a clearing with four pathways branching off it. Which one do you choose?

(a) A narrow path flanked on each side with dense woods?
(c) A pathway cut through jungle undergrowth?
(d) A path along a deep canyon of a dried up river-bed?
(b) A wide pathway between sparse, stunted trees?

4. After many hours trudging, the pathway comes to an end and you are faced with a further walk over:—

(c) volcanic rock?
(d) parched desert?
(b) barren moorland?
(a) green pasture?

5. As dusk deepens into night, you are weary and dispirited, and in need of a rest. Where would you take shelter?
(b) In a subterranean cave?
(a) On a mossy bank?
(d) In an olive grove?
(c) In a hollow of dried leaves?

6. Night falls suddenly, the moon shines through wispy branches and the trees creak in the wind. There is no immediate sign of danger, but your imagination builds up horrors of it's own. Do you imagine you are tormented by:—
(d) snakes?
(c) rats?
(b) ghosts?
(a) murderers?

7. Too terrified to stay where you are, you get up and continue your travels with trembling legs and a thumping heart. The moon has gone behind a cloud, and it's pitch black. Suddenly something happens to make you cry out in terror. What is it?

(a) Have you scratched your leg on a thorn?
(b) Has a bat brushed against your hair?
(d) Is a giant spider crawling over your shoes?
(c) Have wet leaves brushed against your face?

8. You run on in panic. Your foot kicks against something in the dark. Is it:—
(d) the stump of a tree?
(a) a dead rabbit?
(b) a huge, bloated toadstool?
(c) an ant hill?

9. By now you are in such a state you feel you would like to sink into the ground and die. The only thought that keeps you going is:—
(a) your love for the ones you've left behind at home?
(b) your fascination with this mystical journey?
(c) the sheer physical will to survive?
(d) the heroine's welcome soon awaiting you?

10. Dawn is breaking, you look up at the sky. Is it:—

(c) full of angry storm clouds?
(d) fiery red, with dark, menacing clouds on the horizon?
(b) overcast with a floating white mist?
(a) streaked with clouds and gentle rain?

11. Feeling better after the gruelling night, you can just make out in the distance:—

(b) a lost city from some ancient civilisation?
(a) a land of fairy-tale castles?
(c) a primitive native village?
(d) a weird space-age town?

12. Thankfully you walk towards habitation, and when you get there you are:—
(d) greeted and wined and dined like royalty?
(c) viewed with suspicious hostility, but grudgingly given something to eat?
(b) mistaken for the reincarnation of a mythical goddess?
(a) taken pity on like an orphan from the storm?

13. You thank your hosts and begin your journey home, less afraid this time, but tired and lonely. After a few hours your are delighted to find that you have company in this God-forsaken wilderness. Do you meet up with:—
(b) a hermit?
(c) an explorer?
(a) a wood-cutter?
(d) a businessman on a safari holiday?

14. For a while you are travelling-companions, until your paths part. Feeling strong and happy on the last lap of your journey, you cross the Forbidden Lake:—
(a) on a gondola?
(d) in a hovercraft?
(b) on a raft?
(c) by swimming across?

15. You arrive home to a tumultuous welcome, hugs, kisses, hot food and a warm, cosy bed. Lying awake in bed you try to think of the most valuable thing you've learned from your great adventure. Is it:—
(c) self-reliance?
(d) pride in your own abilities?
(a) courage?
(b) a new awareness of life?

SCORING

Now count your scoring. If you ticked mainly (a), read the conclusion for (a), (b) the conclusion for (b) and so on.

CONCLUSIONS

Mostly (a). You are a very romantic, feminine person, and in a world of women's lib types, you should be very popular with the opposite sex. You want your journey through life to be filled with beautiful things, because you appreciate beauty, and have an ideal of what you want life to be. Of course, the dull day-to-day routine of life doesn't match up to your idea of perfection, and consequently you tend to spend a lot of time day-dreaming. You have an affectionate nature, you are kind-hearted and can't bear to see anyone unjustly treated or suffering. You probably love children and animals, and you trust people and always want to believe the best about them. This can sometimes lead to you being rather gullible. You tend to be shy, but once the barrier has been broken, you are a very sincere, warm person with a lot to offer. You must try to overcome your nervousness to enjoy the beautiful life ahead.

Mostly (b). You are an intuitive person. You act on instinct and rush into things impulsively. You are probably artistic, creative and rather uncoventional. A surface knowledge of things isn't enough for you, and you like to delve deeply into things; for you have a great curiosity about the world around you. However, you tend to be impatient. You have rapid changes of mood, up in the sky one minute and down in the dumps the next, and for this reason you are quite a difficult person to get on with. Your temper leaves something to be desired, too. On the bonus side, however, you like your own company, and you are fun to know because you are always full of ideas and could never be accused of being dull. You also have a great sense of drama, which results in the fact that you sometimes 'tell stories' and exaggerate. You go a lot for the mystical and magical and are fascinated by anything spooky. You are lively-minded, but could do with coming down to earth a bit sometimes.

Mostly (c). You are very sociable and should be very popular. You are full of go. You probably talk a lot and you're not backward when it comes to being the life and soul of the party. You seldom become bored. You are practical and cheerful, and think of life as a great challenge. You know you can always cope with most problems which crop up, and you have the self-confidence to branch out and be adventurous. You are forthright in your views; in fact some people might accuse you of being tactless. Because you are so full of energy, you tend to leave people exhausted, but they admire your vitality. You are a bit of a fighter in your way, and you want to succeed. It doesn't matter how difficult the challenge is, you will carry on with determination until your ambition is achieved. Someone like you is bound to do well in any career you choose. Boys find you good company, and you are easy to get along with because you are naturally friendly. It might be a good idea for you to sit down quietly and think a bit more; for you tend to overdo the action and neglect the pensive. However, your independence and vitality will be an asset wherever you go.

Mostly (d). You like comfort, luxury and glamour, and you believe that diamonds are a girl's best friend. You want to be loved and admired. You don't want to be the same as everyone else—you want to feel really special, and you are usually very successful at impressing people and being the femme fatale. You have good taste and a natural flair and sense of colour and design. Other people have to admire your style, but when you don't feel you are getting your share of attention, you can become jealous and moody. It's nice if you can get away with being the Queen Bee all the time, but you should also think more deeply about other people and try to understand their feelings. You must admit you're a bit selfish sometimes. No wonder other girls often envy you though—you have a certain star quality which makes you unusual.

Nina's Natter

I DON'T say I've never scrounged anything in the whole of my life. Other people's clothes are always nicer than mine for some reason. I don't know if you've noticed the same thing.

I've often been sitting there, thinking what I can wear for that party tonight, and a tantalising vision of me in Jane's dress floats into my head, and refuses to go away. I go and look in my wardrobe to see if by any chance I've bought a dress like hers while sleep walking, and forgotten that I had it.

I get more frantic trying to find it, and give up, and wonder how on earth I'm going to ask her if I can have hers. Another vision floats into my head, which is me in Jane's dress and Pauline's boots. Then before I can help it, I put this vision of me into Nicky's long purple coat.

In fact, Nicky's long purple coat is a necessity if I'm going to wear Jane's dress, because my coat is too short. This is succeeded by the totally accessorised me, in Susan's boa, Ann's little woolly hat, and while I'm at it, I might as well borrow Nicky's handbag.

After all, it goes with the coat, it's only fair I should have that too. I mean, if she's going to let me borrow the coat, there's no reason why she shouldn't throw in the handbag as well. It wouldn't hurt her. And so on. But I've got nothing on a borrower I used to live next door to.

I think she was probably the most irritating person I ever knew. She really had this borrowing thing all worked out.

I'd be sitting quietly in my room when there would be a timid little knock, a little head would be poked round the door, and she'd clear her throat nervously.

She gave this appearance of diffidence, to take you off your guard. When I first met her, I thought, "Oh, poor little thing, she's shy, I'd better be nice to her". In fact, it was all part of her fiendish technique.

Eventually it would dawn on me that she had invited thirteen of her friends round and was going to entertain completely off me. The interesting thing was that she never seemed to realise that she was going a bit far. Nobody who knew her would have been a bit surprised if she'd asked to borrow their beds, knickers, boyfriends, or mothers. She seemed to be utterly insatiable.

I was once standing cleaning my teeth peacefully in the wash room, but nowhere was really safe.

"Ah-hum! Hello! I suppose you haven't got any sugar I could borrow, have you?"

"Oh, all right, there's some in my room."

"Ah-hum! I suppose I couldn't possibly borrow your hair-dryer, could I?"

"Oh, I suppose so, you know where it is by now, I expect."

"Ah-hum! I suppose you couldn't possibly let me have a bit of shampoo, could you?"

"Good heavens! Yes, I suppose if you must, you must."

"Ah-hum—"

At this point I snapped and, spitting viciously into the washbasin, I turned on her, brandishing my toothbrush in her face. She leapt backwards and cowered in the doorway, clearing her throat at a greatly increased rate, and managed to stammer out, "I suppose you wouldn't—er—like to come to my party, would you?"

Prints Charming

WHATEVER happened to those plain summer frocks? These are some of the goodies you'll be seeing in the shops from now on, most of them knee- length, some higher, some longer . . . it's up to you to decide which you prefer.

As for style, you won't know which way to turn . . . straps, bows, buttons, belts, they're all here in a range of colours and fabrics that'll take your breath away.

Short-sleeved dress with button front and pointed collar, with lady pattern print, by City Swingers.
Style No.: 5445. Price: £9·50. Fabric: 100 per cent Acetate. Colours: Beige background with two colourways. Sizes 10 to 14.

Sandals with wooden heel and sole and twisted sandal front, from Ravel.
Style: Athis. Price: £6·99. Fabric: Leather/wood. Colours: Black, white, navy/beige, brown/beige. Sizes 3 to 7.

Sunshine dress in printed summer cotton with a low-cut front and buttoned halter, from Silhouette.
Style No.: L620. Price £5·95 approx. Fabric: 100 per cent cotton. Colours: Navy or yellow with clover pattern, green, red, tan with cherry pattern. Sizes: 10 to 16.

Canvas open-toe sandal and basket weave sole, from Ravel.
Style: Rain. Price: £6·99. Fabric: Denim upper, straw platform.

Short-sleeved dress with square neck, dropped waist and printed in a bag and stick design, from City Swingers.
Style No.: 5412. Price: £9·50. Fabric: 100 per cent Acetate. Colours: Beige background with two colourways. Sizes: 10 to 14.

Open-toed, sling back shoe with snake-look crossover front, from Ravel.
Style: Whistle. Price £7·50. Fabric: Leather. Colours: Black, brown, beige. Sizes: 3 to 7.

Super, multi-print dress with thin shoulder straps, panelled skirt and belted waist, by Shubette.
Style No.: 3053. Price: Approx. £11. Fabric: Cotton. Colours: Multi-print in red/green/blue/yellow. Sizes 10 to 16.

Patent shoe with criss cross snake-skin front and open toe, from Ravel.
Style: Shimmer. Price: £7·99. Fabric: Leather. Colours: Black, beige/brown, navy, brown. Sizes: 3 to 7.

WHERE TO FIND THEM

For City Swingers stockists write to City Swingers, Shirley Anne Young Ltd., 89 Great Portland Street, London WIN 5RA. Shubette dress from Gilda, Oxford Street, London W.1.; Joan Barrie, Long Mill Gate, Manchester and branches; Enquiries to Liz Forster, Shubette of London, 42-48 Great Portland Street, London W.1. Silhouette dress from Daly's and Binns of Glasgow; A. Caird, Dundee; Hammonds of Hull; Isaac Walton, Newcastle; Co-op, Plymouth; Bonds of Norwich; Keddies of Southend; Dickens and Jones, Regent Street, London W.1; D. H. Evans, Oxford Street, London W.1.; Civil Service Stores. Ravel shoes from all branches or by post from 103 New Bond Street, London W.1.: All enquiries to Margaret Hicks at the same address.

All prices approximate.

Remember the super Glynn Manson cardi, style 8012, in our Cut It Out page February 23?

We've just heard that the price is approx. £6·50 instead of £3·25 as originally stated.

ARE YOU GAME

Be one of the gang or go it alone — these super sporty looks and clothes will make you a winner!

ANYONE FOR TENNIS?

Delicate white sun-top with pink trim, by Knitcraft at Morley. Style No.: F8020. Price: £4.10. Fabric: 100% Acrylic. Colours: Delphinium, white, pink, navy, pineapple. Sizes: Medium only.

Matching short-sleeved cardi with button front. Style No.: F8400. Price: £6.30. Sizes: Small, medium, large. Fabric and colours as for sun-top. Both from Selfridges of Oxford Street, London W.1.; Rackhams, Birmingham; Claydons, Bradford; Walsh's, Sheffield.

White towelling zip-front shorts with 2 slant pockets, from Marks & Spencer. No Style No. Price: £2.50. Fabric: Cotton towelling. Colours: White, pink, blue, navy, lime, strawberry. Sizes: 34 to 40 hip. Available from most branches of Marks & Spencer.

Flat sandal with loop toe and straw embroidered flower on strap, from Dolcis. Style No.: A15/92403. Price: £4.99. Fabric: Leather upper. Colours: Tan, white. Sizes: 3 to 8. From main branches of Dolcis. By post from Dolcis, 350 Oxford Street, London W.1. + 30p for postage and packing.

MAKE-UP

If you really are going to play tennis, you won't need too much make-up. Keep your hair back off your face . . . it can be an awful nuisance if it's always flopping over your eyes. (You'll find that you're *cooler*, if your hair's tied back, too!)

You'll need a good deodorant to keep you feeling fresh and nice. Try Body Mist in Wild Rose, Dawn Fresh or Spring Whisper, 29p each, or Linden Voss extended life anti-perspirant at £1.06 for the roll-on if you need something extra strong. Give yourself a liberal dusting afterwards with talcum powder, preferably a non-scented one such as Johnson's Baby Powder.

Steer clear of loads of eye make-up, just a touch of mascara will do! Use lip-gloss rather than thick lipstick, try the Max Factor roll-on Lip Gloss in Natural or Mint flavour, price 45p.

CROQUET ON THE LAWN

Pretty white camisole top with long sleeves, from Marks & Spencer. No Style No. Price: £3.99. Fabric: Cotton. Colours: White. Sizes: 32 to 36 bust. From major branches of Marks & Spencer.

Long blue skirt with frill at the bottom, from Shubette. Style no.: 0355. Price: £8.80. Fabric: Cotton/polyester. Colours: Blue, red, green, pink. Sizes: 10 to 16. From Gilda, Oxford Street, London W.1.; Joan Barrie branches; Guys and Dolls and branches; Just Looking, Kings Road, London S.W.3.; Enquiries to Lorraine Beverley, 42 to 48 Great Portland Street, London W.1.

Cork wedge clog with denim front and open toe, from Marks & Spencer. No Style No. Price: £3.99. Fabric: Denim and cork. Colours: Blue, pink, beige. Sizes: 3 to 8. From a selection at major branches of Marks & Spencer.

Large straw hat with flower trim, from Barnett Hats. Style No.: 18/12. Price: £2.95. Fabric: Natural straw. Colours. Natural. From Halperin, Clapham Junction, London S.W.11. No mail order, but enquiries to Miss Dickson, Barnett Hats Ltd., 21-22 Poland Street, London W.1.

MAKE-UP

Pretty as a picture, that's the look to aim for. Try colours from Gala's new Garden Collection, for eyes, lips and nails.

There's Almond Blossom, a dusty petal pink with a touch of beige — lipstick 43p, and nail polish to match, 35p, or Apple Blossom which is a rich cerise pink. For eyes there's Blue Nettle Matte Shadow, 44p, and Sweet Pea Eye Gem which is a soft silvery turquoise. 36p.

Add a touch of colour to your cheeks with a hint of blusher, try Mary Quant's Cheeky blusher in Golden Plum, 62p, Outdoor . Girl's Cream Blusher in Tawny, price 19p

FOR ANYTHING?

V-neck, stripy, cable jumper with long sleeves and little collar, from Bellmans. Style No.: 5124/25. Price: £3.99. Fabric: Acrylic/polyester. Colours: Pistachio, calabash, delphinium, all with striped trim. Sizes: 12 to 16. From all branches of Bellmans. By post from Bellmans, 172 High Street, Hounslow, Middlesex TW3 1BQ, - 30p for postage and packing.

Smart cream trousers with zip front from Bellmans. Style No.: 7958/04. Price: £5.99. Fabric: Viscose/acetate. Colours: Cream only. Sizes: 12 to 16. From all branches of Bellmans. By post from Bellmans at the above address - 30p extra for postage and packing.

Woven canvas wedge sandal with twist strap at the front, from Saxone. Style No.: A52/6501/87. Price: £7.99. Fabric: Hopsack linen. Colours: Beige, brown, black. Sizes: 3 to 8. From main branches of Saxone or Lilley & Skinner. By post from Lilley & Skinner, 360 Oxford Street, London W.1. + 30p for postage and packing.

MAKE-UP

Shade your eyes with a nice hat . . . the sun in your eyes makes you screw them up to see, which isn't any use at all! If you're going to be out and about, especially in the sun, make sure that you use plenty of moisturiser to care for your skin.

Try Oil of Ulay or Boots No. 7 Moisture Plus which is great for dry skin. The Ponds range of moisturisers is great, too. Choose Ponds Light Moisturiser or Ponds Lemon Cream moisturiser for greasy skins.

Keep lips really soft with a lip salve such as Boots' own or Lipsaver.

BE A LITTLE BATTY

BELLE OF THE BEACH

Super zip-up towelling top with collar from Tesco. Style No.: P0682/4. Price: £3.25. Fabric: 100% cotton. Colours: Emerald, red, gold, turquoise. Sizes: 12 to 16. From larger branches of Tesco with Home 'N' Wear departments.

Red halter-neck T-shirt, from Etam. No Style No. Price: 95p. Colours: Assorted. Sizes: medium and large. From all branches of Etam.

Fabulous white shorts with turn-ups and four red buttons on the side, from Bus Stop. No Style No. Price: £6.95. Fabric: Cotton mixture. Colours: Assorted. Sizes: 8 to 14. By Lee Bender for Bus Stop at all Bus Stop branches.

Suede wedge sandal with buckle detail on the white strap front, from Dolcis. Style No.: A15/95402. Price: £4.99. Fabric: Leather uppers and suede-covered wedge. Colours: White, tan. Sizes: 3 to 8. From main branches of Dolcis. By post from 350 Oxford Street, London W.1. + 30p for postage and packing.

MAKE-UP

If you're lucky enough to be able to get down to a beach for a bit of a bake, you'll need to take some sun-tan lotion with you. Even if the sun isn't all that hot it's surprising what the sun and wind, combined with the salty air, can do to your skin.

Try the Skol sun-tan products . . . which are effective and not too expensive. Skol Sun Tan Lotion is a good sun-screen, for all types of skin, price 50p for a 135 cc tube.

If you can't find the sun you'll need to fake it. Try Outdoor Girl's Tanfastic, price 35p for the small size lotion, or Ambre Solaire's Duo Tan 55p a tube.

Hair may suffer from the sun and wind, too, so use a shampoo with a built-in conditioner such as Alberto Balsam or Protein 21, available for all the different hair-types.

All prices approximate.

—BUT WHAT'S YOUR REAL AGE?

YOU can BE 14, and act like 40—or BE 40, yet act like 14! Neither is really a happy way to be. And though that's a bit extreme as an example, it's perfectly true that your age in years can be quite different from the stage of maturity you've reached.

Of course, it doesn't matter that you're a little young for your age—as long as you go on maturing, and don't shut up shop! Some people NEVER really mature in the fullest sense of the word, and they're the kind who always feel dissatisfied with themselves and everything around them. They don't stick at things, have difficulty in making decisions, and basically are still playing at being grown-up, however old they get.

On the other hand, nobody wants to be TOO mature, TOO early. You miss a lot of fun that way, and it's fun that is lost for good, because you can't go back and be a teenager all over again at some future time.

The best way to be is just right for your years—but how do you tell? And what can you do about it if you're not? Well—try this quiz on for size, and then go on from there! Be as honest as you can with the answers.

1. Imagine you have an older sister who is more beautiful, talented, witty and clever than you, and she is also a nice person. One day, you overhear your mother saying to a friend that she wished you were more like your sister. Would you reaction be:

a) To go upstairs and tear something of your sister's into tiny shreds, in an absolute uncontrollable fit of rage and temper?
b) To burst into tears, and tell Mum you wish you could leave home forever?
c) To burst into tears—but keep it to yourself?
d) To resolve to ask your sister's help in making the best of yourself in future?

2. You have a boyfriend, let's pretend, who teases you because you have a lot of freckles and he says when you don't wear make-up you look about 8. Your reaction?

d) You exaggerate the freckles with make-up, and wear young-looking clothes.
b) You feel faintly annoyed, but can't do much about it.
c) You realise it's his way of saying he loves you, and just laugh.
a) You feel really mad, fly into a temper, and try more sophisticated make-up and clothes when you know you'll be seeing him.

3. You have been left minding somebody's baby for the day, and your boyfriend wants to take you out. He says he has younger brothers and sisters, so won't mind a spot of pram-pushing—but you feel . . .

a) Extremely embarrassed to be seen out with him and a baby?
b) It would be best to leave the baby at home?
c) It would be rather funny to go out as a threesome?
d) You promised to look after the baby, so shouldn't go out with him?

4. There is a tremendous row at home between your father and mother, and you are uncomfort bly aware that it's you they are fighting over! Would you:

c) Leave them to sort things out their own way?
a) Take your mother's side?
d) Try to show them they shouldn't row over you?
b) Take your father's side?

5. An argument with your boyfriend blazed up into a big row, but when you cool off later, you discover that you had got your facts quite wrong, and later, when he calls round to see you . . .

b) You feel too embarrassed to admit being in the wrong, but make up the quarrel without really apologising?
d) You humbly admit your mistake, and explain you must have got your facts mixed up?
a) You yell at him some more, to cover your confusion, and say he had no business shouting at you in the first place?
c) You make-up first—admit your mistake later?

6. Money is taken from your coat pocket, while you are having lunch in the canteen. Some girl you don't like very much has been saying how hard up she is, recently. Would you think . . .

a) She must have taken the money, and accuse her of it?
b) She may have taken the money, but you can't prove it?
c) Anyone could have taken the money, and it's not more likely to be the girl you dislike than anyone else?
d) It's unimportant, who took the money—it is as much your fault for leaving it carelessly lying around as the person who stole it?

7. You get a chain letter, which says that unless you send money to the top four names on the list, and send out copies of the letter to 20 friends, you will bring bad luck to yourself, and darkly hints that fatal accidents have been known to happen to people who broke the chain. Would you:

d) Report the letter to the authorities?
c) Tear the letter up without another thought?
b) Tear the letter up, but feel worried about it?
a) Send the letter on, and forward the cash?

8. You spent an hour and a half over lunch break one day, and the boss was furious, and told you to make up the time tonight. At six o'clock, you still have half an hour to do, and you notice the boss has left the office. Your boyfriend is expecting you to meet him for a date tonight, so . . .

b) You work twice as fast for 15 minutes, then leave early?
a) You leave at once, but feel sneaky?
c) You work the half-hour, but feel mad about it?
d) You work the half-hour, and leave a note on the boss's desk saying you have done so?

9. You and a girl-friend sneak into a X-certificate film just for giggles, but get spotted by a neighbour on coming out. Her parents think it is rather a joke, though they tell her not to go to such a place again. YOURS throw a blue fit, and ban you from seeing your friend ever again! It IS unfair, but what would you do about it?

a) Sulk, and throw tantrums till you got the ban lifted?
b) Argue constantly about it, trying to keep your temper, and say it was more your idea than hers, in the first place?
c) Let the whole thing cool down before raising the subject quietly?
d) Admit you were wrong, but say their reaction is stupid, and refuse to give up your friend?

answers

***A* answers** *are perfectly reasonable reactions . . . if you are aged ten, or less. If you are up to five years older than this, you are a little immature for your age. You haven't yet learned that things (and people) aren't always as straightforward as they seem, and you are sometimes bitterly hurt by things that shouldn't have been taken too seriously at all!*

This only means that you are a little slow at maturing, but you will find life much easier if you don't try to be too independent just yet. You still need the protection of your family and friends, and would not be happy if you cut yourself off from them, however much you hate them at times! You shouldn't get upset if you sometimes feel real hatred towards your parents. This is quite normal when you are growing up, and it might surprise you to know they don't always find you all sweetness and light, either . . . but they still love you!

If you are over 18, and scored more than 3 A answers, you are really immature for your age, and you should try to act with more responsibility. Before you take on any permanent relationship, you should make quite sure you know enough about yourself to make decisions on your own two feet!

B ANSWERS *are normal teenage reactions . . . if you are aged around 15. You probably know you aren't always in control of your emotions, and are subject to difficult moods when you are awkward and can't get along with anyone. This doesn't mean you are immature at all, it is all part of the process of growing up, and it would be ABNORMAL if a teenager was too self-controlled!*

If you are younger than this, you are mature for your age, and it may be hard for you to accept that although you are quite able to make decisions and look after yourself, your age on paper is against you, and your parents may still want to treat you as a baby. You'll just have to prove them wrong!

If you are older than 18, and scored more than 5 B answers, you are rather immature for your age. You know what you SHOULD do in a given situation, but sometimes react in a totally different way. You feel unhappy sometimes, because you feel you can't cope. It may be that you have tried to grow up too fast, at one stage of adolescence, and this is nature's way of slowing you down. Don't worry about it. Don't let it bother you if other people start getting engaged, while you feel unready—it's not a badge of success to wear an engagement ring, and you must learn to live life at your own speed, and only accept responsibilities when you feel you are ready for them.

C ANSWERS *are the mature reaction of a normal young adult of around 18-20 or so. If you're a good deal younger than that, you have matured fast and have a tolerant, sensible approach to life and this will give you a good start because you'll be able to handle situations and responsibilities as they come along. Don't get too smug, however. You may be at the stage when you can see what should be done, and feel you have all the answers, but only because your emotions haven't, as yet, been deeply involved.*

When you fall in love, or feel really angry or hurt about something, you will tend to forget your sensible, mature reactions and revert to the automatic response which is expected of your age group. For this reason, although you feel quite capable of tackling a big responsibility, it is not always wise to tackle anything alone.

D ANSWERS *are those of a person, of any age, who feels mature, but is really not able to face up to reality alone. If you are under 20, this is understandable, because you are coming into contact now with situations you may not have come across before, and it is perfectly normal to turn to someone else for advice when you are stuck for what to do! In fact, if you are between 12 and, D answers mean you take a very serious, responsible view of life. Maybe too serious. Being a teenager isn't exactly a licence to have fun, but it IS a time for making mistakes and learning from them.*

If you aren't very adventurous, and are willing to take other people's advice all the time, you aren't really developing your own personality very much. It's a good thing to learn by someone else's experience, now and again—but you must also stand on your own feet. Otherwise, you'll find when you are 25 or so, you feel you have never had much fun, and it is then a bit late to do all the mad things you should have done when you were 15!

STAY TRIM WITH NO GYM

Hands up those who daren't wear sleeveless dresses! Flabby arms certainly don't enhance anyone, so tone 'em up with our easy isometrics.

Remember, exercises work both ways—too fat, they'll slim you down, too thin, they'll build up muscle!

And these ones are the simplest yet . . .

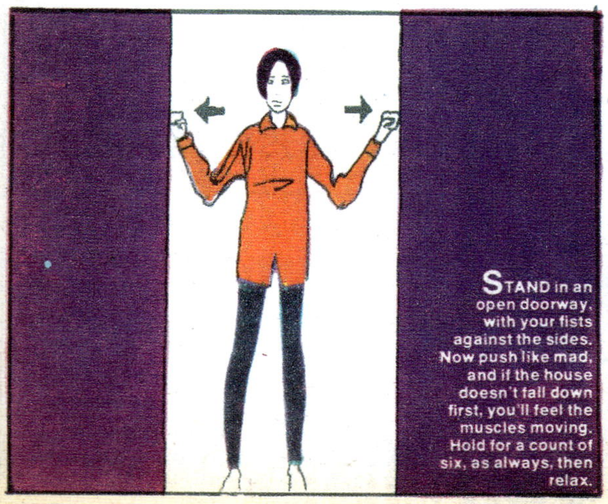

PATCH WORK

PAPERCHASE

Follow the trail — to Paperchase! It's a super shop we've discovered which sells the most amazing collection of paper goodies you ever saw — greetings cards, gift tags, notepaper, wrapping paper . . . the list is endless! We've picked a small selection of items to show you, but do try to see the shop yourself, if you're in London. It's well worth a visit!

For the items shown here, the prices are: pencil bookmark/gift tags (use them as either!) 8p each. Animal gift tags, 5p each. Teddy bear notepaper, 20p for 8 sheets and envelopes. Lion and owl stickers, 20p a sheet.

The address is: Paperchase, 216 Tottenham Court Road, London W.1.

MAKE YOUR PRESENTS FELT!

This week the "Your Patch" idea comes from Gillian Leng of Chester. Gillian makes and collects these gorgeous mice, but parted with Fred to send him to us. We couldn't resist him and know you couldn't either!

The mouse is very easy to make — just — **1.** Cut out 3 pieces of felt — shaped roughly like this — for the

base and 2 sides. **2.** Now stitch together the tops of the two sides and add the base to the bottom of the sides, leaving a small hole for stuffing. **3.** Stuff with foam chips or bits of old (clean!) tights and sew up hole. **4.** Make eyes, tail, nose, ears and whiskers from wool and felt, and sew on.

If you have any ideas for 'Your Patch' send them to 'Your Patch', Patchwork, Jackie, 185 Fleet Street, London EC4A IBL. We'll pay £1 for every idea printed, so what are you waiting for?

WHAT A CARD!

Cards these days are so nice it seems a pity to throw them away after your birthday or whatever is over. And sometimes they're so expensive we feel we might as well make the most of them.

Now, thanks to Concertina publications you can keep your cards — and learn from them! You see, Concertina have brought out "Cards To Keep," a super range of greetings cards which open up to reveal a mine of information about various subjects — from cats to kites, from wild flowers to magic. Being obsessed by food, our favourite is "Homemade sweets."

"Cards to Keep" are available from major stationers, price 30p each.

If you can't find them, write to: Concertina Publications Ltd., 11-13 Broad Court, Covent Garden, London WC2 (enclosing an SAE) for your nearest stockist.

SATURDAY NIGHT AT THE MOVIES!

Have you noticed how many disaster films there are around lately — *"The Poseidon Adventure"* started it all a couple of years ago with the riveting spectacle of an ocean liner swept upside down by a gigantic wave. Everybody was on the edge of their seats as the handful of survivors fought their way through fire and water to the top of the boat, where they were rescued by a timely helicopter!

Since then of course we've had *"The Towering Inferno"* in which an enormous skyscraper catches fire and Paul Newman, Steve McQueen and Fred Astaire struggle to survive!

Followed by *"Airport 75"* in which, you all remember, a plane plunges through the cockpit of a Jumbo Jet killing the pilot and leaving only a stewardess and Charlton Heston to bring the Jumbo down safely.

Not forgetting *"Earthquake"*, where we were transported to San Francisco and yes, an earthquake was recreated so realistically that the sheer force and volume actually had cinema foundations trembling!

Why you might ask in these days when the news is full of death and destruction do people want to go and see more death and destruction? We don't know, but it's interesting to note that disaster films were in fashion immediately before the Great Depression of the Thirties. And of course, going back a bit, death-defying spectacles were very popular just before the fall of the Roman Empire!

Talking about films, after an absolute dearth of pop films for years, we've suddenly had a rush of them. There's been Slade's *"Flame,"* David Essex in *"Stardust"*, Roger Daltrey in the Who's Rock-Opera extravaganza *"Tommy"*. And now we're looking forward to *"Never Too Young To Rock"* (Mud, Rubettes, Glitterband) to be released in June. Also making a film in June are Ron and Russell Mael, with distinguished French film director Jacques Tati.

Sadly there'll be no music, it's a dramatic comedy and the boys will just be acting.

Wonder when we'll be seeing the Osmonds film we've all heard so much about????

PICK A BIC PACK!

If, like us, you're all tied up in knots metres and centimetres, then this is for you. It's a set of ten "Bic" school pens, in black, blue, red, and green, complete with a handy metric conversion chart — something no-one can afford to be without at the moment!

The set costs 60p and is available from most stationers. The pens are also available singly, price 6p each.

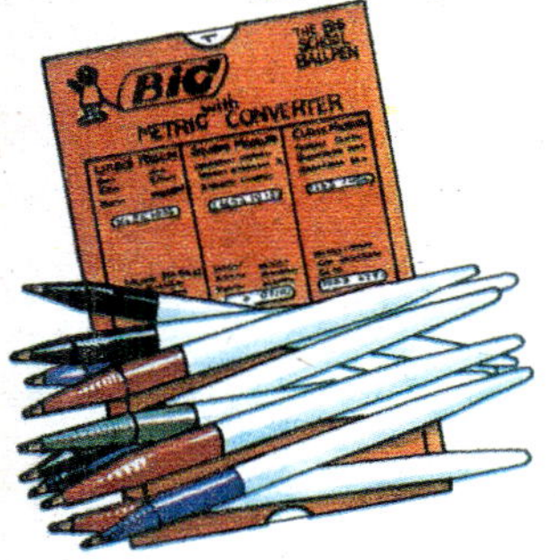

BILBO'S LAST SONG

Lovers of "Lord Of The Rings" will be delighted to know that a Tolkien poem has been brought out — "Bilbo's Last Song."

The poem, previously unpublished, is printed in poster form against a background of a dreamy, misty painting. It'd look beautiful hanging on your wall.

Price 75p, it's available from most stationers.

ANYONE FOR TENNIS?

Do glorious summer afternoons find you sitting within darkened walls, studying every move of Bjorn Borg and Chris Evert on your T V screen? Well, your time is almost here. Wimbledon fortnight (do we need remind you?) is 23rd June to 5th July, and if tennis is all you can think about, maybe you'd like to get some practice yourself.

Luckily, tennis isn't one of those sports that needs tons of expensive equipment. You can trot round to your nearest park, where you'll usually find tennis courts, dressed in any old shorts and T-shirt, and the only thing you mustn't forget is, of course, your racquet! Any good sports shop, or department in a large store, will help you choose one suitable for your height, weight and standard.

If you want to get a bit more serious about it all, go in for the proper gear which does make you feel more the part! Have a look round sports departments and see our fashion special on page 25.

If you really fancy your chances one of these summers, the first thing to do is to get proper tuition. Send an s.a.e. to the Lawn Tennis Association, Baron's Court, London, W.14., and they'll post the details of tennis coaches in your part of the world. They hold classes as well as giving private lessons. You could also find out if your local Education Authority (ask for them at the town hall) organises lessons, too.

Meet you in the championships!

MARS MUNCH

Here's a scrumptious recipe made with just two ingredients — cornflakes and a Mars Bar! For skinnies only . . .

Melt a Mars bar, and beat with a wooden spoon until smooth. Add 2oz. crushed cornflakes, mix well, drop onto a plate in clumps and leave to cool.

A JACKIE SPECIAL

CAN YOU FACE

DONNY OSMOND

Perhaps like many girls you've spent hours gazing at Donny's gentle features wondering what kind of boyfriend he would be! Well Donny has the straight, finely shaped and evenly proportioned nose of a sensitive, poetic person so he must be very sentimental and romantic with girls. But the hollow space under his nose is a sign he's shy with girls and lacks confidence.

His full lower lip shows he would be warm and affectionate once he's overcome his shyness and the downward slant of the corner of his eyes tells us he would try in every way to be agreeable to her. This feature also reveals he's the chatty, not the quiet type.

Several curves in the formation of Donny's upper lip are a sign of his emotional, dramatic nature so his girlfriend could expect some very sentimental, emotional moments with Donny.

The only flaw to romantic bliss is the jealousy shown in his eyebrows which meet!

BRYAN FERRY

Gazing into Bryan Ferry's deep eyes will tell you just what kind of boyfriend he would be. The almond shape shows he's a thoughtful guy — definitely not the chatty type! The slight downward curve of the corners of his mouth and the long, bony shape of his face indicate he would be serious and loyal in love. He's not shy with girls as we can see from the extreme length between his nose and upper lip.

The thickness in Bryan's forehead just above the eyebrows and the narrowness of the bridge of his nose are two signs he's a very sensitive man who could size up a girl's true feelings for him straight away. His medium full lips show he'd be affectionate, but the smallness of his mouth means he can be selfish in love!

His long narrow jaw and chin and his high forehead are also signs he would be stubborn, and domineering!

ROD STEWART

Rod Stewart's thick eyebrows, strong nose and chin tell us he would be a domineering boyfriend. His chin also shows his stubbornness and his heavy eyebrows are a sign he can be abrupt. His deep-set eyes with the lids slightly drooping also reveal he's not one for idle chatter.

The fullness of his lower lip shows his affectionate nature but his flaring nostrils are a sign he lacks romanticism. He's more interested in a girl's physical attributes than her personality. Although he's basically quiet he has a fine sense of humour.

The upward slant of his eyes combined with the concave, scooping shape of his nose tell us he is too critical of women to fall in love easily!

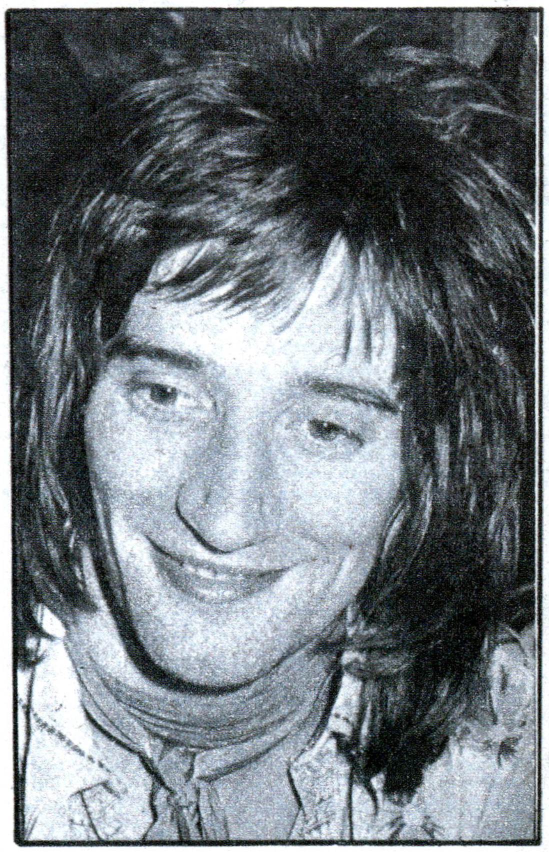

NOW we show you how to do it, in our easy step by step guide to analysing your own face.

All you have to do is look over all the illustrations marking the ones which are similar to your own features and read the analysis underneath to find out about your romantic nature!

In some cases you'll find you have contradicting features. For example, you may have the nose of a sensitive, poetic girl, but the jaw and chin of a practical, unemotional girl! This means that you have a little of both qualities.

Remember that it's best to have a friend to help you. We rarely see ourselves as we really are and someone else will probably be a better judge of your features than you are! OK?

Then why not try out your new face reading skill on your boyfriend and see what those handsome features reveal!

NOSES

Straight and slightly pointed
Very romantic, impractical, idealistic, sensitive, poetic.

Curved inward
More practical than (1), but sometimes fickle with several boyfriends on the string.

Snub
Romantic, sensitive but easily pushed about and taken for granted.

Tip tilt
Very flirty, vivacious, impulsive, reckless in love.

FOREHEADS

High
Very romantic, impractical, idealistic and sensitive with many romantic daydreams.

Low
Often shy and silent with boys — makes bad decisions in love.

Slightly rounded
Very chatty and friendly with boys but over-romantic and easily deceived.

EYES

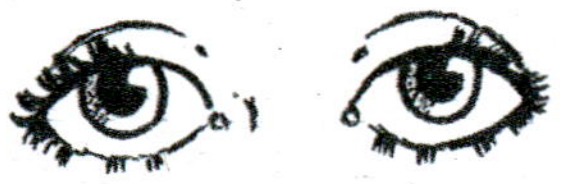

Very large rounded eyes with white under iris
Over-emotional with very strong feelings that are easily aroused.

Large round eyes with curved upper lid
Emotional and sympathetic.

Very deep-set eyes
Can size up a boy quickly but worries too much.

Deep set eyes with upper eyelid drooping halfway over eye
Cautious and rarely falls in love.

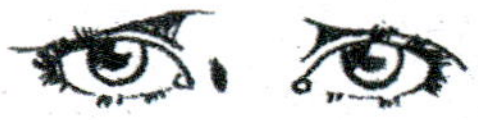

Deep set narrow eyes with less than space of eye between eyes.
Could be secretive, moody and irritable.

Slanting eyes
Can be selfish.

Full upper eyelid droops over eye
Strong emotions and quick temper.

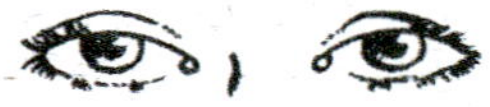

Upper lid covers one third to one half of pupil
Head rules heart.

Upper and lower eyelids close together
Very shrewd in love.

Eyes slant downwards
Very agreeable and tries hard to please.

YOURSELF!

CAN you tell at a glance how romantic a boy is?

Yes — if you know the secrets of face reading!

Jackie's physiognomist (that's the fancy name for a face-reader) has analysed some of our favourite pop stars to reveal how romantic they are. So read on to find out what kind of boyfriends they'd make.

GARY GLITTER

The most striking feature revealed by Gary's face is his changeable, unpredictable personality shown by the way his eyebrows arch upwards and then hook down! His girl-friends would rarely know how he felt about them. His moods change rapidly. On the one hand he can be sociable and friendly — shown by the upward curve of the corners of his mouth — but the way his upper eyelid droops over his eye reveals a harsh temper. This feature is also a sign he is easily irritated and the thickness under the lower eyelid is a sign of lack of control over emotions.

The horizontal line cutting across the bridge of his nose between his eyes is a sign he'd be domineering with a girl. While his fairly thick lower lip shows a warm, generous nature but there are not signs of the romantic in Gary's face.

In fact the squareness of his face tells us he takes a practical, unsentimental attitude towards girls!

DAVID ESSEX

David Essex's face reveals that he would be a gentle boy-friend hiding a quiet strength. His strong chin combined with thick eyebrows reveal a firm, energetic personality with strong likes and dislikes as far as girls go. The corners of David's mouth turn up telling us he is a sociable, friendly, optimistic person. Since the outer edges of his eyes turn downwards we also know he tries hard to please his girl.

The short space between David's nose and upper lip reveals a lack of confidence and the need for approval from girls. His full lower lip shows his generous warm nature while his well-formed soft eyes indicate a romantic, sentimental nature.

The fullness running under his lower lid is a sign of strong emotions — but suspicion and jealousy in love are revealed in the meeting of his eyebrows over the bridge of his nose.

LES GRAY

Should you, would you accept a date from Les Gray, and if you did what kind of guy would he be? Face-reading tells us you'd have a wonderful evening with him. The curved shape of his nose shows he has a great zest for life but it also tells us of his love of change and variety so you might not be the only girl in his life! But he would always treat you fairly since love of justice is shown in the two faint down-ward lines between his eyebrows.

Is he romantic and affectionate? The fullness of his cheeks just below the cheekbones and the medium fullness of his lower lip say he is. The shape under his lower eye-lids tells us his emotions are quickly aroused and he falls easily in love. However, he might hesitate to tell you, since the short space between his nose and mouth shows he lacks confidence.

He's probably shy but the cleft in his chin is a sign of his excellent sense of humour!

EYEBROWS

Heavy eyebrows
Very bold with strong opinions about the way a boy should treat a girl.

Thin delicate eyebrows
Mild, sensitive, nervous personality.

High arched eyebrows
Very emotional, impulsive and jealous.

Low, usually thick eyebrows
Not easily deceived but sometimes too suspicious.

Eyebrows that meet
Suspicious and jealous.

Eyebrows low over nose with outer ends slanting upwards.
Changeable and rather scheming.

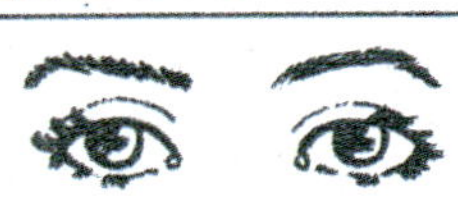

Outer edge of brows high and rounded, hooking downwards
Unsociable and a bit self-centred.

LIPS

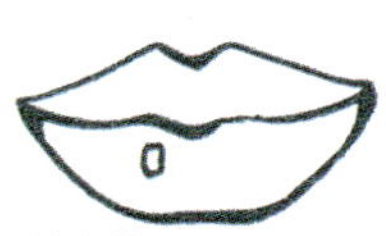

Large, thick lips
Strong and sometimes uncontrolled passions.

Medium full lips
Very warm and affectionate.

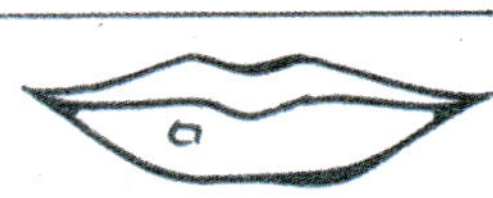

Medium thin lips, wide mouth
Affectionate but rarely shows feelings.

Narrow lips wide mouth
Head always rules heart — cool and calm.

Full lips with upper lip protruding
Heart always rules head.

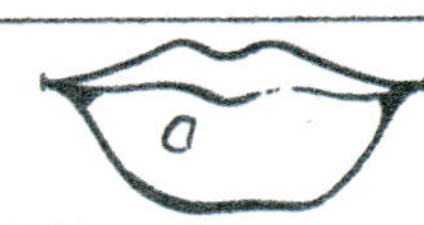

Very full lower lip
Very sympathetic, affectionate and kind.

Short space under nose
Nervous, excitable and lacks self-confidence with boys.

Turned up corners of mouth
Sociable, friendly, full of fun and likes to flirt.

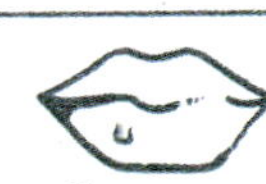

Small mouth
Sometimes selfish in love.

Lips apart when mouth relaxed
Bashful with boys.

CHINS

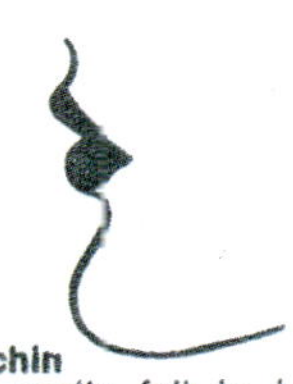

Strong chin
Doesn't easily fall in love — head rules heart.

Weak chin
Her emotions rule her life.

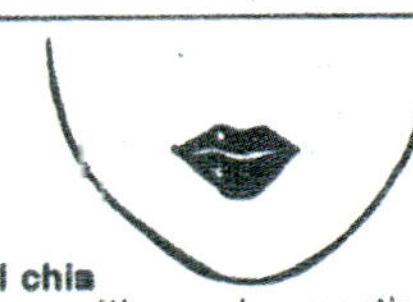

Oval chin
Very sensitive and romantic.

Square chin
Very practical and unsentimental.

Pointed chin
A witty, chatty girl who is a bit flighty.

A JACKIE QUIZ

SSHHH... YOU KNOW WHO

Do you like yourself? What a silly question, you might think, but it's not as silly as it seems, and not one many people could answer honestly. If you don't believe in yourself, no-one else will. So if you want to know what you really do think of yourself, answer this quiz and see what your subconscious comes up with!

1—Do you usually smile at shopkeepers and bus conductors?

2—Do you really believe the compliments boys pay you?
3—Can you make decisions quickly?
4—Do you have frequent headaches or stomach pains?
5—Are you as fresh and sweet-smelling as you should be?
6—Do you become easily envious of your friends?
7—Do you spring out of bed like a lark in the morning?
8—Do you often have hysterical fits of the giggles?
9—Do you like fresh air?
10—Do you eat/drink/smoke too much?

11—Have you usually got an instant opinion about most things?
12—Do you ever worry that you might have bad breath or smelly feet?
13—Do you spend long hours in front of the mirror?
14—Do you often blush or stammer?
15—Do you like boys to whistle or call out at you?
16—Do you gossip about people a lot?
17—Do you admire your body in the bath?
18—Do you find it difficult to say 'no' to people?
19—Can you talk to your parents about emotional things?
20—Do you sometimes feel overwhelmed by people's kindness to you?
21—Have you a special hobby, interest or sport (apart from boys and pop, we mean!)?
22—Do you often think, If only . . . . ?
23—Do you carry on day-to-day routine as normal during periods?
24—Are you a bit squeamish about blood?
25—Can you easily live down making a fool of yourself?

26—Does a pimple on your chin ruin the whole weekend?
27—Are you a good sport, having a go and joining in usually?
28—Do you often get upset over remarks people make about you?
29—Do you always question people when you think their remarks are incorrect, unfair or misguided?
30—Have you ever apologised to someone when they stepped on your toe or bumped into you?

NOW: Ignore all the questions to which you have answered 'no'. If you have more 'yes' answers to questions with ODD NUMBERS (1,3,5, etc.) turn to SECTION A. If you have more 'yes' answers to questions with EVEN NUMBERS (2,4,6, etc) turn to SECTION B.

SECTION A

1—Do you think your best friend is—
(a) not so pretty as you are?
(b) prettier than you are?

2—If someone asked you to make up a foursome on a blind date, would you worry most—
(a) that he might not like you?
(b) that you might not like him?

3—When you're all dressed up to go to a party, do you feel—
(a) absolutely fantastic and full of confidence?
(b) really marvellous, but still slightly apprehensive?

4—Do you naturally assume that people always admire you and say nice things about you?
(b) not particularly.
(a) yes, more or less always.

5—Do you ever feel lonely?
(a) never.
(b) occasionally.

6—How do you feel when the boy you're with ogles longingly at another female—
(b) angry and hurt. But you accept it?
(a) madly furious. And you don't accept it—you challenge him about it?

7—Which alternative would best sum up your attitude to people in general. Especially nasty, aggressive people—
(a) No-one can push you around—you're capable of looking after yourself?
(b) You'd make an effort to stand up for yourself, but you'd keep out of their way if you could?

8—When someone (Mum, Dad, teacher, boss or friend) criticises you in a hurtful, personal way, do you—
(b) feel worried, and think whether there might be some truth in their criticism?
(a) feel wronged, and usually have faith that the criticism is unjust and untrue?

9—Do you worry about the future?
(a) No. Not at all.
(b) Yes. From time to time.

10—Do you get bored when other people talk about themselves?
(b) Yes, quite often.
(a) No, not a lot.

11—Are your thoughts and daydreams—
(a) nearly always pleasant and positive?
(b) positive and negative, pleasant and unhappy in more or less equal parts?

12—How d'you get along with money?
(b) a bit silly and spendthrift, but you try to be careful?
(a) What's money! You tend to be very generous, very indulgent in your spending.

SECTION B

1—When you break down and cry, which is your most usual procedure? Do you:-
(a) have a short burst of uncontrollable tears and wracking sobs?
(b) weep softly on and off for hours?

2—Are you more likely to feel—
(b) that people don't understand what makes you tick?
(a) that you don't understand what makes other people tick?

3—Do you enjoy hearing all the personal details of your friends' love life?
(a) yes.
(b) no.

4—Do you—
(b) wear make-up only when you're going somewhere special?
(a) always wear make-up whenever you can?

5—When you're kissing a boy for the first time, are you thinking—
(a) how much you're enjoying the kiss?
(b) how much he's enjoying the kiss?

6—If you could wave a magic wand, which would you most like to change—
(b) your personality?
(a) your appearance?

7—Suppose a boy you really fancy phones you for a chat. Would you—
(a) accept the conversation more or less at face value?
(b) delve into the meanings behind his words and read volumes into them?

8—Imagine you're really upset over some gorgeous, thoroughly inconsiderate boy who's given you the brush off. Would your reaction be—
(b) to hibernate from the rest of the world?
(a) to seek comfort from a friend?

9—When you have a difficult and important decision to make, do you—
(a) have a good think, then ask the advice of one special friend?
(b) ring round lots of people to get as many opinions as you can on the matter?

10—Do you get that horrible, cringing feeling of embarrassment on average—
(b) almost every week?
(a) at wider than a week's interval?

11—When you make a resolution, how often do you stick to it—
(a) sometimes?
(b) hardly ever?

12—Do you sometimes get the feeling that people are laughing and sniggering at you behind your back?
(b) hardly ever.
(a) never.

CONCLUSIONS

SECTION A

Mostly (a)
Sorry, love, but we sense that someone is bluffing somewhere! Perhaps you don't even realise it yourself, but it's our bet that you filled in the answers you **wanted** to believe, and not always the ones which might have been nearer the mark. It seems you're a bit wary of admitting there is anything about you which leaves room for improvement. The truth is that no-one as young as you could be quite so sure and confident, nor could they like themselves so much. 'Cos, you don't **know** yourself well enough yet. You need a few more years on the face of the globe to become acquainted with yourself. But never mind, the will and the spirit are there. You can convince yourself what a wonderful person you are on the surface, but you don't want to go through life kidding yourself, and having to avoid too much deep thinking which might give the game away. All you need is a good, hard, honest look at yourself, and you'll be well on the way to making friends with yourself.

Mostly (b)
You genuinely like yourself, and this is reflected in everything you do. You are self-assured, you trust your own judgement and you believe you are a worthwhile person who can create a good and happy life. You also admit that you have human weaknesses, and that, like everyone else, you go through stages of awful doubt, depression and failure. Admitting these things only goes to show how much you like yourself. It shows that you can face up to the bad things about yourself as well as the good things; it shows that you can learn by your own mistakes; and that you have enough faith in yourself to be able to stand up to criticism. Because you like yourself, other people will like you too. You don't have to go round proving yourself or showing off, because you are naturally at ease with people. There isn't any advice we can give you. Just go on liking yourself, and you'll be all right.

SECTION B

Mostly (a)
This may come as a shock to you, but you actually like yourself; basically that is. You haven't quite realised that you like yourself, however, and this causes you difficult problems, like a lack of confidence, and a feeling that you don't come up to scratch. All you really need to do is to be a bit more positive about yourself. You brood too much about your failings and unlikeable qualities and forget about the good things. Sit down some time soon and think about your good qualities. Give yourself a chance. You deserve it!

You are sensitive, emotional and have a natural sympathy for other people, and it's a pity that your modesty and reserve sometimes prevents you from showing your true worth. Try to trust and have more faith in yourself. Don't be shy—just keep saying that you are very pleased with yourself and you like yourself. Deep down you know you do!

Mostly (b)
You're not exactly crazy about yourself, are you? Perhaps you were in a bad mood when you answered this quiz, or it's your off-day. But you are doing yourself a disfavour by dismissing yourself so uncaringly, and not giving yourself enough credit for your good qualities (and you **do** have them, you know). You are easily led by other people, and you tend to think that other people know better than you do. You have just got into the habit of thinking about yourself in a rather negative way, and you'd be surprised at the difference if you started to think more positively. Forget other people for a bit and rely on yourself. Stop worrying about what other people think of you, and start being yourself. Once you have done this, you will find out you like yourself a lot better than you thought. Your feelings go very deep, and for this reason you will obviously find it more difficult to sort yourself out. It's much easier for your shallow sisters to sail through life. But being a deep and complicated person can eventually be more interesting and more rewarding. So don't worry. Get introduced to yourself, break the ice, and you might go for yourself in a big way!

THE CATHY & CLAIRE PAGE

We can't promise the perfect solution, but we'll do our best. If you're stuck with a problem and you can't see the way out, write to us at this address: Cathy & Claire, Jackie, 185 Fleet Street, London EC4A 2HS. Please remember to enclose an S.A.E.

DEAR CATHY AND CLAIRE — My boyfriend Robbie is almost perfect, except that he won't cut his hair. I've told him long hair is out now, and it doesn't suit him — he's got such a little face, it gets lost in that jungle. I'm not the only one who thinks so; everyone tells him he'd look better with it short, but he's so stubborn.

Wouldn't *you* be, if everyone kept telling *you* you'd look better if you looked different? You're treading on pretty shaky ground here — nobody likes having their appearance criticised. So give it a rest — after all, you say there are plenty of other people pointing out the error of his ways.

Robbie probably will get his hair cut when people stop hounding him, but the point is, he's got to do it in his own time. So just love him, hair and all, for the time being! You say he's almost perfect — plenty of girls would consider that good enough!

DEAR CATHY AND CLAIRE — My best friend is a real boy-chaser. She's always flirting like mad. It doesn't matter who the boy is, or what he's like, she'll chat him up. She's even tried it on another girl's boyfriend.

Well now she's getting herself a bad reputation. Lots of people, especially girls we know, think she's a bitch. But she isn't at all. We get on great together and she'd do anything for anyone, truly she would. Her only fault is that she enjoys talking to boys in this way.

I don't want to fall out with her, but I don't want us to be talked about, either. Do you think if I told her what people were saying, she'd stop flirting?

If you think she'd be upset by this gossip — then by all means, tell your friend what people are saying, and try to make her realise that not all boys are taken in by girls who bat their eyelashes and flirt madly — they can see through this sort of act just as well as girls can.

The only difference is that they enjoy being on the receiving end, even though they realise that it means very little; and they usually respond to girls who flirt, because they're flattered.

On the other hand, lots of girls think that flirting in this manner is both silly and pointless. But at the same time they still get extremely jealous of others who manage to carry off such an act successfully. After all, a flirt is usually the centre of attention, isn't she?

However it is a false and very temporary sort of attention. It's all right on occasions but we think you'd be wise to warn your friend against doing it all the time, before she sacrifices her personality to the habit of merely flirting.

DEAR CATHY AND CLAIRE — My friend Ann gets £2 a week pocket money and I only get 75p. We're both 16 and I think I should get the same as her. I've asked my parents but they think £2 is a ridiculous amount.

Ann always has more money to spend than me and is very generous, whereas I have to be pretty mean because I can't afford to be otherwise. This makes me feel very bad.

Don't you think I should be getting more pocket money?

Well, the amount of pocket money we think someone should get, is a question we're always being asked, and we can't really solve it. This decision is really your parents' and we can't do much about that.

If you really want to have more money, think of other ways you can get it. You're old enough to get a Saturday job, you know. Have a look in your local papers or ask at supermarkets. Or, if you like young children, why not try babysitting? There are bound to be some young families in your area, so ask around to see if a babysitter is needed.

Working part-time or on a Saturday can give you a great sense of achievement because you really have earned the money you get at the end of the day. It helps to make you independent, too!

Do try not to think of money as a status symbol, though. People won't think you're mean just because you don't throw your money around. And you don't have to have a lot of money to be generous . . .

DEAR CATHY AND CLAIRE — I don't know what to do about my parents; they're so old-fashioned and set in their ways. Our house looks like something out of a museum — and they just aren't interested in up-to-date ideas of decorating. We haven't had any new furniture or carpets for as long as I can remember. I keep trying to nudge them into getting some new stuff, but they just aren't interested. I'm almost ashamed to bring my friends back to this terrible old place.

It's well-known, of course, that people's surroundings can affect their moods, and you're certainly getting depressed by yours. But have you thought why this might be?

You don't say what your dad's job is, but if he's not in very highly-paid work, the reason he doesn't do much decorating could simply be that he can't afford to — painting and wallpapering a room and fitting a new carpet and curtains can run away with a hundred pounds quite easily.

If he *does* make a reasonable salary and hasn't got expenses that take most of it, then drab as it is, it's obviously the way your folk like it. Tastes differ, but in their own home, people are entitled to have things their way.

There's not much *you* can do in either of these cases, but it might be possible to make your own room bright and beautiful. Buy a few magazines to give yourself some ideas, plan out what you'd like and work out the cost. Then tell your parents about your plans and say you'll get a Saturday job to pay at least part of the cost. Who knows, the sight of one gay room may spur them on to smartening up the whole house, especially if you leave the magazines lying around where they can read them!

What you mustn't do is keep nagging your parents. After all, it's pretty insulting for them to be told the home they've given you isn't good enough. And it must have a friendly atmosphere, as you're obviously not *completely* unable to bring your friends in.

And remember, new curtains and carpets are cheerful and pleasant, but it takes a lot more than that to make a house into a home . . .

DEAR CATHY & CLAIRE. — I met this boy at a dance and I like him a lot. So I took him back to our house for coffee one night. He met my mum and dad and seemed to get on with them okay.

But my mum said she didn't care for him and I'm not to see him again. She won't say why, but just forbids me to go out with him. No amount of me going on at her will get her to change her mind. I don't want to keep nagging about it, else she might not let me back to the dances. But he's so nice and I do want to go out with him.

What can I do?

You don't say how old you are but we feel that though your mum doesn't mind you going dancing, maybe she feels you're too young to have a steady boyfriend?

If you can make it clear to her that you only want to see this boy at the disco, or occasionally for coffee and a chat, then she might relent.

If not though, then ask your Mum just what her objections are. If, as we suspect, it's because she feels you're too young to have a steady boyfriend, then we're afraid there's not much you can do. You'll just have to give way on this point, otherwise you might indeed lose the freedom she already allows you. If you obey the rules she lays down for you at the moment, then gradually she should come to accept that you're growing up, and she should give you a little more freedom as regards going out with boys.

If, however, there's some *other* reason for your mum objecting to this boy, then, in all fairness to you, she really should tell you what she dislikes about him. Perhaps it's something you can do something about or discuss with her. Who knows? Maybe she doesn't like him because his mum once cut her dead in the supermarket! It *could* be something as silly as that, but you'll never know unless you *talk* about it.

Whatever happens, though, we think you should tell this boy your mum won't let you go out with him. That way, he'll know you haven't suddenly gone off him, and he may wait until such time as your mum decides you *can* go out with him.

It's difficult just now, we know, but do try to have patience, meanwhile!

HOW CAN I GET HIM TO STOP?

DEAR CATHY AND CLAIRE — Jeffrey is nice-looking and usually quite affectionate, but on Friday and Saturday nights he does sometimes get in with some boys who like to drink a lot, and when he's had a couple of beers, he changes completely.

He becomes extremely rude and shouts vulgar things at me, orders me about and generally makes me look a fool.

I keep telling him I'll leave him if he goes on like this, and although he always apologises for his behaviour next time he sees me, come Friday he's in the pub again. Is there any way I can stop him acting like this, without him hating me for nagging?

Are you really as worried by Jeffrey's behaviour as you make out? Or have you got the idea that this is something you just have to put up with if you want to keep a boy friend? Because you don't, you know. Not all boys get nasty with drink, and Jeffrey can obviously manage without his beer most of the week.

But while you *are* putting up with it so meekly, why should he bother to change? You threaten to leave him, yet here you are still going steady with him. No wonder he doesn't take your threats seriously.

You hold the answer to this problem. Arrange to spend Friday and Saturday nights at the cinema or in a disco — preferably a non-licensed one. Tell Jeffrey at the start of the week that he makes you feel small when he gets drunk, and that if he does it again you'll walk out.

And if, despite your plans, you end up in the pub and he starts on you, don't wait till he's thoroughly upset you — don't even say anything to him. Just get up and walk out. If you're old enough to go out with boys, you're old enough to see yourself home. And do go straight home — don't lurk outside the pub to see if he's going to follow you.

All Jeffrey needs is to be shown you mean what you say. You might have to walk out on him two or three times before he really believes you — but if you really want him to change, you'll do it.

But if he persists in being rude, we suggest that you leave him to his beer and boring behaviour, and get yourself a new and more considerate boy friend.

Printed and published by D. C. Thomson & Co., Ltd., 185 Fleet Street, London, EC4A 2HS.

SEEING

WANT to save money and look good at the same time? Buying something basic and dressing it up in different ways is the answer . . . and if you stick to one main colour it makes things even easier. Have a look at the fashions we've chosen below and see what we mean!

Separates are simple to swop around. Just substitute a pair of trousers for a skirt and you've got two really nice outfits.

Cream shirt with short puffed sleeve and embroidery trim, from British Home Stores. Style No. 8007/5099. Price: £3.50. Fabric: Polyester/cotton. Colours: Cream only. Sizes: 10 to 16. From major branches of British Home Stores.

The flowery pinafore has a tie at the back, a square neck and frill trim at the bottom British Home Stores, Style No.:8005/5099. Price: £5.50. Fabric :Cotton. Colours: Turquoise/cream, pink/cream. Sizes:10 to 16. From major branches of British Home Stores.

Lovely long skirt with double frill at the bottom and lace trim, from Marks & Spencer. Style No.: 147/6350. Price: £5.50. Fabric: Cotton. Colours: Green, navy and maroon. Sizes: 12 to 18. From selected branches of Marks & Spencer.

Cream T-bar shoe with slim heel and no platform, from Dolcis Style No.: A11/58417 Sarah. Price: £6.99. Fabric: Synthetic. Colours: Beige, navy and black. Sizes: 3 to 8. From main branches of Dolcis. By post from Dolcis, 350 Oxford Street, London W.1. plus 30p for postage and packing.

ALL PRICES APPROXIMATE

DOUBLE

The green cord jacket has two pockets and three buttons and is from Etam. Style No.: 60112. Price: £8.99. Sizes: 10-14. Colours: Brown, mint, navy and light blue. From all main branches of Etam.

Green floral print shirt with pointed collar and turn-back cuff is from Woolworth. Style No.: G25/5. Price: £2.99. Fabric: Cotton mixture. Sizes: 34 to 38. From larger branches of Woolworth.

Green zip-front, knee length skirt with 2 buttons and waistband elasticated at the sides, from Woolworth. Style No.: A513S. Price: £3.99. Fabric: Polyester/viscose. Colours: Navy, dusty green, camel. Sizes: 10 to 14. From major Woolworth branches.

Dark green trousers with zip front and two-buttoned waistband, from Littlewoods. Style No.: 316/2. Price: £4.50. Fabric: Trevira/viscose. Colours: Assorted. Sizes: 10 to 18. From all Littlewoods branches.

High-heeled shoe with printed cloth detail on the front and 1 inch platform, from Lilley & Skinner. Style No.: 55/8369/82 Aurora. Price: £8.99. Fabric: Pearlised leather. Colours: Pearl cream, pearl blue and black patent. Sizes: 3 to 8. From main branches of Saxone or Lilley & Skinner, 360 Oxford Street, London W.1. plus 30p for postage and packing.

Look Out

DYEING TO PLEASE

If you're sick of the colour of your shoes/belts/bags, why not change them? It's really easy to do and there are all sorts of leaflets you can get to help you. Dylon dyes come in loads of different colours for suede, leather, plastic, wet-look and patent leather — not to mention a huge range of cold dyes and multi-purpose dyes and tints for all sorts of fabrics.

Colours for spring and summer are going to be light and clear (what a relief after all the browns, blacks and rusty colours of winter!), in beautiful colours like peach, pink, dusty blue and clear apple green. Dylon have lots of colours at the ready, like Spring Light, Dusty Pink, Forget-Me-Not, Peach and Carnival (a deep pink).

Shoes are really easy to dye with Dylon, as long as you follow the instructions and use a conditioner first to remove any dirt or grease! Miss Dylon Instant Shoe Colour costs

49p and comes in a choice of 25 colours, the Conditioner costs 16p and the Suede Dye costs 33p. You can use the Instant Shoe Colour on leather, plastic, wet-look, and patent leather . . . here's how!

First, pack the front of each shoe tightly with newspaper to smooth out cracks and creases, then apply the conditioner, which must be rubbed on briskly until the surface is thoroughly clean. Shake the Shoe Colour well and apply the colour sparingly with the special brush provided, using light, even strokes. When the first coat is dry, apply a second and a third later if really necessary. Leave the shoes overnight before removing the packing and buff with a soft cloth for a normal shine.

If you have any questions or need advice about dyeing, write to Annette Stevens, Consumer Advice Bureau, Dylon International Ltd., London SE26 5HD.

THIS week we look out for special beauty offers . . . So make the most of the more expensive brands at cheaper prices while you can! Send away for two great leaflets we've discovered — and belt up . . . with some super belts we found at Boots branches!

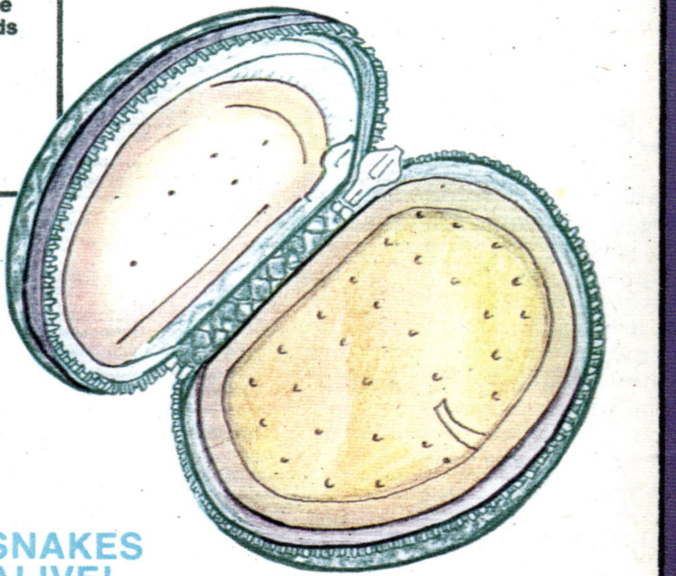

BELT UP!

Boots have a super range of belts in their larger branches which look expensive but aren't! 1 — A leather belt with a heavy buckle, in brown or tan. Price £1.45. 2 — A super narrow leather belt in black, dark brown, black or navy patent with a tremendous slim buckle. Price £3.45. 3 — Slim leather belt with an attractive buckle, in a choice of brown or camel. Also available in black, navy or black patent. Price £3.45.

Leather belts start from 95p, but you can get nice plastic ones for as little as 75p! For evenings you can buy thin plaited belts in gold, silver or black, for £1.25 each.

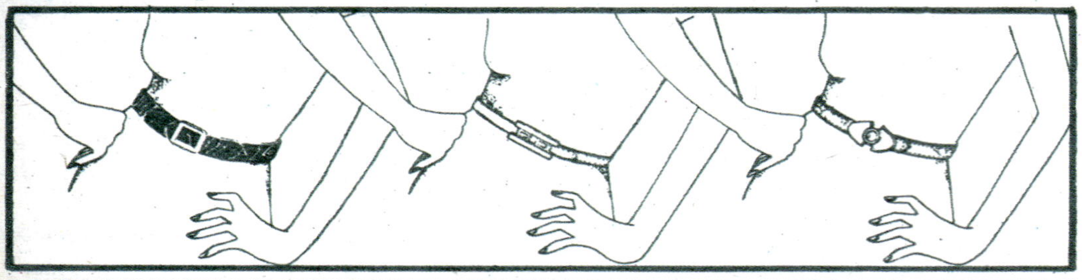

SNAKES ALIVE!

Not *real* snake, of course, just imitation is what this tremendous zip-up powder compact from Bombacha is made of. It's for loose powder only and has its own mirror in the lid. Price is £1.50 from Bombacha, 104 Fulham Road, London S.W.3, plus 30p for postage and packing.

SO FAR SEW GOOD

Cheap and Cheerful Fashion Ideas

Keeping You In Stitches

Men's shirts are great for the baggy look, but if you don't want them to *look* too much like men's shirts, try a bit of stitching to brighten them up. Here's how . . .

A mans work shirt makes a super over-shirt for you. Roll up the sleeves and sew them up with giant sized herring bone stitch (shown below) using thick embroidery thread or wool. Sew on big, bright contrasting pockets and decorate these, and perhaps the yoke seams as well, with the same big herring-bone stitch.

SOMETHING FOR NOTHING!

Loads of girls worry a lot about B.O., which can be a big problem if you don't know how to cope with perspiration, hot feet, etc. Well worry no more! There's a great leaflet you can send away for called, "How Well Do You Know Yourself?" compiled by the makers of Cool and Body Mist, which tells you all sorts of interesting facts about why you perspire and how you can make sure you smell nice all the time.

There's also a leaflet on hair, called Caring For Your Hair, which tells you all about dandruff, damaged hair, split ends, etc. Write to Richard Heath Ltd., 17 Golden Square, London W1R 4HS, enclosing a stamped, self-addressed envelope. Mark *your* envelope to *them* "Leaflets" so that it doesn't go astray and tell them which one (or both!) you want.

BE A BIG BABY

Johnson's Baby Shampoo is specially formulated for babies which is exactly why it's good for your hair, too! It cleans hair without destroying the natural oils which are so essential for shiny, healthy hair, and leaves it really soft and nice.

There are two sizes to choose from, large (205cc) at 54p and medium (100cc) at 29p, available from all good chemists and stores.

BUDGET BITS

Shoes aren't cheap these days, so when we do find bargains, we let you know!

Here's a super, wedgy shoe with a high front, that'll look great under trousers, from Miss Curtess. The style number is CO98, price a modest £4.99, and the shoe comes in a choice of black or brown synthetic, in sizes 3 to 8, from all main branches of Curtess.

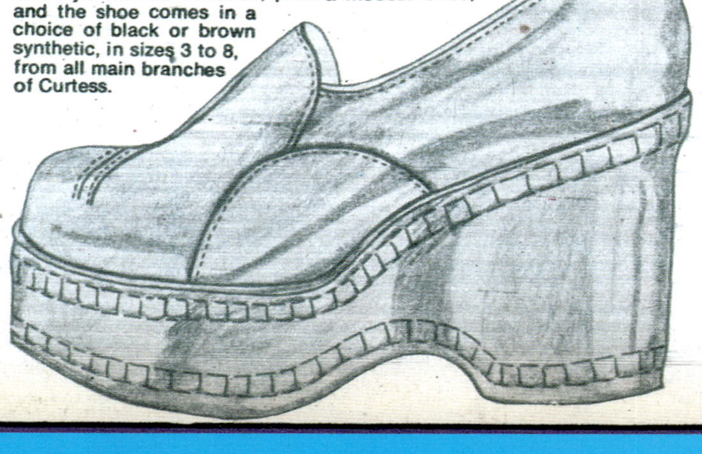

FOOT NOTES

Throughout January you'll be able to make the most of all the beauty products on offer in the shops — like these from Almay which are great value . . . Moisture Lotion (220cc) for 90p; Cream Cleanser (200cc) for £1.10; Skin Tonic (190cc) for 85p; and Moisture Cream (200cc) for £1.30.

Helena Rubinstein also have a tremendous offer of Skin Dew . . . Skin Dew Emollient Cleanser will cost 98p for 340cc; Skin Dew Freshener and Toner will cost £1.08p for 340cc; Skin Dew Herbal Lotion will cost £1.08p for 340cc and Skin Dew Emulsion will cost £1.41 for 340cc.

If you've always thought you'd like to try more expensive products but haven't had the money, now's your chance . . . so make the most of it!

ALL PRICES APPROXIMATE

A JACKIE GUIDE TO THE FIRST THINGS YOU NOTICE ABOUT HIM

AT FIRST GLANCE

FIRST impressions of a boy mean so much, and they can tell you a lot about his temperament. So just for a bit of fun check on our "Jackie" list if you want to know what makes HIM tick!

THE-SAY-NOTHING-BUT-CLING-CLOSE-TYPE

First impressions can be dangerous with this guy.

When you're dancing with him don't jump to the conclusion that he's just after ONE THING and that he's not interested in your mind! "Wait and see," tactics are best here. Maybe he's just a sensible guy who can't be bothered with the "Do you come here often?" bit unless he's got something interesting to say.

On the other hand, he could be a big head who thinks he doesn't have to bother chatting you up as any girl would be proud and grateful to dance with him!

So give him a chance to prove himself a nice, intelligent guy who is a bit unconventional and uninterested in social chit-chat. But don't be all that surprised if he turns out to be yet another Romeo who thinks girls were just made for him to demonstrate his fantastic technique on!

THE NOT-SO-PRIVATE EYE

There's a glint in his eye whenever you look at him, the sort of look that makes you feel you and he share a burning secret.

This is the unmistakeable sign of a wolf. He's very attractive and knows how to turn on the charm, he doesn't have to say anything — it's all in the way he looks at you!

And, for the moment, it's true he's absolutely wild about you and wants to show it; no matter which way you look, you can't avoid those eyes. For him, you see, the pleasure of girls is in the chase, but once he knows he's got you hooked, he'll soon lose interest and turn to new conquests. So don't expect a long term relationship from this boy.

Enjoy his attention and be flattered. Wolves usually only bother with girls who they think will make other guys jealous.

Enjoy the fact that he's temporarily smitten with you and string him along if you feel like it. But don't make the mistake of falling too heavily for him — or you could end up with a broken heart. Of course there are exceptions, but don't make any gleaming, glinting,secret looks back until you're sure he **is** the one!

THE DEMON HAIR COMBER

He's nervous

Every time he passes a mirror or a handy shop window, he just can't resist the urge to comb his hair. And it isn't just a quick flick either! He spends ages and takes elaborate care to make sure his coiffure is as gorgeous as possible! This boy hasn't really grown up yet and he's more concerned with himself and the impression he makes on other people, than he is with you.

His obsession with combing his hair is an outward expression of his obsession with his own feelings which are in a constant state of change. He feels that by putting his hair into immaculate order, he will somehow make his mind and emotions more ordered, too. He's unsure of himself with girls and feels that if his hair's OK it's a kind of good luck charm.

So treat him gently and don't think his constant hair combing is due to vanity. In fact it means quite the opposite, this boy is insecure, he needs encouragement and reassurance. When he gets it and finds a good relationship, you'll find that just like other boys, he'll never have a comb on him and that you'll have to lend him yours!

THE CHANGELING

One time you meet him and he falls on you as if you're his long lost love from another planet.

You feel terrific and think what a fantastically nice, open, friendly boy he is. Then the next time you see him, he almost passes by without recognising you and has tremendous difficulty dredging up your name from the darkest depths of his memory! What's happened? Nothing, he's always like that.

You see, he's a tease. He thinks the only way to get a girl interested is to blow hot and cold. He likes to keep you dangling while he makes his mind up whether he really wants to go out with you or not. The only way to hurry him up one way or the other is by talking to other boys. This sometimes gets him thinking you're not totally obsessed with him, and he'll be so intrigued by this strange phenomenon he might even make a move.

One fatal mistake is to assume that this boy is really shy, because believe us — he isn't!

FOOT TAPPERS AND MAD MONEY JINGLERS

They have a sort of "Not quite with you" look and are often dreamy and introverted.

They find it hard to concentrate on what you're saying, are easily distracted and their minds tend to drift aimlessly over a large number of subjects.

If he taps and jingles when he first meets you, it may well mean that his thoughts are elsewhere. You should tread carefully with this boy if he keeps on rhythmically tapping his foot or jingling his money when you're speaking to him, as this can show irritation and annoyance. Perhaps he disagrees with what you're saying but is too polite to say so openly. So ask him what he thinks and give him a chance to tell you.

This boy is a bit restless too, though, and it could be that he's just plain bored, so try to keep his interest and you'll probably find that these irritating signs will disappear!

This guy is very demanding and hard to please. He won't settle for second best, but if you hook him, you could find that when he's not being vague and dreamy, he's terrific company and great fun to be with.

THE HEAVY CAMOUFLAGE BOYS

They're the ones who don't like to come out into the open, so they hide behind the covering protection of their mates, although they keep looking your way.

And then a girlfriend tells you that she's heard from a friend that he fancies you! Try encouraging him with a smile or two because his reluctance to approach you could be due to shyness.

On the other hand, don't depend on it. If he doesn't thaw out and act pretty soon, it's probably because he's just too tired to make the effort — perhaps he prefers the company of his mates after all!

THE GIRL HOG

He won't let anyone else get within shouting distance of you and he spends all night blocking you from the eyes of other boys.

If you're dead certain he's the boy for you and if you enjoy being the bird in a gilded cage, then go ahead, go out with him.

But this boy can prove a problem if you're still interested in other guys. So keep him at arm's length (if you can!) until you've had a good look round at all the other types!

JACKIE FASHION

THE GREAT

LOTS of last minute holiday extras to throw in your suitcase . . . they're easy to cart about and easy to care for!

Square blue glasses from Boots, price £1.99. Buy them from most Boots department stores.

Stripy sun top by Bairnswear. Style No.: 2831. Price: £3.75. Fabric: Courtelle. Colours: Milk/cactus, milk/blue, milk/marron glace. Sizes: 34 to 38. From Hull Co-Op; J. T. Black, Cole Street, Birkenhead; Collins Bros., Mill St., Stafford; Hutchinson & Co., Cochran St., Barrhead, Glasgow; Hailey's Casuals, Seabourne Road, Southbourne, Bournemouth.

Brown cord jeans from Levi. Style No.: 61817. Price: £7.50. Fabric: Cotton cord. Colours: Ice blue, navy, brown, bottle green, black, mushroom. Sizes: Men's waist sizes 28 to 36. From Milletts branches; Army and Navy Stores; Jean Machine; John Lewis branches; House of Fraser branches.

Super, stripy sundress with halter ties, from Marks & Spencer. No Style No. Price: £5.50. Fabric: Cotton towelling. Colours: Brown/cream, blue/cream. Sizes: 10 to 16. From major branches of Marks & Spencer.

Greeny sunspecs by Polaroid, price £2.70 in a choice of Cedar or Mint. Buy them from all good chemists and department stores.

Strappy suede wedge sandal from Sacha. No Style No. Price: £4.99. Fabric: Suede. Sizes: 3 to 8. Colours: Buffalo only. Also comes in leather. Price: £5.99. Colours: Red/black, cream/black. From all branches of Sacha.

Checked cheesecloth wraparound skirt, from Girl. Style No.: 560602. Price: £3.99. Fabric: Cheesecloth. Colours: Assorted. Sizes: One size to fit 10 to 14 waist. From all Chelsea Girl branches.

Thick cheesecloth men's shirt with one breast pocket, from C & A. No Style No. Price: £2.95. Fabric: Cotton cheesecloth. Colours: Natural. Sizes: 14 to 16. From all branches of C & A.

TAKE-AWAY

Pretty v-neck towelling top with short sleeves, from Erica Budd. Style No.: C5017. Price: £3.50. Fabric: Cotton/nylon. Colours: Assorted. Sizes: Small, medium, large.
Long-sleeved zip-up top to match, also from Erica Budd. Style No.: C5016. Price: £5.90. Other details as for top. From Jane Norman, Oxford Street and branches; Peter Richards, Cheltenham and branches; Bentalls, Kingston.
Flat sandal with white strap upper, from Sacha. No Style No. Price: £3.99. Fabric: Leather. Colours: Assorted. Sizes: 3 to 8. From all branches of Sacha.
Blue towelling short shorts with two slant pockets, from Marks & Spencer. No Style No. Price: £2.50. Fabric: Cotton/polyester towelling. Colours: Blue, white, yellow, brown, green. Sizes: 10 to 16. From most branches of Marks & Spencer.
Blue checked cheesecloth shirt with tie waist, from C & A. No Style No. Price: £1.75. Fabric: Cotton cheesecloth. Colours: Assorted checks and stripes. Sizes: Small, medium, large. From a selection at all branches of C & A.
Sunspecs with two-tone red/black frames from Boots, price 75p. From larger Boots department stores.
Halter neck 'string' vest top from Palmers. Style No.: 2134. Price: £1.75. Fabric: Nylon raschel knit. Colours: White only. Sizes: One size. By post from Palmers, 3 Forum Way, Edgware, Middlesex HA8 7HA, plus 10p for postage and packing.
Pink, cheesecloth calf-length skirt with gathered waist, from Ann Green. Style No.: 320. Price: £7.30. Fabric: Cheesecloth. Colours: Pink, green, natural. Sizes: 10 to 14. From Ann Green, 13 Brighton Square, Brighton; Pot-Pourri, 39 Station Road, Beaconsfield, Bucks.
Rope weave wedge sandal with white canvas upper and ankle strap, from Elliotts. Style: Cari. Price: £9.95. Fabric: Canvas. Colours: Pale blue, navy, red, white, khaki. Sizes: 3½ to 7½. From all Elliott's branches.
Wedgy espadrilles with denim uppers and long navy laces, from Elliotts. Style: Philly. Price: £9.95. Fabric: Denim. Colours: Blue, white. Sizes: 3½ to 7½. From all branches of Elliotts.

A Jackie Psycho-quiz.

Are You A Natural?

EVERYBODY responds to the world around them, even without realising it. And the way you react to your surroundings reveals a lot about your personality.

So look closely at each of our illustrations and decide which statement is closest to the way you feel. Then count up your score and turn to the conclusions to find out the hidden personality secrets you've revealed!

1) CLOUDS

a) They make you forget the everyday world and feel like floating away.
b) They make you sad because they cast shadows.
c) They're dramatic, striking and sometimes sinister . . .
d) They leave you quite indifferent.
e) You enjoy trying to see faces, castles or weird animals in them.

2) TREES

a) They make you feel secure, you want to shelter under them.
b) You're not interested in trees.
c) You'd love to paint them.
d) They make you feel a bit creepy as they're full of insects.
e) You like to think of birds nesting in them and furry animals burrowing under them.

3) MOUNTAINS

a) They make you think of eternity because you know they'll still be there, long after you've gone.
b) They make you feel lonely and very insignificant.
c) You think they're hostile because men die trying to climb them.
d) You've never stopped to think about them.
e) They give you the impression that they're protecting you and keeping you safe.

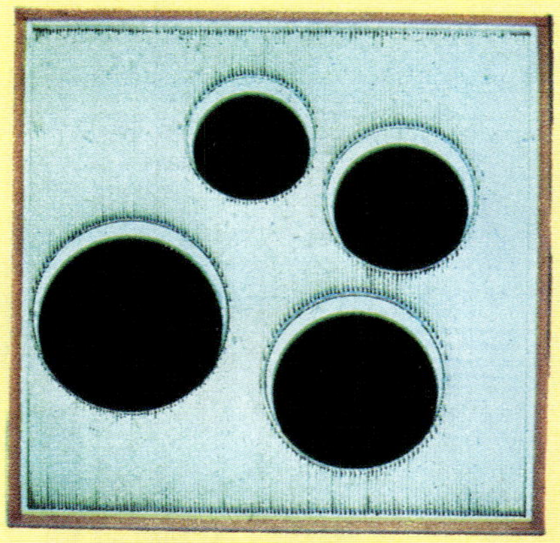

4) BLACK HOLES IN SPACE

a) They're scary, some hideous monster might come out of them.
b) You'd love to be able to measure how deep they are.
c) They're strange and unfathomable.
d) You wish you could travel on and on down the black hole until after an eternity you discover what's at the bottom.
e) They don't interest you.

5) THE ROOFS OF HOUSES

a) You love to see them when they're wet and gleaming after rain.
b) You dislike them.
c) You're always worried in case they fall down.
d) You imagine crafts from outer space landing on them.
e) When you look down on them, it seems as if they're just part of a child's building set.

6) RAINDROPS

a) They don't affect you.
b) You'd like to see them through a microscope.
c) You love their strange and interesting shapes.
d) They make you feel like singing to their pitter patter rhythm.
e) They make you think of tears and tragedy.

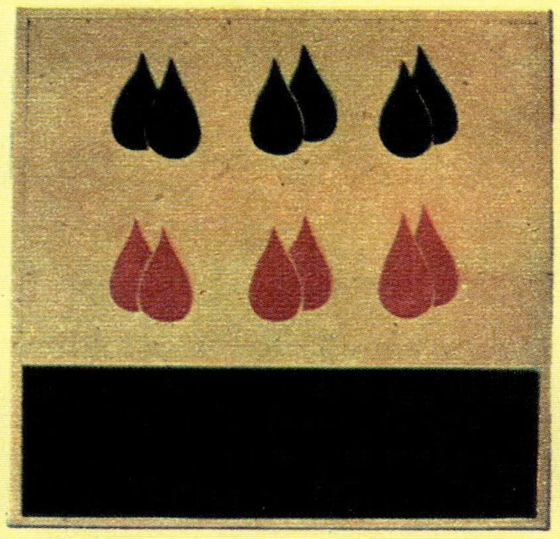

7) STONES

a) You love to hear your feet scrunching over them.
b) Their shapes are really interesting, like modern sculptures.
c) As far as you're concerned, a stone's a stone.
d) They're grey and dreary.
e) They make you think of the end of everything.

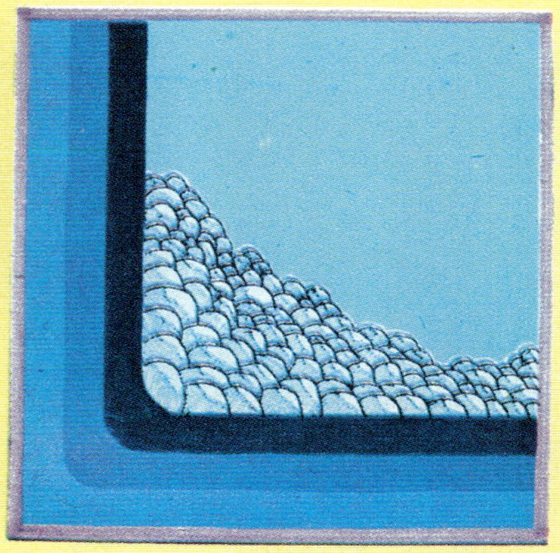

CONCLUSIONS

FROM 60 TO 70 POINTS:

YOU'RE inclined to see the world through grey-coloured glasses, and to dwell on the sad side of life.

Perhaps, in fact, you have real reasons for unhappiness which you haven't yet been able to overcome. Or perhaps you've just got into the habit of thinking the worst.

Now's the time to start afresh and look positively at your surroundings and the people you know. In the past you've tended to try to escape from what you see as harsh reality by retreating inside yourself. Instead of letting your worries get on top of you, talk them over with a good friend. That way you'll prevent tension from building up. Get out and about more, make a real effort and soon you'll find that the world's looking a whole lot brighter!

FROM 71 to 80 POINTS:

YOU love nature, you find it endlessly fascinating and you enjoy life too.

You can always be relied on to see the bright side of every situation. You're never bored and always ready to laugh.

You're imaginative, artistic and try to express yourself through writing and painting. As far as you're concerned all's right with the world and you tend to live in an ivory tower. You should be aware of the darker side of nature and life too, or when you're suddenly faced with it in reality you could collapse!

FROM 81 to 90 POINTS:

YOU refuse to respond deeply to nature and almost seem to want to deny yourself pleasure and contact.

This carries over to your relationship with other people too, most of your friendships are pretty superficial as you never want to get too deeply involved.

You dislike poetry and anything else that you think is romantic or sloppy. You never give free reign to your imagination, you're only interested in facts. And at your best you have a strong practical sense which leads you to enquire into the world around you, just to see how it functions.

But be careful — your one-track-mind approach to life could eventually dry up your emotions and make you a bit of a passionless person!

FROM 91 to 100 POINTS:

YOU respond dramatically to the world around you and very often you see it as hostile.

You see the dangers in life and this makes you tread cautiously. You tend to look for problems even where they don't exist.

Almost all this is due to your heightened, flourishing imagination. So there's a conflict in you between your responsible side and you ability to savour every experience and sensation to the full. You want to be practical and yet you long to abandon yourself to all your deepest emotions.

So at the moment you tend to feel frustrated and unable to express yourself completely. But once you've overcome this conflict, you'll lead a very full and happy life.

8) SHADOWS

a) They make you shiver and feel anxious.
b) You pay no attention to them.
c) You think they look like cartoon figures of people.
d) You sometimes imagine they could start to live an independent life of their own.
e) You're interested in studying how they're actually formed.

9) SPLASHES OF PAINT

a) Each one is bright and gay and makes you think of something funny.
b) Every splash troubles you.
c) Each one is like a modern painting to you.
d) You wonder how the paint splash came to be there, was it by intention or mistake?
e) You think it's sloppy and wasteful to splash paint about.

10) HUMAN BODY

a) It's so awkward looking.
b) It's a poem of harmony.
c) It's interesting from a scientific point of view.
d) It looks as though it just came about by accident.
e) It's rather ridiculous.

POINTS

1) 7 POINTS for A; 6 for B; 10 for C; 9 for D; 8 for E.
2) 10A 9B 8C 6D 7E
3) 7A 6B 10C 9D 8E
4) 10A 8B 6C 7D 9E
5) 9A 6B 10C 8D 7E
6) 9A 8B 10C 7D 6E
7) 8A 7B 9C 6D 10E
8) 10A 9B 6C 7D 8E
9) 7A 6B 10C 8D 9E
10) 6A 10B 8C 9D 7E

Patchwork

INSTANT SUCCESS!

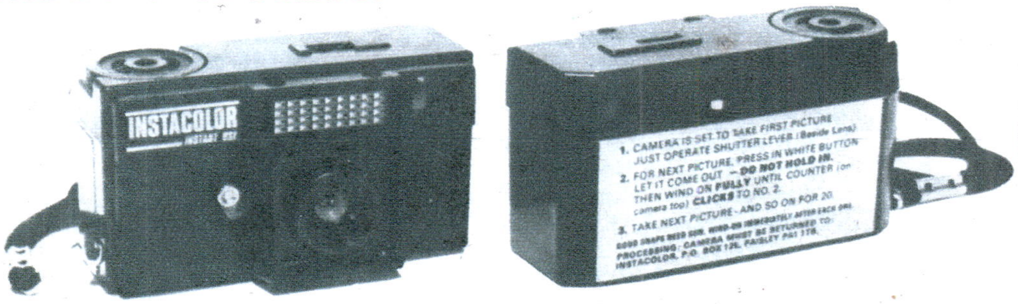

If you don't already have a camera, now's the time to get one! Then you'll have plenty of time to practise before going on holiday!

If you want an inexpensive but efficient camera, we can recommend the "Instacolor", shown here. It weighs just over 3 oz. and is small enough to fit into a pocket, so is a very handy thing to carry around with you!

What makes the camera really special, though, is that it works through the "Free Film Service." This means that once you've taken the 20 colour shots in the spool, you simply send the whole camera back to the Free Film Service laboratories, where your film is removed and processed, and another film replaced in the camera for you. You pay only £2.65 for the processing of each spool — and receive another one free, every time! Can't be bad, can it?

The initial cost for an "Instacolor" camera complete with film is just £1 — and you must admit, that's quite a lot less than any other camera around!

"Instacolor" cameras are available from most major photographic centres and chemists.

SPONSOR A SHELTER SUNFLOWER!

How do you fancy growing a sunflower for charity? — Really!

"Shelter," the National Campaign For The Homeless, have come up with a really novel idea for raising money.

All you do is send off 20 pence this month to them, and they'll send you sponsor forms, labels and sowing instructions for your sunflower. Then — it's all stations go! Start sowing your sunflower seeds (try saying that in a hurry!) and, at the same time, start collecting sponsors — the idea is that they sponsor you at a certain rate for every inch your best sunflower grows.

When your sunflowers have grown to their full size, you collect the money and send it off to Shelter, along with details of the sizes they grew to. Shelter are offering prizes for the best ones!

Sounds like fun? We thought so too! The address to write to is: — The Youth Campaign, Shelter, 86 Strand, London WC2R 0EO.

Please enclose an S.A.E.

NOW LOOK HERE!

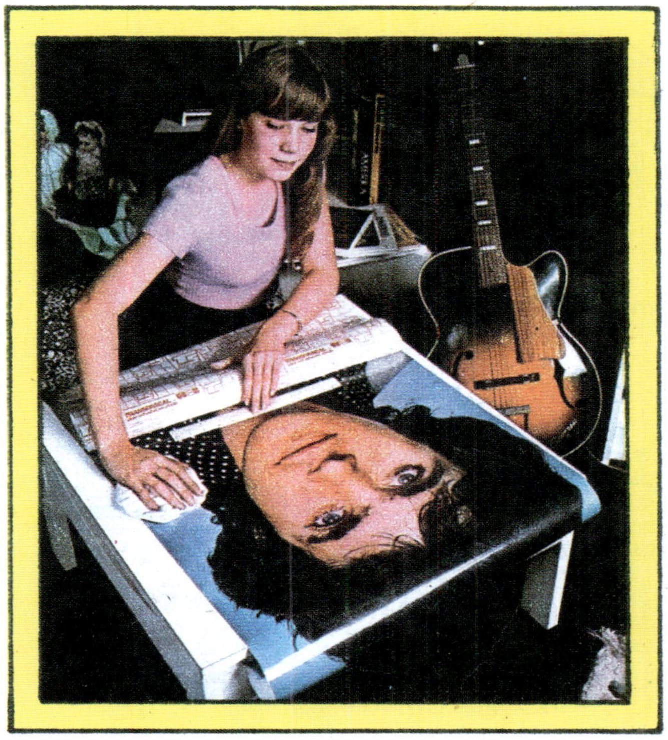

Have you ever cut out a pop picture from a magazine, put it away carefully in a drawer and then, at a later date, found to your horror that it was crumpled, dirty and covered in ink blots?

If so, invest in a roll of Web Transpaseal. This is, as its name suggests, a special adhesive film which you can cover all sorts of things with — like posters and pictures, school books, mementos — anything at all which you'd like to keep clean and well-protected. Transpaseal is completely transparent, so you can cover anything with it and still see through it perfectly.

It's available in five sizes of rolls and comes complete with instructions. From 34 pence a roll. Available from most stationers and department stores.

GIVE US A (KEY) RING!

These attractive key rings are hand-crafted in leather in the U.S.A. — then sent over here so that you can buy them in any Boots store! Available in a wide range of styles, they cost just 49p each. The ones we particularly liked were (left to right) a seagull flying over the sea, "Think" and a super tree design. So why not go along to Boots and treat yourself today?

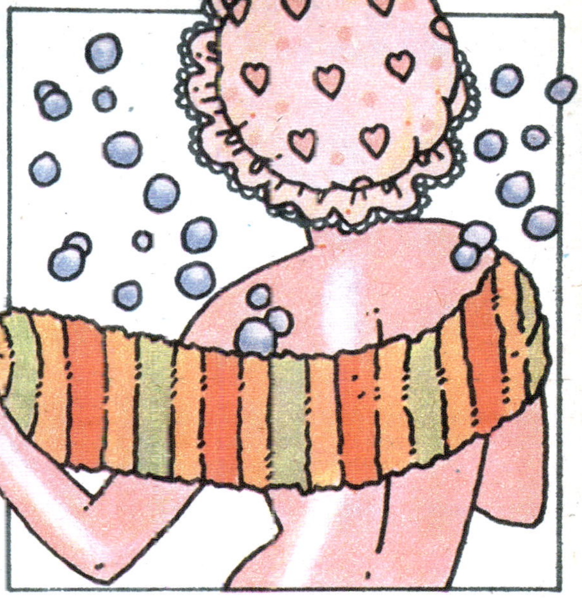

YOUR PATCH — THROW IN THE TOWEL!

Gillian Stewart of Liverpool is our lucky contributor this week — lucky because she sent in the following super idea to "Your Patch" and won herself £1.00 for it!

Gillian's idea is to make a "bath flannel," as she calls it, from an old towel which has some threadbare patches (ask Mum's permission first though!). Cut a piece of material lengthwise from the better part of the towel — about 7 in. wide is the right width. Hem it all round and then sew the ends round two strong plastic bangles. Result? A cheap and cheerful bath flannel which will last for ages.

If you'd like to win £1.00, send your ideas in without delay to "Your Patch", Patchwork, Jackie, 185 Fleet Street, London, EC4A 2HS.

CAST YOUR EYES ON THIS!

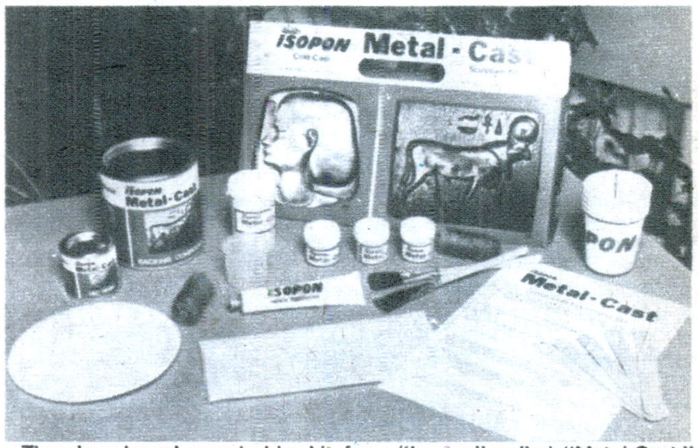

There's a brand new hobby kit from "Isopon" called "Metal-Cast." The idea is to make your own wall plaques from a very effective metal-like substance. The results, as you can see from the photograph, look amazing — really authentic. The kits contain everything you need to produce a wall plaque, and there's a whole range of different moulds available. At £4.86 the kits *are* a bit expensive, but they're really worth it if you're at all interested in arts and crafts.

"Metal-Cast" is available now from most large hobby and toy shops.

QUICK AND EASY RECIPE

Say cheese, please — and smile! 'Cos there's something about cheese which is — well — cheerful! It's nourishing and tasty, very good for you, and can be served in hundreds of tempting ways. So why not cheer up a chilly February by inviting your friends round for a cheesy buffet party? Just serve a selection of tasty cheese snacks like the ones shown here, with lots of hot soup to go along with them, and we guarantee an instant success!

Left to right:

1. Inch-thick slices of cucumber with centres hollowed out and filled with grated Cheddar.
2. Prunes stuffed with cottage cheese.
3. "Baby Beets" stuffed with crumbled Danish Blue cheese.
4. Cold ham rolls filled with grated Cheshire mixed with mayonnaise.
5. Dates stuffed with cream cheese.

Add your own variations to this theme — we're sure you could think of lots more cheesy goodies!

A JACKIE QUIZ

HOW SEXY ARE YOU?

Are you a sizzling sexpot — or a prune-faced prude? Do you enjoy being a girl — or might you just as well've been a boy? And if *you* think you're fairly sexy, does the opposite sex agree with you? Find our just where you stand, with our quiz!

1 What kind of casual clothes do you like to wear?
(d) Old, comfortable jeans and a jumper.
(a) Tight-fitting jeans and T-shirts.
(c) Floppy trousers and layers of tops.
(b) Long, flowing skirts.

2 What would you wear to a party?
(c) A pretty, feminine, knee-length dress.
(d) Smart trousers and top.
(b) A long, fitted dress with a low neck and a swirly skirt.
(a) A curvy, clinging slither of a dress, guaranteed to turn all heads.

3 Which fabric would you choose for your bedspread?
(b) Velvet.
(d) Crisp, flowery cotton.
(a) Fur, real or fake.
(c) Old-fashioned lace or patchwork.

4 When a boy stares at you, do you —
(a) stare right back,
(b) let your eyes just glance his way in passing,
(c) look the other way,
(d) blush furiously?

5 You fancy him right away; do you —
(c) hang around hopefully,
(b) make up excuses to go and see him,
(a) make it perfectly obvious to him how you feel,

(d) go all tongue-tied every time you meet?

6 Would you rather people thought you were —
(c) beautiful,
(d) sweet-natured,
(a) sexy,
(b) attractive?

7 Do you dress and make up mainly to —
(a) attract the opposite sex,
(d) look as nice as you can,
(b) please yourself,
(c) follow fashion?

8 When you enter a roomful of people, do you —
(b) look around to see who's there,
(a) hope every eye is on you,
(c) feel self-conscious,

(d) hope nobody notices you?

9 Which footwear do you like best?
(c) Fashionable T-bars.
(a) Strappy black platforms.
(d) Jolly clumpers.

(b) Knee-length boots.

10 What kind of hairstyle best suits your personality?
(b) Some variation on whatever is 'in' at the moment.
(c) You're still looking for your ideal style.
(d) You prefer it short.
(a) You like it long.

11 Do you worry about your weight?
(a) Hardly ever.
(c) Constantly; you diet every now and then.
(d) You're too thin.
(b) You like to try to keep to a certain weight.

12 How many children do you hope to have one day?
(c) Two.
(a) None.
(b) Four or more.
(d) You're not sure yet if you want children.

13 What attracts you most about a boy?
(b) Good looks, definitely!
(c) A really attractive personality.
(a) He just turns you on!
(d) He's specially nice to *you*.

14 What kind of music gets you moving?
(b) Rock 'n' Roll and Soul.
(c) Reggae.
(d) Victor Sylvester.
(a) Anything!

15 Whose voice turns you on most?
(b) Paul Newman.
(c) David Essex.
(a) Steve McQueen.
(d) Robin Day.

Now count up your score — mostly (a), (b), (c) or (d), and turn to the conclusions

QUIZ CONCLUSIONS

MOSTLY A's
Wow! You're certainly conscious of the fact that you're female! In fact you emphasise it so much that no-one could fail to get the message. This is OK, if that's what you really want — though it could lead to trouble, like the wrong kind of boyfriend for example! So ask yourself if it *is* what you really want; thinking of only yourself all the time could lead to a lot of unhappiness eventually. If you really want to have a successful and deep relationship with a boy, you should begin by calming things down a bit! That come-on attitude of yours is silly and superficial — oh, it's fine if it's only for fun, but if *you're* the one who's taken in by it, it can only lead to unhappiness. Forget about being a flirt and concentrate on being a nice person instead!

MOSTLY B's
You have the nicest kind of sex-appeal! You manage to be very attractive to boys without making it obvious that you *want* them to be attracted. You aren't even being clever; it comes naturally! You probably have lots of male admirers, as you realise how important it is to concentrate on being friendly and interested in people, rather than sizing boys up as prospective boyfriends. You have a strong sense of humour and a genuine interest in other people. You don't seem to worry too much about how attractive you are, as you seem to be basically doing OK so far! If you can avoid getting smug about it, you're all set for a happy and contented life, and the males in it will mostly be the right ones!

MOSTLY C's
You're going through a rather self-conscious phase at present, so you aren't quite making the best of your attractiveness to the opposite sex; in fact, you tend to be a little bit scared of boys. This situation will improve with time, but you can help things along by having more confidence in yourself and your appearance, and trying to enjoy yourself more in male company. Boys *will* accept you for what you are, you know; you don't have to turn them on all the time, just be a good friend. Just relax and let life take its course, and soon you'll be wondering why you used to be so worried!

MOSTLY D's
You just aren't trying! Nobody can be attractive or sexy if she doesn't like herself a bit more than you do! Your prickly exterior is putting people off, and no wonder! You've just got to get it together; you have only one life to live, so go ahead and start living it! First, recognise that you are a person, and start to learn how to make the best of it. Even if *you* think you don't rate, be sure there'll be someone who thinks you *do*. So try to make it worth their while and start on a course of conscious self-improvement. Take a critical look at yourself, your hair, your clothes, the expression you usually wear on your face — it can't all be bad! And it *can* all be improved upon. Go on, smile at yourself in the mirror; that's a pretty good start!

A JACKIE SPECIAL ON ELTON JOHN.

"I WASN'T ALLOWED TO WEAR TRENDY CLOTHES!"

Elton with his Watford mug!

DEPRESSION must be one of the gloomiest feelings in the whole world. We all know the feeling — suddenly everything's gone wrong and life doesn't seem worth living any more. Everybody feels like that at some time or another — no matter how glamorous and exciting a life they lead. Even a famous pop star like Elton John admits that he still gets fed up!

"Of course I still get depressed at times," Elton told me. "But the most depressing time of all for me was when I was in my early teens. I used to get very upset about little things — particularly my weight. In fact it was my weight more than anything else.

"I can remember going into shops and trying on trendy trousers and then having terrible trouble getting out of them again! It gave me a terrific inferiority complex, which I still have to some extent.

"I really was enormous though. I have the sheet music of 'Come Back Baby,' which was the first record I made with my first group Bluesology, and you just wouldn't believe the photo of me that's on it. I was huge — I looked like Billy Bunter!

"The thing about it is that the more weight you put on, the more depressed you get, and so the more you eat to cheer yourself up! When I'm depressed, I just eat everything in sight. I'm a human dustbin!"

His weight wasn't the only thing young Elton used to get depressed about. On top of that, he had all the same problems with his parents as any other teenager.

"I used to think my mum didn't understand me, because she would never let me wear Hush Puppies or Winklepickers, which were the fashionable shoes in those days! I thought that was ridiculous. In fact I still think it was ridiculous.

Elton's record collection

"It caused a running battle between us, because for a teenager, that's a crippling blow. It's like the end of the world, knowing that you have to go to school wearing these horrible shoes, when everyone else will be wearing Hush Puppies.

"I really used to get fed up with those stupid rules. When Mods came into fashion, everyone went around wearing anoraks and Parkas, and I wasn't allowed to have one.

"Another fashion that my mum disapproved of was that craze for those military great-coats that everyone wore in the Carnaby Street days. I found one in a jumble sale for 50p that was full of moth-holes and went right down to the ground — I loved it! But when I met my mum in the shopping centre near where we lived, she took one look at it and ran the other way! She wouldn't walk home with me!

"In fact that's probably why I dress the way I do now — I'm still rebelling against all that."

And luckily, Elton's clothes no longer cause arguments between him and his parents!

"My stepfather walks around in my shoes now," he laughed. "He's the same size as me, so he just takes any of my shoes that he fancies!

"My mum doesn't particularly like my clothes, but she hasn't really got any choice now. She just takes them with a pinch of salt!"

THESE problems, of course, are the sort you can laugh at when you look back on them. But there are lots of things which can still make Elton feel depressed.

"I don't often get very depressed now," he said, "but when I do, I'm utterly impossible! Some people seem to expect me to be in a sparkling form all the time, which is ridiculous.

"I know it sounds crazy, but it's silly little things like running out of sugar that really irritate me. If I realise I have to go over to the shops to get more sugar, that can really add to my depression."

And when Elton's in a bad mood, everyone knows about it!

"No one really knows what I'm like when I'm depressed," he said, "because no one dares come near me! They stand outside my window with a megaphone, shouting 'Are you ready to come out yet?' while I hurl things at them!

"The only thing that can get me out of that mood is a good laugh. Everyone around me knows how to cheer me up. They ring me up and make jokes, and say things like, 'We're sending the coffin round in three minutes. I hope you've left all your money to me!'

"That really helps. I'm lucky, because I'm surrounded by people who're great to me — everyone at Rocket Records for instance.

"In fact, as long as I'm involved with music, I never get depressed for long. Music's the most important thing. Sometimes I get really depressed with things and decide that I can't go on, so I rush away for a change. After only three days I usually have to come zooming back to find out what's been happening while I've been gone! I just can't stay away.

"I enjoy the life I'm leading now, but at the same time I think I'd be just as happy working in a record shop somewhere. I did that years ago, at the time of the 'Elton John' album, and I loved it.

"I love records, and I was fascinated just watching people coming in and buying them. I got really involved in it all. I suppose I just love being involved with music, on any level."

Elton has a huge collection of records, and often relaxes by sorting through them all.

"I never get tired of filing my records," he said. "I don't often have the time to do that nowadays, and that really upsets me. At the moment I have about 2 or 3,000 records that I still haven't filed, and I feel really guilty about them. I keep going and looking at them all. You see, I think inanimate objects have feelings just the same as us. I'd never treat anything like that badly — I even talk to my records!

"I'd never, ever lend anyone any of my records. When I see anyone even fiddling with my records, I want to go and slap their hands!"

His record collection can cheer Elton up in other ways as well. When he's really fed up, he'll put on a record by one of his favourite groups or singers and let them calm him down!

Elton with his juke box — another cheerer-upper!

But one thing Elton says he never does when he's in a bad mood is to start throwing things about and taking his temper out on the furniture!

"Oh no, I hate that sort of thing," he said. "I could never smash up hotel rooms or anything like that. Sometimes I feel like it, but I've never actually done it!

"The only thing I ever did was to throw a plate of fried eggs at a wall, but that was done in jest, not in anger. And I spent the next fifteen minutes clearing up the carpet!"

Obviously, Elton is the kind of person who never stays gloomy for long. Like everyone else he has bad moods, but he soon snaps out of them and gets back to enjoying life.

So I wondered, what did he think was the best way to cure the blues?

"Try to see the funny side of things," he said. "Try and look at both sides. There's a funny side to most situations — like when things go wrong, or you have a broken romance — the sort of things that bring you down. Try to find that side of it. And remember, there's always another day.

"I'm the great believer in Fate, too, and I think that things always happen for the best — no matter how awful they seem at the time. If you can believe that, things won't seem nearly so bad!"

A JACKIE SPECIAL ON THE SECRETS OF YOUR HANDWRITING

SERVES YOU WRITE!

THE way you write can tell you a lot about your character and personality . . . It can also be a fun thing to know about . . . So dig out an old sample of your handwriting and check up on what really makes you tick. By the way, you can also use our guide to analyse your boyfriend's writing, so get out the love letters you've been squirreling away and then find out if he's all he says he is!

(1) Are your a's and o's
a.) open,
b.) closed,
c.) knotted?

I like the open air — cold and comforting — how old did you

If they're: 1. (a) You're a talker and everyone knows it . . . no secret is safe with you and your favourite occupation is gossip.

(b) You can keep a secret and how! You're never going to tell all you know and you're the kind of friend other people cling to.

(c) You have lots of pride in your own achievements and those of your family.

(2) Do you cross your t's to the
a.) left,
b.) right,
c.) straight across?

the time to — the time to give — the only thing that

If they're: 2 (a) You're cautious and not likely to make a move until you're certain other people agree with you. You're also bad at making decisions and are not going to rush into relationships.

(b) You're a natural leader and boys have to follow you if they want you . . . you're go ahead and you don't look back. You don't regret things — the future is what matters to you.

(c) You're well balanced in your outlook and very mature for your age, but you can be a little bit too over-organised and very fussy over small details.

(3) Are your capital letters
a.) large,
b.) small,
c.) medium?

George — John — James

If they're: 3. (a) You think about yourself too much . . . you're likely to be a little bit vain and have quite an opinion of your abilities where romance is concerned.

(b) You've got a small inferiority complex — a chip on your shoulder — you need to be constantly reassured to bolster up your ego.

(c) You're a well-balanced girl with good head and heart control. You're not going to be swayed by other people and you know your own mind.

(4) Is your signature
a.) circled round,
b.) underlined,
c.) without any adornment at all?

Sheila — Ingrid — Julia

If it's: 4. (a) This is a warning sign — "Keep Off." You're a loner and you prefer it that way . . . some boys find it difficult to understand you're not the most sociable of girls.

(b) You're good at blowing your own trumpet and you like to seem important . . . You desperately need to be 'someone' in your own right.

(c) You're logical and intelligent with no wish to stress your own importance of your views. You're capable and competent and you show it.

(5) Does your writing run
a.) uphill,
b.) downhill,
c.) or is it completely straight?

I miss you — I miss you — I miss you

If it's: 5. (a) You're an optimist and always look on the bright side of things. You don't let things or people get you down and you have a lively sense of humour.

(b) You're a bit of a pessimist carrying the worries of the world on your shoulders. You may be a bit of a drag and sometimes not too much fun to be with, when you're in one of your 'down' moods.

(c) You have lots of common sense and think things out before you act. You're a logical girl and should go far.

(6) Is your writing
a.) large,
b.) small,
c.) medium?

I love you — I love you — I love you

If it's: 6 (a) You're inclined to boast and like to show off a little in front of your friends. You're loyal though, and you know the meaning of friendship . . . you're kind and generous.

(b) You could be a little shy and reserved and you may have to make an effort to start conversation. You're not exactly the life and soul of the party, but you're very intelligent.

(c) You're thoughtful and kind, the type of girl who always remembers a birthday.

(7) Does your writing slant to
a.) the left,
b.) the right,
c.) or is it upright?

left slant — right slant — upright slant

If it's: 7 (a) This is the sign of the introvert. You'll find it hard to mix. You'd rather sit in a corner with a book.

(b) You have a sentimental and affectionate nature. You love to be loved and you can give love too . . . you'll enjoy mothering your boyfriend.

(c) A trifle cool and calculating, you'll weigh up the pro's and con's before you agree to go out with a boy. If you like someone they're in — if you don't — they most certainly are out!

(8) Are your small d's
a.) short,
b.) tall,
c.) looped?

don't delay in writing — don't delay in writing — don't delay in writing

If they're: 8 (a) You're very down to earth and have a lot of respect for the material things of life. You're not interested in poetry or music and the arts leave you cold.

(b) You've lots of ideas and you want to get so many things off the ground you don't always succeed. You're the bright ideas girl — the live wire who gets things done.

(c) You've got more than a touch of vanity in your make-up and you have a strongly developed sense of the dramatic.

(9) Are the stems of your g's and y's
a.) straight down,
b.) looped,
c.) non-existent?

give me your — give me your — give me your

If they're: 9 (a) You're a fatalist and believe that what will be will be. You probably read other people's hands and the tea leaves and you're pretty serious about it, too.

(b) You have a well developed imagination and enjoy the artistic and romantic side of life.

(c) You don't want to know about romance . . . you lack energy and you enjoy mental work more than getting out and about.

(10) Are your f's
a.) two loops,
b.) like a cross,
c.) knotted?

your funny face — your funny face — your funny face

If they're: 10 (a) You've a lot of pride and other people find you difficult to please . . . you always want to be right and this can be irritating.

(b) You take what comes and don't expect too much from the people you're involved with. You're capable of devotion and you have a well adjusted attitude to love.

(c) A little too crafty for your own good . . . you're secretive, inventive and you'd love to be a female James Bond. But watch out, you could find yourself tied up in knots and unable to get yourself out of the intrigue you've got yourself into.

(11) Do you dot your i's
a.) high,
b.) low,
c.) to the side?

if we live nearer — if we live nearer — if we live nearer

If they're: 11 (a) You're a dreamer with your head in the clouds most of the time — but providing you find a boy with his feet on the ground, all will be well!

(b) You're careful and excellent at remembering details — you have a good memory and lots of concentration — especially on boys — if they're on your wavelength.

(c) You're quick thinking with frequent changes of mood and many bright ideas for getting on in the world. A boy will have to be on his toes to keep up with your quicksilver mind!

(12) Are your margins
a.) narrow,
b.) broad,
c.) no margins at all?

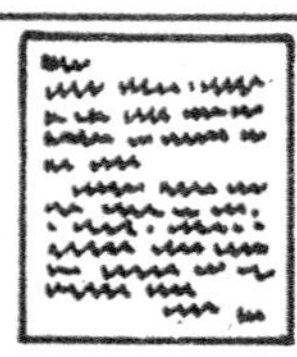
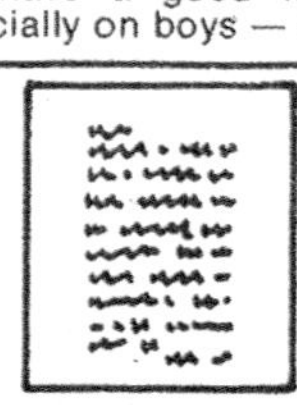
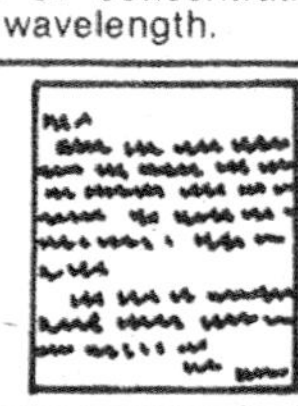

If they're: 12 (a) You're careful with money . . . almost, but not quite, mean. You have a good sense of economy — if you like to put it that way . . .
(b) You're a lover of luxury and you can be madly extravagant and wildly generous at times . . . you'll lavish lots of presents and gifts on people you're fond of.
(c) You're a bit of a miser and you're going to make sure you get value for money. Not a big spender, you like to look after your pennies and the pounds, too.

what will the world be like in 2075?

ON THE SPOT INTERVIEWS where our roving reporters find out what *you* think.

MIKE BATT (ORINOCO WOMBLE)

It's obviously going to be very crowded, but apart from that I doubt if it will be very different from today. I think we've got to such a state of scientific advancement, all that's going to happen is that people are going to realise there will be a lot of overcrowding but they will adapt as we've adapted to a changing world at other times. So basically I reckon it will pretty much be the same as it is today.

Linda King, London, S.W.19.
If the world hasn't been destroyed by war by then, I think people will probably be living on the moon or in cities under the sea.

Yvonne Turner, Bradford, Yorkshire.
I try not to think so far ahead as it's kind of frightening, but I imagine by that time it could well be like something out of the very worst science-fiction. Of course, if over-population, inflation and pollution continue there might not even be a world in 2075 . . .

June Ellis, Motherwell, Lanarkshire.
I think man can only progress so far, before some catastrophe sends him back to square one. Probably by 2075 people will be living in caves again. There are plenty of signs around the world of previous advanced civilisations which have vanished without trace.

Lesley Fellowes, Maidstone, Kent.
It'll be a great place! No work, just lots of fabulous-looking robots, nothing ugly at all, and the towns will be like gardens! There'll be tremendous advances in music and films, and no schools. We'll have pocket computer-brains to tell us all we need to know. Wish I could be there!

Karen Clark, Ely, Cambridgeshire.
Sorry to cast doom, but I'm sure the world is going to be horrific in a hundred years' time. People will be born in test tubes and there will be massive factories manufacturing all the food we need. So there will be little for us to do.

Mick Bradley, Keighley, Yorkshire.
I think by that time it'll be possible for a lot of the population to emigrate to some other planet, leaving a nice peaceful earth behind for 117-year-olds such as me!

Linda Green, Dewsbury, Yorkshire.
I'd like to think it'll be a much happier world in which cures have been found for all the diseases which are still present in our society, and people are living in peace and plenty.

Susan Anderson, Folkestone, Kent.
I think life will be much the same as it is today, but the world will seem much smaller. For instance, Britain and Europe will all be part of one State, and as air travel is bound to be more advanced, places will be more accessible and men will be able to fly from one side of the globe to the other in no time!

Virginia Griffith, Shady Bower, Wilts.
I believe there will be some sort of vitamin tablets to keep people young so no-one will ever get old! I have a feeling that things which we take for granted, like coal and steel, will be extremely rare and therefore very valuable. I don't think people will have a working life as we now know it; computers will be used. And of course there will be people living on the moon!

Lucy Richie, Ashford, Kent.
It all depends on what we do now! If we can manage to stay at peace, to ration our resources, to cut down population, to be less greedy and selfish, and think about the future — then there might be a beautiful world in 2075. But I doubt it. I think it'll be even more ugly and concrete-ridden than it is now!

Norma Patterson, Renfrew, Renfrewshire.
Pretty much the same world it is now. Conditions change a lot over the centuries but people remain the same. Their emotions, hopes, and fears don't alter all that much; and the best things in life will still be free, like love.

Davy James, Battle, Sussex.
I think there's a grim picture ahead. We'll have exhausted most of our natural resources; we'll be disastrously over-populated (unless there's a plague or a world war); the climate will be colder; we'll all be vegetarians; and there'll be 1001 channels on the telly! Ugh! I'm glad I'm here today and gone tomorrow!

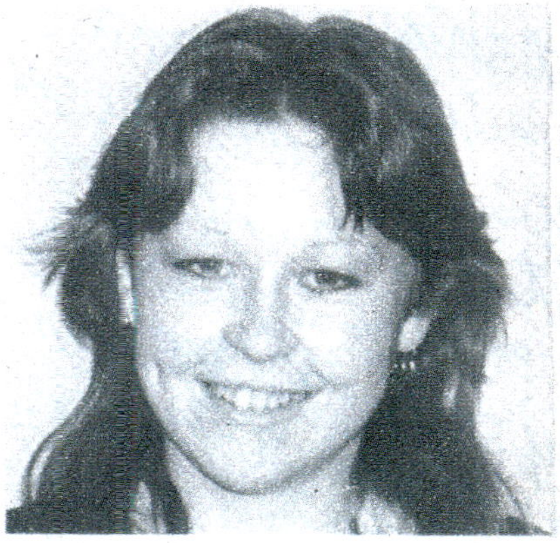

Susan Woodhams, Welling, Kent.
I've always imagined it to be full of people going around dressed in space suits eating tablets instead of food. So I think that in 2075 things will be very different from today.

LOOK OUT

LOADS of wise buys to look out for on the fashion and beauty scene . . . see what's new and where to buy it.

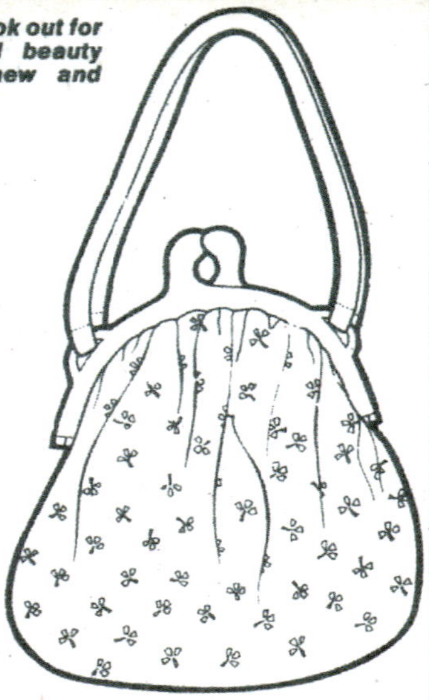

LOOK SNAPPY

Super cord handbag with flower print comes from Dolcis. It's got a snap fasten top and big loopy handle and comes in a choice of black, brown or beige. Price is £2.99, style Matilda, and it's on sale at most Dolcis branches at the moment.

HIP-HUGGER

The new autumn looks include loads of slinky, long-line cover-ups, usually striped or tweedy with short sleeves to be worn over shirts or polo-necks or just a scarf.

We chose this stripy one from the Bairnswear range to illustrate the look. The Style No. is 2877, price £7.25 in courtelle/celon boucle. It comes in a choice of parchment/camel/opal or parchment/camel/filbert (a sort of mushroomy pink) in sizes 32/34 and 36/38.

Stockists include Henry Wigfall and Son, Brandon Street, Sheffield; Mansfield Co-Op; A. Shortland, Bourne End, Bucks; M. Rees, High Street, Gorseinon, Swansea.

SO FAR SEW GOOD

Cheap and Cheerful Fashion Ideas

oops-a-daisy!

Go daisy-crazy now that summer's here. Buy lots of artificial daisies and sew them onto fine ribbon or elastic to make daisy-chains for your neck or your arms. Pin a daisy in your hair, sew some onto your belt or waistband, or around the hem of your skirt or just pin a bunch onto your pocket.

BUDGET BITS

Save, save, save with a pretty cotton pinafore from Van Allan for £4.95. It has a square neck, two big buttons, patch pockets and a tie belt at the back, comes in sizes 10 to 16 in a choice of green, blue, brown, navy, beige or grey.

Pop it over shirts or jumpers or wear it on its own when the sun shines. Buy it from Van Allan branches throughout the country.

SHORT SHORTS

Short of a pair of shorts for your holiday? Try making a pair yourself with this simple Simplicity pattern, No. 6946.

It takes one yard or less for each pair of shorts shown and you can make them up in all sorts of fabrics such as cotton, denim, gaberdine, flannel and a host of others as suggested on the pattern.

BEAUTIFUL BELTS

Three belts from Woolworth to suit all moods, at a reasonable price! The top one is an elasticated belt in three colourway stripes, red/white/navy, red/beige/navy, or plain rust, navy, beige, brown or black, price 59p from larger Woolworth stores.

The middle belt has an art deco touch, with a choice of buckle shapes and comes in brown, beige, pink, navy, bright blue, lime or fuschia, price £1.25 from larger Woolworth branches.

At the bottom is a soft, wide sash belt with a round buckle which comes in cream, mid-brown, chocolate, fuschia, pink, bright green, orange, jeans blue, rouge or black, price £1.59 from Woolworth fashion stores.

FRESHEN UP

Here's something that's really nice to have . . . a multi-coloured drum of Fresh Up lemony tissues. They're moist and refreshing and come in a long strip so you tear off sections as required and the rest stay really moist inside the drum. You can also buy Make Off face cleansing tissues which are slightly medicated and cleanse the skin without removing those natural oils from your face. Price is 59p each for Fresh Up and Make Off and you can buy both from good chemists and department stores.

LOOK OUT FOR . . .

New hair styles like these created by Francis at Steiner are just right for the mood of the moment, especially if you're looking for something new and different. Choose from soft, young curls on the left or the dramatic, geometric look on the right.

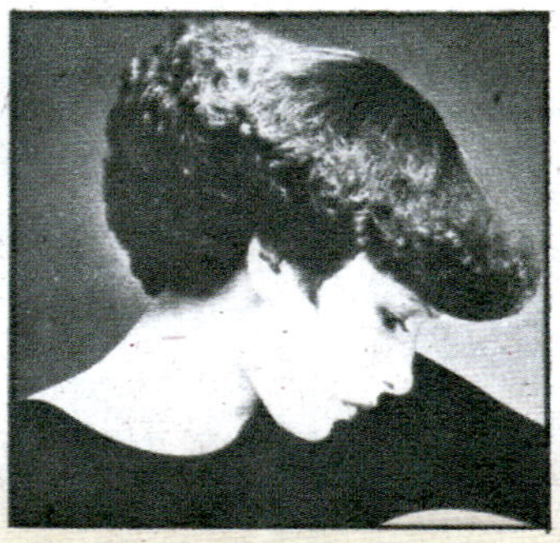

ALL PRICES APPROXIMATE

THE look is soft and full, wide skirts belted tightly at the waist or tiered dresses falling gently from just under the bust. Separates girls put a loose shirt over polos and below- the-knee skirts for the baggy look.

JACKIE FASHION

HIT THE BIG TIME...

1 Full, peachy-coloured dress with belt and short sleeves, from Shubette. Style No.:2156. Price: Approx. £9.80. Fabric: Polyester/cotton. Colours: Green, pink, cream, blue, red. Sizes: 10 to 16. From Gilda of Oxford Street, London W.1.; Just Looking, and branches; Marshall Fashions, Kent; Best Wear, Thundersley; Lucienne, Northampton. Enquiries to Lorraine Beverley, Shubette, 42 to 48 Great Portland Street, London W.1.

Brown polo-neck jumper from a selection at Chelsea Girl. Style No. 412178. Price £2.49. Fabric: Acrylic. Colours: Assorted. Sizes: One size to fit 10 to 14. From most branches of Chelsea Girl.

Bronze-look, strappy wedge shoe with open toe and sling back, from Saxone. Style No.: A55/6806/62. Price: £6.99. Fabric: Synthetic. Colours: Bronze, black patent, black suedine, gold lurex, silver lurex. Sizes: 3 to 8. From main branches of Saxone.

2 Beautiful blue tiered dress with tie at the neck, from Dorothy Perkins. Style No.: 0221. Price: £9.99. Fabric: Jersey Courtelle. Colours: Blue, tan, brown, black. Sizes: 12 to 14. From main branches of Dorothy Perkins.

Black patent shoe with strappy front, open toe and sling-back, from Saxone. Style No.: A55/6540/02. Price: £5.99. Fabric: Patent. Colours: Black. Sizes: 3 to 8. From all main branches of Saxone.

3 The layered look . . . brown over-shirt with pin-tuck front, tie belt and buttons down the front, from Dorothy Perkins. Style No.: 9064. Price: £3.50. Fabric: Polyester/cotton. Colours: Navy, brown, cream. Sizes: 10 to 16. From main branches of Dorothy Perkins.

Polo neck jumper from a selection at Chelsea Girl. Style No. 412178. Price £2.49. Fabric: Acrylic. Colours: Assorted. Sizes: One size to fit sizes 10 to 14. From main branches of Chelsea Girl.

Brown fleck calf-length skirt with buttons down the front and two patch pockets, from Chelsea Girl. Style No.: S53/007. Price: £6.95. Fabric: Tweed Mixture. Colours: Assorted. Sizes: 10 to 14. From a selection at main branches of Chelsea Girl.

Brown studded shoe with canvas twist detail on the front, from Saxone. Style No.: A52/8708/60. Price: £7.99. Fabric: Leather/stud trim. Sizes: 3 to 8. From main branches of Saxone.

4 Super green dress with short, full sleeves and belt at the waist, from Chelsea Girl. Style No.: X51/052. Price: £7.95. Fabric: Jersey. Colours: Assorted. Sizes: 10 to 14. From main branches of Chelsea Girl.

Cream wedge shoe with T-bar front, sling-back and cork wedge. Style No.: A52/8705/80. Price: £7.99. Fabric: Leather, cork. Sizes: 3 to 8. From main branches of Saxone. All the Saxone shoes also obtainable from Saxone, 360 Oxford Street, London W.1. plus 30p for postage and packing.

Prices Approximate.

ARE YOU SORRY FOR YOURSELF?

A CATHY AND CLAIRE SPECIAL ON SELF PITY

"EVERYTHING'S gone sour on me since my friend Jenny started going steady with a boy," Susan wrote to us recently. "I'm so miserable it takes me all my time to get out of bed in the morning. Mum and Dad call it moodiness and tell me to snap out of it. They don't even try to understand what I'm going through.

"Not so long ago they were raising the roof because I was always out and now they never stop nattering about me mooning around the house. But how can I go out when I don't have a friend to go out with?

"Of course Jenny's tried to fix up foursomes with her boyfriend's mate, but I don't want her sympathy, they're only asking me out with them because they feel sorry for me. Anyway I couldn't expect any boy to fancy me at the moment. I'm so depressed I can't stop eating and I must have put on about a stone, but I can't be bothered weighing myself to see.

"My mother keeps on at me that I'm letting myself go and she's offered to buy me some new clothes to try and get me interested in my appearance again. But what's the point? It's a horrible feeling, knowing that if I disappeared off the face of the earth no one would care. Life just isn't worth living any more."

Poor Susan. She really is feeling sorry for herself, isn't she? And of course you wouldn't react to a problem like that in such a self-pitying way, would you?

Or would you?

Everyone feels a bit sorry for themselves when things go wrong and once you start sliding into self pity the most trivial setback can grow in your mind to mountainous proportions. Having a strip torn off you in front of your friends can make you feel everyone has a down on you and being stood up by a boy or having a friend go off you can make you feel unloved and unattractive. Setbacks at work or school or having the sort of day when everything goes wrong can also trigger it off.

"THERE'S this teacher at school who really has it in for me," Alison told us. "He always chooses a night I'm planning to go out to give us extra homework. The dates he's ruined for me! I'd tell him what he could do with his homework only I need maths 'O' level if I'm going to get to college.

"It's not that I slack in class. I don't. But he still piles the extra work on, even when it's not officially maths homework night. The trouble is I get so worked up and mad about it I sit there fuming all night, thinking about all the fun I'm missing and end up with no work done. Then he accuses me of not trying! I might just as well have not bothered with the homework and gone out anyway."

Alison has discovered that self pity, rather than solving problems only makes them worse. She spends so much of her energy feeling sorry for herself she has none left to do the work. Whether the teacher really has a grudge against her is neither here nor there. It's Alison who needs the 'O' level, not him.

If she can only take the extra work philosophically, knowing the rest of the class is in the same boat and get down to it early in the evening without wasting her energies on fretting how unjust it all is, she could find there's still time left for some fun!

SO when it's such an obvious waste of time why do some people seem to ENJOY wallowing in self pity? Well it's a way of getting extra attention. The self pitying girl is basically insecure. She desperately wants to be liked but she's not sure she's a likeable person. She's an introvert, worrying far too much over what other people think of her.

Of course everyone wants to be liked but we have to accept the fact we can't hit it off with everyone all the time. There are bound to be differences of opinion and misunderstandings.

Everyone has problems and friends can help, but only if you're prepared to listen to advice and not if you only want their sympathy. Because that's what the self pitying girl is after, *sympathy.*

And feeling sorry for yourself can become a never ending circle. You start off feeling sorry for yourself because something rotten's happened to you. Then you start over-eating or not eating at all, so that your health suffers and you start to look very unattractive. So you have something else to make you feel gloomy. Then when you're with friends all you can talk about is the rotten thing that happened to you, how fat/thin you're getting and how miserable you're feeling. Soon all your friends are avoiding you because they don't want to listen to your catalogue of woes and you've got something else to feel sorry for yourself about!

So how do you get off the roundabout? Well you have to realise that feeling sorry for yourself is a negative emotion and to beat it you have to take a more positive attitude to life. Instead of moaning to the world "What have I done to deserve this?" try asking yourself, "What can I do to make things better?" When things aren't going too well, don't just limply sit back and let them get worse, comforting yourself with the feeling that everybody's got it in for you. Instead, tackle the problem, make an effort to overcome your difficulties and you'll be surprised how people rally round to help!

Look at it logically. What's so special about you that everyone should have it in for you? In this busy old world people have better things to do with their time than wait for opportunities to put you down. And who wants pity anyway? Isn't it better to gain respect and admiration for the cheerful way you handle problems? Convinced? Then pick yourself up, dust yourself down, and start all over again!

ON-THE-SPOT-INTERVIEWS

WHICH MODERN INVENTION COULD YOU GIVE UP QUITE HAPPILY?

Kay Lillburn, Balunie Avenue, Dundee.
The electric toothbrush. It's such an extravagance. After all, what's wrong with a little elbow power?

Mary Ruxton, Bilby Terrace, Irvine.
The motor car. Riding horseback, or travelling in a carriage along leafy lanes would be so much pleasanter than driving along bleak, concrete expanses of motorway, even if it did take longer to reach your destination. I think people who go everywhere by car lose more than they gain.

Alison Grimes, Wallisdown Road, Poole, Dorset.
I'd be quite happy if my mum got rid of her deep freeze. There's always so much food in the house these days that I can't take my mind off it. It's very difficult when you're trying to diet and trying to pretend food doesn't exist.

Sandra Hills, Foleshill Road, Coventry.
The telephone. It always seems to ring at the wrong time. Either when I'm in the bath or just about to eat a meal and when I want it to ring it never rings at all. And when I ring people up the line's usually engaged. The telephone can be terribly annoying at times. I could easily do without it.

Susan Paul, Marsh Barton Road, Exeter.
I could give up having showers quite easily. I'd much rather lie for hours in a lovely hot bath. Showers are quick and efficient but they take all the luxury and fun out of bathing.

Shirley Maskell, Doveton Road, South Croydon.
The packets they put biscuits in. In our little corner shop there used to be tins of biscuits and you could choose your own mixture. Now you have to take the dull ones with the yummy ones — when you manage to get the packet open.

Ann Purkiss, Glenister Park Road, London S.W.16.
Motorways! They're so boring. They do save time, but I'd rather go the long way round and enjoy the countryside.

Fay Newman, London Road, Wendover, Bucks.
Bathtubs. It's so silly to wash off your dirt and then sit in it — much better to have a shower.

Stephen King, Muswell Hill, London N.10.
Concorde — I've always found it perfectly easy to manage without it — in fact I'd rather the government put the money spent on it to better use.

Tricia Dunton, Bicester Road, Aylesbury, Bucks.
Oh, I don't know — I'm happy with most inventions! I suppose I could manage without television as I much prefer listening to records!

Pat Creasey, Fallowfield Avenue, Birmingham.
Instant mashed potato. I wish it had never been invented. It tastes like chalk mixed with water, but being lazy, everyone uses the stuff, and it's hard to get a real potato with your lunch anywhere now.

Ina Green, St. Michael's Road, Aldershot, Hants.
That's easy — multi-storey flats. They're ugly, they spoil the landscape . . . I think that's two good reasons, don't you?

Rosslynn Kerley, Woodside Road, Salisbury.
Exploration of outer space. It's a complete waste of money when there are thousands of people starving on *this* planet.

Jackie Waites, Howden Avenue, Kilwinning.
I would be very glad to see the end of platform shoes! Tall girls look as if they are on stilts, and small girls seem to be all feet! It's a very unflattering fashion, no matter who's wearing those ungainly shoes.

Emma Cox, Fieldway, New Addington, Surrey.
Planes. They scare me stiff, I'd never go up in one unless it was a matter of life and death.

Hazel Weaks, Maison Dieu Road, Dover, Kent.
Lifts. I really hate them. When they start going up I always feel I've left my stomach somewhere on the ground floor. In fact I don't use them unless I'm in a real hurry. I'd rather walk up nine flights of stairs than go in a lift.

THE CATHY & CLAIRE PAGE

We can't promise the perfect solution, but we'll do our best. If you're stuck with a problem and you can't see the way out, write to us at this address: Cathy & Claire, Jackie, 185 Fleet Street, London EC4A 2HS. Please remember to enclose an S.A.E.

DEAR CATHY & CLAIRE — My friends laugh at me because I'm so interested in sport. I spend nearly all my spare time taking part in sporting activities and I have a great time. There are lots of boys at the club I go to and I don't think I'm missing out on anything but all my school friends won't stop teasing me.

How can I make them understand that I'm having a great time and really enjoying my life?

Well, if they insist on teasing you just because you enjoy yourself in a different way from them, they probably won't ever understand or believe that you *are* having a good time.

These school "friends" of yours sound a bit narrow-minded to us. It's our guess that they think people can only possibly have a good time at a disco or party. They don't realise you can meet lots of boys and have a great if not better social life, just by being a member of a club or interested in a certain activity.

So try to ignore these girls' remarks and keep on enjoying yourself! And if they really knew how *much* you enjoyed yourself, they'd probably all be green with jealousy!

DEAR CATHY & CLAIRE — I went out with Neil for three months before I met his brother, Danny. Danny's 25 and he's married but I really fancy him. He's always really nice to me and puts his arm round me and things when we go and visit him and his wife.

Neil knows this but he only laughs and teases me about it. I don't think he knows I'm serious about Danny.

I keep hoping that Danny will ask me out. Do you think he will?

Well, we're sorry if this sounds cruel, but we very much doubt that Danny will ask you out. We think you've mistaken Danny's friendliness for something else. He obviously just feels affectionate towards you because he's fond of you — not because he fancies you.

You're his brother's girlfriend and he likes you, but you'd be very wrong to try and make more of this. Remember that Danny is *married*. He's not free to go out with you, even if he wanted to.

Neil laughs about this because he knows Danny isn't serious. He'd probably think you were very stupid if he thought *you* were serious.

So don't let your imagination run away with you. Enjoy your relationship with Neil . . . and your friendship with Danny.

DEAR CATHY & CLAIRE — I know it's stupid but I fancy my friend Kathy's boyfriend. He's the best person I've ever met. I used to get on great with him but then I realised I fancied him so I kept out of their way.

Well, now they both keep phoning me and asking me why I don't go down to see them anymore. You see I used to go down about twice a week to her house to see them and play records. It used to be a good laugh, but now I can't bear to see them together.

I can't tell her my real reason for not going down so I make up stupid excuses and I know she doesn't believe me. When Simon, her boyfriend, phones me up I find it impossible to talk to him.

I think I've really offended them now and I don't know what to do. Do you think I should just go and see them anyway and try and hide my feelings?

Well, that really depends on how good you are at hiding your feelings. If you're going to go down and be really miserable, we don't think there's much point in you going.

But, if you feel you could go and try and learn to accept this situation we think it would be much better.

Try to accept the fact that he's your friend's boyfriend and try to keep your relationship friendly.

It would help, too, if you found yourself some new friends to go out with at weekends. Go to discos and parties and we're sure you'll soon find a real boyfriend of your own . . . and you'll still have Kathy and Simon as friends.

DEAR CATHY & CLAIRE — Our mother died just over a year ago and although we still miss her very much, my sister and I have gradually accepted the situation. The problem is our father. His attitude towards us has really changed. He never allows us to go out with friends — never mind boys — and we seem to spend all our time doing housework or watching T.V.

Neither of us have been out with a boy yet, although we have been asked out by quite a few. We just can't seem to talk to our father at all. Do you think there is anything we can do to change this situation without causing a row? I'm 15 and my sister is 14.

You really should try to talk to your father — we bet he's very sad about this communication barrier between you two and him, and we're sure he'd welcome a serious talk with you both.

Explain to him that you'd like to go out with your friends and if he still isn't keen, ask him if it's okay for you to bring a crowd of your friends, both boys and girls, home, so he can meet them. When he sees what a reliable bunch you are, we're sure he'll relent.

Your dad is probably worried that he won't be able to bring you up well enough alone, so do your best to show him you won't let him down. And be nice to him. He's lost his wife — your mother — and he must still be feeling that loss. So let him know you understand — and try to be patient with him. OK?

DEAR CATHY & CLAIRE— A couple of months ago, my friend and I met these two boys at our local youth club. They were really friendly and my friend and I fancied them a lot. The third week we had been there, one of the lads came up to me and told me that he liked my friend. I told him that she liked him too and he was really pleased. So he asked her out.

A few days later the other lad phoned me up asking me out too and now we go out in a foursome. The trouble is, I can't help thinking he just asked me out for convenience — just for the sake of the foursome. This is making me really unhappy. Can you help?

We think you're making a mountain out of a molehill! We honestly don't believe this boy would have asked you out if he didn't *want* to go out with you. So just try to enjoy yourself with him — and don't take things too seriously. We're sure you'll find out in the near future how much he likes you — and meantime — have a great time! And don't worry!

DEAR CATHY & CLAIRE — I used to be really keen on my boyfriend but now I'm afraid I've gone off him. The trouble is, though, that it's my birthday in a week and I know he's bought me a solid gold locket I admired recently.

I really don't know what to do about this. Obviously I want the locket but I think I'd feel guilty about accepting it because I intend to finish things. What do you think I should do?

Well, it would be a bit unfair of you to accept a present as expensive as a gold locket if you're intending to finish with your boyfriend shortly afterwards.

It's a bit awkward, we know, when he's already bought this locket for you, but we still feel it would be wrong to accept it.

We know it's going to be difficult, but we really think you should finish with him before your birthday. He may still want to give you the locket anyway — in which case, if he insists you take it, well, you'll just have to accept as gracefully as possible.

It's a horrible situation, we know, and we hope everything turns out well for you.

DEAR CATHY & CLAIRE — My boyfriend, Scott, is very dependent on me and I feel this is quite a responsibility. You see, he comes from a children's home and he's never known his parents. I don't really know if that has anything to do with it, but he seems to need the security of a steady relationship.

My mum and dad think the world of him and he often stays at our house for the weekend.

Well, I'm beginning to feel this is too much for me. I feel as if I've got a weight round my neck all the time.

I really think I should finish with him but I'm scared to. Can you help?

Well, this is rather a difficult situation but if you really are beginning to feel tied down and unhappy, you *must* do something about it before you get more involved.

Scott is *not* your responsibility, you mustn't feel guilty if you want to finish with him. If you do finish, though, you could always try and stay friendly. This isn't easy, but he'd probably appreciate it if he could still come and visit your home.

Going out with Scott because you feel sorry for him won't do him any good. He's got to learn to stand on his own two feet and, strange as it may sound, your finishing with him might help him do just that.

So try not to worry and do what you think is best — we're sure everything will work out fine.

DEAR CATHY & CLAIRE — I was at a disco last Saturday with my friends and we were all pretty bored. There was this really weedy boy there and one of my friends dared me to ask him to dance.

Well, I did and all my friends started laughing at him and I felt really ashamed that we'd made a fool of this boy. Just before the dance ended, he turned round and said, "That was a really horrible thing to do. I hope you're pleased with yourself." Then he just walked away.

I feel really sorry about it and we all want to apologise to him. It was just a stupid thoughtless action and we feel really bad about it.

Do you think we should approach him at the next disco and apologise?

We're glad you realise this was a really nasty thing to do. This boy was obviously very hurt and he probably lost a lot of confidence through your actions.

We don't think that all of you should approach him if you intend to apologise to him and, since it was you who asked him to dance, and you who accepted the dare, we think it should be you who apologises.

It won't be easy but we think you should do it as soon as possible because the longer you leave it, the harder it will be.

We think you've learned your lesson so we won't lecture about this, but do think twice before you do anything like it again.

Just think to yourself — would you like it?

I DON'T WANT TO END UP LIKE HER!

DEAR CATHY & CLAIRE — I get so depressed when I think about growing up and getting married — the thing all girls are supposed to want.

You see, my nineteen year old sister's married and I really don't fancy her sort of life at all. There's her and Jim and the baby living in one room, they have to share the kitchen and bathroom, and the place is always a mess, with nappies drying everywhere.

I'm sure my sister never cleans up, and when they come round to our house, Jim wolfs his food as if he hasn't had a proper meal in months. My sister used to be so pretty and full of fun, but now she looks a mess all the time and never stops moaning.

Is this what I'm going to be like in four years time?

Why on earth should it be? There's no law that says you must be married by nineteen, and even if you are, you can put off having a family till you've got somewhere decent to live.

There's no reason at all for you to suffer what you consider your sister's awful fate — in fact, simply by observing what's happened to her, you can take steps to see you *don't* go the same way! At present you seem to see marriage as the only thing you can do in the future. Why not think a bit more about getting a good job — travelling around a bit — growing up yourself before you have to help your children grow up? You're in control of your own life, and you can make it as good or as bad as you like.

Meanwhile, don't be too hard on your sister. Getting married doesn't instantly make a perfect cook and housewife out of a lively, pretty girl — that's something she'll need time to learn, and it'll be harder for her with a baby around.

So why not help her out a bit? Go round after school and offer to take the baby out and get her shopping, so she can tidy up the room. Or send *her* out while you do the cleaning up. It'll be a great help to her and it might make you a bit more tolerant of what she's going through . . .

Printed and published by D. C. Thomson & Co., Ltd., 185 Fleet Street, London, EC4A 2HS.

WELL, WHAT DO YOU

A JACKIE SPECIAL SURVEY

YOU may think you're just one of the crowd, but it's amazing how different you probably are from your best friend even! To prove it, we've been rushing around the country asking various "Jackie" readers about all kinds of topics. From items that cut deep into the pocket (like money!) to those that pierce the heart (like boys!) these girls have told all! So now we proudly present to you our latest, revealing, "Jackie" survey!

Eileen Rains, Bexleyheath, Kent, age 16.

Evelyn McLellan, Dundee. age 14.

Fiona Lincoln, Co. Durham. age 17.

Elizabeth Ramsden, Manchester. age 15

ABOUT...

clothes

Eileen: Mostly I buy T-shirts and jeans from shops like Jean Scene. My favourite outfit, though, is a soft green pleated dress which I got from Wallis for £10.

I have two pairs of shoes both from Dolcis which cost £7 each.

Evelyn: I buy clothes mostly at Van Allan boutiques. My favourite outfit is a tweed knee-length skirt with matching waisted jacket. My most expensive article is a pure angora jumper which cost £14.

I have three pairs of shoes from Saxone which cost £7 each pair.

My parents spend about £10.50 per month on clothes for me.

Fiona: I buy most of my clothes from Fenwicks or C & A. My favourite outfit is plain brown trousers and tan jumper matched up with a suede belt.

My most expensive outfit is a chocolate velvet suit costing £20 from Fenwicks. I've got 2 pairs of shoes at £7 and one pair of cream boots for £10 bought at Freeman, Hardy & Willis.

On average I spend £20 a month on clothes.

Elizabeth: I always shop at Miss Selfridge where I bought my favourite outfit. It's a blue midi-length dress with long sleeves and padded shoulders. The most I've ever spent is £10 on a calf length silky skirt with zebra stripes which I've only worn once!

Usually I spend £8 on dresses. I've only one pair of shoes which also cost £8, from Ravel.

make-up

Eileen: I hardly wear lipstick, usually it's only cream and foundation from Outdoor Girl. I spend about £1 a month on make-up.

Evelyn: I mostly wear Miners pearly eye shadow and Max Factor mascara which costs about £1 a month.

Fiona: During the day I wear Boots No. 7 foundation and Rimmel lipstick. At night I usually add Miners dark brown eye shadow to match the browns in my clothes.

Elizabeth: I wear quite a lot during the day. I'm crazy about Biba's red eye shadow and wouldn't go anywhere without it. I spend about £1 a month.

entertainment

Eileen: I go out about four nights a week, either to the Black Prince Folk Club, Woolwich Polytechnic or the Marquee in London. But there are lots of things to do in Bexleyheath especially if you're sporty like me — there's bowling and swimming.

I stay out till about 11.30 and don't usually pay for my entertainment, but if I do it's only £1 a week.

Evelyn: I go out five evenings a week, usually to play table tennis at Grey Lodge youth club. I'm allowed to stay out till 10.30. I spend nearly £1 a week.

Fiona: I usually go out with a crowd of friends to the Southern Club in Newton Agcliffe or the pictures. I stay out till 11.30 and manage to get through £4 a week.

Elizabeth: I go out every night and usually end up at our local youth club, the Forum Civic Centre. I'm allowed to stay out till 10 p.m. which is just as well as by then I've spent all my 50p!

pop

Eileen: I like the Beach Boys or folk music depending on my mood. I usually watch the Pelicans, the band my brother-in-law's in!

Evelyn: I only have one favourite star and that's David Essex! I play his records over and over. Unfortunately I've never seen him perform, but I queued for hours in the hope of getting tickets.

Fiona: I like all types of music except soul. Wishbone Ash are the group I'm most into at the moment.

Elizabeth: I quite like Alice Cooper and Elton John, but my favourite is David Bowie. He's also the last person I've seen in concert.

boys

Eileen: I've got a steady boyfriend, Kev, who I've been going out with for about three months. My ideal boy would be very tall, about 6 foot, with a fast car.

I don't think there's any right age for marriage, just when you're ready for it.

Evelyn: I have a steady boyfriend, Pete, who's sixteen. My ideal boy would be someone rough and rugged like Ben Murphy who would make all the decisions for me.

I don't have many thoughts about marriage — I've still got plenty of time!

Fiona: I have a steady boyfriend, Nick, who's 20. We have a perfect understanding and never row over money when we go out. If he's short I'll pay my way.

What I'd expect from my ideal boy above all else would be security. 22 seems a nice age for marriage, though I'll gladly wait till my ideal boy comes!

Elizabeth: I don't have a steady boyfriend at the moment, but that's only because I'm too shy to speak to Peter Green. He's 18 with dark wavy hair, quite small but extremely gorgeous.

I'd like to get married at 18.

yourself

Eileen: My ambition is to do social work with the homeless. What I'd most like to change is my nerves. I'm not scared of exams or anything like that but I get nervous about the unknown.

Evelyn: My ambition is to be a professional dancer and dance in a group like the Young Generation or Pan's People.

The most important thing I'd like to change is my shyness.

Fiona: My ambition is to be happy and successful and to pass my City & Guilds in photography which I'm studying hard for. I'd like to lose weight, though Nick says he likes me the way I am!

Elizabeth: My ambition is to have a nice family with lots of children. Beautywise I'd like to have fair, bubbly, curly hair.

family

Eileen: I get on so-so with my parents, but then I'm hardly ever at home. Up to now I've been on holiday with the family to the South Coast, but next Easter I'll be going with the school to Greece. I'm looking forward to that!

Evelyn: I get on OK with my family, but have the inevitable rows with my dad who disapproves of Pete.

The last time I went on holiday was to Blackpool, but that was ages ago.

Fiona: I get on well with my parents, but my two sisters annoy me as they're always playing soul music.

Still, next year I'm going on holiday to Majorca for the first time so I'll have some deserved peace!

Elizabeth: My father's dead but I get on very well with my mum, though I feel guilty about not doing more housework. I don't go away every year but when Mum and I go away it's great as we visit relations in Germany.

money

Eileen: I get £1.50 pocket money a week which I find I can save, but there seems no point with the value of money going down so fast. If I had £100, I'd give some of it away to "Help the Aged" and use the rest to visit a health farm.

Evelyn: I get £1.50 a week pocket money, and when I get in debt, which is very often, I do some babysitting. If I had £100 I'd either have lessons at the Dance Centre in Covent Garden or spend it all on clothes in one mad day in London.

Fiona: I find it easy to save as I've got a job but still live at home. If I had £100 I'd rush out and buy an old car.

Elizabeth: I start with a £1, though it's usually doubled by the time I've cadged more off Mum! If I had £100 I'd treat Mum to a holiday in Germany.

THINK?

Gwyneth Sharr Evans, Cardiff. age 17.

I buy clothes from Etam or Richard Shops and sometimes from jumble sales. My favourite outfit is a gypsy blouse with embroidery, gypsy skirt with a frill from Etam, a headscarf and big hoop earrings from Corocraft, while my most expensive one is a grey and white cotton pinafore from Girl boutique which cost £14.50.

I have two pairs of shoes, clogs for £5 and sandals at £7 from Dolcis. I spend £10 a month on clothes.

Mary Quant eye shadow and highlighter. Almay hypo-allergenic mascara. I always wear Mary Quant "Bloody Mary" nail varnish as it's so striking! I spend £1.50 a month on make-up.

I go out two or three evenings to parties or concerts at Cardiff Students' Union and sometimes to discos at the Top Rank. I spend as much as I can afford. It's usually £4 a week.

I like David Bowie, the Rolling Stones and reggae music. The last group I saw was 10CC. who played in the beautiful grounds of Cardiff Castle.

I have a steady boyfriend, Mark, 21, who's an art student from America, thought I must admit I sometimes have dreams of a tall boy with dark curly hair who smiles a lot!

My ambition is to visit Greece, and if it's not too greedy, to be a successful fashion artist. I'd also like to be thinner.

I get on great with my mum and dad who really like Mark, in fact he helped us with the decorating all last year. He also painted pictures of all the family. I haven't been on holiday for two years as I've been saving like mad to go to America with Mark.

I get £23 a week for my work as a fashion artist. If I had £100 I'd like to go to one of the Paris fashion shows.

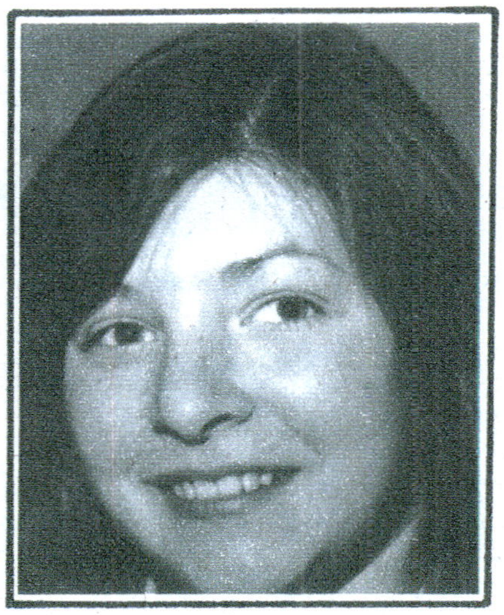

Helen Laird, Glasgow. age 16.

I buy most of my clothes from boutiques, mainly Virgo. My favourite outfit is a red and white polka dot halter neck dress from Van Allan, while my most expensive one is a peasant style tiered dress in a floral pattern which cost £20 from Laura Ashley in Edinburgh.

I have three pairs of shoes costing about £8 from Lilley & Skinner. I spend £6 a month on clothes.

I wear foundation, mascara and lipstick from the Mary Quant Special Recipe range. In the evening if I'm feeling lively I'll add Miner's beauty spots and beauty transfers to selected parts!

I only go out at weekends, usually to friends' parties or a disco in Glasgow called Clouds. I spend £2 a week and am home by midnight.

I like rock and roll and country and western which I think will be very popular over here soon. My favourite artistes are David Essex and Tammy Wynette. I saw her recently at the Apollo Centre and I thought she was great!

I have a steady boyfriend, Willie, 19, who's a commercial artist, but if anybody came along who looked like David Essex, I'd think twice about going with Willie! I think the ideal age for marriage is 21.

My ambition is to be happily married and a top rate audio typist. If I could I'd like to change my face, get some high cheekbones, etc!

I get on well with my parents who approve of Willie and always invite him round so that I can show off my cooking! But I think it's Mum's way of getting me into the kitchen. Last year I went away on holiday with the family to Portugal.

I get £5 a week pocket money on which I save as much as I can. If I had £100 I'd buy everyone on my huge list of relatives, from great-grandmother to second cousin, a present.

the HEART WAY CODE (just for fun!)

Roadsigns are there to give you information or warn you of danger. We couldn't do without them on the roads, but — have you *another* use for them? We have! So read on, about —

Always be on the lookout, and avoid following any path which might leave you with 'No Right Turn' at the end!

Take care — and stop if he starts offering to teach you about love!

Emotional crossroads happen when your boyfriend isn't as keen on you as you are on him.

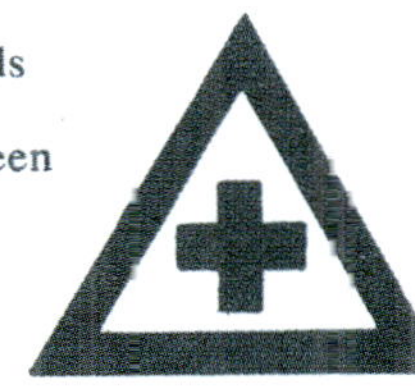

Means to be avoided unless you want to find yourself on a 'slippery road'!

If this is the case, you'd be much better to make a 'sharp turn' away. To follow the other road might mean danger!

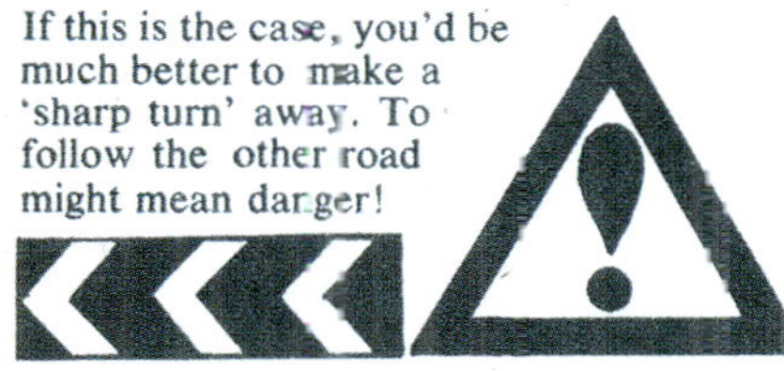

Try to make sure he's around your own age!

Level-crossing — it isn't safe to be near the track. But on the highway to romance it's different — it's much safer to stay on the rails —

No waiting, i.e. — no hanging around if he's clearly not keen!

— even when approached by 'Roundabout' ways!

He's getting more deeply involved — are you ready for it?

Strictly no over-taking when you fancy someone else's boyfriend!

No doubling back on promises you made to him!

The surest and the safest way of reaching romantic happiness is to stick to the straight and narrow motorway, neither bending to left or right.

Let's face it, you're just not travelling in the same direction, love-wise!

You may find the going hard at times. But in the end, if you persevere, you'll make it.

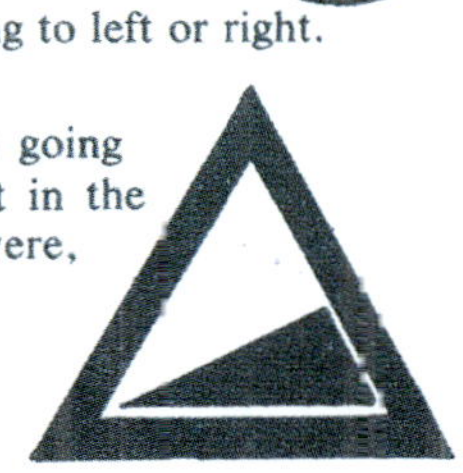

Emergency telephone. If you've quarrelled, don't wait for him to make the first move — phone him up immediately and apologise!

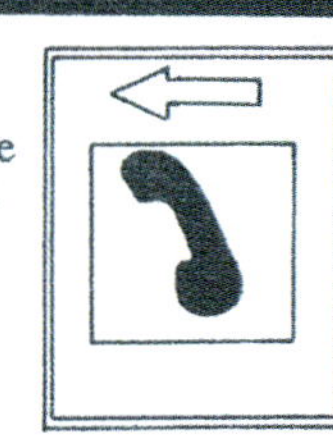

Keep well within your speed limit.

No entry if he has a girlfriend already or is obviously not interested.

But, if you feel your heart driving you faster than your head reckons is safe, it's time to obey this sign!

Staggered junction — don't worry if you miss out on an opportunity for romance — there'll probably be another one soon!

A JACKIE QUIZ

CAN THIS BE LOVE?

WELL, can it? Or is it just a passing fancy? You might *think* you have all the symptoms, but how can you tell if you're really in love? Is it just infatuation, or a love meant to last forever? Do our quiz and find out!

First, answer yes or no to the following questions:-

1. Do you go all breathless when he talks to you?
2. Is it impossible to hold a conversation which isn't about him?
3. Is the thought of being kissed by him enough to send you into a hysterical collapse?
4. Would you sacrifice all your personal ambitions for him?
5. Does your heart miss a beat whenever the phone rings?

6. Do you torment yourself thinking of all the things which could stop the romance from flourishing?
7. Do you believe you're the only girl in the world to have felt such overwhelming passion for someone?
8. Do you believe Fate has ordained that you and he are the only ones for each other?
9. Do you live solely for the moments you can be with him?

Mostly yes — go on to Section A
Mostly no — go on to Section B

SECTION A

1. Does he make you feel —
(a) attractive and special as a person,
(b) endowed with strange magical powers?

2. Can you imagine this great passion you feel lasting for ever?—
(a) you can't imagine the future. You're too consumed with the present,
(b) yes. It will last for ever and a day?

3. When your friends tell you he's not right for you, do you think —
(a) they don't understand the wonderful relationship you have together,
(b) they only want to hurt and spite you because of their jealousy?

4. When you're together, do you feel —
(a) a wonderful sense of excitement and understanding,
(b) an uncanny, almost spiritual togetherness?

5. When you're away from him, do you mostly —
(a) wonder what he's doing, and whether he's thinking of you,
(b) daydream about the next time you're going to be together, and about the future with him?

6. When your friends ask you about him, do you feel —
(a) you want to talk about him endlessly so that they understand how you feel,
(b) that whatever you say, you cannot convey the very special quality of your love for him?

7. Do you think he loves you as much as you love him?—
(a) you desperately hope so,
(b) you have an absolute conviction that he does, even though he might not show it?

8. Are you willing to forgive him his faults —
(a) within reason,
(b) unquestionably?

THE FIRST IN OUR 'HOW DO YOU KNOW' SERIES

YOU KNOW YOU SHOULD GO ON A DIET WHEN...

. . . your bicycle tyres need pumping up three times a week.

. . . if you want a belt to fit you, you have to shop at the men's counter.

. . . on a day-trip to the Zoo, a hippo starts trying to chat you up!

. . . the ceiling of the room under your bedroom starts to sag.

. . . you can't remember the last time you saw your feet.

. . . a whaling ship chases you three times round the harbour when you're out for a swim!

. . . you get a sneaking suspicion that three lettuce leaves might be better for you than three Mars Bars!

. . . your friends start turning their cameras sideways when they take your photograph.

. . . they won't let you ride at the Pony Club any more, following a complaint from the R.S.P.C.A!

. . . your boyfriend doesn't ask you to sit on his knee any more!

. . . your friend, the sweet-shop lady buys ANOTHER mink coat.

. . . they won't let you in the Leaning Tower of Pisa!

. . . your boyfriend keeps telling you how much he likes soft, cuddly girls . . . but you notice his eyes keep following the skinny ones!

. . . you're wearing your favourite smock-top, and a friend tells you tight shirts are out of fashion.

. . . they ask you if you'd mind sitting at the back of the plane.

. . . your kid brother says your new coat would make a super wig-wam.

. . . your mum says you're still a growing girl — and watches you tuck into your tenth helping of egg and chips.

. . . the bath-water slurps over the top of the bath when you get into it!

. . . the lift-man says "Full up!" when you're the only one inside!

. . . you can't telephone your boyfriend from a kiosk any more!

9. If he sent you a dozen red roses, would you —
(a) waltz round the house, singing,
(b) faint with joy?

If you answered: mostly (a), turn to conclusion 1, mostly (b), turn to conclusion 2

SECTION B

1. When other girls obviously fancy him, do you feel —
(a) resentful of them and jealous of him,
(b) rather proud they fancy him, while *you're* the one he belongs to?

2. When you have a quarrel, how do you feel?
(a) you're upset and worried, and have awful nagging fears that this might be the end of a beautiful friendship,
(b) you're not seriously worried. You're sure underneath it all, that he'll come back to you?

3. You've planned to see a film together, but you go down with 'flu, so he says would you mind if he went to see the film with his best friend instead. Would you —
(a) feel disappointed, but think it's only fair to let him see a film he's been looking forward to,
(b) feel rather insulted and think he ought to sit by your bedside and talk to you instead of going off enjoying himself in your hour of need?

4. What do you admire most about him?
(a) his wonderful personality,
(b) his devastating good looks?

5. Which evening would you enjoy most with him?—
(a) a quiet dinner — just the two of you,
(b) going to a party, dance, or disco?

6. When he criticises you, are you —
(a) hurt,
(b) offended?

7. No-one's perfect, and there must be some things about him, which annoy you (biting his nails, being too jokey, sniffing a lot, etc.) Do you —
(a) try to get used to it,
(b) keep wishing he wouldn't?

8. Could you imagine yourself being happy with anyone else?—
(a) no, I couldn't,
(b) only with someone better than him, and there just isn't anyone better than him?

9. When he looks pale and seedy after a bout of 'flu, do you feel —
(a) sorry for him,
(b) disappointed he doesn't look his usual dishy self?

If you answered: mostly (a), turn to conclusion 3, mostly (b), turn to conclusion 4.

Conclusions

Conclusion 1 — Well, it's not exactly love. It's a passing fancy, which could develop into love, given a chance. You're not really seeing him as a person in his own right at the moment, but rather as the image of all your dreams come true. You try to be sensible about the relationship, and that's half way to finding out whether you really love him or not; but a bit more sense and a little less day-dreaming is needed before you can think straight about this boy. Maybe you haven't known him very long, maybe you're just a romantic at heart, but either way it's obvious that your feelings are genuine. You're not trying to kid yourself — you really do feel something for him, and he makes you happier about yourself as a girl and as a person, which can only be good. If you haven't known him for long, stay starry-eyed, but try to look at your relationship more carefully to see whether it will stand the test of time. If you've known him for a few months or longer, it's time to stop being starry-eyed and get down to working out your motives a bit more carefully. Either way, the relationship has possibilities, so keep working at it. Good luck!

Conclusion 2 — This is a case of pure infatuation. Your imagination seems to be working overtime, and the boy of your dreams appears to be a combination of David Essex, Tarzan and a Greek God! If he is, we'd like to meet him, too, but we do feel you're getting carried away by your own image of a perfection which doesn't exist. You're obviously a very sensitive and aware person, and your creative abilities make you unusual, but love isn't just a beautiful idea, you know — it's a real experience which you can only get at by being strictly honest with yourself. So think about yourself a bit more realistically, and try to see your dream boy as a human being. Perhaps when you've come to terms with reality, you might really be capable of falling in love

Conclusion 3 — You're really in love, and it's the genuine thing. It's easy to get carried away by dreams, it's easy to believe the wildest compliments in the moonlight, but in the hard light of day, you can look at your boy and still love him when the first flush of romance has worn off. This is the real test. You can be in love without being starry-eyed, you can accept his faults, you can tolerate him having other interests besides you. In other words, you have a mature, honest view of yourself and of the boy you love. You don't expect miracles, but you believe in the special quality of love. Your realistic view of the relationship doesn't stop you from being sensitive to his moods and feelings though so you never take him for granted, and there is always just a slight twinge of doubt at the back of your mind. You realise he's a person in his own right, that he's special and unpredictable, and no matter how long you know him, you'll always respect him. Your love for him can be unselfish, but you'll never be a doormat, and it seems as though this is a perfectly balanced relationship. Hang on to it!

Conclusion 4 — Are you kidding yourself, or do you know deep down in your own heart that you don't really love him? You expect him to make all the running and you're entirely confident that whatever you do, he'll always love you and want you. You think about yourself far too much and tend to take him for granted. You expect a lot from him — but how much are *you* prepared to give? You feel some affection for him, you appreciate him, but be honest and admit that your motives tend to be selfish. Perhaps he's good for your ego — especially if he's good looking and considerate. He makes you feel good to be seen with him, and his love for you gives you the knowledge that you're a very attractive and desirable person. But what about *him*? If you really love him, think less of yourself and more about him. If you don't love him, it's not fair to keep him like a pet dog on a lead, so let him go and find someone who can keep you in your place. And if you discover you really want him and need him, show more respect for the poor guy!

ON-THE-SPOT INTERVIEWS

WHICH JOBS DO YOU THINK OF AS GLAMOROUS?

Linda Slimming, Hyndford Place, Dundee.
Working as a make-up artist for a television company must be a very glamorous job. Meeting actors and actresses and television personalities and working with them is bound to be very exciting. But I suppose once the novelty wears off, you'd be left to get on with the job and no doubt the glamour would soon wear off.

Bridget Scott, Riverside Terrace, Stapleford.
I think a model's job must be the most glamorous one there is. As you're trained to look good, people always see you at your best, don't they?

Linda Cook, Lochlie Road, Saltcoats.
Television dancers, like Pan's People, always look glamorous to me. Much more so than fashion models who have to adopt unnatural poses and stay in them or walk in an affected way to exhibit clothes. There must be a lot more satisfaction in being a dancer.

George McKay, King's Lynn, Norfolk.
The dictionary definition of glamorous is: "bewitching, alluring etc." The dictionary definition of a job is: "a piece of work, labour etc." Therefore the only glamorous job I can think of is an attractive, fully-employed witch.

Jacqueline Gibson, Skelmorlie Place, Kilwinning.
I'm always attracted by pictures of nurses. It's a smashing uniform, especially the cloak. Of course it must be very hard work being a nurse, but I hope to become a children's nurse myself. Helping people to get well is quite glamorous enough for me.

June Redman, Knowle Road, Bromley.
Secretary to the Queen, Lady in Waiting to Princess Anne — or even her hairdresser, in fact any job connected with royalty must be very exciting and glamorous.

Denise Smith, Bolton, Lancashire.
I think it must be quite glamorous to be one of those super-secretaries who take temporary jobs all over the world, going for a fortnight here and a month there, and always meeting new people.

Jan Buckley, Coniston Road, London N.10.
I'm sure singers like Carly Simon must have very glamorous jobs. Travelling around the world and singing songs to everyone is my idea of bliss.

Beth Mead, North Avenue, Chelmsford, Essex.
I've just seen a programme about Bunny Girls on television, and I think it looks like a fantastic job! If I had the figure for it, I wouldn't mind trying it. Of course the work can be hard, but so are plenty of other jobs and they don't have the same sort of perks.

Laura Butler, Baldwins Lane, Birmingham.
I can't imagine anything more glamorous than being a professional beauty queen — providing you can keep winning all the time!
It must be a fantastic feeling to be picked out of a crowd of beautiful girls as the most beautiful. It must do wonders for your confidence — and for your social life!

Lou Leask, School House, West Dean, Wilts.
Oh, a Bunny Girl's — even though that costume looks decidedly uncomfortable! They get paid jolly good money.

Mary Haines, Alleyn Road, London.
Air hostesses have very glamorous jobs, meeting many famous people, and visiting foreign countries. They don't work very hard, either, but I don't really think I'd fancy being an air hostess these days. What would I do if the plane was hijacked, or if one of the engines failed? Come to think of it, I'll keep my feet firmly planted on the ground.

Vicky Jackson, Heston Road, Earlswood.
Lots of jobs *seem* glamorous to me. Pop stars, models, racing drivers, actors, probably all have glamorous jobs, but they do work very hard so indeed it's not all glamour.

Lindsay Cheetham, Bury, Lancashire.
I imagine it's very glamorous to be an actress in one of the historical series on television. Wearing those beautiful costumes is my idea of a heavenly way to spend a working day.

Dawn Matthews, Hyde Road, Purley.
I think I have a glamorous job — I work in a florist's and to me, working with flowers is a really glamorous way of earning a living. It's also romantic as we often send flowers from young men to their girl friends and it's especially romantic helping to make up wedding bouquets.

Mandy Phillips, Godstone Road, Whyteleafe, Surrey.
I regard working on T.V. as the most glamorous job. Not that I'd like to work on television myself, I'd be scared stiff, but I still envy pop stars and actresses who make regular television appearances. I only wish I had the chance to find out if it's as glamorous a job as I imagine it is.

HOW TO LOOK~ HORRIBLE!

BEAUTY BOX

IT'S not easy, you know — in fact, learning how to look perfectly horrible is quite an art! But we'll tell you how — if you really want to know!

Have a quick look at the girl in our drawing — how many beauty faults can you see? In fact, there are over twenty things wrong with her! She's done just about everything she could possibly do to make herself hideous!

Obviously, no-one in real life is going to look *quite* as bad as she does (we hope!), but just in case you're guilty of one or two of her faults, we're going to tell you what to do about them all!

So, starting at the top, let's deal with hair. Our girl has done all the wrong things to hers, so let's have a look.

For a start, she's got lots of split ends. She obviously hasn't been to the hairdresser for ages! It takes hardly any time to go along to the hairdresser for a 6-weekly trim, and it's the only way to prevent split ends. No amount of conditioning or anything else will prevent split ends forming — so be warned!

Secondly, she's dyed her hair blonde, which is all very well, but she's let the brown roots grow out so badly that she's beginning to look like a zebra!

There's no excuse for this happening. Retouch your dark roots yourself, or go along to your hairdresser as soon as they become noticeable, not when they're six inches long!

The *style* of her hair is all wrong, too. A round, fat face needs a hair style to slim it down, like a pageboy for example. The last thing it needs is a mass of short, "off the face" curls which only make her look like a balloon!

You may be stuck with a round face, but there's no need to be stuck with a fat face! No matter what your basic face shape is — round, square, long or whatever, it'll look ten times better if it's thin, not fat and bloated. You'll discover cheekbones you never knew you had! And the chances are that if you're dieting, you'll be doing your complexion a lot of good, too.

You see, fattening foods like sweets, stodgy things and greasy fried foods are also the foods which will give you horrid spots and blackheads just like our 'model'. So you can see that you'll be doing yourself a double favour if you give them up and start eating healthy foods, like fruit and cheese, instead!

Our model's eyebrows are also a big giveaway. Not only are they horribly bushy, but they're a telltale brown — even though her hair is meant to be blonde! If you're going to lighten (or darken) your hair, it's essential to make sure your eyebrows match, otherwise you'll probably look more than a bit odd! Ask your hairdresser about brow lightening — much safer than trying to bleach them yourself. And, of course, your eyebrows should never be left to straggle all over your face.

If yours have never been plucked, and you're a bit unsure of the shape to suit you best, have them done professionally the first time. Lots of hairdressing salons and beauty salons do this nowadays, for around 50p.

After that, it's just a matter of keeping them tidy by plucking away odd 'stragglers' whenever they appear. Always remember, though, to pluck from *underneath* the eyebrows — never from above, as this can ruin their natural line.

NOW then! Who's got her make up all wrong, then! There's no need to be absolutely slap bang up to date in your make-up all the time, but there's not much excuse nowadays for still wearing a blob of boring old blue eyeshadow, when there's such a variety to choose from!

So no marks to our 'model' for originality! Nowadays you can choose just about any colour imaginable for your eyeshadow. Rust, pink, gold, silver — you name it!

The best way to try out a variety of shades is to buy a 'palette' of several colours. Rimmel do lots of these, at very reasonable prices. Then you can experiment all you want at a fraction of the price it would cost you to buy six separate shades. Alternatively, you could try swopping eyeshadows with your friends, that'll hardly cost you anything!

As for that black eyeliner and those disgusting false lashes — well! As we said, there's no harm in being a little old fashioned, but that's no excuse for being about six years out of date! And not only does it look old fashioned, but it also tends to make eyes look a lot smaller!

So remember, if you want to make your eyes look bigger (and who doesn't?) — harsh, black lines and huge, heavy false lashes do nothing for your eyes but make them look tiny and piggish — ugh! Light colours and a slight, subtle line of colour under the lower lashes will make your eyes look bigger, as will using a highlighter near the browbone or outlining an eye socket with a line of dark colour.

As you might expect, our model's got her foundation all wrong, too. She's tried to use a heavy foundation to cover up her spots, but she's just succeeded in giving her face a horrible cementy look which is definitely *not* attractive!

For a start, she's using a shade which is far too dark for her, thinking that it would make her look more healthy. In fact, as it's far too dark, it just makes her face look dirty.

The secret is to choose a shade as near as possible to your own skin tone. Test this by putting a little on the inside of your wrist and blending it in — the colour it appears there is how it'll look on your face.

Don't make the mistake of using a really thick foundation if you're trying to cover up spots. It's far better to use a medicated make-up specially made for the purpose, like Boots 17's "Take Cover" (around 27p) or Helena Rubinstein's "Bio-Clear Coverfluid" (around 95p).

These are fairly light, liquid foundations which manage to cover up minor spots and flaws while still giving a natural look to your skin. For really stubborn spots, try a spot-concealing stick, such as Rimmel's "Hide The Blemish" (approx. 27p). Never, ever do what our 'model' did and stop the foundation just at chin level, without blending it down into your neck. Otherwise, it'll look just like a dirty great "tidemark"!

LOTS of girls seem to have the idea that if they've got greasy skin, they shouldn't use moisturiser as it will make their skin even greasier. This just isn't true!

Everyone needs to use moisturiser, otherwise dirt and make-up will just sink into the skin and cause all sorts of damage. Do remember to choose a moisturiser suited to your skin type, though — a fairly creamy one, like 2nd Debut, for drier skins, a fairly light one, like Vedra, for normal skin, and a *very* light one for greasy skin. Try Helena Rubinstein's "Moisture Response" (around 98p). It's super, as it works according to your skin type, so can be used on a combination skin.

If you find your face going a bit shiny (see our model's glowing nose) after a couple of hours, try 'setting' your make-up first with an 'Anti-Shine' powder like Rimmel's, when you make-up.

You may not like your mouth shape, but you can do a lot about it, if you try! Wearing the right colour of lipstick has a lot to do with it. For example, our 'model' has a very small mouth, which looks ten times worse because she's wearing a very dark shade of lipstick!

Dark colours really only look best on big mouths — medium to light shades look far better on small mouths. If your mouth is a bit uneven in shape — or if you'd simply like to make it look bigger or smaller, invest in a lip brush. You really should have one anyway, if you want your lipstick to have that professional touch!

But a liphrush is absolutely essential if you want to change your lip shape. Simply load the brush with colour, and paint on the shape you want, keeping within your own lip lines if you want to make it smaller and extending it beyond them to look bigger!

Blusher is one thing you simply cannot plonk on and hope for the best, like our girl did. For a start, you should choose the right shade to suit the rest of your make up. Something pinky for an 'ice-cream colours' look, something browny for a more rusty look. And never just stick it in the centre of your cheeks, unless you have incredible bone structure which can take anything!

Experiment with your blusher until you've found the right place on your face to give it shape. On most people, this means down the sides of the cheeks in the "hollows" but remember that *you* can create all sorts of looks by putting your blusher in different places — i.e., a tiny little bit stroked on your temple will make your face seem thinner, while a touch blended into the tip of a long nose can make it seem much shorter.

FINALLY, hands. Our model's hands are in just as much of a mess as the rest of her! Her nails are uneven and all different shapes.

No excuse for this, when a couple of minutes with an emery board (not a metal file — it's too harsh) would get them all into shape. Remember always to file in one direction, from the sides to the centre, as a "see-saw' method can ruin your nails.

She's been biting her nails, too — tsk, tsk! If you bite your nails and can't find the willpower to stop, try painting "Sally Hansen's "Nail Biter" (around 49p) on them. The taste should keep them well away from your mouth! Alternatively, you could invest in a set of false nails, and wear them till your own ones have grown to a reasonable length underneath.

The same rule applies to nail polish as to lipstick. Dark colours reduce, light colours enlarge, so if you have short nails like our 'model', *don't* wear blood red nail polish.

Leave that until your nails have grown a bit, and meanwhile stick to a pale colour. Transparent nail polish looks nice, and goes with everything. Rimmel's "Nail Strengthener" (around 29p) does a double job, it looks like a high-gloss clear nail polish, and protects them at the same time.

And, of course, no matter what colour of nail polish you're wearing, it should never, ever be chipped! Carry a tin of nail polish remover pads around, and your bottle of nail polish, so that you can carry out quick repairs anytime. Never try to paint over a chipped bit, it'll look all lumpy and horrid if you do.

As for what she's holding in her hand — anyone for a cancerette? Apart from being bad for you, smoking *looks* so hideous!

So there you are. Do you want to look like our model? The choice is yours — but we're sure you'll make the right one!

All prices approximate.

PATCH WORK

Collecting for Fun: Paper Knives

GETTING THE POINT!

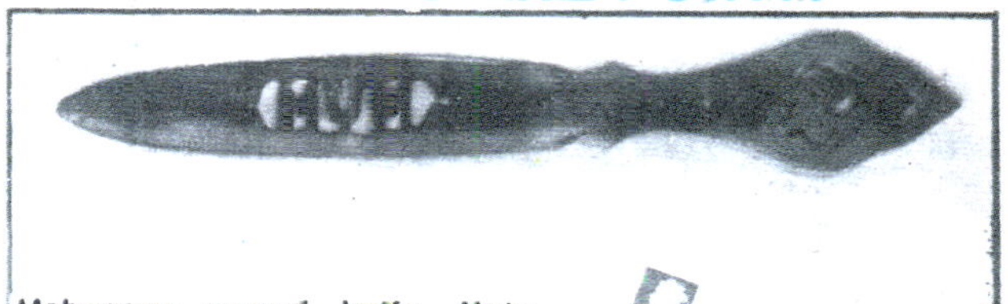

Mahogany carved knife. Note the word "Mum" on the blade!

How do you open your letters? With a finger or pencil, we bet! But you could use a proper antique paper knife — they're not expensive, and they make even bills look better!

Long ago, there were no envelopes. A letter was just the piece of paper it was written on, folded in three and tucked in at the ends. The edge was sealed with a sticky disc or blob of sealing wax. And a pointed paper knife was used to cut round that seal.

After 1840, proper envelopes and stamps came in. But knives often kept their round, smooth handles. The handle was used to make a sharp crease on letters — it was the mark of a top secretary!

You'll find paper knives in wood, ivory, silver, brass, shaped like birds, painted and plain. The big ones opened parcels — or newspapers. It's true! Some snobs liked to have their papers delivered "uncut" round the edges. That way, their servants, up at the crack of dawn, wouldn't know the news before the master, who rose much later in the day!

Tiny knives were used to cut open the pages of new books. And sometimes the book knife had a little flap in the blade, so you could slip it over the top of the page and keep your place!

There's a knife with the postal rates printed on it for nearly 100 years ago. That's called "The Popular Paper Knife" and is worth picking up.

Others we've seen were carved to look like flowers or the neck of a violin!

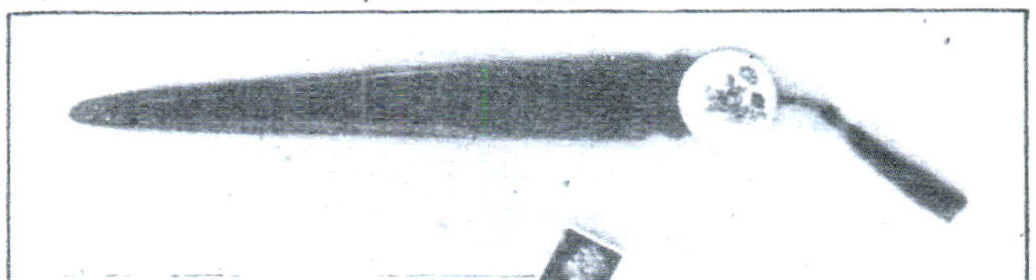

Green mottled imitation sharkskin knife with hand painted bottom.

IT'S MAGIC!

The Airfix people have been busy lately — thinking up lots of super new ideas. This is one of our favourites — "Magic Miniatures" The idea is to paint the picture as you would any paint by numbers set, on an easy to use large size board, then reduce it, by a special magic process (!), to miniature size. The effect is tremendous — and your friends will be really impressed!

There are several different 'magic miniatures' sets available — you'll find them in department stores and art shops, price £2.65.

Make It Snappy!

Here's just the thing to give as a present to your friends or to yourself! These super little photo albums from Boots come in three different sizes, and each one holds 32 prints. They're available in bright, shiny colours with cheerful designs on the front. 59p for the small square album, and 69p for the two larger albums.

Available from major Boots stores.

HOT ORANGE ICE!

Here's an unusual autumn recipe you'll want to eat all year round!

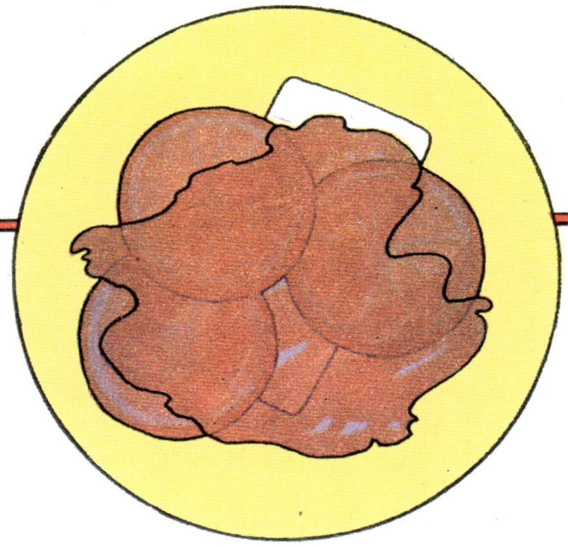

Hot Orange Ice

1 block of ice cream, 1 small sliced orange, 1 tablespoon marmalade, heated.

Put the ice cream in a dish, place the sliced orange on it, and pour over the hot marmalade.

MINI MIRROR!

We all know how fond of themselves Virgoans are — so if you want to give a Virgoan the ideal present, give her a mirror! This handy-sized mirror comes complete with its own plastic carrying case, and has an attractive design on the back. The mirror costs 25p plus 10p postage and packing, from Zodiac, The Astrological Emporium, 3 Kensington Mall, London W.8. *(Incidentally, it's available in all the other zodiac signs, too.)*

BUSY BOOKS!

That's what we'd call them, 'cos W. H. Smith's new range of "Look In" books will keep you busy all winter long! The six paperbacks, all very well written and illustrated, are on fascinating subjects — "Origami," "Wildlife," "Outer Space," "The Wild West," "Exploring Woods," and "Ponies and You." Hopefully, you won't just read them and put them away on the bookshelf, but will be prompted to follow up the subject of the book further — by trying out origami for yourself and becoming an expert in it, by discovering a whole new world of nature when you go out exploring woods on your own, etc.

By the time summer comes around again you'll be amazed at all you've done and learned over the winter! So if you're feeling bored at the thought of those long, dull winter evenings — buy yourself a "Look In" book. They're all available from W. H. Smith & Son branches, price 50p each.

Your Patch — Eggstra! Eggstra!

Brighten up your breakfast — with an egg cosy! Jackie reader Susan Tibbenham, of Bracknell, Berks, has sent us this great idea for keeping your boiled egg warm while you have an extra five minutes kip! To make her cheerful felt hen, just cut out two 'tulip' shapes and sew them together down the sides, leaving the pointed ends free. Now simply decorate with embroidery threads in your own style. You can sew on felt eyes, a beak, a "plume" or a fancy pattern — anything, in fact!

If you have any ideas you'd like to pass on, send them to: Your Patch, Jackie, 185 Fleet Street, London EC4A 2HS. We'll pay £1 for each idea printed!

The Art of Self Defence . . .

Fancy being a black belt? You must admit, saying you're a judo expert sounds a lot more impressive than saying you're any other sort of expert! It's a lot more useful, too!

If you're interested in judo, it's worth enquiring locally about night classes and sports clubs. Judo's becoming more and more popular nowadays, so no matter where you live (unless it's on the top of Ben Nevis) there should be a club of some sort near you!

You won't need any expensive equipment at all, or special clothing, usually, though some clubs might ask you to supply a special judo robe after a while.

Nor is it a man's sport — Janet Fox of Leeds, shown here "strangling" her boss(!) has been chosen for the British National Judo Squad, though she's only 20, and is within 15 points of being a "black belt."

Bet she's not worried about walking home alone at nights!

EVERYBODY SAY AAH!

If you've been in London recently, you're bound to have noticed that the London buses are looking a lot nicer these days — thanks to Jim Lee. Jim, one of London's top fashion photographers, has been splashing out on putting what he calls "my most romantic pictures ever" on the sides of buses, so that everyone can see them. What a lovely idea!

The photographs are part of a series called "Young Lovers", with Mark Lester of "Oliver" fame, and Carin Miller, a young Swedish girl, as models. If you liked them as much as we did, you'll be glad to know that the series has now been made into a tiny little booklet, just right for a gift to your boyfriend! It costs 75p and is available from selected bookstores or by post from; The South Wharf Consortium, 16 South Wharf Rd., Bay 8, London W2 1PF. (Enclose 7½p for postage & packing.)

Train Your Dog!

If you own a dog, you give him food, exercise and affection, (we hope!) But a dog needs more than that — he needs to be trained. An untrained dog can be a real menace, both to yourself and to other people. So Pedigree Petfoods have brought out a helpful wall chart to show you how to train a dog to sit, walk to heel, and all the other necessities. You'll find it a great help in training your dog, and it's available from Pedigree Petfoods Education Centre, 43-44 Albemarle Street, London W1X 3FE, price 30p and 12p postage and packing.

DOWN - large dog

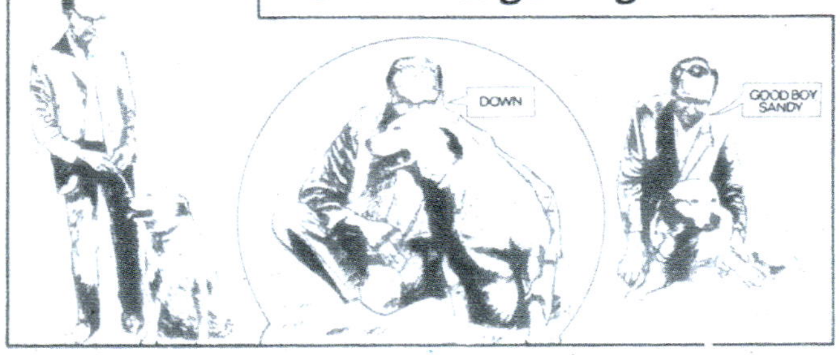

A large dog may try to resist the attempt to make him assume the 'down' position. Here the method is slightly different to the one for small dogs. Adopt a crouching position . . .

With all the slack of the lead gathered in your right hand, command . . 'Down!' – at the same time using your left hand to pull the dog towards you so that he is slightly off balance. If necessary, raise his left forepaw.

A firm but steady downward pull on the lead whilst holding on to your dog's left forepaw, will bring him into the 'down' position. Again, do not forget to praise him – *but only when the correct position is achieved.*

DO YOU ENJOY BEING A GIRL?

Everyone knows what they think about boys! But what about girls? What do you think of them? Do you treat them as your friends or foes? Try our quiz and find out the real truth — but be warned, what you think of other girls will reveal a lot about yourself!

1. What do you think of best friends who become 'blood sisters' and promise eternal friendship?
(b) It's good. It shows they are really genuine friends.
(c) It's nice, but a bit unrealistic.
(a) It's OK for young kids.
(d) It's daft!

2. Your best friend comes to you in tears about a row she's had with her boyfriend. Do you —
(a) secretly enjoy the drama, and are pleased it hasn't happened to you,
(d) get bored with her problems after a while,
(b) really feel sorry for her and sympathise with her,
(c) try to comfort her, telling her it's not as bad as she thinks?

3. When you see a really ugly girl in the street, do you —
(c) think, "Oh, well, **someone** must love her",
(b) feel sorry for her,
(d) dismiss her from your mind,
(a) think, "Thank goodness I don't look like **that**!"?

4. Your friend wants to borrow your best dress for a party. You know you *have* to lend her it because she can't afford to buy many clothes of her own and she doesn't have much fun. Do you feel —
(a) very virtuous, but a bit worried she might spoil your dress,
(d) a bit grudging about the whole thing, so refuse,
(c) pleased to have made her happy,
(b) so pleased to be able to help, that you lend her your best shoes as well?

5. A new friend of yours comes to tea, and when she's gone, Mum raves about her and says what a lovely girl she is. How do you feel about that?
(d) You immediately go off your friend — imagine sucking up to your mum like that!
(b) You're delighted your mum likes her and it makes you think even more highly of your friend.
(c) You're pleased your mum likes her, but it doesn't change **your** view of your friend in any way.
(a) Since your mum is always criticising *you*, you're a bit peeved she thinks someone else is so wonderful!

6. Your mate has just started a new job, and she wants you to go to the firm's dance with her because she's scared to go on her own. Would you —
(b) feel a bit apprehensive about it, but say you'll go, because you know what it's like feeling like that,
(a) feel flattered that your friend has asked you,
(d) refuse to go if you don't want to,
(c) say you'd love to go — it might be fun?

7. Your friend gives you a blow by blow account of the tremendous evening out she had with a boy she's just met. Do you feel —
(b) fascinated — you have to admire her style,
(a) curious — it sounds fantastic and you keep wishing it had been you,
(c) amused — you enjoy sharing her experience,
(d) resentful — she's a boastful twit and she's probably making the whole thing up anyway?

8. A girl you've never seen in your life gets chatting to you in the bus queue. Do you feel —
(d) annoyed because you don't want to talk to her,
(b) a bit shy — you can't think what to say to her,
(c) pleased that someone is being so friendly towards you,
(a) non-commital. You chatter away, but think underneath that perhaps she's a nut?

9. A group of girls are being very catty about a girl you like but don't know very well. Would you —
(c) defend the girl like mad,
(a) warn the girl that some people have it in for her,
(d) ignore it (or possibly join in),
(b) feel upset about it but still do nothing about it?

10. You see this girl at the disco with a boy. She's clinging on to him like she won't ever let go and he looks obviously embarrassed. Do you think —
(d) "What a fool she is",
(c) "I can't understand how she could do that when it's obvious he doesn't like her",
(b) "She must be madly in love with him",
(a) "She thinks she's making a supersexy impression, but honestly, who is she trying to kid?"?

11. You meet a boy and start to go out together regularly. The trouble is that your best friend feels hurt and left out. What would you do about it?
(b) You'd feel guilty, and see her as often as you could between dates with your boyfriend.
(c) You'd try to fix up one of your boyfriend's mates for her so you you could go out in a foursome sometimes.
(a) You'd keep your boyfriend away from her, in case he took a fancy to her; but you'd see her as often as possible on your own.
(d) You'd feel a bit mean, but after all, she should be able to get her own boyfriend.

12. You see an absolutely stunning girl in the street — beautiful face, hair, figure and clothes. How do you *honestly* feel about her?
(a) Very jealous — some girls have *everything*, and it's not fair.
(b) Wistful, imagining the wonderful life she must have.
(c) Admiring — you have to hand it to her, she's fantastic.
(d) She doesn't make any impression on *you* — you couldn't care less.

Now count your score to see whether you have mostly (a) (b) (c) or (d), **turn to page 12 and read the conclusions.**

WHAT T.V. PROGRAMME WOULD YOU LIKE TO BE ON?

ON-THE-SPOT INTERVIEWS where our roving reporters find out what *you* think

Heather Sherwood, Salisbury.
Oh, I should like to be the person Eamonn Andrews comes up to and says "This is Your Life" to! Admittedly, there's only seventeen years of it so far, but it would be a laugh!

Diane Winterbourne, Leeds, Yorkshire.
I'd like to be in one of the 26-part historical serials, based on the life of some famous person or book. I'd just love to wear all the beautiful costumes and watch the characters develop through the serial. Also, I'd know what was coming next, before anyone else did!

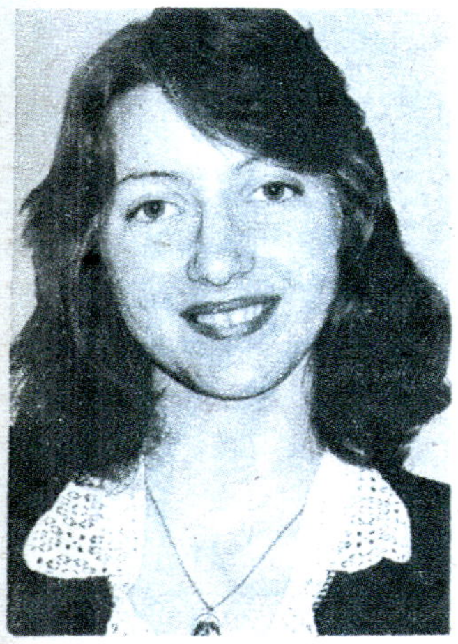

Gillian Indge, St. Pauls Cray, Kent.
I'd like to star in a comedy programme, particularly "The Liver Birds". I think I'd prefer to play the role of Sandra, but I wonder whether I'd be able to stand the strain of being able to share a flat with Beryl!

Sally Oakley, Fordingbridge, Hants.
I'd choose to be one of the girls who hang around the "Six Million Dollar Man"! Of course, I should have to go to America to star in it — that's the main attraction!

Verity Haworth, Cheam, Surrey.
I'd like to play the leading lady in a costume series, like "Upstairs, Downstairs" or the "Forsyte Saga". I'd really live the part, and get right away from the nasty, scientific, money-mad modern world!

Susan Kellett, Bradford, Yorkshire.
My all-time favourite programme is "The Magic Roundabout." I'm not sure how I would appear on it, but I'd love to be in it just to find out how they manage to make Brian the snail come in and out of his shell!

Kathy Price, Weston Turville, Bucks.
Well, I watch "Blue Peter" and I think they do lovely things — always going on journeys, visiting lovely places and doing interesting things in the studio too. I think I'd really love to do something like that.

Paul Griggs (Guys And Dolls)
I'd love to star in "Match of the Day". As I'm a Liverpool fanatic, I'd love to take the place of one of their players, probably Kevin Keegan. But as I haven't played football for years, I'd probably only be good enough to prop up the goalpost!

Caroline Jones, Woodfalls, Wilts.
"Kojak" — as his girl friend. I might even get to try one of those yummy-looking caramel lollipops!

Sue Jones, Aylesbury, Bucks.
"Top Of The Pops", of course — only not as a singer. I'd like to be the DJ who introduces all the acts, because I bet they have great parties afterwards with all the groups!

Jackie Andrews, Salisbury, Wilts.
I'd like to have a show similar to Parkinson's. My guests would range from politicians to quite ordinary people. One person I'd interview would definitely be Reg Prentiss, the Minister of Education, because I'd like to know what advantages there are in introducing a four-part school holiday system instead of three.

Davina Stewart, Leatherhead, Surrey.
I fancy being the nice lady who reads the story on 'Jackanory'. It seems such a pleasant, relaxing job — and as I love reading to little kids it'd be smashing to do it for lots of them at once!

Pamela Downs, Ham, Surrey.
I think I'd like to be a newsreader for "Nationwide". They seem to have a lot of fun in the studio, and they meet the most interesting people around. I like dressing up, and I enjoy talking to people, so I think it'd just suit me fine.

Jo Heap, Blackheath, London S.E.3.
I'd like to be in "Alias Smith and Jones" and play the part of a young damsel in distress so that I'd have to be rescued by gorgeous Ben Murphy.

QUIZ CONCLUSIONS

Continued from page 5

DO YOU ENJOY BEING A GIRL?

Mostly (a)
You like and need your friends, but basically you don't trust other girls, and you tend to treat them as rivals rather than close companions. You probably have one or two really genuine girl friends, but other members of the female sex send you worrying about what they think about you. Trouble is, you're always comparing yourself with other girls instead of enjoying friendships in a relaxed way. You always want to be one better than them, and you're always looking for signs of *them* scoring points off *you!*

You can't see a friend's new dress or hairstyle without thinking, 'is it nicer than mine?' And, this of course can lead to terrible jealousy. You could find a great deal of fun, enjoyment and sympathy from your mates — but you spoil it all with your continual quest to be better, prettier, sexier than they are.

Try treating them as people — stop competing with them all the time, and you'll find you'll be more relaxed and nicer to know. Have more faith in yourself, which will in turn make you have more faith in others!

Mostly (b)
You're kindness itself to your friends — let's hope they appreciate you! You enjoy close companionship with other girls, and are a good and faithful friend to them — sympathetic, understanding and open-natured. But you have such a good heart and such a trusting personality that you're sometimes disappointed in your friends — they can't *all* be as good and kind as you are.

The true gift of being able to give and receive friendship is one of the best, most rewarding things in life, but don't you think you tend to depend on other girls a bit too much? It's fine to have friends, but you must also branch out on your own sometimes. Maybe you lack confidence and need their reassurance, but you tend to be too easily led and too easily influenced by them.

You genuinely want to please, but that doesn't mean making a martyr of yourself. Think what *you* want to do, and not always what *they* want you to do. All you need is a little bit more self-confidence. And at least you're free from the horrible envy and jealousy which can spoil someone's view of life. You may wish you had some of the things your friends have — but you'd never become bitter about it.

Mostly (c)
You have just the right attitude to other girls. You don't feel you have to compete with them and create an impression all the time (like type a), you're not too dependent and trusting (like type b), and you are not a girl-hater (like type d). You can accept other girls on an equal footing, without having to weigh up whether they're better or worse than you are.

You treat other girls as people, in other words, and although you're very aware of feminine things, you have enough confidence and faith in yourself as a person to get along naturally with other girls, whether they look like a film star or the back of a bus!

You're out-going and sociable, you enjoy the company of your friends and can have a good laugh with them. You're also sympathetic: you can look after your friends and be sympathetic when the occasion demands it. But you don't expect too much from them. You're realistic enough to know that nobody is perfect (including you!), so rows and differences don't get blown up in your mind, and you are not too easily hurt by others. You have the natural gift of getting along with other girls, without always taking friendships too seriously. And if they could be as sensible and naturally sociable as you are, they'd be a lot happier!

Mostly (d)
You simply **hate** other girls, and have very little time or sympathy for them. In general, that is. Perhaps you're different with your very special girl friends, but not much, we suspect! Your jealousy doesn't just make you treat other girls like rivals, but like out-and-out enemies!

Yes, we all know boys are far more interesting, but in fact, you miss out on a lot by avoiding communication with your own sex — girls can comfort each other when they're down, can have fun, have heart-to-heart talks and simply enjoy genuine trust and friendship.

Perhaps you feel that you're far too superior to confide in other girls, or even to admit that you are "one of them" — perhaps you genuinely don't **need** female company. Still, you might find it worth making the effort sometimes — you might just enjoy a girlish giggle from time to time! If your life is full and happy without much feminine company, that's all very well, but if you're often unhappy or lonely, you must break down the barriers, swallow your pride, and join the hen-party. Well, it's better than brooding alone, isn't it?

Jackie Fashion

BEST OF

WE'RE having a party . . . a garden party to be exact, with long floaty skirts, tops and smocks to wear, and flowers everywhere. Care to join us?

1. White overshirt with deep v-neck, wide collar, tie belt and blue lady print on the back, comes from Van Allan. No Style No. Price: £4.95. Fabric: Polyester cotton. Colours: White, blue, green. Sizes: 10 to 14. From Van Allan shops; Just Eve; Weston's; H & J. Wilson of Warrington, Swindon, Plymouth, Oxford, Hastings and branches.

Long swirly skirt is by Paul Separates. Style No.: M138. Price: £7.90. Fabric: Courtelle. Colours: Black, brown, olive, damson, airforce. Sizes: 22 to 28. From Jane Norman, Oxford Street, London W.1.; Alders of Croydon; Mackross of Cardiff; Lamports of Portsmouth; Shinners of Sutton; Farnon of Newcastle; Medhurst of Bromley; Page of Camberley.

2. Blue and white flowery print smock top with long sleeves, v-neck and tie belt from Laura Ashley. Style No.: S100. Price: £6.50. Fabric: Cotton. Colours: Assorted. Sizes: 10 to 14.

Matching long skirt also from Laura Ashley. Style No.: LSK/97. Price: £5.50. Other details as for top. Both from all branches of Laura Ashley.

3. Black suit with long skirt and ruched top with cap sleeves comes from Dorothy Perkins. Style No.: 9010. Price: £9.99. Fabric: Polyester. Colours: Blue, black, green. Sizes: 10 to 14. From all branches of Dorothy Perkins.

4. Beautiful overshirt with long sleeves, tie neck and elasticated waist, by Neil McGowan. Style No.: E523. Price: £5.00 approx. Fabric: Acrylic jersey. Colours: Black, red, yellow, tan, navy, brown, dark green. Sizes: Small and medium. From Figgy, 29 Holland Street, London W.8.; Mary Mary, South Woodford, London E.18.; Jennifer Ann, 106 Barlow Moor Road, Didsbury, Manchester; Brown Thomas, Grafton Street, Dublin; By post from Figgy, 29 Holland Street, London W.8. plus 20p postage and packing.

Long dark green skirt comes from the Co-Op. Style No.: BE/336. Price: £4.99. Fabric: Polyester. Colours: Black, chocolate, bottle. Sizes: 12 to 18. From most Co-Op branches.

THE BUNCH

5. Pretty-as-a-picture flowery suit with long frilled skirt, and short-sleeved top with buttons, tie-belt and lacy trim, from Dorothy Perkins. Style No.: 9011. Price: £10.99. Fabric: Cotton. Colours: Brown, green. Sizes: 10 to 14. From main branches of Dorothy Perkins.

6. Soft cream smock with long sleeves and flower trim, from Hampstead Bazaar. Style No.: 2066/4. Price: £5.90. Fabric: Calico. Colours: Natural only. Sizes: Small, medium, large. From Hampstead Bazaar, 30 Heath Street, London N.W.3.; Richmond Bazaar, 6 Duke Street, Richmond.

Bright red crepe culottes with wide, wide legs come from Irvine Sellars. No Style No. Price: £3.95. Fabric: Crepe. Colours: Assorted. Sizes: 10 to 14. From a selection at all branches of Irvine Sellars. Enquiries to Irvine Sellars, Sellars House, Lancelot Road, Wembley, Middx.

7. Tan overshirt with short sleeves, v-neck and elasticated waist from French Connection. Style No.: 5331/4. Price: £3.90. Fabric: Cotton. Colours: Blue, brown, tan beige. Sizes: Small, medium, large. From Hampstead Bazaar, 30 Heath Street, London N.W.3.; Richmond Bazaar, 6 Duke Street, Richmond.

Long black skirt with brown print by Irvine Sellars. No Style No. Price: £5.95. Fabric: Cotton. Colours: Assorted. Sizes: 10 to 14. From all Irvine Sellars branches.

8. Coffee and white long flowery top with tie belt from Laura Ashley. Style No.: S196. Price: £6.00. Fabric: Cotton. Colours: Assorted. Sizes: 10 to 14.

Matching long skirt also from Laura Ashley. Style No.: LSK/92. Price: £5.50. Other details as for top. Both from all branches of Laura Ashley.

All prices approximate

WHAT MAKES YOU LOVE THEM?

IF you had to choose between a date with the nice, good-looking boy next door, or with a wild, romantic stranger, we bet you'd choose the latter any day, even though you know full well that the relationship is likely to lead to a broken heart — yours, not his!

It's just a fact of human nature that we tend to fall for the rotten boys. We have this romantic idea that men should be tough and dominating, and most girls are automatically attracted to the worst ones out! It *sounds* very romantic, taming the wildest boy in town, but when you actually have to cope with a difficult boy, it's not always such fun. So here's our catalogue of difficult boys and how to cope with them. See if you recognise any of your boyfriends, past, present or future!

THE HARD TYPE — WITH A SOFT CENTRE!

This isn't really the worst type of boy, but he can make you despair sometimes, as Linda, aged 15, found out. She's been dating Roddy for six months, and much as she loves him, she admits that he's a bit of a mixed blessing.

"He's really nice to me when we're alone together," she told us, "but when we're in a crowd with his friends, he becomes a totally different person. He's inconsiderate and rude to me, he ignores me most of the evening, and I get really angry and upset. I *know* he cares about me, so why can't he show it when we're in company? But he gets so angry when I challenge him about it and he tells me I'm possessive. I don't want to lose him by nagging, but he just doesn't understand how hurtful his behaviour can be."

Naturally Linda gets upset about this, even though she knows Roddy loves her basically, but perhaps she doesn't understand just how insecure he is.

There are a lot of boys like Roddy. He loves Linda very much, but he's embarrassed about his feelings and frightened of being labelled "soft" or "hen-pecked" by his mates. So he acts big in front of them, and tries to make out he's the great man-of-the-world who has all the girls at his beck and call. This so-called manly act he puts on is hurtful and often humiliating to his girlfriend.

So if you ever have to cope with this kind of boy, it's best to try not to be clinging or possessive, which will only embarrass him more and make him act even tougher. It's more than likely that if you're patient and understanding, he will soon feel self-confident enough to be able to drop the act and be as nice to you in company as he is when you're a romantic twosome.

This is a very common type of problem, and it must be remembered that the boy genuinely doesn't mean to hurt your feelings — it's just that he's a bit immature and is trying to protect his self-esteem, and gain admiration from his crowd of friends.

THE UNOBTAINABLE TYPE

The Unobtainable Type is enough to turn any sane girl into an hysterical wreck! If you really fall for a boy who keeps his distance and plays it cool like this, you can let yourself in for a lot of unhappiness. Fair enough if the boy really isn't interested in you — in which case you should get the message fairly quickly, but some boys (usually the best-looking ones) get a kick out of keeping a girl on a puppet-string.

Cathy is a pretty 16-year-old from Cardiff, and she explains what a terrible time she had when she fell for Martin The Unobtainable!

"He goes round in our crowd" she said, "and he always used to single me out to talk to me, but he'd never go any further than that. He was very good-looking and popular, and used to getting his own way. I knew he was conceited from the beginning but I couldn't help falling for him. I knew he liked me, and I just couldn't understand why he was so aloof.

"It was ages before he even asked me out, and I went through a terrible time just waiting, and hoping. I must admit, I did chase him — I couldn't help showing my feelings for him. Sometimes he'd ignore me, which upset me terribly; sometimes he'd be nice to me and give me new hope again.

"In the end I tried very hard to get over him by going out with another boy in our crowd, and as soon as that happened, Martin started to get interested in me and asked me out. Well, we've been going out for two months now, but I'm still not sure of him. I know I love him more than he loves me, but I dread the thought of losing him."

Boys like Martin treat love as a kind of emotional contest, to score points in. Basically, they lack affection and are afraid to show their feelings for a girl. It makes a boy like this feel superior to play around with people's emotions, and he feels really great when he's in a position of power. He actually enjoys leading girls on and then switching off the charm and seeing them suffer.

Let's hope boys like Martin will one day come to their senses and find out that love is a genuine two-way experience. Meanwhile, our best advice is never to fall for The Unobtainable Type in the first place — give him the treatment he deserves. But once you've fallen for him, it's not so easy. It's possible, though, that if you can show him enough genuine affection, he may eventually realise what he's been missing all these years and give in to love!

THE UNROMANTIC TYPE

This boy is infuriating! Every girl wants to feel loved and appreciated, but although the unromantic boy might love you desperately, he can't actually bring himself to *say* those sweet words you long to hear. No wonder you begin to think he doesn't care. No wonder you long for a glamorous stranger to come along and sweep you off your feet with love-letters and flowers.

The unromantic type is emotionally shy and cannot express his feelings. But if you challenge him with his lack of gallantry, he's likely to retire even more into his shell. He's scared to commit himself, and terrified of giving his feelings away in case he gets hurt. It will help if you can be extra loving to him and show him how much you feel for him. Then he may just get round to trusting you enough to utter those three difficult little words!

At least you have the consolation of knowing that the unromantic type is sincere and his feelings go very deep. When he eventually gets round to declarations of love and passion, you can be sure he means every word he says. He doesn't say anything lightly or for effect. Much better than the guy who puts on a big, insincere act at the beginning and you discover to your cost — and your heartbreak — that he never meant a word of it. It was all a sham and he never really cared for you at all.

So if you find you're stuck with an unromantic type — hold onto him with all you've got!

THE LADY KILLER

This brings us to the Lady Killer. He's the original insincere smoothie, and when he first crashes into your life, you're in seventh heaven. He's so charming and he makes you feel so loved and treasured, so feminine. Recognise him? But the act soon wears thin, or worse still, you find that the pretty girl down the road is getting exactly the same treatment, with the full blast of his fatal charm.

There are all sorts of ways of dealing with this boy. You can pretend you don't care; you can flirt with everyone in sight and play him at his own game; you can create jealous scenes; you can turn into an ice-berg. But nothing really works, and unless he *really* falls deeply in love with you, he spells trouble.

The awful thing is that he can't help being a lady-killer. He feels this need to go around proving himself all the time, reassuring himself that he is attractive. The conquest is all-important to him. He needs challenge and variety, and although he may genuinely care for you, he simply cannot help hurting you.

If you must go out with him, try to keep it casual and don't get too involved. Better still, drop him, leave him to his own dubious devices and find a nice steady boy. The lady-killer is almost untameable, and even if you *could* tame him, do you really think he's worth the effort?

THE POSSESSIVE DOMINEERING TYPE

The possessive, dominating type can make your life a misery. He's demanding and difficult, jealous and suspicious. He watches you like a hawk in case your eyes stray; he questions you like an interrogation squad when you've done nothing more devilish than going to visit your best friend, or taking the dog for a walk.

Some girls are very attracted to this type of boy, and it's quite understandable. Firstly, if a boy is jealous and possessive you tend to think that he loves you desperately, and secondly, there's no doubt that most girls respect a boy who is manly and dominating. The trouble is that he often goes too far with his pushing ways and you are likely to end up either giving in to him all the time, which reduces you to the status of a doormat, or fighting against him all the time which is unpleasant not to mention energy consuming!

Margaret, a 17-year-old secretary from Hull, went out with Peter for 2 years, until she just couldn't stand the strain any longer.

"Peter just wore me out," she said. "We had so many rows. He wanted his own way all the time, and he was always making awful scenes because he thought I was being unfaithful to him. He just wanted to *own* me, and I began to feel like a prisoner. However much you love someone, you want your own life, too. That was

impossible with Peter. He even got jealous of me going out with my best friend, Jean. I broke it up in the end. I just couldn't stand the strain. We were fighting more and more and, believe me, it was no fun."

Margaret kicked against Peter's domination, but there *are* girls who like the man to be the boss. If you're one of them, you could get on perfectly well with a boy like Peter. It's wise to remember, though, that this type hasn't any real respect for a girl as an individual. He expects his girlfriend to be a shadow of him and live up to his standards without any regard for her personality or what *she* wants in life. Could you take it?

THE PLAIN ROTTEN TYPE

Last but not least, the Plain Rotten Type, which includes most boys at some time or another, because no-one can be perfect, after all! It's very strange how we're always attracted to the worst side of a boy's nature. If he's moody and strong-willed, he somehow becomes more manly in our eyes. If he's casual and thoughtless, we fight all the harder for his love. If he's cool and distant, we pine away for him, and somehow think that his aloofness makes him far more intriguing and attractive.

It's just female nature to be attracted to the mean, domineering, or downright rotten boy. It all goes back to the times when the man was the brave hunter and warrior and the little woman sat at home sewing the bear-skins, you see. Traditionally, men are *supposed* to be dominating and women are supposed to be gentle and submissive. So, even if you think you are a Women's Lib. girl, the chances are that in your emotional life, you're the cave-woman who wants her man to be powerful, strong and just a little bit mean! Just make sure you're always sufficiently in control of yourself to take the vital steps *out* of the relationship if it comes to the crunch!

PATCHWORK

SNOOPY'S BACK IN TOWN!

Yes, the range we've all been waiting for has arrived . . . Snoopy and Gang are in town!

Hallmark, the firm who brought out Peanuts candles recently, have now gone completely overboard for Peanuts and have brought out a whole range of goodies . . . including stationery, stickers, birthday cards and even a gorgeous Snoopy pincushion!

The best thing about Snoopy is that he appeals to everyone from the age of about 2 upwards, so you can be guaranteed to please everyone if you present them with a Peanuts gift! We must admit, though, we'd rather keep them all for ourselves!

The prices are very reasonable — for the items shown here, the prices are: notelets — 30 pence a box, stickers — 30 pence a pack, booklets — 48 pence each.

The Peanuts range is available from most major stationers. So don't delay — say it with Snoopy today!

YOUR PATCH — Handkerchief Holder!

Here's a super-simple, super-effective idea from reader Alison Hutchison of Leeds — a holder for your tights, made from handkerchiefs! It couldn't be simpler to make — you just take two large, coloured handkerchiefs, fold them over and sew them into a "pouch" shape, attach a press stud, and that's it! A colourful, cheerful way to store your tights.

Alison wins £1 for sending in her idea — if you'd like some extra money (and who wouldn't?) send your ideas to "Your Patch," Patchwork, Jackie, 185 Fleet Street, London.

A GOOD ALL-ROUNDER

If you enjoy doing — or even just reading — Weekspots, then you'll love this new book from Piccolo — "The Piccolo All The Year Round Book" by Deborah Manley.

It's absolutely packed full of things to do all the year round — starting with January and working through month by month to December. You'll find details of monthly festivals and events, what to see in the countryside, even what weather to expect! (No, not rain all year round!) It's really an invaluable book which'll keep you interested and amused for ages. Don't miss it!

"The Piccolo All The Year Round Book" is available from most major bookstores, price 50p.

HOME TYPING

If you've always wanted to learn to type, but never had the opportunity — here's your chance!

"Eurotone" have brought out a home typing course with a cassette tape, booklets, and a keyboard "trainer." Or, for people with a record player, there's a choice of a kit with three records instead of a tape.

The course costs £4.50, which may seem a lot, but it really is a good investment if you want to learn to type at home. The course will take you from a basic introduction to the keyboard of the typewriter to the skills of speed typing, and you can more or less progress at the speed you want to.

Available at most major department stores now.

CHOCOLATE CRUNCH

Here's a delicious recipe to make up in a spare moment.

You need; 1 oz. butter, 3 tablespoonfuls golden syrup, 4 oz. seedless raisins, 1 pkt. chocolate polka dots, 1 oz. puffed wheat.

Melt butter and syrup in a pan, bring to boil. Boil for 5 mins. Remove from heat — stir in raisins, chololate drops, puffed wheat. Press into greased tin, leave to set. When cold, cut into squares.

BUSY BEE

Isn't he lovely? His wings and legs move, his eyes look around him, and he's attached to a long wire. He's great fun for children to play with, or to give to a friend, or best of all, just to keep for yourself! He'd look great hanging from a ceiling or the top of a window. Busy Bee costs 6p (plus postage and packing — 9p for up to a dozen bees) from Jacksons, 171 Piccadilly, London W.1.

MAKE A MODEL . . .

Here's another great idea from "Airfix" the Arts and Crafts people — a model kit. It's rather like making aeroplane kits — but a lot more fun!

The one we've shown here is Anne Boleyn, from the "Famous Women of History" range. The kit comes in small pieces which you stick together with glue to form the model. Then you simply paint it in bright colours — and hey presto! One instant Anne Boleyn to decorate your room.

The kits cost 42p approximately, and are available from most craft shops.

SOAP SHOP

Definitely one of the most original ideas we've seen in ages — stay on soaps! Let us explain . . . these gorgeous soaps, decorated with the famous Toulouse Lautrec designs, are made with a special process that makes the picture "stay on" right throughout their use. So that even when you're down to the last sliver of soap, the picture's still there! The set of 3 soaps costs only 65 pence (excluding postage and packing) and is available from a super shop called "Rosalinde" which stocks an amazing range of interesting soaps, like ones with "Smiley" on, or ones with a Gatsby girl face! Why not write away today, for a catalogue, to "Rosalinde," 8 Brompton Arcade, Knightsbridge, London S.W.3. (Enclosing an S.A.E. please!) They're a mail order company, so you can order your soap selection by post. What are you waiting for?

Are you the

WELL, are you? He'll know by the way you're dressed — so check up with some of your favourite people and see what they like their girls to wear!

DONNY OSMOND

"I guess I'm just a romantic at heart. I like to see girls in long print dresses with narrow waists and full, flared skirts. Makes me feel romantic just thinking about it!"

BRYAN FERRY

"I like to see a girl with a sense of good taste and style, dressed in well-cut, fashionable clothes. It's especially good when a girl can adapt high fashion to suit herself. My favourite is a long black slinky dress, worn with thin, high heels . . . I really dislike great ugly platforms!"

Long navy and white flowery dress with high neck and lace trim, pin tuck front, tie belt and frill at the bottom, from Laura Ashley. Style No.: L172. Price: £8.75. Fabric: Cotton. Colours: Assorted colours in prints or plain. Sizes: 10 to 14 From Laura Ashley shops: Enquiries to 157 Fulham Road, Chelsea, London S.W.3. or 9 Harriet Street, Knightsbridge, London S.W.1.

Beige open-toe sandal with suede wedge, leather upper and brown detail on upper, from Ravel. Style: Esma. Price: £6.50. Fabric: Leather. Colours: Beige, brown, blue and tan. Sizes: 3 to 7. From all branches of Ravel.

Long black dress with wide sleeves and v-neck with lace trim, from Top Shop. Price: Approx. £9.99. Fabric: Acrylic. Colours: Assorted. Sizes: 10 to 16. From a selection of long dresses at Top Shop, Oxford Circus, London W.1. and 42 other Top Shop branches throughout the country.

Brown suede and snakeskin stiletto shoe with ankle strap and cross straps at the front, from Ravel. Style No.: Winds. Price: £8.99. Fabric: Suede/snake. Colours: Beige/brown, black. Sizes: 3 to 7. From all branches of Ravel.

girl for him?

BAY CITY ROLLERS

"Definitely casual! We don't like to see girls looking too dressy or too made up. Jeans and T-shirts or jumpers are best, but girls should still look like girls so we think long hair helps . . . it's much nicer than a short crop. Of course, we really love to see girls dressed in Rollers' fashions — v-neck jumpers, bags and stripy socks!"

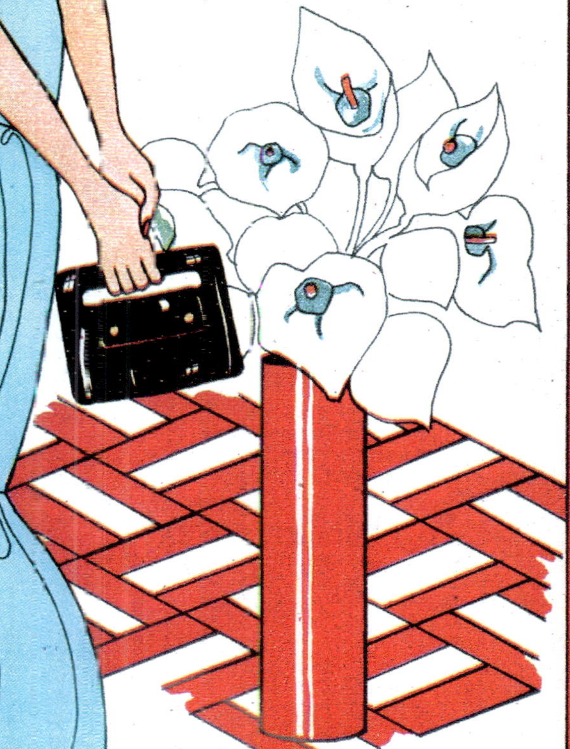

DAVID ESSEX

"I like a girl to look ladylike and I think if she's quietly and tastefully dressed she looks really attractive. Elegant shoes and a handbag look great with a thirties style dress. I hate great big wedgy shoes. As for materials, my favourites are crepe and beautiful old prints."

Navy v-neck jumper with long sleeves and white trim, from Dorothy Perkins. Style No.: 3328. Price: £3.99. Fabric: Acrylic. Colours: Navy with a white stripe, ecru with brown stripe, new blue with ecru stripe. Sizes: Small and medium. From main branches of Dorothy Perkins.

Pale blue denim jeans (rolled up to the knee) with zip front and two slant pockets, from Dorothy Perkins. Style No.: 4651. Price: £4.50. Fabric: Cotton. Colours: Blue. Sizes: 10 to 16. From main branches of Dorothy Perkins.

Super stripy socks from Mary Quant. Style: Alice. Price: 75p. Fabric: Wool. Colours: Assorted combinations of stripes. Sizes: One size. From Selfridges of Oxford Street, London W.1. and branches; Harrods Way In, Knightsbridge, London S.W.1.

Wood wedge shoe with strappy upper, from Ravel. Style: Ace. Price: £8.99. Fabric: Leather. Colours: White, brown, black. Sizes: 3 to 7. From all branches of Ravel.

Pale blue, tiered calf-length dress with v-neck and button trim on the front, by Gene Bernel. Style: Southern Belle. Price: £10.00. Fabric: 100% Courtelle/jersey. Colours: Dusty green, dusty blue, camel, dusty pink. Sizes: 10 to 16. From Dickens and Jones, Regent Street, London W.1.; Patches, Woolwich; Catlins, Lowestoft; Unique, Southsea; Bob In, Harrogate Road, Leeds.

Small black patent bag with flap top, from Saxone. Style No.: Tia, B09/0486/02. Price: £2.99. Fabric: Patent. Colours: Black. From main branches of Saxone.

Black patent stiletto shoe with open toe and twist bow on the front, from Ravel. Style: Lochan. Price: £8.99. Fabric: Leather. Colours: Black, brown, white. Sizes: 3 to 7. From all branches of Ravel: (All Ravel shoes by post from Ravel, 103 New Bond Street, London W.1.)

All prices approximate

YOUR LETTERS PAGE

You all know about Pete's insatiable desire to improve himself, and boy does he need some improving! Well now he's taken up learning Spanish. He sits all day with his grammar book in front of him making horrible gurgling sounds.

He says he wants to be able to chat up the Spanish lovelies in Majorca this summer. Perhaps some incensed Spanish Mama will take a crack at him — I think I'll suggest he takes up judo, it'll probably prove most useful.

Anyway I'm encouraging Pete to learn Spanish, I keep telling him how much happier he'll be in a warmer climate — permanently! I'm also going to encourage you to keep writing me letters, I love reading them, so please drop a line to me — Sam, at "Jackie," 12 Fetter Lane, Fleet Street, London EC4A 1BL. You'll win a quid for every original letter printed and if yours is chosen as the Star letter, you can take your pick of — A Mary Quant Overnighter, a Pifco Go-Girl Hairdryer, a £4 record voucher or £4 in cash.

Adios Amigas!

QUITE RIGHT

My younger brother is an extremely good fencer and has won several trophies and titles in this sport.

As a result of this he has been offered a place in the British fencing team.

But despite the fact that he has great potential in the sport, he can find no sponsors or financial help of any kind.

This seems very unfair and it is no wonder that Britain is behind other countries in sporting activities if they refuse any encouragement for their young prospects. It's possible that he won't be able to accept the place in the team due to the expense of travelling abroad. I think that something should be done to help people who could represent Britain in the field of sport.

Jenny Steventon,
Upminster,
Essex.

This week's winner has chosen £4 in cash as her star prize.

AMAZING!

On an occasion when I had been absent from school, my mum wrote a note saying "I'm sorry Jacqueline did not attend school yesterday, but it was her head. She had it on and off all day, yesterday." Then she realised her mistake!

**Jacqueline Dunbar,
Dundonald,
Belfast.**

NOTHING'S NEW!

While reading a book the other day I came across this line: "The boots had the latest platform sole."

Nothing odd about that, you may think, but the story was set in 1642!

**Jenny Robinson,
Bedford.**

WHAT'S IN A NAME?

I overheard a conversation between my mum and my sister one morning when they were listening to the radio and a certain name was mentioned. My sister said, "If my fiance was called that I'd make him keep my name, you can do that can't you?" "Oh, yes" said Mum, "you can change your name by deed poll." After a pause my sister said, "Oh I don't like Deed Poll I think I'll stick to Spiers." Exit my Mum with convulsions.

**Julia Spiers,
Bristol.**

PLEA FROM THE HEART

Last week my friends and I went into a small paper shop and bought some sweets. When we went outside the shop assistant said to a woman;

"There are a few postcards missing."

The middle-aged woman replied, "It was probably those young girls." When we heard this we were quite astonished. Why do adults always accuse us?

I'm sure it's just because we wear modern, trendy clothes and so they think we're stupid. I just wish that adults would try and understand us and not judge us by our appearance.

**Yvette Martel,
Guernsey,
Channel Islands.**

VERY APPROPRIATE . . .

One Sunday night when I was trying to feed the budgie, I accidentally left the door open and Joey flew out. Just at that moment Des O'Connor came on the TV singing "Spread Your Tiny Wings And Fly Away."

Even my mum, who was chasing him, had to laugh.

**Susan Bennet,
Immingham,
Lincs.**

AND MOTHER CAME TOO . . .

Girls in this country have nothing to complain about. Spanish girls are hardly ever allowed to go out alone with a boy to a disco or the pictures. But my male Spanish pen friend thought the limit had been reached when he found this gorgeous Spanish girl, aged about 19, and he asked her out to the pictures.

On the night, he had a taxi waiting outside her house, he knocked on the door and out came this beautiful girl — followed by her mother, her grandmother and the dog! This was too much for my friend, he jumped in the taxi and drove off. No wonder that when Spanish boys see an English girl they're like flies around a jam pot.

**Maxine Bailey,
Market Drayton,
Shropshire.**

ED'S LETTER.

More adventures of Leonard J. Watkins on page 4 this week! We do hope you like him and his attempt to find true love. Secretly, the whole series was based on Pete's early days — before he became the suave, sophisticated man-about-town that he is!.

See you next week, The Ed.

P.S. I wrote that nice bit about Pete with my fingers crossed, 'cos I didn't really mean it!

A MEMORY

I sit with a hidden loneliness,
wondering if my love for you
is a passing dream, or something
which will go on forever.
I know in my depths,
that I will never see you again,
yet wonder if some day,
our paths of fate may cross.
I wonder, and hope,
but with a hopelessness which
I long to fade into distant memories,
lost together with thoughts of you.

**Diana Hawkins,
London, W.C.1.**

WORKERS OF THE WORLD

When we went after a summer holiday fruit-picking job, the employer said she only took on boys because she considered girls too weak — what a cheek! But seriously, how can women be expected to work if they're not allowed to even pick plums from a tree!

Don't worry, we're not for the burning your bras stuff, but we do need all the support we can get!!!

**Alison and Beverley,
Houghton,
Huntington.**

DEMENTED?

Here is a little tale that my grandad told me.

A butler was asked by a newly appointed maid what the letter "d" stood for painted on the refuse bin outside the back entrance of the mansion. The butler replied, "Damsel, the 'D' displayed on the dustbin denotes that the despairing domestics of this detached domicile, desire that the dustman during his daily diversions, shall deem it his delightful duty to dislodge, deftly and deliberately, all dirt and dust deposited in this disgusting dustbin." Phew!

**Jayne Cangford,
Glamorgan,
S. Wales.**

BE PREPARED

I was talking to my younger brother about a certain television series shown on a Saturday morning. He told me that he had never missed watching it. I asked him how he did it as I always oversleep and miss it. He replied, "It's easy really, I always get up early in case I get up late!"

Pat Cartney,
Gorton.

GOOD MANNERS

People are always complaining about school dinners, well I like them, and if my friends and I really enjoy the meal, we thank the cook. You can believe me, she is always quite surprised because she doesn't get compliments very often. So when you enjoy your school meals tell your cook. You could be making someone a very happy person. And helping the cook to know exactly what you like!

**M. Bell,
Beeston,
Notts.**

NO HURRY

Did you know that in 1802, people began talking about the Channel Tunnel? It is now 1974! And they've only just started making plans! *Only* 172 years later, I might add!

That's what you might call progress.

Janet Burton, Nr. Newark, Notts.

KNOW HOW YOU FEEL!

Oh, this silly school uniform we have
to wear,
Guaranteed to stand up to wear and tear,
The pleated skirt of a dull looking grey,
Seems more and more lifeless every day,
That horrible "tie" of yellow and red,
Would look better to me, if it was "tied
round my head,"
Then there's the cardigan and that great
white shirt,
"Not to be marked by a speck of dirt!"
And to top it all, there's the flat heeled
shoes,
No wonder we get the "School-uniform"
blues.

**Toni Elston,
Nottingham.**

TASTY GEEZER

On opening a sardine tin a few days ago, I noticed the words:- "Smoked Norwegian bristling in olive oil." Poor fella!

**Jackie Fan,
Enfield,
Middlesex.**

TEE-HEE

T-SHIRTS are still tops with us . . . wear them with your usual jeans or be really fashionable and wear them with shorts and stripy socks when the weather's warm enough. 'Smart' skirts are out as far as T-shirts go — choose thicker calico or denim instead.

1
Round-neck, long-sleeved T-shirt with 'sowers in the field' print, from Erica Budd. Style No.: 4650. Price: £2.60. Fabric: Cotton. Colours: Peach, brown, green, pink. Sizes: 1 to 3. From Jane Norman, Oxford Street, London W.1.; Peter Richards, Cheltenham and branches.

2
Stripy polo-neck in cotton jersey with long sleeves, from John Craig. Style No.: 355. Price: £4.50. Fabric: Cotton jersey. Colours: Assorted. Sizes: Small, medium and large. From Fenwicks of Newcastle; Army and Navy Stores, Victoria, London S.W.1.; Che Guevara, Kensington High Street, London W.8.; Sheltones, High Wycombe.

3
V-neck peachy T-shirt with lady print, from Erica Budd. Style No.: 4652. Price: £2.60. Fabric: Cotton. Colours: Beige, blue, peach, green. Sizes: 1 to 3. Stockists as for Fig. 1.

4
Super stripy top with long sleeves, hood and a pouch pocket at the front, from Chelsea Girl. Style No.: 191345. Price: £5.49. Fabric: Acrylic. Colours: Assorted. Sizes: 10 to 14. From most branches of Chelsea Girl.

5
Navy stripy velour top with cream collar, waist and cuffs, from John Craig. Style No.: 338. Price: £5.90. Fabric: Velour. Colours: Assorted. Sizes: Small, medium, large. Stockists as for Fig. 2.

6
Pink, round-neck T-shirt with long sleeves and flower vase print, from Tesco. Style No.: PO6866/8. Price: £1.75. Fabric: Cotton. Colours: Pink, blue, yellow. Sizes: 34 to 38. From larger Tesco Home 'N' Wear stores and departments within supermarkets.

7
Pale blue 'Gaiety Girl' print T-shirt with round neck and long sleeves, from Etam. Price: £1.99. Fabric: Cotton. Colours: Assorted. Sizes: 10 to 14. From main branches of Etam.

8
Bright red sweat-shirt with Oxford University print on the front, from Jean Junction. Price: £4.99. Fabric: Cotton. Colours: Assorted. Sizes: Small, medium, large. From Jean Junction, 337 Oxford Street, London W.1. and branches; By post from Jean Junction at the above address.

9
Cream, round-necked T-shirt with Gatsby print, from Etam. Price: £1.99. Fabric: Cotton. Colours: Assorted. Sizes: 10 to 14. From main branches of Etam.

10
Brown velour-look top with cream and brown knit neck, cuff and waist and two pockets at the front, from John Craig. Style No.: 336. Price: £7.00. Fabric: Velour. Colours: Assorted. Sizes: Small, medium and large. Stockists as for Fig. 2.

11
French cafe print T-shirt with plain long sleeves and round neck, from Etam. Price: £1.99. Fabric: Cotton. Colours: Assorted. Sizes: 10 to 14. From main branches of Etam.

12
Sizzling stripy T-shirt with elasticated waist, from Marshall Lester. Style No.: 1004. Price: £5.50. Fabric: Cotton. Colours: Brown, yellow and orange stripes. Sizes: One size only. By post from Marshall Lester, 50/52 Paul Street, London E.C.2. plus 20p extra for postage and packing.

All Prices Approximate

A JACKIE SPECIAL

WHAT MAKES US GO PINK

ALTHOUGH there are a few people who claim they never, ever do, most of us have to admit that there are times when we just can't help it! What am I talking about? Blushing, of course!

We all have our secret memories of the things that have made us blush — so we thought it would be interesting to find out some of those secrets!

Here in the "Jackie" Office we have some champion blushers — and you might be surprised to know, there are a few in the pop business as well! So here, specially for all you fellow blushers out there, are some ideas about what makes us go pink!

Suzanne Osmond.
(All the singing Osmonds are used to being in the public eye so they hardly ever blush. But it's different for Merrill, Alan and Wayne's wives!).
"I'm even shyer than Merrill's wife Mary, and I get embarrassed quite easily when I find a lot of people looking at me!
"The worst moment ever was just a few weeks after we got married, during our visit to Britain. In the middle of a press conference, Alan made me stand up in front of everyone while he introduced me!
"I still blush at the thought of it!"

Gary Glitter.
"When I fall over on my platform shoes on stage, I really go pink! It happens quite often too. I try to avoid that, because it's really embarrassing in front of all those people!"

Sandy.
"I go pink when boys I like phone me in the office, and everyone teases me about it!"

Noddy Holder.
"You may laugh, but I go pink when girls throw their underwear on stage during our stage act! Mind you, it's quite useful — I clean my guitars with them afterwards!
"The rest of the group agree with me that we all try not to blush. Instead, through our music and stage act, we try to make other people blush!"

Fiona.
"I blush when I'm with a boy who's so shy, I have to take the initiative when I'm with him!"

Sam.
"The most embarrassing thing I can think of is meeting a boy I like when I'm walking down the street wearing my tattiest clothes and no make-up!"

Bryan Ferry.
(Though you might not expect it, Bryan is actually quite a blushy type of person!
"The situation that's most likely to make me blush is when somebody remembers something that happened in my past — something I'd completely forgotten about! That always embarrasses me.
"But I'm a quiet blusher. I don't go dark red or anything like that!"

Alison.
"I get really embarrassed about money mix-ups! I hate anything to do with money, especially when it goes wrong. That's when I go really pink!"

Barry Blue.
"I go pink when someone says something nice about me in front of me!"

Cathy.
"When I've told a lie, and I get found out — that's when I go pink all over!"

Claire.
"What makes me blush is going into a room full of strangers, and finding everyone looking at me!"

Woody (Bay City Rollers).
"I can't help blushing when I first go onstage and see girls screaming at us, because I'm really quite shy.
"After a bit I start getting involved in the stage act and I forget about it. But I always get a bit embarrassed at first."

Sheila.
"It's really embarrassing when a boy finds out that you fancy him, especially at school, because you have to meet him every day!"

Roger Taylor (Queen).
"Not remembering people's names always embarrasses me. And I never do, unless it's repeated to me about six times!
"I always try to avoid using the person's name, but it's a problem if I have to introduce them to someone!"

Ingrid.
"I go all blushy when a boy looks intently into my eyes. I get all hot and bothered, and have to look away!"

Pete.
"I never, ever blush or go red. I'm un-embarrassable!"
(What about the time you came out with David Cassidy after one of his concerts, made a daring leap for his escape car — and missed?! — The Ed.).

A FASHION & BEAUTY SPECIAL OUTWARD

Football crazy

When he suggests taking you to a football match, you'll have to be prepared for anything. You'll want to be warm and comfortable, but look good enough for him to be proud of you at the same time!

Heavy-knit cardi with short sleeves, cable front, collar and two pockets, from Woolworth. Style No.:415/5. Price: £2.99. Fabric: Acrylic. Colours: Emerald, white, navy. Sizes: 36 to 40. From larger Woolworth stores.

Ribby-front shirt with two button cuff, from Dorothy Perkins. Style No.: 9013. Price: £3.50. Fabric: Jersey. Colours: Assorted. Sizes: 10 to 16. From all branches of Dorothy Perkins.

Brown zip-front trousers with two slant pockets, from British Home Stores. Style No.: 7323/3175. Price: £3.75. Fabric: Cotton. Colours: Blue, brown and cream. Sizes: 10 to 18. From most branches of British Home Stores.

Stripy knee socks from a huge selection by Sunarama. Price: 85p. Fabric: Acrylic. Colours: Blue/Cream/Rust stripes. Sizes: One size. From leading shops and stores throughout the country, or by post from Janet Girsman Promotions, 34 St George Street, Hanover Square, London W1R 9FA plus 10p for postage and packing.

Cork wedge clog with brown upper from Curtess. Style No.: A9280. Price: £4.99. Fabric: Synthetic. Colours: Brown, black, beige. Sizes: 3 to 8. From main Curtess branches.

MAKE-UP

If he's the healthy, outdoor type, he won't want to drag a ghost-like, pale little you around. If you're a bit on the white side, try a little fake tan or just add a blush with the help of Miners Cream Blusher in Damask (20p).

Go easy on the eye make-up (just a trace of shadow and mascara will do). Use something like Boots 17 Eye Sheen in Brown, 24p, to cover the lids and outline the socket with a brown crayon for extra effect.

ambles through the brambles

MAKE-UP

Soft, smooth lips, healthy cheeks and pretty eyes are the answers here. Use plenty of moisturiser before you go out to protect your skin from the elements and don't use too much blusher if it's windy as you're likely to go red anyway.

Use a lip gloss instead of thick lipstick . . . Leichner make a tremendous one called Kissers Lip Shiners, in loads of colours. We like the Shine Natural one to make lips look shiny or Shine Rose to give you some colour!

If it's at all windy and your eyes are the kind that water easily, use a tearproof or waterproof mascara like Max Factor's Comb On Mascara, in Black, Brown, Brownish Black, Navy, Plum Burgundy and Midnight Green, 62p each.

No need to go prepared for mountain-climbing when he asks you to go for a walk, but it's best to wear a pair of shoes that'll keep you going. Trousers are best, with a warm jumper and a nice jacket over the top.

Canvas-look jacket with buttons and tailored collar, from a range of jackets at Marks and Spencer. No style no. Price: Approx. £12. Fabric: Cotton. Colours: Blue, brown and cream. Sizes: 10 to 16. From a range of jackets at major branches of Marks and Spencer.

Cabled polo-neck with long sleeves, from Dorothy Perkins. Style No.: 3321. Price: £3.50. Fabric: Acrylic. Colours: Navy, brown, ecru, pale blue. Sizes: Small and medium. From all branches of Dorothy Perkins.

Blue trousers with front zip and flap detail at waist, from City Swingers. Style No.: T1084. Price: £8.00. Fabric: Vincel/polyester. Colours: Sage, grey, airforce, black, brown, camel. Sizes: 10 to 14. From S & U Stores, Birmingham: Jane's Roundabout, Romford, Essex; Merel, Notting Hill Gate.

BOUND!

LOOK your best on every occasion, know what to wear to look good *and* feel good. We tell you how to feel part of the crowd in your own special way!

Tea With His Mum

MAKE-UP

Mums *do* like make-up, you know, not too much of course, but a touch of colour here and there won't go amiss. Keep eye make-up soft and pretty, Leichner's Eyes of Sky or Eyes of Grey in the Kamera Klear cream powder shadow range (42p each) are really nice.

Mums tend to notice the less obvious things, though, like finger-nails, tidy (or untidy) hair, whether your shoes and bag are clean and your tights are hole-less! Nails should be tidy and well-kept, hair well-cut and clean!

No need to panic when you finally meet his mum. Wear something simple that she'll like, but make sure it's fashionable and pretty enough for him as well. She'll probably be seeing you again, so be yourself from the very beginning!

Brown knee-length dress with floral print, tie belt and long sleeves, from Dorothy Perkins. Style No.: 0115. Price: £6.99. Fabric: Rayon. Colours: Green, brown, black. Sizes: 10 to 16. From all branches of Dorothy Perkins.

Brown patent T-bar shoe from Freeman Hardy Willis. Style No.: A4229. Price: £5.99. Fabric: Synthetic. Colours: Brown, navy. Sizes: 3 to 8. From main branches of Freeman, Hardy Willis.

Wining & Dining

If you're meeting him for lunch, you may be wondering what to wear. You want to dress up, but you don't want to look as though you're off to the disco!

Trousers and jackets are still popular because they're so nice and easy to wear, but you could always choose a jacket and skirt if you'd rather. Dress up with one or two bangles, but leave off earrings, heavy necklaces or too many rings.

Blue trouser suit with one-button jacket, tailored jacket and smart trousers, from Littlewoods. Style No.: 70013. Price: £12.50. Fabric: 100% viscose. Colours: Beige, brown, navy. Sizes: 10 to 16. From major branches of Littlewoods.

Cream long-sleeved shirt with two pockets, from Dorothy Perkins. Style No.: 9063. Price: £2.99. Fabric: Polyester/cotton. Colours: White, green, cream, navy, brown. Sizes: 10 to 16. From all branches of Dorothy Perkins.

Blue patent-look shoe with full front, from True-Form. Style No.: A4519. Price: £5.99. Fabric: Synthetic. Colours: Navy and brown. Sizes: 3 to 8. From main branches of True Form.

MAKE-UP

Be clever with your make-up, remember it's day-time and you don't want to put him off his food, so choose your colours carefully. Match your eye colours with the main colour you're wearing, rather than your eyes, Boots 17's new Rocknumbers are really nice, choose the Hard Rock Eye Kit containing three powder shadows, Tourmaline Blue Marble/Granite (35p) or Boots No. 7 new Shadow Mist colours in Mushroom or Town Brown 35p.

Match lips and nails with Miners new Seashore Colours For lips choose from Shrimp, Scampi or Beachcomber 30p (18p for the small size), for nails choose from Catch-a Crab, Starfish, Oyster, Beachcomber or Lobster, 30p.

PATCHWORK

OUT IN THE OPEN A Jackie Recipe

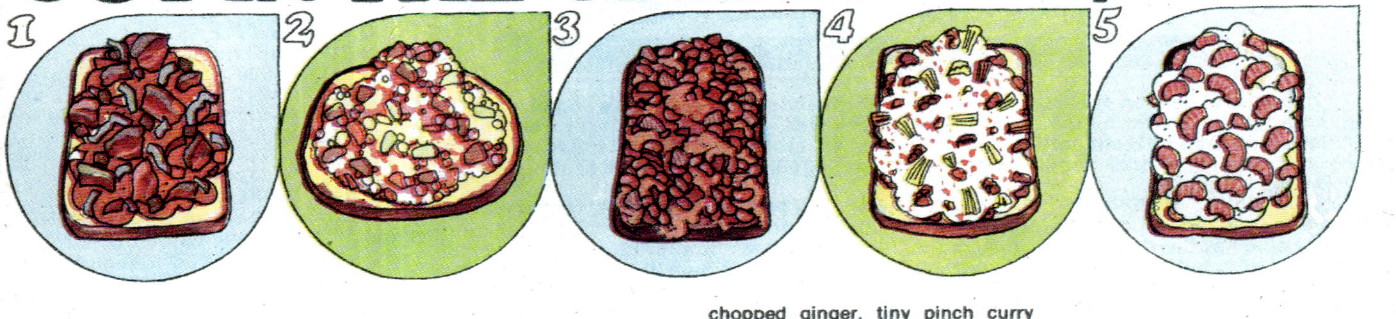

When you're hungry, but can't be bothered waiting for something to cook, open sandwiches are the answer. They're tasty, filling and very easy to make!

Here's a selection of tasty recipes — think up your own variations!

From left to right, they are:

1. Four tablespoonfuls peanut butter, 2 tablespoonfuls chopped, well-grilled bacon, and 2 tablespoonfuls coleslaw, on brown toast.

2. 4 oz. cottage cheese, 1 oz. chopped ginger, tiny pinch curry powder on french bread.

3. This is a toasted one — don't eat it cold! 1 small tin beans, 2 oz. grated cheese, 1 tablespoonful chopped onion and 1 chopped tomato, on toast.

4. 2 oz. cream cheese, 1 oz. chopped walnuts, 2 tablespoonfuls chopped pineapple, a little chopped peach, on fruit loaf.

5. 1 small tin prawns, 3 tablespoonfuls plain yogurt, 1 teaspoonful Worcester sauce on rye bread.

Karen Ruth Debbie
Ann Sharon Jane

ALL YOUR OWN!

Just the thing to make your stationery that little bit more personal — this attractive "named" writing paper by Janet Girsman promotions.

Personal stationery like this usually costs quite a lot, but with this special offer, you get all of 100 sheets, each one printed with the name of your choice, for only £1.25 (this covers postage and packing costs too). The sheets are 8¼ inches x 6 inches, so you can see they're a reasonable size.

To get your paper, send a postal order for £1.25 to Janet Girsman Promotions Ltd., 34 George Street, Hanover Square, London W1R 9FA, not forgetting to give your name and address, and of course, the name you want on the paper! Please allow about three weeks for delivery.

Easy

. . . that's what these ideas from Sellotape are! To make these super items for your room, all you do is: 1. Collect a selection of old tins, jars, etc. and wash and dry. 2. Cover the outside of the containers completely with fabric of your choice, glueing it in place with dabs of Sellostic glue. Decorate the edges with bands of Sellotape plastic tape in a colour to match your fabric. And that's it! You now have a whole new range of jewel boxes, cotton wool containers, waste paper bins . . . see? We told you it was as easy as pie!

PIN-UPS!

Looking for an interesting hobby to fill in those winter evenings? Try new "Pin Pictures" by Airfix. Even if you're not in the least bit artistic, you'll find it easy. All you do is simply pin some coloured sequins and discs onto the black background. Simple! And the effect is really stunning — a shimmering, sparkling picture which everyone will admire. And if you start now, you could even make up a picture in time for someone's Christmas present!

"Pin Pictures" are available from craft stores and toy shops, price £1.95. There's a choice of six designs too — "Flower Arrangements" (as shown), "Peacock Plumes," "Oriental Lady," "Mountain Hut," "Carriage Ride," and "Dragon."

YOUR PATCH

Got an old umbrella which you think is past its best? Don't throw it out – follow the advice of "Jackie" reader Julie Moore, of Wednesbury, and re-vamp your brolly! Julie suggests that you first get hold of a really old umbrella – if there isn't one in the house, you'll probably find one at a jumble sale. Now, cut out a selection of flowers or other shapes from sticky backed "Fablon," and decorate your umbrella with them. If there are any holes in your brolly, so much the better, 'cos you can cover them up with flowers and make it waterproof again!

Now paint the handle of the umbrella in a bright colour, add a gay tassel, and you're all set to sing in the rain!

Got any bright ideas for "Your Patch"? Then send them to "Your Patch," Jackie, 185 Fleet Street, London EC4A 2HS. We'll pay £1 for every idea printed!

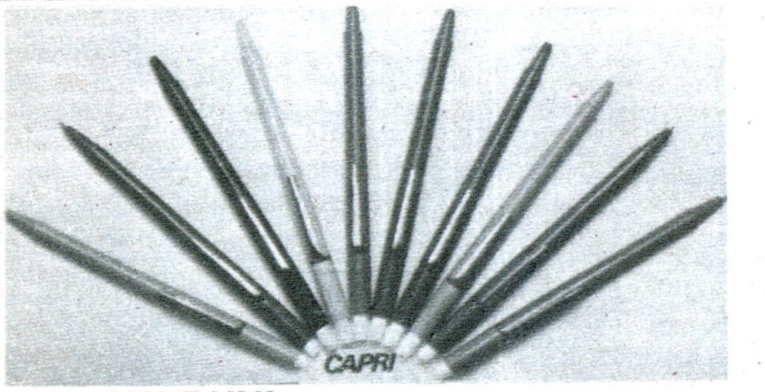

BARGAIN BUY!

Our best buy of the week award definitely goes to these new "Capri" pens by Tempo. Why? Well, Capri pens have some rather special features built in.

For example, they're moulded all in one piece, without the usual plug at the end which pen-chewers find irresistibly easy to chew up and swallow! There's also a large cap which has a flat end for telephone dialling — saves your nails! Capri pens are made from extra tough plastic which makes them difficult to break, and what's more, the ink's extra long-lasting too.

Capri pens come in three ink colours (black, blue or red) with a choice of medium or fine points. And the most amazing thing about them is that they cost just 12p and 8p each.

Available now from most stationers and newsagents.

Meet Archie The Octopus!

More magic from Bowater Scott, the tissue people who come up with all those super ideas for paper decorations, flowers, etc. "Archie The Octopus" is easy to construct, and makes a great mobile for your room.

You'll need a box of "Man Size Scotties," pipe cleaners, glue, ribbon and rubber bands.

To make his head, make a ball of tissue and cover smoothly with two layers of Man Size Scotties. Secure at the neck with a rubber band.

For the legs: take two pipe-cleaners and join them, end to end. Place diagonally across the corner of a tissue, and roll the tissue tightly round. Glue down loose tip of tissue. Repeat once to make sure pipe cleaner is completely covered. Now repeat this seven times to make eight legs.

Flatten the neck of the Octopus and trim off surplus tissue. Secure ends of legs under the neck with glue. Arrange legs, paint face and tie a jaunty ribbon bow round the neck. And there you are!

SNOOPIFIED!

Good news for all Snoopy fans. We've found some super new Snoopy products for you! From "The Gladhand" company comes a whole range of calendars, jewellery, patches, keyrings – all with the unmistakable Snoopy on them! They're ideal for presents, or just little gifts to cheer yourself up. We've shown a Flip-over keyring (55p plus 12p postage and packing,) a Stick-On Snoopy (40p plus 12p p.p.) and a Snoopy patch (50p plus 12p p.p.) – just a few of the items available. Watch this page for details of more products soon!

The above articles are all available by mail order from "The Gladhand Ltd.", 9 Gorst Road, London NW10 6LA. (There's a postage and packing charge of 12p on each article.)

A JACKIE QUIZ

DO YOU SEE YOURSELF AS OTHERS SEE YOU?

YOU can never be certain of what people think of you — you may imagine yourself to be a perfect saint, while others see you as the perfect opposite! So we've devised a crafty way of getting a picture of the impression you make on people.

Just answer our quiz — truthfully! Each answer has a corresponding letter or number, in brackets after it. Shade in the matching letter or number in the diagram at the end to find out the secrets of your image!

1 **How would you describe the usual state of your bedroom?**
In a mess even inside cupboards and drawers. (5)
Slightly messy at first glance, but there *is* a proper place for everything. (24)
Neat and tidy. (E)

2 **Your friend borrows 40p, and doesn't repay you next time you see her. What would you do?**
Forget all about it. (14)
Try to think of some way of hinting, so she won't be embarrassed. (G)
Ask her for it, nicely. (9)

3 **Do you have nightmares?**
Yes, often or fairly often. (A)
Not since you were a child, or rarely. (2)
Only after horror films or cheesey suppers! (3)

4 **A boy you really fancy asks you out, but on the date you find you're really bored by his company! What do you do?**
Make an excuse and cut the evening short, and don't arrange to see him again. (17)
Hope things will be better next time. (F)
Suggest doing something different that may fit in better with his mood. (20)

5 **Which colours do you prefer to wear?**
Bright, strong colours like red and sunshine yellow. (12)
Soft subtle shades like pink, grey and beige. (L)
Dramatic shades like black and purple. (15)

6 **How many of the following types of people do you regularly kiss or hug? Parents, close relatives, boyfriends, small children, close friends of either sex.**
One group only. (D)
Two or three groups. (19)
More than three groups. (18)

7 **A child seems to be drowning in the park lake, and you're the only person who notices. What would you do?**
Dive straight in. (4)
Scream. (7)
Dither. (J)
Run to the park-keeper's hut. (22)
Grab the nearest male and get him to go to the rescue. (13)
Go away, thinking you're probably mistaken anyway. (C)

8 **You're meeting your boyfriend's mum for the first time. From his description, you don't think you're going to get on. Would you take a gift, though you're only going for tea?**
Yes — an expensive bunch of flowers. (H)
Yes — a cheap box of chocolates. (21)
No. (16)

9 **Do you say things you don't mean to, like telling people something you meant to keep secret?**
Never. (B)
Occasionally. (8)
Quite often. (23)

10 **If an enormous party was being arranged, which would you rather do?**
Organise it, help with food, invites and so on. (10)
Go, as a guest. (1)
Have nothing to do with it. (K)

11 **Which dog appeals to you most?**
A spaniel. (M)
An alsatian. (11)
A terrier. (6)

Now fill in the appropriate squares, and read the answers at the bottom of the page to discover the secrets of your personality!

1	E	3	5	F	7
G	2	4	6	8	H
9	10	A	B	12	11
13	14	C	D	16	15
J	18	20	22	24	K
17	L	19	21	M	23

CONCLUSIONS

All you have to do is look at the way your diagram is shaded in and match it with one of the following patterns! Don't worry if your drawing doesn't fit in exactly with any of these, just pick the nearest one to yours.

A square in the centre, with nothing round the edges, means that you have a very positive nature, with a warm, generous personality and enough imagination to help you understand other people's problems. You make a very good first impression as you're lively enough to make people want to get to know you better!

The thing people remember most about you is probably something physical, like your bright smile, twinkling eyes or impulsive giggle! We don't think you'd want to change much about yourself, but if you do yearn to have a moody, smouldering personality — well you could try stubbing your toe, hard, just before you meet people!

A central dark square and shaded areas towards each corner means that you're a very shy, quiet person. In fact you probably don't make much of a first impression at all — people may not realise you're there! (You have lots of imagination though so use it!) Don't allow yourself to be self-centred and only concerned with your own problems. Stop worrying what other people think of you, and concentrate instead on being more outgoing and having a good time.

If you give yourself half a chance, the thing most people will remember about you is your sympathy and your quiet sense of humour.

If there is no real pattern to your diagram with bits everywhere, this means (as you might guess) that you're quite a mixed-up person — in the nicest way possible, of course! You probably make a very good first impression, as you're bright and breezy and naturally interested in everything going on around you. Your only problem is that you tend to lose interest very quickly, jumping about from one new idea to another, leaving a trail of unfinished projects and confused friends behind you!

So if you want people to keep that good first impression of you, make an effort to stick at things more — your efforts will pay off and you'll be a much happier and more fulfilled person!

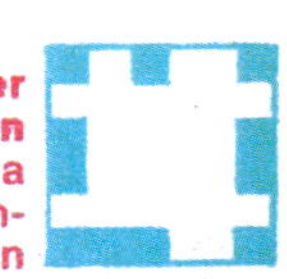

Squares round the outer edges, hardly anything in centre at all — you have a strong, dramatic personality and a similar effect on people — they either love you or hate you, there's no happy medium! If you're one of the lucky ones, you'll be having lots of fun with plenty of close friends. If not, though, you could feel very lonely at times, and that means that your first impression is a very negative one — people instinctively shy away from you. This may be because you scare them or upset them by handing out too many "home truths." Not a good habit unless you know the person very well!

If this is the case, you should try to think before you speak and imagine how you'd feel in their shoes. And then the things people will remember about you will be your ideas, your energy and the fact that you're a girl going places.

PLEASE MR POSTMAN...

A SAM SPECIAL ON PENPALS

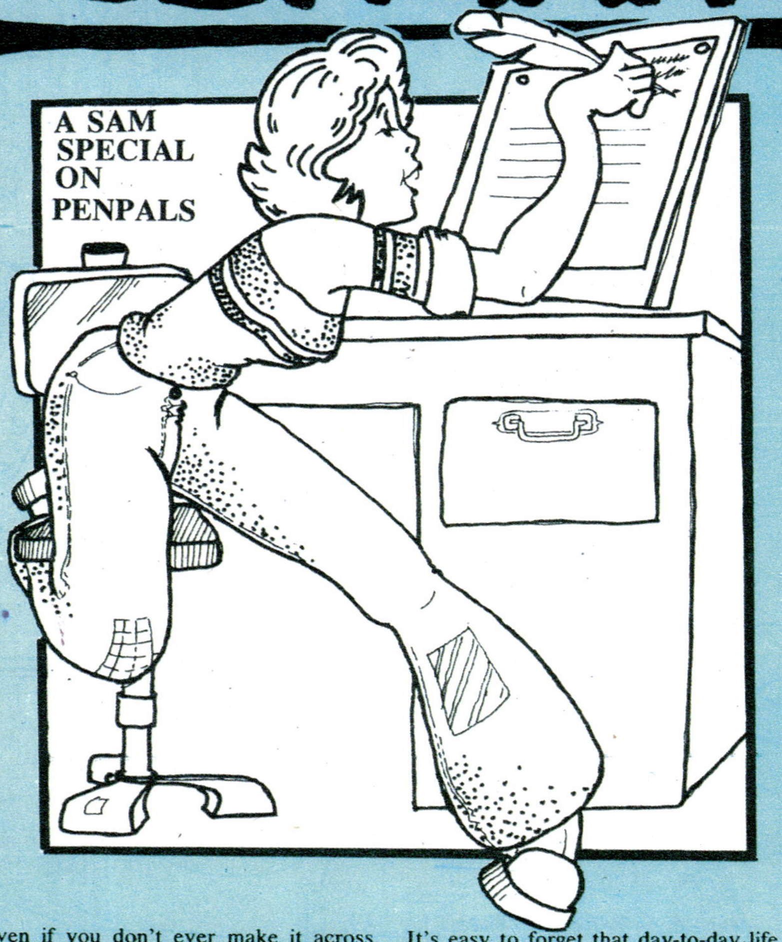

So you're dying to write to someone. You're taken with the idea of scribbling great screeds of news to this distant stranger who you know is just waiting to receive them. And — even better — how great to have all those envelopes full of friendly chat plopping regularly through the letter box, all for you! But, meanwhile, it's me who's been getting all your letters — asking how to go about getting you a penpal. So here's all the info !

Nobody really knows what first sparked off the idea of 'Penfriendship.' But nowadays, of course, it's a thriving activity, and people are linking up not only in the ever-popular European countries but as far afield as Japan, New Zealand, or even Surinam. It's always good to find new friends who have the same sort of interests as you, but with a penpal you start off with the great advantage of getting together because you *know* you'll have the same interests! It's great to hear from someone else who thinks David Essex is gorgeous — yet probably gets very different pictures of him; or somebody who also goes youth hostelling every summer — but nowhere like the Lake District!

Of course, there can occasionally be more to it all than just friendship — there's also the possibility of finding romance! Romances "by letter" aren't as fleeting as holiday romances, nor do they have the pressures of day-to-day ones. After all — he'll always listen to you, and you'll be able to pick and choose carefully what you want him to hear! It's not unusual for penpal romances to get quite serious — but don't pin all your hopes on a penfriend if a romance starts developing between you — he may, after all, meet someone at home, and stop writing, or you may meet up to discover after all that you're totally unsuitable! So do try to keep things *fairly* casual until you've met — that way you'll avoid any possible disappointment. By the way, if you are interested in the romance angle . . . there are thousands of unmarried young British soldiers out in Germany . . !

Romantic reasons apart, there are loads of other goodies to be had from a penpal. A major one is the chance to travel: if you want to visit a particular country, it's far nicer to have a friend to go and stay with, and a family there who can help you see the place from a very different angle to the usual package-deal tourist one. And of course, writing letters is an ideal way for shy people to make friends — there are none of the pressures of having to talk to someone face to face!

Even if you don't ever make it across the Atlantic or the Asian deserts — or even the Channel — you'll most likely pick up all sorts of fascinating information about the place where your penpal lives.

It's easy to forget that day-to-day life can be totally different from life here — in the way people live, work, enjoy themselves and generally think about things. Hearing first hand about Christmas beach parties at a temperature of 90° in Sydney, or going to a school in California where jeans and sneakers are the usual "uniform" can really bring the point home to you! And those boring old school French lessons will seem a lot different, too, when you start reading letters from a real, live French boy! And don't worry if your foreign languages aren't quite perfect. Your penpal will probably get just as much of a laugh reading your grammatical howlers as you do from theirs!

Just one point to remember — penfriendship *can* be very time-consuming, especially if you have several penfriends, so it's no good joining a penfriend club if you're snowed under with schoolwork or go out dancing every night. You'll only get a guilty conscience about all those unanswered letters piling up! (If you join a penpal club, they circulate your name on their news-sheets, so you never know who you're going to hear from next.) I remember going through agonies when I used to get around five or six letters a week from all over the world, and I knew I'd never have time to answer them properly!

Postage costs can prove pretty hefty, too, if you're writing to quite a few people, so bear this in mind, before you commit yourself. It's better to start off writing to one person and then 'acquire' more people later.

Anyway, if you want to get to know a Sparks fan in Singapore, a table-tennis champion in Turkey, a drummer in Denmark or a postcard collector in Poland, here's how to go about it:
Send your name, address and details of the kind of person you'd like to write to (male, female, age, nationality etc.) with a stamped addressed envelope (this is most important) to the following:-

International Friendship League, 16 Beaulieu Road, Portsmouth PQ2 ODN. or: **Teenage Penpal Club, Falcon House, Burnley, Lancashire.**

If you specifically want to write to a soldier, the "Union Jack" magazine, which is circulated to British Forces in Germany, will try to print your details on their penpals page. Write to:
The Editor, The Union Jack, C/o F.P.O. Hamm, British Forces Post Office 103, Germany.

But remember, we can take no responsibility for any correspondence entered into.

Hope this helps you find a lasting friendship — and remember, I'll want lots of lovely letters telling me all about your penfriends!

YOU KNOW YOU'VE GOT A FRIEND WHEN...

. . . She gives your telephone number to the dishy boy who asks for it!

. . . She deliberately misses her bus so you can stand and talk while you wait for yours.

. . . You went to the party with her, but when he asks if he can take you home, she fades away like snow!

. . . She doesn't let on to your mum whose idea it was to go to that notorious new disco.

. . . She lets you know you've got lipstick on your teeth *before* you smile dazzlingly round at all the talent.

. . . She tells you about the dress she can't afford, but would suit you down to the ground — while there's still time to buy it.

. . . You can talk and talk and talk for hours and it only seems like minutes.

. . . You can pop round to each other's house at any time and you're always glad to see each other.

. . . You can insult each other without hurting each others' feelings.

. . . She doesn't start asking for her Slade record back the very next day.

. . . After your boyfriend drops you, *she* cries!

. . . She gets David Essex's autograph — for you!

. . . She says 'what spots?' when you're complaining about your complexion.

. . . Not a soul is gossiping about your secret three weeks after you told her.

. . . She doesn't yawn once while you're telling her about your new boyfriend — for three solid hours!

. . . You can introduce her to your latest boyfriend without a qualm.

. . . You never feel ashamed or envious of each other.

. . . She gives up sweets when you're slimming.

. . . You can laugh about 'old times' together.

. . . You accept each other for what you are, and don't try to change *anything!*

FAN CLUBS

Wizzard Watch'a Society, 29 Mulberry Road, Bournville, Birmingham B30 1SX

Jackson Five, c/o Caroline Schloss, 9 Ranelagh Close, Edgware, Middlesex.

Sparks Fan Club, c/o Joseph, 8 Basing Street, London W.11.

Mud, c/o Linda, 4th Floor, 62 Shaftesbury Avenue, London W.1.

David Cassidy, c/o Susie Miller, 58 Parker Street, London WC2

Enclose a stamped addressed envelope when writing.

THE CATHY AND CLAIRE PAGE

If there's anything worrying you which you can't work out for yourself, why not drop us a line? Address it to Cathy & Claire, at Jackie, 12 Fetter Lane, Fleet Street, London, E.C.4.

DEAR CATHY & CLAIRE—I can't make friends at school. I used to go around with a girl called Maureen, but she moved to a school in another district, so I only see her during the holidays now.

I'm in fourth year and all the rest of my classmates have their own special friends and I don't want to butt in or split anyone up. I always feel out of things and it's no fun going to galas and things on my own. Some girls take pity on me and include me sometimes, but it never lasts and I'm left on my own again.

I'm beginning to hate school because of this. Do you think I should leave if I'm not happy?

No, we don't think you should leave school. Are you SURE you're trying hard enough to make new friends? Have you joined the drama clubs, the debating society or the swimming club? You may not make friends in your own year, but you *will* meet people—we guarantee it!

And look at it this way, luv. It's the *work* you do at school that's important, not your popularity rating.

DEAR CATHY & CLAIRE—I like this bloke called Sandy, and he's started taking an interest in me. The thing is all my friends are very catty to him and make it plain they don't like him one bit.

For the past few weeks I have been going along with their opinion, because I never thought I'd have a chance with him. But if I suddenly start declaring how lovely he is, they'll all turn on me and call me "two-faced" which I'm not. I really like him, but I don't want to make any enemies.

If your friends act like that, who needs enemies?

Why do you think your pals don't like him? Bet we can guess. They all secretly admire him (just like you did) and don't want to admit it in case they don't get off with him.

Go ahead and encourage him. And if you do go out with him, you'll know for *yourself* what he's really like. If your mates act up, take it in your stride—it's probably jealousy, but they'll get over it. Don't spoil your chances with Sandy because of what your friends say. You've got a mind of your own haven't you?

We think it was pretty dumb of you to say you didn't like him because of what they said—the poor bloke's getting a reputation he knows nothing about—and all because of some neurotic females. Go out with him and spread it around what a great guy he is. We think he deserves it.

DEAR CATHY & CLAIRE—I wear glasses and that in itself isn't a problem, as I don't think they look too bad on me, it's just that I don't know what to do with them when a boy asks me to dance.

If I don't wear them, I can't see a thing, but if I keep them on while I dance, they dig into the boy, so I'm not relaxed because I'm trying to avoid him all the time. Do you think I ought to hold them in my hand while I dance, or will that look stupid?

Please help, and don't suggest I buy contact lenses because I'm 14 and couldn't possibly afford them.

This needs a leetle bit of cunning and female ingenuity. You realise specs suit you, so play them up to their best advantage. So they dig into him a bit—make a joke of it! A boy appreciates a girl who can laugh at herself, and anyway, if you get that close to him, they can't be such a disadvantage, can they? And surely a little thing like a nudge from your specs isn't going to put him off if he's really keen?

Explain to him before you start dancing that you'd take 'em off but he'd probably end up with 10 cracked toes if you do—we're pretty sure he'll see the sense in that!

DEAR CATHY & CLAIRE—My friend just doesn't seem to want to meet any boys. Every time we meet a couple of lads who seem keen, she puts them off by being purposely catty and bitchy (which is quite unlike her), and if they ever get as far as asking us out, she puts them down in a very nasty way. They never stick around long and I don't blame them.

If I tell her I fancy a certain boy, she'll do anything to keep me away from him or put him off, with the result that I'm 15 and have only been out with one boy! (That was before I started going around with her).

She's a great friend in every other way, but she just seems to have an aversion to meeting any members of the opposite sex. I've tried talking to her, but she changes the subject. She won't even speak about boys.

She's got a giant-size inferiority complex, luv. She probably feels she wouldn't stand a chance of getting a boyfriend, and it's probably because of you! You sound very confident and well-adjusted to boys, so your friend most likely feels that she can't keep up to you. We reckon she's so cripplingly shy, she feels no boy could possibly want to know her, so she shuns away, which is wrong, very wrong.

Try building up her confidence very gradually. Get her to go to a youth club with you, have a beauty parley and try to brighten her up a bit, and make her look attractive, and *convince* her she's okay. It's up to you, as her best friend, to bring her out of her shell.

She is getting too dependent on you, and this is bad for your relationship. You must both get out and meet new people, and not just go out together all the time. Never get rid of a boyfriend just to please her—don't let her ruin your social life, too.

DEAR CATHY & CLAIRE—My boyfriend is the same age as me, 16, and he behaves very childishly. We go around in a crowd most nights, and there is nothing Phil likes better than showing off. Nothing is too outrageous, and I've never known him to refuse a dare yet.

I usually laugh like all the others, but his behaviour does worry me sometimes. He also has another side to his character that no-one sees except me. Sometimes he is so withdrawn and moody, I just can't get through to him. It's as if there's some kind of barrier blocking any kind of communication between us.

Phil's motto seems to be "Laugh and the world laughs with you." He feels so unsure of himself, so insecure, that he thinks he must always have some sort of facade—whether it's playing the fool or being so hyper-sensitive no-one can get through this shell he has built around himself.

Most young people go through this phase—they feel they must always prove themselves—but they usually grow out of that when they realise that no-one expects them to be perfect or super-human.

Don't nag or mock Phil—he'll only go deeper into his shell. Build up his confidence. Tell him how marvellous he is, and let him know that you appreciate having him around.

He'll grow out of his daredevil phase—that's unimportant—but try to coax him out of his black moods. And don't go out with the crowd so much. Have plenty of time to get to know one another. He'll drop his defences when he sees you really care about *him*, good or bad, and don't just want him around when he plays the comedian.

DEAR CATHY & CLAIRE—I'm 14 and badly want to go to college when I leave school. Art is my best subject and my art teacher encourages me a lot, so I'd like to have a career to do with that.

The trouble is, my parents are dead against it. They say I have to leave school next year and get a job to help out at home. I just can't get through to them that this is something really important to me and that I could do well if I have the correct training.

We're not that badly off, although there are three younger than me and the thought of a dreary office job or working in a factory repels me. Please tell me what to do for the best as we keep having rows about it and it's making me very unhappy.

When somebody has an obvious talent for something and is getting forced into something they don't want to do, it's very frustrating. The fact that you're encouraged at school means you can make something of yourself in that line of work, and we think it's a crying shame to see talent being wasted.

We sympathise, but we think you should also look at it from your parents' point of view. Their reasons are obviously financial—the fact that you don't think so is probably due to your mother's good management!

We suggest that you ask your art teacher to have a talk with your parents and let them know that your chance of success in this field is very real. If they decide to let you stay on, they will be giving up a lot for you, and we hope you appreciate it, and do your bit to help, too. A Saturday job, for instance, would provide you with your own pocket money and keep you in tights and all the little extras that you take for granted, but which raise the bill for your parents that little bit higher.

Find out from your careers officer at school about grants for further education—we're pretty sure you'd qualify. And don't be afraid to give up a few things. It's all in the cause of Art! Good luck!

THIS IS THE KIND OF PERSON I AM....

TOMORROW will be my new beginning. If I had a pound for every time I said that, I'd be rich.

Let me tell you the kind of person I am. I'm weak. And I'm lazy. And I'm honest.

I can sit down and quite calmly and cold-bloodedly draw up a list of all the things that are wrong with me. I'm overweight. I daydream too much. I'm sloppy about my looks and careless about my schoolwork. O.K., so I plan. I get hold of a copy of the latest quickie diet.

And I plot out a timetable for myself: so many minutes a day to be spent getting my appearance up to scratch. So many hours to be spent improving my mind: learning French, perhaps.

Fine. Tomorrow will see the start of the new high-speed beautiful me. And being a lazy time-killing slob, tomorrow never comes.

Maybe it would be easier for me to accept my true nature if I wasn't surrounded by a family of keenies: a father and four brothers who hike and hill climb. A mother and sister who think an evening's telly-viewing's wasted if they haven't managed at the same time to run up at least one stunning garment apiece.

They worry about me, my family. They see me slouch, evening after evening, in the direction of my bedroom with a huge box of chocolates to sustain me. They can't quite come to terms with someone so close to them whose ideal of physical activity is turning over the pages of a book and getting to work on a caramel.

I'm 16, after all. Shouldn't I be out dancing at some discotheque? Covering thirty miles in a sponsored walk? Maybe. They could be right. I'll start making like a regular whizz-kid soon. Say tomorrow?

The thing is, I've always been the family dreamer so my mother can't console herself with the thought that I'm going through a phase. If I am, it's one that looks like lasting all my life.

I'm sure she thinks I'll pull myself together—my family's favourite phase—when I fall in love. I thought so, too, at one time. But I've got news for both of us. It hasn't worked.

I'm in love at the moment. His name is Dave. He's two years older than I am. We met at a party my sister dragged me to, and in the classic tradition bells rang, birds sang, and my heart felt fit to burst.

How can I describe him? Well, he's gorgeous. The outdoor type. A touch of the Robert Redfords, maybe.

The thing is, he likes me. He's asked me out a couple of times on casual dates. No great big, hearts-and-flowers romance but at least he likes me. It's a start.

If I had any sense I'd be taking myself in hand right now and working like fury to get my weight down, clear up my spots, and brush up on my tennis technique. (I did say he's the outdoor type).

I don't have any sense. I find myself even more dreamy than before, because now I have something to dream about: Dave.

The more I think about him, the more I'm convinced I love him. The more I think I love him, the more I despair that he'll ever love me, since he has another girl friend or two on the string.

The more despairing I get, the more chocolate I eat. The more chocolate I eat, the fatter I get. The fatter I get, the lazier I become. The more I'm lazy, the more I dream . . . it's a vicious circle.

My sister says that anyone can do anything if they want to hard enough. Well, I want to win Dave's love. I want that more than anything else in the world right now. But I don't see it happening at the rate I'm going.

I'm trying to change. I know that Dave likes long hair, so I'm growing mine. He says I'd look a knockout if I lost just half-a-stone, so I'm determined I'm going to stick to my diet.

He likes pretty hands, so I'm going to stop nibbling my nails. He likes all kinds of sport so I'm furiously trying to work up the enthusiasm and energy to like it too. Oh, the things I'm going to do, the supergirl I'm going to become . . . starting, of course, tomorrow!

LOOK OUT

LOOK out for everything that's exciting and new and start thinking about Christmas . . . it's just around the corner!

ALL-IN-ONE

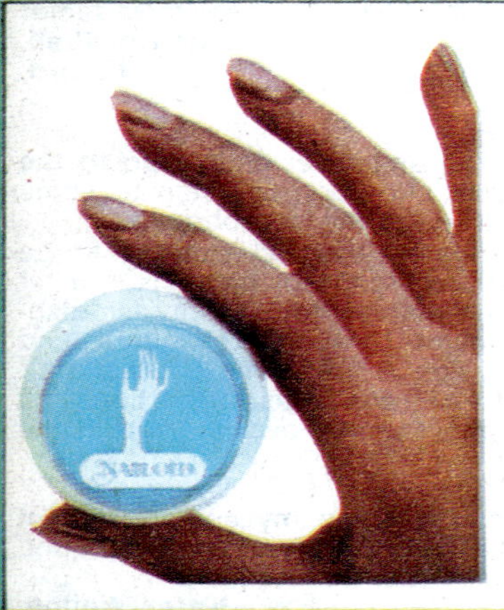

Give yourself a manicure with Nailoid's new all-in-one manicure cream. It helps to strengthen, nourish and condition the nails, while softening the cuticles at the same time.

Follow the instructions carefully and help to keep your nails in tip-top condition all the time. Nailoid cream costs 18p, or 33p for the economy size from chemists and department stores.

If your nails are flaky and just won't grow past your finger-tips, try using a nail strengthener like Mavala, 69p, Woltz Gro-Coat 75p, or Sally Hansen's Hard as Nails, 35p. Use them regularly according to the instructions on the bottle, for longer, tougher nails!

ONE . . . TWO . . . THREE

Trio is a brand new fragrance from No. 7. It's young, French and very subtle, a blend of flowery, sultry and woody ingredients.

Prices are £2.20 for the Perfume Essence, £1.75 for the Eau de Toilette, £1.35 for the larger spray and 69p for the smallest size. All are on sale at Boots.

What's more, No. 7 are giving you a chance to enter their fantastic competition to find the special Trio girl. They say that Trio was created for the 'jeans-and-T-shirt girl, the hamburger and Coke, lunch with the boys, row-on-the-lake girl,' so if you think that's you, why not have a go?

The winner will, a) win the chance of a new career as a model with the Peter Lumley Model Agency b) have her hair done at Michaeljohn and her face made up by top make-up artist Barbara Daly c) have £50 worth of No. 7 cosmetics and a set of Trio fragrances!

Collect an entry form from your Boots No. 7 counter and find out more . . . the competition doesn't close until the 31st December, so there's plenty of time left.

LOOK OUT FOR . . .

Purple! There's loads of it about in the shops. Wear lilac and purple accessories, pouches, belts, shawls, etc. Wear purply plummy shades with grey and pink . . . mmmm, delicious.

Christmas . . . it's just around the corner as you'll notice if you look round the shops! Look for presents that mean something this year, no matter how small, and think carefully about the person you're buying for.

Ankle boots . . . they look fabulous with thick tights and below-the-knee skirts. Also look out for flying boots, wedgy calf-length boots with trousers tucked in the tops. Thick platforms are OUT, so don't be caught wearing them this winter!

KNIT A POUCH

Everybody's wearing them . . . little woollen pouches and bigger cloth ones worn singly or together slung round your neck. If they fasten, keep your small change and keys in them, if they're open keep your hanky inside.

Buy them from Top Shop and Selfridges from between £1 and £2, or make your own like this one we made up. Here's how to knit a pouch very quickly and very cheaply.

For a pouch that measures approx. 4 inches wide and 4½ inches deep we used one 25 gram ball of Lewis' own double-knitting wool, price 10p and one pair of child's size 8 needles, also from Lewis price 10p.

Cast on 25 stitches (ask your mum or your gran to show you if you don't know how) then knit 21 rows of garter stitch which is straightforward knitting.

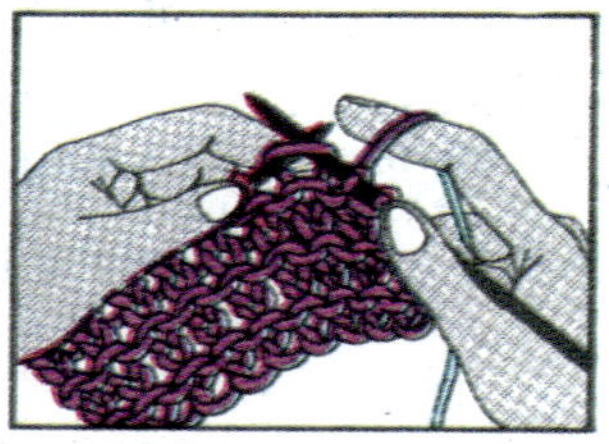

When you've reached 21 rows, cast on another 12 stitches and carry on knitting for another 21 rows. Cast off and sew up two sides and the bottom. You'll find you're left with a flap to go over the top . . . sew on a toggle and a loop to fasten it with or just use a press stud.

Make a long loopy handle by twisting three strands of wool, each approx. 2 ft. 6 ins. long. Sew them on to the sides with the same colour wool and the darning needle.

Look out for our pattern for a cloth pouch soon!

Garter stitch diagram from the Children's Clothes Pan Craft Book, price £1.

TWEET TWEET!

Cheer yourself (or a friend) up with this "Tweety" bra and briefs set from Sunarama! The bra is for smaller sizes 32 to 34 A or B cup with quite wide stretchy straps and a fastening at the back, while the briefs are one-size.

Choose from white, pink, cream or sky blue all with "Tweety" on the front, prize £1.10 for the set from most department stores, or by post from Janet Girsman Promotions Ltd., 34 St George Street, Hanover Square, London W.1., plus 20p for postage and packing.

Photo by Mike Crockett

HAIR CARE

There's always something exciting happening to hair, new styles being created, new shampoos and conditioners appearing in the shops, etc.

Here's a super new wedgy style by Malcolm at Scissors, 46a Kings Road, Chelsea. It's permed at the back to give the hair 'body' and permed lightly round the sides for "lift." Highlights around the edge give it a soft, textured look.

Although it's quite a wide style, it's the kind that you could have done without fear of people roaring with laughter as you walk down the street!

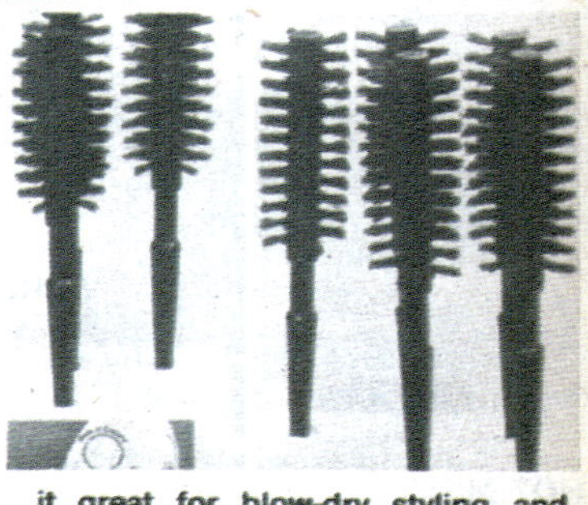

Then if you need a new hair brush, try Kent's Curly. It's an "all round" brush . . . the bristles go all the way round which makes it great for blow-dry styling and for brushing quite thick medium to long hair, especially if you twist your wrist when you brush!

The Curly comes in two lengths, short price 99p and longer, price £1.25. Find them both in most good chemists and department stores.

BUDGET BIT

We're trying to make winter as warm as possible . . . and as cheap! We've found a cream polo-neck jumper at Tesco for only 95p and put it underneath a long wrapover cardi with wide sleeves and a tie belt, also from Tesco, price £3.50.

The polo is made in nylon, style no. 593/4, comes in extra small, small, medium and large in a choice of 12 colours. The cardi is acrylic, style no. 197/8, comes in sizes small, medium and large in brown/parchment, purple/parchment, lake blue/parchment, and dark green/light green.

Buy them both from Tesco branches with Home 'N' Wear departments.

GIVE US A THONG!

SO FAR SEW GOOD CHEAP AND CHEERFUL FASHION IDEAS

COULD YOU BE A STAR?

Diamonds, mink coats, rich men in fast cars, fan mail, applause, red carpets, grand hotels, holidays in the Bahamas . . . is that the life you want? Well who doesn't, but have you got what it takes to be a big star? Try our fun quiz and find out.

Simply put a tick at the answer you think is correct for you personally, add up whether you have more a, b, c, or d answers, then read the appropriate conclusions. We can't guarantee to make you a star, but we can guarantee to bring a smile to your face as you do our quiz. Have fun!

1—Can you tell your mum a lie with-ut giving the game away?
(a) I'm smashing at it.
(b) I'm getting better and practising the art.
(c) I'm not as good as I'd like to be.
(d) I never tell my mum a lie!

2—Do you ever practise making faces nd posing in front of the mirror?
(a) Only in the spring.
(b) Yes, all the time — it's my favourite hobby.
(c) No, but I used to when I was a kid.
(d) No — I'd feel silly.

3—What do you feel when you see a irl who is altogether more charming nd beautiful, and better-dressed than ou?
(a) There aren't any.
(b) I feel mad with jealousy.
(c) I feel slightly envious.
(d) I just admire her.

4—Would you steal your sweet, nnocent cousin's boyfriend?
(a) Yes, and the expensive bottle of perfume he bought her.
(b) All's fair in love and war.
(c) Only if I really and truly loved him.
(d) No, I couldn't do such a thing to my sweet, innocent cousin.

5—What's your reaction when your admirer asks "Hasn't anyone ever told you what fantastic eyes you have?"
(a) "Yes, of course, all the time."
(b) Actions speak louder than words. You just give him a smouldering look through your long lashes.
(c) "Oh, thank you for the compliment."
(d) You blush, giggle and look down at the carpet in embarrassment.

6—The leading lady whom you are understudying goes down with flu a week before the grand first night. Would you —
(a) Keep telling her about the killer-virus that's going around, and reminding her how sick she looks?
(b) Just pray her illness will be a nice long one?
(c) Start rehearsing her part just in case?
(d) Visit her with grapes, a big smile, and a miracle influenza cure?

7—When you are in your boyfriend's arms, do you imagine that —
(a) You are Sarah Miles?
(b) He is Oliver Reed?
(c) You're both yourselves, acting in a film?
(d) You're too busy enjoying the clinch to imagine anything?

8—Your rich boyfriend has just bought you the most expensive dinner in town, plus a nice little emerald brooch. Trouble is, the next thing he has planned on the agenda is a proposal which you don't fancy. Would you —
(a) Grab the brooch and run for it?
(b) Tell him you're recovering from a serious operation and have to go to bed early?
(c) Tell him it's all been a terrible mistake?
(d) Apologise profusely and offer to pay half the cost of the evening?

9—You're late for a very important date when an old lady asks you to see her across the busy road. Would you —
(a) Say "Sorry, dear, take a deep breath and run?"
(b) Ask the next person walking along the street to take her across?
(c) Take her across yourself?
(d) Take her across and ask the poor old lady if she'd like you to walk her all the way home?

10—You bump into an old childhood sweetheart who's announced his engagement to your ex-school chum. What would you say?
(a) "She's so charming, I'm sure you'll be happy. Pity she's got cross-eyes and fat legs."
(b) "Congrats, darling. Fancy you settling down with the girl next door."
(c) "Rather her than me, that's all!"
(d) "Congratulations. What would you like for a wedding present?"

☆ conclusions ☆

Mostly (a) — You really are a gas, aren't you? It's our bet you don't really want to be a star at all, but no one can accuse you of not having a sense of humour. You could steal the show from Morecambe and Wise any day. Carry on enjoying yourself, but careful the joke doesn't misfire. People might really start believing you're mad and start ignoring you! And you don't want that to happen, do you?

Mostly (b) — Well, you **could** be a star. You possess some of the important qualities. Namely, you're not fussy who you tread on, no inconvenient morals hold you back, and you're working at putting on the passion with a cold heart. You're a nice person underneath it all, but if you harden your heart a bit more, you're destined to make it to the top in a very big way.

Mostly (c) — You might be surprised to hear that you could be a star — if you have any acting ability, that is. You are not the glamorous, tempestuous, tantrum-throwing starlet type, but all that isn't important any more.

The new young stars shining up into the headlines these days are more likely to be serious, mature, nice people with real talent. Join your local amateur dramatics group and see how it goes. One day soon you could see your name in lights!

Mostly (d) — You're a lovely person, and we'd all like to know you. You'd trip over the stage-props before you got within a mile of the microphone, but who wants to be a star, anyway? A wonderful person like you doesn't have to show off under the spot-lights to be noticed. Go on being super and sincere, and good luck for the future.

A LITTLE OF WHAT

Bright red zip-up jacket, with hood and side pockets, comes from C&A. No Style No. Price: £3.50. Fabric: Acrylic. Colours: Assorted. Sizes: 12 to 16. From all branches of C & A.

Stripy gloves with turn-back cuff, from Boots. No Style No. Price: 55p. Fabric: Acrylič. Colours: Brown, beige, red/navy, green/yellow. Sizes: One size only. From larger Boots branches.

Stripy polo in amazing colours comes from John Craig. Style No: 1459. Price £6.00. Fabric: Acrylic. Colours: Assorted. Sizes: Small, medium, large. From Just In of Liverpool and branches; Unisex of Tottenham.

Plastic pouch bag with red trim, from Bombacha. No Style No. Price: £1.10. Colours: Assorted handles. Fabric: Plastic. From Bombacha, 104 Fulham Road, London S.W.3., by post from Bombacha, plus 20p postage and packing. Also from Selfridges and Fenwicks branches.

Green knee-high boot with high slim heel from Emma. No Style No. Price: £14.99. Fabric: Leather upper, synthetic sole. Colours: Green, black, brown, navy. Sizes: 3 to 7. From Emma in Garb, 285 Oxford Street, London W.1. Emma, Westway Acton, London W12; Emma, 193 Portobello Road, Kensington, London W.11., or by post from that address plus 50p for mail order.

Stretchy "jeans" belt with gilt clasp, from British Home Stores. No Style No. Price: £1.25. Colours: Navy/white, beige/navy, beige/red. Sizes: One size only. From major branches of British Home Stores.

Red rose brooch for popping on hats, dresses, anything you like, comes from Baggage & General. No Style No. Price: £1.25. From Van Allan branches; Top Shop, Oxford Circus, London W.1. and branches.

Green chenille pull-on hat with turn-back brim, from Boots. No Style No. Price: £2.25. Fabric: Chenille. Colours: Bottle green, petrol blue, rust, brown, stone. From larger Boots branches.

Zodiac carrier bag by Paul Stephens. Style No.: F1791. Price: £1.50. Colours: Assorted with different zodiac signs. From D. H. Evans, Oxford Street, London W.1. and department stores throughout the country.

YOU FANCY...

FEELING blue? Cheer yourself up with a little something. It needn't cost a fortune but it must be something fun! We've found loads of bits and pieces that are bound to make you smile!

Stripy stretch belt with round clasp by Paul Stephens. Style No.: 031397. Price: £2.45. Colours: Assorted stripes. Sizes: One size only. From Bourne & Hollingsworth, Oxford Street, London W.1. and department stores throughout the country.

Patterned "Toe Socks' by Mary Quant. No Style No. Price: £1.25. Colours: Assorted colours and patterns. Fabric: Wool. Sizes: One size only. From D. H. Evans, Oxford Street, London W.1. Barkers, Kensington High Street, London W.8., and other department stores.

Flowery print cotton dress with elasticated frilled top, from Marks and Spencer. Style No.: 0523. Price: £6.99. Fabric: Cotton. Colours: Black, green or rust. Sizes: 10 to 16. From major branches of Marks & Spencer.

Cream jumper with Coke and Pepsi print, from Little Lisa at Twomax. Style No.: 438. Price: £5.60. Fabric: Acrylic. Colours: Ecru (creamy beige) only. Sizes: Small, medium, large. From Girl of Oxford Street, London W.1.; Cyril Clapham, 22 Howard Street, Rotherham, Yorks; New Penny Boutique, 29 Broad Street, Seaford, Sussex. Enquiries for further stockists to Twomax Ltd., 187 Old Rutherglen Road, Glasgow C.5

Blue bead necklace with bright plastic flowers, by Baggage & General. No Style No. Price: 99p. Colours: Assorted. From Van Allan branches. Top Shop, Oxford Circus London W.1. and branches.

ALL PRICES APPROXIMATE

FASHION AND BEAUTY SPECIAL

WHAT'S NEW...

AUTUMN HINTS!

NEW shapes, new colours . . . Autumn's on the way, so we show you the latest looks in clothes and tell you about the new make-up colours and how to wear them.

Outdoor shoes are heavy, just right for colder weather. These brown ones with brogue-style front and thick ridge sole come from Curtess. Style No.: A6245. Price: £5.50. Fabric: Synthetic. Colours: Black, brown. Sizes: 3 to 8. From main Curtess branches.

Stripes are all the rage for autumn knitwear and this long-sleeved jumper from Richard Shops is one of the nicest we've found. It even comes with its own long woolly scarf! Style No.: 4221. Price: £6.95. Fabric: Acrylic. Colours: Tomato, brown, laurel. Sizes: Medium, large. From main branches of Richard Shops.

One of the nicest jackets we've seen around is this long stripy one from Left Bank. It's got long sleeves with big cuffs, tie belt, flapover pockets and toggle fastenings down the front. Style No.: AJ206. Price: £10.30. Fabric: Acrylic. Colours: Rust/beige/grey, navy/blue/beige. Sizes: 10 to 14. Write to Left Bank, 106 Great Portland Street, London W1., for stockists.

Rust calf length skirt with two pleats in the front from Top Shop. No Style No. Price: £5.95. Colours: Assorted. Sizes: 10 to 14. From a selection of skirts at all Top Shop branches.

Low, wedgy shoe that will look great under trousers and will be comfy too, from Ravel. Style: Zem. Price: £6.99. Fabric: Synthetic. Colours: Black/tan, brown/beige. Sizes: 3 to 7. From all branches of Ravel. By post from Ravel, 103 New Bond Street, London W1., plus 30p for postage and packing.

MAKE-UP

NAIL colours go deep and glossy for autumn, with really rich reddy browns and reddish golds being the most popular colours.

Rimmel's new shades are extra nice especially the ones laced with gold . . . Ruby In Gold, Russet In Gold and Coral In Gold, 22p. Rum Baba, Peony Ice and Burgundy are also super shades in the Rimmel cream polish range, price 17p each.

Miners new School's Out range has four pearly polishes . . . Teachers Pet (dusty pink), Tell Tale (pretty plum), Dunces Cap (rich beige) and Playing Hookie (gentle rust) all 30p each.

Other great colours we've discovered are Tangee's Cherry Red, Love's Bluebottle, while Mary Quant predicts 'a really dull autumn' with super sludgy colours in Camouflage Colours like Sam Browne, Dawn Patrol, Under Canvas and Last Post, price 43p.

EYES AND LIPS

EYES and lips are soft and luscious for autumn. Lips match nails so buy colours in the same ranges or be clever and mix and match different ranges. Rimmel make things easy by giving their lipsticks the same names as the polishes . . . look for Ruby In Gold, Russet In Gold, Rum Baba and Peony Ice, push-up size 18p, twist-up size 29p.

Miners have three new shades in their School's Out range, Bully Brown (rusty brown), Artful Dodger (smoky pink) and Brain Box (rich plum), push-up size 18p, swivel 30p. Mary Quant's Camouflage lipsticks match the nail polishes . . . chose from Rustberry, Pink Drab, Feveille Rose and Night Watch, price 70p.

Eye colours are beautifully soft, either sticks or powders. One of our favourites is Hot Chocolate in the Boots 17 Pearly Shadow range, price 17p. Just stroke on to lids or brow-tones for really subtle colouring. Other Pearly Powder shades are Pearly Azure, Clean Green and Pearly Slate, or try the new Smudge Liner/Shadows in Bronze, Jade, Plum, Grey, Mid Blue Deep Blue, price 28p.

Also new are four liquid mascara shades, Bottle, Aubergine, Maroon and Charcoal, price 28p, in bigger bottles with really good brushes . . . well worth a try!

Miners are introducing a new product called Deep Colour Frosted Eye Shiner in Brown, Grey or Grape price 30p. There are also three new shades in the Magic Crayons range, Pretty Turquoise, Rich Lavender or Silver Blue, price 30p each.

Our favourite colour in the Rimmel Shimmering Shadow range at the moment is Silver Birch, a fantastic silvery grey with a hint of blue, price 35p. Other colours in the range are Alpine Blue, Misty Mauve or Marron Glace.

Mary Quant has three new shades of Peep Eyes duo powder shadows. Eyes should look huge and smudgy, Mary tells us, so surround them with colour, swept up and out from below the eye. Choose from Steel Blues . . . muted bluey grey and dark airforce blue, Jungle Greens . . . dark bottle green and sludgy khaki green or Desert Browns . . . light sandy brown and dark tobacco brown, price 75p each.

Knobbly, chunky knits are the other knitwear success story at the moment, as are tunic tops like this one from Erica Budd with v-neck and two patch pockets. Style No.: A6077. Price: Approx. £10. Fabric: Acrylic. Colours: Brown, blue, grey, rust, green. Sizes: 1 to 3. From Jane Norman, Oxford Street, London W1 ; Bentalls, Kingston; Peter Richards, Cheltenham and branches.

Airforce blue and rust look great together. This waistcoat is by Knitcraft at Morley with button front and airforce band at the bottom. Style No.: F5441. Price: £4.10. Fabric: Courtelle. Colours: Tan, silver grey, litchen, airforce, mocha. Sizes: Small, medium, large. From Jeannie, Heddon Court Parade, Cockfosters; Seal of Pershore; Mabel Brunt's Hat Shop, Buxton, Derbyshire.

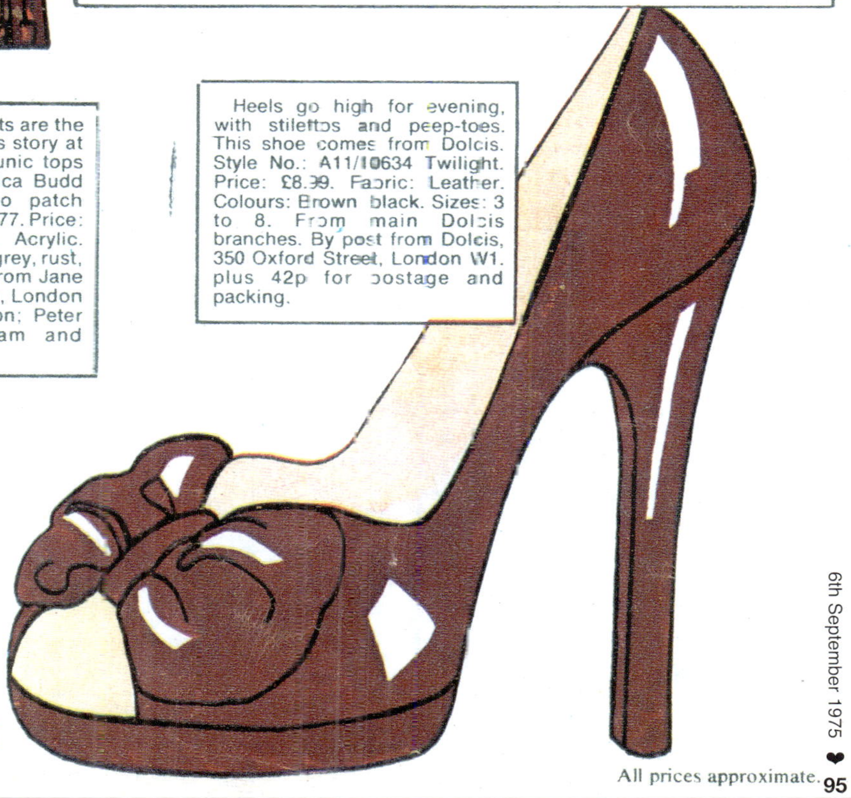

Heels go high for evening, with stilettos and peep-toes. This shoe comes from Dolcis. Style No.: A11/10634 Twilight. Price: £8.99. Fabric: Leather. Colours: Brown black. Sizes: 3 to 8. From main Dolcis branches. By post from Dolcis, 350 Oxford Street, London W1. plus 42p for postage and packing.

So, that's the mood for autumn so far. Look out for much more in Jackie in the weeks to come; more make-up, more clothes, more ideas to keep you right up to the season!

All prices approximate.

BYE BYE '75...

BEFORE we go into the new year, we thought it would be fun to stop just for a moment and take a last look back at 1975 — and at the people, places and events that made it such a special year!

So cast your memories back twelve months, and let's remember just what was happening then.

IN 1975 . . .

. . . we all started the year still humming Mud's Christmas hit, "Lonely This Christmas".

. . . everyone was wrapped up in huge, baggy overdresses, and baggy boots, topped with layers of warm, woolly scarves, all in the favourite winter colours of brown and rust.

. . . we were still wearing platforms!

. . . the springtime colours were those ice cream shades — peach, cream, pale blue, and peppermint green.

. . . our favourite models were Belinda and Rusty.

. . . soul music continued to be one of the most popular kinds of music.

. . . dancing became popular again — although not too many people were able to copy the incredible dance, "Footsee" which was made famous by Wigan's Chosen Few!

. . . everyone was making up with pencils and crayons in all sorts of beautiful colours.

. . . everyone was wearing belts in all shapes and sizes.

. . . youth hostelling holidays were more popular than ever with young people.

. . . we were sad when Biba, the most spectacular store in Britain, closed down.

. . . David Essex' second film, "Stardust" caused quite a stir when it was given an 'AA' certificate instead of an 'X'.

. . . espadrilles were our favourite summer footwear.

. . . it was the hottest summer in years and for once we all got nice and brown!

. . . the summer hit was "Barbados" by Typically Tropical.

. . . drainpipe jeans became fashionable — but only for those with drainpipe figures!

. . . new sweets like Welcomes and Nutties came along — but we still loved the good old Mars Bar the best!

. . . long nails went right out of fashion.

. . . we all started watching a new TV show about a New York cop called 'Kojak'. There were two attractions — Telly Savalas himself, and his fanciable assistant, Crocker, played by Kevin Dobson.

. . . still on the subject of Telly Savalas, he had a number one hit with his very own, unique (!) version of the lovely David Gates song, "If".

. . . pop stars like Rod Stewart were forced to quit Britain and move to America.

. . . knitwear came back in a big way — especially beautiful, bright Inca styles.

. . . David Bowie made his debut as an actor in the science fiction film, "The Man Who Fell To Earth".

. . . lots of exciting new pop shows came on television — "Pop Quest" "Supersonic" and "Look Alive".

. . . we wore socks with toes, and gloves without fingers!

. . . women were given equal pay for the first time.

. . . the little blue salt bag reappeared in crisp packets!

. . . we all loved the new pouch bags, because they were so easy to wear — and to make!

. . . the first singing Osmond brother became a daddy when Merrill Osmond's wife Mary had a little boy called Travis.

. . . Elton John flew 128 people — including our Ed — to Los Angeles for a week. (More about that later!)

. . . disaster movies like "Earthquake" and "The Towering Inferno" scared us all to death. But we were still waiting for the best of them all — "Jaws!"

. . . we were all glued to our TV sets for two whole weeks while the tennis was on at Wimbledon.

. . . Purple was the favourite colour this winter — closely followed by grey.

PEANUTS CHARACTERS COPR © 1950, 1965 UNITED FEATURE SYNDICATE, INC.

. . . our favourite cartoon of all time, Peanuts, celebrated its 25th birthday!

. . . and last, but definitely not least, the group of the year — yes, you've guessed it, the Rollers! What would we do without them!

PATCHWORK

MICHAELMAS DAY(S) IS . . .

You've probably heard of Michaelmas daisies, which'll give you some idea that there's something called Michaelmas around this time of year!

In fact it's on September 29, and Michaelmas is the festival of St Michael, the great prince of all the angels. In the Middle Ages, St Michael was looked on as the spirit of the planet Mercury, and the bringer to man of the gift of prudence. He's often shown in pictures as a severe-looking but beautiful young man, winged and with a lance or a shield, fighting a dragon.

There's a custom of eating goose at Michaelmas — it used to be followed closely, and is many centuries old. Probably it arose because geese were plentiful and in good condition at this season; but the popular story is that Queen Elizabeth 1 received the news of the defeat of the Spanish Armada while she was eating a dinner of goose on that day.

Another Michaelmas Day custom was that young girls living in the West of England gathered crab-apples from the hedges then. They carried them home, put them into a loft, and formed them into the initials of their boyfriends' names. The initials which kept in the best condition were supposed to be those of the boy who'd make the best husband!

GIVE THEM A RING!

COLLECTING FOR FUN — TELEPHONES

You're probably quite used to talking on the telephone — but have you ever tried an antique telephone? It can really be quite exciting!

One of the most popular of all old phones is the "sit up and beg" gangster type. You might have seen them in old movies. They look like a shiny black candlestick with the dial in the base.

The part you speak into, the mouthpiece, is on top and points straight out. At the side of the "candlestick" hangs the earpiece, which looks a bit like the rubber stamp the person in the post office uses to date-mark your postal orders!

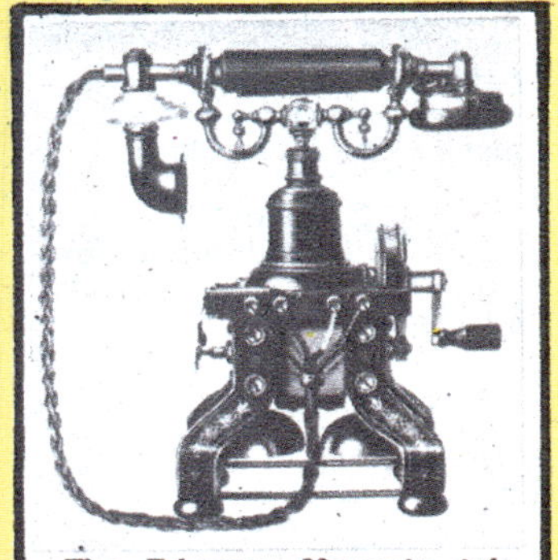

The Ericsson Magneto telephone was adopted by the post office in 1906 and used until about 1935.

Some antique dealers strip off the black plastic casing and shine up the metal underneath. But gangster phones are more valuable in their original condition.

Also much in demand are pretty phones like the Swedish-made Ericsson model. This is another table-top telephone and has an elegant handset — the proper name for the part you lift off, speak into and hear through — and handsome gold engraving all over the black base.

At the side there's a handle the caller would wind up to get through to the exchange. The Post Office adopted Ericsson phones in 1906 and used them for nearly thirty years.

Telephones meant to be used in country areas open to wind and weather were often especially designed to shut out the noise. One model had a padded leather ring around the earpiece to rest your head snugly against and keep the noise out.

Another phone, known as the Gower bell, had two earpieces on long tubes, one for each ear, to give a kind of stereo reception!

Surprisingly, the plainest phone of all — known as the Post Office Model No. 1 — is also the most valuable. Stuck on the wall, it looks just like a wooden box. But these can fetch over £1,000 if they are in good condition.

Alexander Graham Bell, the man who invented the telephone in 1876, would have been amazed with the progress being made today. Dial phones should soon be a thing of the past. Fast push-button phones are now being installed in places all over the country. You simply press a button for each number you want.

The most advanced phone machines are known as "call makers," and these can actually put the call through for you, to save time and energy. Suppose a secretary wants to ring up a regular business contact. She simply chooses a specially punched card that represents the number.

She then slots the punched card into the call-maker which is connected to her phone. The call maker "reads" the number on the card and automatically calls it.

So it looks as though the telephone you use every day will soon be an antique, too!

New push-button telephones will soon make those with dials look like antiques!

FLYING HIGH!

Getting all tangled up in kites? If you were interested by our mention of kite-flying in last week's "Jackie," you might be interested in a new Penguin book all about this subject.

The Penguin Book of Kites tells you all about kite-flying, from its history to how to construct a kite and fly it in all sorts of conditions.

One of the nicest things about the book is its colourful illustrations. They range from fantastically decorated Japanese Sanjo kites to a man-carrying kite built in 1905, and there are also detailed diagrams for making kites like the Chinese Centipede and the Bermudan Three-stick – and very simple ones that you can do in minutes from folded paper!

The Penguin Book of Kites costs £1.95 – it's a super present for someone who wants to get in on a fascinating new hobby, too.

IT'S WILD!

Buffalo Bill (Paul Newman) and the producer of the Wild West Show.

Introducing William F. Cody —, or Buffalo Bill, to you — the legend of the Wild West!

Buffalo Bill, though, was also the undisputed lion of show-business in 1885. His incredible Wild West Show was known throughout America, with acts like Annie Oakley, the world-famous sharpshooter, dare-devil trick riders, and Buffalo Bill's cowboy band, the Deadwood Stage.

The thrilling story of this rip-roaring show, with all its legendary characters, can be seen in the exciting film, "Buffalo Bill and the Indians."

An EMI film, it's on general release now. And with super Paul Newman as Buffalo Bill it can't fail to hit the target!

JACKIE RECIPE

Here's a snack that's easily prepared, popped into the oven to cook and which will fill an aching void!

CHEESY BEANS

Put a layer of sliced cheese in a small ovenproof dish, then the contents of a small can of baked beans. Cover with another slice of cheese, and put a rasher of bacon cut into neat pieces on top of this. Bake for approximately 20 minutes near the top of a hot oven (425 deg. F., or Gas Mark 6). Increase the quantities to feed the number of people you want!

MEET THE WINNER . . .

Monica's collage, "Saturday In The Garden."

She's 15-year-old Monica Wells, from Ashford, in Kent, who this summer was lucky enough to come first in a competition organised by the Observer magazine and sponsored by Copydex (the people who make glue).

The competition entailed making up a collage – a picture composed of anything and everything and the subject was Family Life.

As you can imagine, you'd have to be pretty imaginative to make up this unusual sort of picture. We asked Monica what she used to depict her family, and she told us it was a mixture of foil, matchsticks, wool, material and egg boxes, all stuck on to cardboard. But from all this came a recognisable outdoor scene of her father digging the garden, mother hanging out the washing, her sister skipping and Monica herself sunbathing – not forgetting the family cat, right in the foreground!

You'd think a detailed picture like this would take weeks of work, but Monica told us she managed it just by spending about an hour every evening, for two weeks.

"First of all I worked out the design in pencil, then I started to stick all the pieces on. Actually the first one I started went wrong, so I had to start all over again!"

This is really "third time lucky" for Monica – she's entered the competition for the past three years, and come out as runner-up the other times.

She thinks what put her out there in the front this time was, "the variety of materials I used. Though in fact, I didn't have to buy any of them, apart from the cardboard and the glue. Everything else was lying around at home!"

We wondered whether Monica's a really arty person, but she told us she's got loads of other interests.

"I'm very keen on sports – I like playing tennis, squash, badminton – and I like photography, too. But what I really want to do when I leave school is to be a surveyor!"

It's the first time Monica's won a competition, though she spends "an awful lot of time" going in for them. She certainly wants to keep doing her collages in any spare time, though. "I really enjoy putting all the bits and pieces together," she says.

Anyway, this one's certainly proved its worth for Monica. She won a beautiful portable television set with it.

"I've got it in my bedroom – I was able to watch all the Olympics on it!" she said excitedly.

If you live in the North, you'll be able to see Monica's collage in a tour of the complete exhibition of the 100 best pictures that were entered for the competition. It's in the Lantern Gallery, Worsley, Manchester, from October 2-8, and later goes on to Belfast.

Congratulations, Monica!

Monica receiving her prize from Carol Chell, presenter of B.B.C.'s "Playschool."

YOUR PATCH — JUST PICTURE IT!

If you think you'd like to have a go at making a collage, here's a very simple idea you can try to start off.

Katie Wings of Gloucester sent us the one she made, which was really pretty and decorative. All you've got to do is make up a simple design which you draw clearly, then get a few oddments of material together and cut them out according to your design, with different colours for the different bits.

Make a background frame by sticking plain material on a cut out shape of cardboard, and stick the pieces to this to form your design. You can add bits of lace, beads, sequins, etc., if you want to be really creative!

Thanks, Katie, for sending your idea to us. We pay £1 for each one we print, so if you've got one you think we'd like, send it to Your Patch, Jackie, 185 Fleet Street, London EC4A 2HS.

A JACKIE QUIZ

ARE YOU ONE OF THE IN SECT?

There are lots of similarities between people and insects. No, seriously, we've all used phrases like 'buzzing around' and 'flitting here and there', all phrases originally intended to describe insects but now in common use in referring to people. Maybe even you! Don't believe it? Then just try our quiz and find out—we dare you! You might even be surpriz-z-z-z-ed at the answers!

1—Somebody gives you a nice fat cheque for a birthday present, on condition that you spend it all in one day! Would you:—

a) Spend all week going from shop to shop looking for something really nice to buy, then dash out on Saturday morning and get it?

b) Decide you haven't time to mess about, so make out a list of every single item you're going to get, map out a route between shops and nip out one lunch hour and buy everything?

c) Get yourself in such a tizzy trying to make up your mind, that you annoy everyone around you?

d) Just go out with no real idea what you want and think of buying the first thing you see. Then change your mind and leap off into another idea, till you've wasted the whole afternoon and simply worn yourself out—and got nothing?

2—A friend is giving a party. It's to be a great affair. You're dying to go. But you want something special to wear. Do you:—

a) Flutter between a gorgeous new long dress you've seen in a shop, or your favourite long skirt and blouse, without making up your mind till the day of the party?

b) Go out and buy some material and get busy sewing straight away?

c) Complain and nag at home that you've nothing worth wearing, till your mum says she'll treat you to a new dress if it will make you happy?

d) Think one day you'll wear jeans and a sweater; the next that you'll maybe not go at all; the next that you'll wear a mini dress; and so on till the party day when you rush out and buy a maxi skirt and a frilled blouse?

3—You've made a resolution not to eat between meals. You meet a friend who invites you to go with her for coffee. Do you:—

a) Go, but say you won't have any, then change your mind when you get in the café?

b) Tell her definitely you haven't time?

c) Go with her, have coffee, then blame her for making you break your resolution?

d) Say, "Gosh! I was just waiting for somebody to tempt me!" and go with her?

4—You're with the 'crowd' at the disco when this new boy comes over. He looks super. But he's shy and seems more inclined to talk to the boys rather than the girls. Do you:—

a) Flit from boy to boy all evening to show him how popular you are?

b) Get on with the business of enjoying yourself regardless?

c) Say something sharp about boys being slow these days?

d) Leave the boy you've been dancing with and flash over to greet the newcomer?

5—It's your mum's birthday soon. You want to give her something, of course. Do you:—

a) Spend several weekends prior to her birthday looking in shops for something special, then buy her the scarf you'd thought of first of all?

b) Make her that crocheted waistcoat she's been fancying?

c) Spend hours meticulously embroidering a tablecloth for her, then decide you hate it, and buy her some perfume instead?

d) Plan to buy so many things then forget it's her birthday after all, till your dad brings her a bunch of flowers, and you have to rush to the corner shop for a box of chocolates and a card just before tea's ready?

HOW TO SCORE

Mostly 'A's.

You're the sweet, charming BUTTERFLY who flits through life full of day-dreams and only comes down to earth when the sun stops shining. But you can be definite about things, can't you? Whether it's boys, friends, clothes, or resolutions. As long as the sun shines you're quite happy to flit around or bask in the warmth. You don't appear to take life too seriously, it's a lovely, lovely world full of gay times.

But there is another side to you. The side that comes down to earth and makes the decisions that have to be made sometimes, and stuck to. Because you're not as delicate and frivolous as you sometimes appear to be. After all, many of these fragile-looking butterflies fly thousands of miles across the sea every year to get away from the cold. So if you're a butterfly take heart! You have hidden strengths. No matter what happens, you'll always get through, by using your initiative at the right time.

Mostly 'B's.

You are the busy, no-nonsense BEE. A pity you haven't a little more sense of fun. Everything you do, even your pleasure, is so full of purpose it might be hard work. You're the person people can rely on though, if they want anything done. You make decisions and stick to them. It's because you're so reliable that people make friends with you. Which is a good thing, because if it was left to you, you wouldn't have time to make friends or go out to a party or disco.

And yet, you know, you love being lazy sometimes, don't you? You love soaking up the sun and the pleasant things of life—the honey, that is. Only after you've enjoyed yourself being 'thoroughly' lazy, you feel you have to buzz off and work twice as hard as before to make up for lost time.

Just try to remember life isn't all work. So when you're out, relax, have fun and just show people there's something more in you than work, work, work!

Mostly 'C's.

No need to worry that being a WASP means being nasty all the time. Wasps have got other qualities, you know. Don't forget they are very clever little insects, and not nearly so bad-tempered as they seem. Just a bit nervous. They always seem to think the other person's going to be nasty to them, and that's why they tend to sting first and think afterwards.

In fact wasps are smart, neat, clever and well organised little people. No muddling through for wasps. They plan. They don't get caught out.

And they like fun too. They must do, when you think how they come zooming back close to your ear after you've been trying to swat them.

So don't worry. Just remember that everybody isn't out to play tricks on you or do you a bad turn. Lots of people admire you. Just be cautious and let them get to know the better side of your nature, and you'll be friends for life.

Mostly 'D's.

You're the GRASSHOPPER, the little fellow in the green jacket that sings so pleasantly when the sun's shining and then leaps away like a streak of lightning after some new idea he's got.

You don't like to be pinned down to anything for long, do you? You're here, there, everywhere, and you almost make people dizzy trying to keep up with you. You rather scare people a bit with your changes of mood, which is a pity, because you're really friendly and sincere, very good at parties and social gatherings.

It's just that you jump from one idea to the next so fast you get lost sometimes, a bit forgetful. Not intentionally. You like people and like them to like you. But you're a bit shy, and when they hem you in too close—you're off!

If only you'd stay still for a bit you might find life is really a good thing, even at ordinary level. But you're so full of ideas that it's just too difficult, isn't it?

THE CATHY & CLAIRE PAGE

We can't promise the perfect solution, but we'll do our best. If you're stuck with a problem and you can't see the way out, write to us at this address: Cathy & Claire, Jackie, 12 Fetter Lane, Fleet Street, London EC4A 1BL. Please remember to enclose an S.A.E.

DEAR CATHY & CLAIRE — This year my friend and I went on holiday together expecting to have a great time, but when we got there we were horrified to discover that the place was overrun with girls and that there was hardly a boy in sight.

What we would like to know is — where do all the boys go in the summer? If you know of any male-infested holiday resorts for next year, we'll be your friends for life.

One theory has it that all the members of this rare species go into hibernation over the summer months and only come out when the football season starts.

We think a hunting trip would be your best bet next summer and if you by any chance manage to track down any of that rare and elusive species, do send us a telegram and we'll come and join you.

DEAR CATHY & CLAIRE — I have been going out with my boyfriend for three months now. He is genuinely kind and thoughtful and we've had lots of good times together.

But, there's only one slight problem, he keeps referring to his old girlfriend he went out with for two years. He doesn't actually compare me with her (at least I hope he doesn't), but he will keep mentioning the things they used to do together, the places they went to, and things like that.

I'm really fond of Paul, but this is getting on my nerves. Should I tell him how I feel about this ex-girlfriend, or would he think me jealous? I don't want to lose him.

Well love, if you don't tell him how you feel, then he'll probably continue to refer to this ex-girl in blissful ignorance. He probably has no idea that he's hurting you and if you let him know that he is, then we reckon he'll try not to mention her so much.

Try to understand how he feels, though, and be subtle about how you put this matter to him.

Even if he didn't love this girl, two years is a long time. It's not really much wonder that he talks about the things they did together.

And remember he's talking about the things *he* did, and places *he* went to, during the past two years. He's not specifically saying how wonderful this girl was.

Try to get him to live more in the present, instead of remembering the past. When you're with him try to be your happiest and most friendly. He should enjoy himself so much that he stops thinking about the old days with his other gir. Then you'll both be much happier.

DEAR CATHY & CLAIRE — I really need help, so I'm writing to you, though I wouldn't usually have the nerve to ask for advice. I haven't really got a single problem — I've got dozens. I'm tall, fat and ugly! Really, my face has nothing nice about it, and I've no shape to speak of, or rather I have far too much shape! Wherever I go, I'm always getting looked at, and it's really upsetting me. It's got to the stage where I'm scared to go out. I just stay at home in the evenings and watch TV. But I think I'll go out of mind with boredom.

If I'm not watching TV, I'm spending pointless hours in front of a mirror, trying to improve my looks. But it's no use 'cos I know the real awful me is underneath. I'm 17 and I've had boyfriends, but never anyone special. Please give me some information on how to improve my looks so that people will stop staring at me, and I can get a nice boyfriend.

Look, love, it's not your looks that need drastic improvement, it's your outlook. If you can overcome your self-consciousness, you'll be able to appreciate all those second glances, people are giving you. To stand out in a crowd, to be noticed — is great! That's what most girls strive for, and you're running away from it. Obviously, you are *not* unattractive because you do get boys. It's when they find out you're self-conscious, that they're put off.

Is it possible, by any chance, that you spend the time refusing their compliments and bringing yourself down? If you don't have a decent opinion of yourself, then it'll show, and you'll convince others that this opinion is right! You must have some faith in yourself, love.

Your looks are obviously getting you noticed, so don't bring them down. Instead, build on this. After you've met boys, talk to them about other things — about anything, in fact, apart from yourself, and your faults. If you don't make a big issue out of them, boys won't see them, and gradually you'll forget about them yourself. OK?

DEAR CATHY & CLAIRE — Recently my friends seem to have turned against me. They're really quiet when I'm around, but as soon as I leave their company, they start chatting normally again. Sometimes, they even ignore me completely.

I can't think what I've done to cause this reaction. I'm not normally outspoken, in fact, quite the opposite. Do you think they find me boring and this is the reason they're acting so strangely? Or do you think it could be something else?

What we think is that you should ask your friends what *they* think! After all, they're the ones who're acting strangely, and they're the only ones who know why. It's going to be very difficult for you, we know, but the only way to get to the bottom of this is to march straight up to them and say, in as calm a voice as you can manage, "I've obviously done something to upset you, and if you just tell me what it is, maybe we can work something out." Then wait and see what they say.

If there's been a genuine misunderstanding, well, you can all clear the whole mess up right then and there. If there's been *no* misunderstanding, though, obviously your so-called "friends" aren't worth bothering about anymore, and you should just leave them to their own devices and go and find some other people to go around with.

It's not as easy as it sounds, we know, but surely it's better to make the effort to get to know nice people than to waste your time on not-so-nice ones . . .?

DEAR CATHY & CLAIRE — What can you do with a jealous boy? I've only known Barry for six weeks, but it feels like much longer. He's very open and straightforward, and we've been out most nights during this time, so we're very close already.

I really like him, except for one thing — he gets really jealous. Whenever I speak to or even look at another boy, he goes all quiet and huffy. But last week was the worst so far — I was talking to my ex-boyfriend, just about some friends, and Barry stormed past us, ignoring me completely. Later I found out that he'd threatened to beat up my ex-if I ever spoke to him again.

I tried explaining that it was nothing, but Barry just wouldn't listen. He says that if I ever look at another boy, he'll get him.

He's not really a violent type, but I'm afraid he might keep to his word. I'm not going to give him up as I do love him, but I don't want to lose my friends.

Well, you must realise that this kind of jealousy can ruin a relationship. No matter how close a couple is, it's still necessary to retain some of your independence. Otherwise you risk losing much of your individuality, not to mention your friends.

We feel that as you and Barry have only been together for a few weeks he still feels insecure about your feelings towards him. Because he feels so strongly about you, and he's not sure that you too, feel as deeply as he does, he sees all other boys as a threat. Everyone you talk to, he regards as possible stealers of your affections.

The only solution would be for you to have a straight talk with him. Explain that you *do* return his feelings but that his jealousy does upset you. Make him see that you really do care for him more than for anyone else, and that other boys are just friends.

He may need lots of convincing, though, and, unless you've got loads of patience, maybe you should think twice about him if he doesn't start improving . . .

DEAR CATHY & CLAIRE — I don't know what it is but my mother just doesn't trust me. Even though I'm fifteen she still treats me like a kid and whenever I go out I have to tell her exactly where I'm going, who I am going there with, and I ALWAYS have to be in at eleven o'clock.

Whenever I bring any friends to the house my mother always embarrasses me by bombarding them with questions about where we go and what we do when we're out. I've had to stop bringing them home because of this and now my mother is always complaining that I never bring any of my friends to the house.

What can I do — her behaviour is really getting me down.

Your mother only asks you all these questions and makes these restrictions because she CARES about you. And you aren't really doing anything to set her mind at rest by being so secretive about your social life that she has to drag any information out of you.

Why don't you *tell* her where you're going instead of waiting for her to ask you? That way if you show you don't resent her knowing about your social life, she just might be willing to let you out a bit later occasionally if you want to go to a late dance or disco

We agree that your mother's questioning of your friends might be a bit annoying, so why don't you try to talk to her about this? Just tell her as tactfully as possible that you think your friends are a little embarrassed by all her questions. Your mother may be surprised to hear this, because she probably doesn't realise the effect her questions have, but hopefully she'll calm down a bit and stop giving your friends the third degree every time she sees them. After all, she won't need to ask questions any more, because you'll already have told her where you've been etc., won't you?

We hope you and your mother will come to a better understanding in the future — all it needs is a little give and take from you both.

DEAR CATHY & CLAIRE — All the spending money I get from my mum goes on clothes. I always dress in the latest fashion and enjoy people looking at me. My boyfriend is a trendy guy, too, or so I thought.

Anyway I arrived for a date, dressed in my latest gear, which he hadn't seen — and he wouldn't take me out! He said he was embarrassed to be seen with me. We had a blazing row and he walked out on me. I want him back but what can I do?

Well, as we see it, you've got a choice. Either you keep your trendy gear and lose your boyfriend, or you dress a little more conventionally and try and get your boyfriend back. If you want him back, that is.

Seems to us that he acted a little bit childishly, but then, it depends on what you were wearing, we suppose. I mean, if you turned up in multi-coloured socks, red jeans rolled up to the knee, sparkly green platforms and shocking pink bomber jacket, we'd say he had a point! If, on the other hand, you were dressed trendily but neatly, we'd say he possibly over-reacted.

Only you know the truth of the matter love, and only you know if you want him back. If you do — then you'll just have to go round to his house and apologise and, if you go back with him, leave all your trendy gear at home. It'll be safer that way.

I'M SCARED TO KISS HIM!

DEAR CATHY & CLAIRE — I have a terrible problem — I'm really worried that I'll never be able to kiss a boy. I'm 14 and up till now, I've only had one boyfriend, Geoffrey. But I've known him nearly all my life, and don't really like him all that much. I never let him kiss me. Whenever he tried, I would turn away — I just couldn't help it. I didn't really *want* him to kiss me, but I didn't really know *how* to, either.

Now I've been asked out by Keith and I just have to go, because I've fancied him for ages. The trouble is, what if he tries to kiss me? I just don't know what to do, I'm so worried.

Look love, don't worry about this. The reason you couldn't bring yourself to kiss Geoffrey is possibly because you felt no physical attraction for him. And this is perfectly natural. It would take a very shallow person indeed to go around kissing every boy in sight whether she fancied them or not!

You probably look on Geoffrey as a good friend, but no more than that. With Keith, though, the situation's quite different — you *do* fancy him and, pretty soon, you're going to want to kiss him.

And as to the problem of *how* to kiss him, well, you've really no cause for worry here, either. Remember — everyone has to have a first time — including Keith! It's our guess that he'll be just as nervous as you — not because he's never kissed *anyone* before, but because he's never kissed YOU before.

So — when you're out with him, don't spoil your evening by thinking about what you're going to do when he kisses you. Forget all about it if you can. Concentrate on building up a more relaxed relationship between you and Keith. Make friends with him — then, on the way home, or when he says goodnight, it'll be quite a natural thing to kiss him.

Of course, you don't *have* to kiss him on your first date. And, if you like, and if you think he'd understand (which he probably will) you could explain your worry to him. Then he'll know to approach the whole business of kissing slowly, carefully and gently.

Then, when your first kiss happens — which it will do very soon! — relax, close your eyes, and enjoy it! It's really very nice! Honestly!

Approximate size 1½–2 ins.

Peeplkins & Pomkins...

They're taking over! These weeny furry "thingies" all have distinct characters of their own – both the little human ones and the little animal ones! The idea was first thought up from pompoms hanging on the edge of curtains, then they started to be made up by people living on isolated farms in Minnesota in the U.S.A. Now they're catching on everywhere!

Peeplkins and Pomkins have so much personality that a children's TV series is being planned around them, so they're bound to become quite familiar figures! It's interesting that they're all still being individually made, "down on the farm" in a sort of co-ordinated cottage industry. Everyone who's working on them thinks up their own designs – at the moment there are about 50, from a chef to a sheriff, a squirrel to a walrus, each with a small magnet on its back for perching it on tins or typewriters, etc.

Though they're so simple, they're incredibly appealing – it's easy to grow to love 'em!

If you can't find them locally (in big stores like John Lewis price 35p each), you can send away for them, though you'll have to take pot luck on which you're sent; also they'll only send them packed in twos, fives or tens (perhaps they like to travel with company?!) Including post and packing, two cost £1; five, £2, and you can get 10 for £3.50. The address to send off to is Philyum Ridd Ltd., The Water Mill, Newnham, Cambridge.

THE CORONA FIZZICAL!

A special offer from Corona, whose sparkling fizzy drinks are bound to be refreshing you this summer.

If you buy a bottle of Corona with the special T-shirt offer label on it, all you have to do is fill it in and send off 80p to receive the cotton T-shirt with its orange "chest-expander" bubble on the front. It looks different on everybody, because it expands according to the size of your chest!

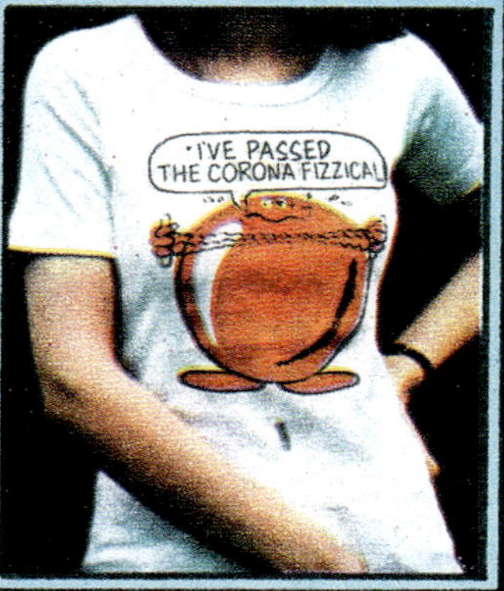

Would you like to help keep an old traditional craft going? Well, here's your chance. Craftsmith shops are now stocking a range of easy-to-make hessian figure kits to meet the demand for traditional toymaking.

Each pack contains hessian, wire, tape, thread, glue and a pattern for the figure and accessories.

Molly Malone, Mother Hubbard, Sailor and School girl cost £1.45 each; "Shopping Day" and Jack and Jill are £1.99. You can get hessian figure kits from Craftsmith shops in Hemel Hempstead, Richmond, Southend and, very soon, in Exeter, too!

A Jackie recipe —

We couldn't resist giving you this recipe using luscious strawberries, which everybody we know takes every opportunity to guzzle, while they're about!

STRAWBERRY SHORTCAKE
¾ lb. self-raising flour.
Just under ¼ pint milk (about 4 fluid ounces).
3 oz. butter.
2 oz. sugar.

FILLING
1 lb. strawberries.
2 oz. sugar.
½ pint whipped or double cream.

Rub the butter into the flour until the mixture resembles breadcrumbs. Add the sugar and mix to a stiff paste with the milk. Roll out or gently pat the mixture until it's about ¾ inch thick. Cut into 2-inch rounds with a pastry cutter. Bake on a greased baking sheet in a hot oven (425 deg. F., Gas Mark 7) for 12 to 15 minutes, until well risen and firm. Allow to cool on a wire rack.

Meanwhile, wash and dry strawberries carefully, reserving the same number of whole ones as there are shortcakes. Slice the rest, mix with sugar. Whip the double cream until it is just stiff.

Split the shortcakes into two or three when cold. Spread each layer with cream, then strawberries, and replace top. Top each one with a blob of cream and a whole strawberry.

GAME & SET...

Time for tennis again – and if all the tennis talk that's going around now has made you determined to learn properly this year, here's a new idea from Slazenger that should help.

The Slaz Ball is a tennis trainer ball with all the characteristics of a standard tennis ball, but it's made from entirely different materials, which causes it to rebound at a constant pace. This helps you develop timing and co-ordination, and also, since you can use the ball on any surface (carpet, stones, or whatever), you can practise safely indoors or in any confined space.

Whether you're practising seriously or just knocking about, the Slaz Ball will help you get the most from it! It costs 95p and you'll get it from sports shops and department stores.

Oh, and – looking for a new tennis racket? You'll have to be a tennis fanatic if you go for this one – it's the first tennis racket in Britain to cost over £100! Slazenger's "Phantom" is a one-piece construction made entirely of the space age material, graphite, which they say gives ultimate control, power, balance and feel. Definitely for the tennis player with everything!

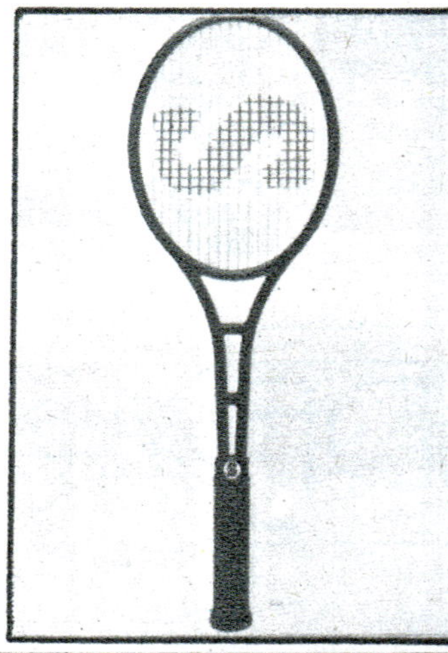

YOUR PATCH — Tidy-up

On The Rack!

E. Bracken, from Rugby, tells us that it's very cheap and easy to make a holder to keep all your Jackies neat and tidy.

What you'll need is four of those wooden boxes that hold garden bulbs, etc. (your grocer or garden shop may have some, if you can't find any lying around in the shed at home). Make sure that these are all the same size and shape. Then you'll need some pretty canvas material (or anything else that's quite heavy), and some strong glue, such as UHU.

First cover your boxes with the material, cutting it to the approximate size first and glueing in the odd ends. Then you stack the boxes, and stick them together firmly, starting with one flat downwards, and standing the next one with its top uppermost. Then repeat so you've got two wide compartments which'll nicely hold all your Jackies!

Of course if you don't want to cut and stick down the material, you could always just paint over the boxes, but it won't give so neat a finish, and you'll have to watch out for splinters!

We pay £1 for all ideas we print on Your Patch, so if you've got any you think we'd like to put on the page, please send them to us at 185 Fleet Street, London EC4A 2HS.

ALL THE PRESIDENT'S MEN

'All The President's Men' is the film of how two American reporters cracked the Watergate scandal, which eventually led to the resignation of the President of the United States. All very heady stuff — and what's more, the film stars two of our very favourite men — Dustin Hoffman and Robert Redford!

Robert Redford says the film is a 'Howdunnit about a Whodunnit!'. It's on release now and if you fancy either Robert Redford, Dustin Hoffman or both (and who doesn't!) you shouldn't miss this chance to see them together. So look out for them at your local cinema. It should be quite a treat!

GET AHEAD OF HIM!

Reading your boyfriend's palm is one thing, but reading his head is something else! The ancient art of phrenology — or head reading — can tell you a lot about the boy in your life. Is he romantic, fun-loving, a show-off — or what? His head can tell you!

EVERYONE is born with certain natural bumps on their head. And, just like the lines on your palms, for instance, your head bumps can tell a lot about your personality! For instance, you can tell whether someone is sympathetic and affectionate or jealous and bad-tempered just by reading their bumps.

The ancient art of bump reading (or phrenology) goes back thousands of years, but we've brought it up to date with our simple, fun, step-by-step guide.

So find out all about the boy in *your* life by reading his bumps. And, if at first you don't succeed, well, think of all the fun you can have practising! "Excuse me, can I read your head?" is much more interesting than, "Do you come here often?"

And, of course, you can try it out on yourself or a girlfriend, too. So start now — and get ahead!

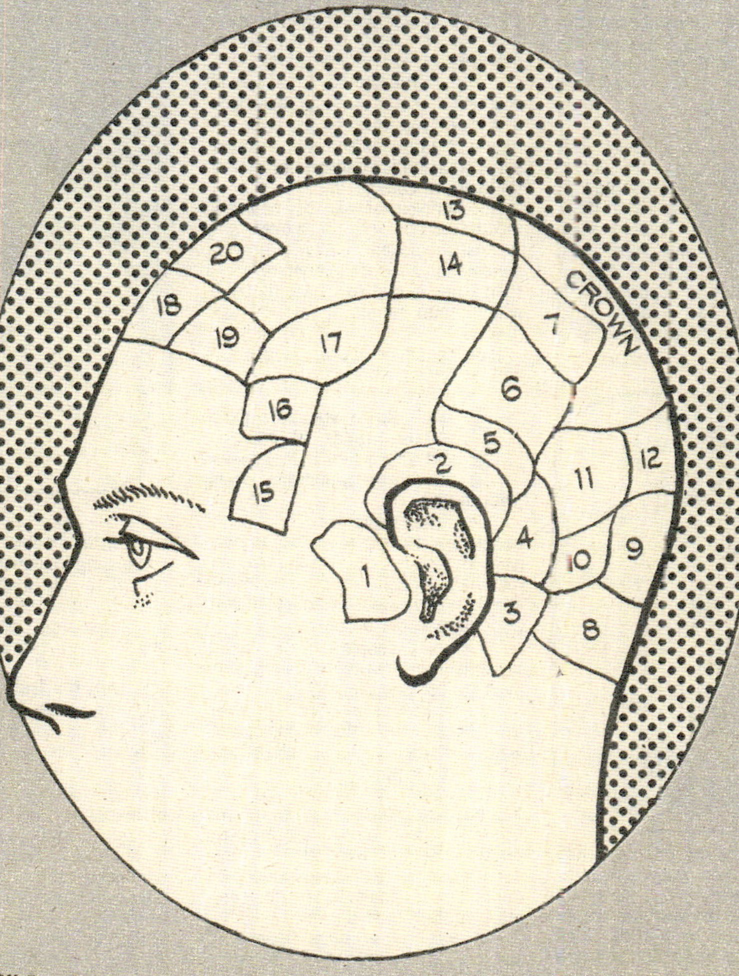

SECTION 1 — IS HE THE EXTRAVAGANT TYPE?

Place your fingers gently on the tips of his ears. Then move your fingertips forward over the area between the tips of his ears and the hollow of his temple. As you move your fingers back and forth you should feel a hollow directly in front of his ears and then a rising bump and then the hollow of the temple. A large bump here tells you you've met a boy who will spend his money entertaining you. But if there's no bump you can expect to spend your evenings in front of the telly!

SECTION 2 — IS HE DOMINEERING?

Place your fingers down behind the tips of his ears and move them over the area covered by section 2. You should begin to feel a moon-shaped ridge that curves down behind the ear. If this ridge is quite pronounced here's a boy to be wary of, unless you enjoy being pushed around.

SECTION 3 — IS HE A FUN-LOVING GUY?

Place your fingers on his ears just above the lobes. Move your fingers backwards behind the ears. You will feel a hard ridge running down toward the neck. A large ridge in this area means a boy who is full of the love of life — probably an optimistic, happy-go-lucky type of boy. If only a slight bump is present you've met a gloomy sort who moans that life isn't worth living.

SECTION 4 — DOES HE LOVE ROMANTIC QUARRELS?

Bump number 4 begins behind the middle of the ear and runs in a ridge upwards and on a slant toward the crown. If this bump is very large you're guaranteed many romantic quarrels. When this bump isn't pronounced, you may have met a hen-pecked type of boy — or perhaps he would just rather make love than war!

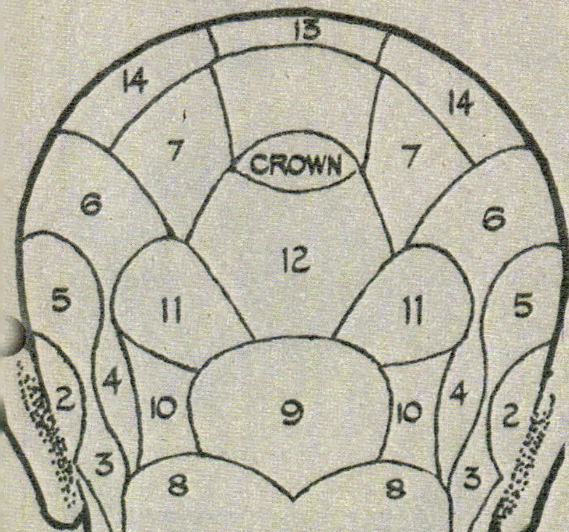

SECTION 5 — IS HE SECRETIVE?

Place your fingers on the tips of his ears. Move your fingers upwards and on a slant backwards toward the crown passing over bump number 2. A large bump in section 5 means a boy who may be too shy to reveal his feelings — or he could be the two-timing kind. He's definitely a bit of a mystery and someone to watch carefully. A slight bump here means an open, frank boy.

SECTION 6 — IS HE CAUTIOUS IN LOVE?

If you find a bump directly above and slightly behind bump number 5 then you've met a boy who takes his time and moves very carefully in romantic matters. Trying to push him into romance will only frighten him away.

SECTION 7 — IS HE A SHOW-OFF?

He may be if he has a bump directly above and slightly behind bump number 6. He's certainly susceptible to flattery and if you want to keep him you'll have to give him your undivided attention, otherwise he'll sulk.

SECTION 8 — IS HE ROMANTIC?

To find these two bumps place your fingers on the middle of the neck at the back of the head. Move your fingers upwards to the base of the skull on a line with the middle of the ears. You should feel a slight depression in the middle of the base of the skull just under bump 9. On either side of this depression are bumps 8. The larger these bumps are the greater his interest in girls!

SECTION 9 — IS HE A MUMMY'S BOY?

A large bump in the middle of the base of the skull could mean he's very attached to his parents, in particular his mother. And he will also be kind to children.

SECTION 10 — IS HE A ONE-GIRL GUY?

Place your fingers on the section 9 area at the back of the head. On both sides of bump number 9 are two small but very important bumps. A boy without these bumps doesn't have any interest in getting tied to one girl and will probably never marry. But a boy with large bumps in these areas is definitely a one-girl boy, who won't mess you about!

SECTION 11 — DOES HE MAKE FRIENDS EASILY?

Find section 12, the most prominent part of the back of the skull just below the crown. On both sides of this large bump are bumps 11. If these bumps are quite noticeable he is a very extroverted, friendly person with an active social life. If no bumps are present he is an introvert with few friends.

SECTION 12 — IS HE THE HOME-LOVING TYPE?

Find the crown at the back of the head just before the back of the head rounds off to form the top of the head. Just below the crown is bump 12. A large bump here indicates a boy who is a stay-at-home. You'll have difficulty getting him to go out — or take you out!

SECTION 13 — IS HE STRONG-WILLED?

Place your fingers on the tips of his ears and draw a perpendicular line upwards to the top of his head. Move your fingers back toward the crown about half an inch. A large bump in this area means he's a boy with grit and determination someone you could rely on in a crisis. But if this area is very flat he's definitely not the strong, he-man type lots of girls dream of.

SECTION 14 — WILL HE PLAY FAIR IN LOVE?

Find section 13. Move your fingertips sideways from section 13. On both sides of section 13 just before the skull begins to slope toward the sides of the head you will find bumps 14. If these bumps are well-formed he will always treat you fairly, but if no bumps are present he believes that all's fair in love and war!

SECTION 15 — WILL HE LIKE MUSIC AND DANCING?

The bumps at the front of the head are difficult to find but don't give up! Place your fingers at the outer end of the eyebrows near the temples. Move your fingertips up over the top of the eyebrow toward the centre of the forehead. Above the temple depression and the eyebrow you will feel a ridge of bone which forms the outer edge of the forehead. A large thickness in these areas indicates a boy whose idea of a good time is a rock concert, a disco or simply music in full glorious stereo!

SECTION 16 — IS HE FULL OF FUN?

Find section 15 and then move your fingertips above it about an inch above the eyebrows. A bump in this area means he's a boy who will bring a lot of sunshine and fun into your life.

SECTION 17 — IS HE IDEALISTIC IN LOVE?

Find section 16. Section 17 runs along behind and slightly above section 16 at the side of the head. A large bump here means he's a boy who puts the girl he loves on a pedestal. Only a slight bump in this area would mean he has a more realistic attitude to love and sees and accepts his girlfriend's faults.

SECTION 18 — CAN YOU USE YOUR FEMININE WILES ON HIM?

The best way to find this bump is to draw a line with your fingertips from between the eyes up over the forehead to the area just above the hairline. A large bump in this area indicates a boy who can see right through girls! You won't be able to pull the wool over his eyes but on the other hand, he'll understand your moods and will comfort you when you're feeling low.

SECTION 19 — IS HE EASY TO GET ON WITH?

Having found section 18, feel with your fingertips for bumps on either side of section 18. Bumps in these areas mean a boy who goes out of his way to get on with his girlfriend. He's also a very persuasive boy who will use charm rather than willpower to get his own way.

SECTION 20 — IS HE KIND-HEARTED AND SYMPATHETIC?

You can find section 20 just above section 19 where the front of the head curves to form the top of the head. A large bump in this area shows he is compassionate and kind. If there's only a small bump here, though — watch out!

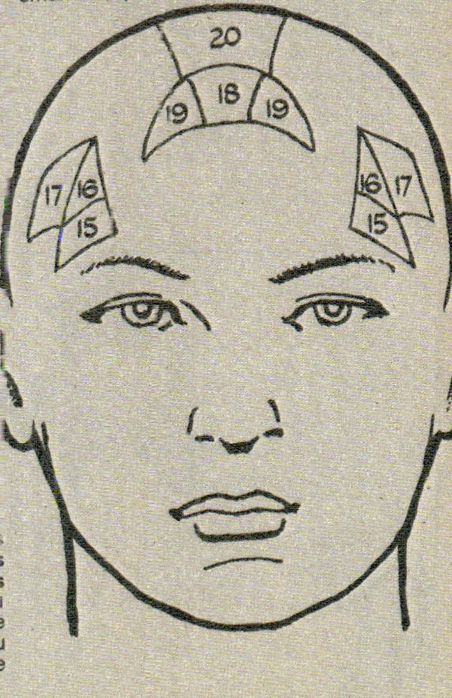

ROOM FOR IMPROVEMENT

NOW that summer's almost here, take a good look round your room. How does it strike you? Drab, dull, boring? Then help's on its way. Take a look at our two very different bedroom designs — both can be achieved with very little money and a bit of hard work! So what are you waiting for?

HOW to make your bedroom as feminine as you are!

1. Cover the walls with murals painted by you — landscapes with lots of blue sky, puffy clouds, rainbows, green fields, birds and flowers, make it as romantic and imaginative as you like!

2. Make a pretty border to run round the ceiling by cutting up wrapping paper or a string of flowers from wallpaper.

3. If you have a small (unused!) fireplace and a narrow mantelpiece over it, you can easily turn this into a special beauty closet like ours.

First, clean the shelf and fireplace surround, and push a piece of strong cardboard up into the chimney so that no soot can fall down! Next, fit shelves into the empty fire-place, to take cosmetics, cleansers, cotton wool — all your beauty stuff and things you don't use every day, like a hair dryer. If you can't knock up shelves yourself, and don't have a handy boyfriend or brother, stand a couple of plastic-covered wire plate or storage racks inside — you can buy these in department stores.

While you're shopping, get enough ordinary cup-hooks to be able to fit one every 6 inches along the sides and front of your mantel-shelf. Screw these along the underneath, near the front edge, and make a curtain from a pretty remnant of any material you like.

To work out how much material you need, measure the HEIGHT from floor to shelf, and add on about 4 in. for hems, and then measure the WIDTH along the side of shelf, width of shelf and the other side, and add HALF this amount again. Fit a length of curtain-wire through the top hem, and hook this on to the cup-hooks.

Finally, cover the top of the shelf (if necessary) with a bright plastic like Fablon, glue an adhesive-backed mirror to the wall, and there you are!

4. Trace a simple design on to your mirror and paint it as a silhouette (see our artist's sunset scene).

5. Finally make a stool like ours to go with your beauty closet. You should be able to buy an old one in a junk shop to do up yourself. Cut a piece of fairly thick (2 in to 3 in.) foam rubber just the size of the top of the seat, and glue this into place. Cover with a piece of any firm material cut larger than the top of the seat — so that it'll come down over the foam rubber and fix under the seat. Make sure this is put firmly into place with drawing pins all round, to gather the fullness in as neatly as possible.

Now make a long "skirt" from the same material which you hem at floor edge, and gather at the top with shirring elastic. Glue this to the rim of the seat with a really strong glue like Copydex. Finally, using your Copydex again, glue a band of strong braid or tape all round to cover the pins and rough edges. And there you are, a frilly, romantic, stool.

6. If you want a cheap, cheerful room divider like ours, keep your eyes peeled for the type of wooden crate that fruit comes in, go to local markets — or ask your supermarket, greengrocer, etc.

The sort you want is fairly strong, measuring roughly 20 in. by 10 in. by about 6 in. deep. You'll want at least five. Make sure they're thoroughly clean, and then put them together as in the illustration, and fix them permanently that way with plenty of small nails or tacks, driven right through the two layers of wood where two boxes come together — both sides and bases.

Also, buy four small pieces of dowelling or rounded wood from your local Do-It-Yourself shop, cut the same depth as the outside height of the boxes. Put these at the unsupported outer corners of the middle layer, and fix them with a nail or tack driven from the inside of the boxes into the dowel.

Now smooth any rough bits of wood with sandpaper, and either paint all the wood you can see, or cover it with wallpaper and glue, or stick-on plastic. Stand the divider at right-angles to a wall, or use it to separate two beds, or even stand it against a wall. You can use it to store books, shoes, records, goldfish, school-work, bags — anything you like!

7. Wardrobes take up a lot of space and often look clumsy and ugly. So instead why not hang your clothes on a bamboo rod? Attach two chains to the ceiling with rawl plugs so that they hold really firmly. Put large curtain rings through the last links in the chains and slide the bamboo pole through them. Now hang up your clothes!

(Try your local hardware shop for bamboo poles and your local Do-It-Yourself shop for the chains and rawl plugs.)

8. Disguise shabby lino with lino paint available in hardware stores — and invest in a brighly patterned rug.

9. Cover your bedside table with a pretty circular table cloth.

10. Add a super mushroom lamp from British Home Stores.

11. Blinds like the ones in our room can be made from roller blind kits available at most large stores or specialist shops.

12. We've got rid of the bed and instead we've put a mattress on the floor. It takes up less space and looks less "bedroomy" especially when surrounded by bright, cheerful cushions.

(See instructions on how to make the cushions in our thirties style room.)

13. The hanging lampshade in our room is an old shade frame covered with crepe and coloured paper to make a super original light. (Be careful to keep the paper well away from the light bulb though.)

14. Create your own miniature garden inside a brightly painted garden tub. Fill with earth and plants and add interesting ornaments — plastic frogs, little people, etc. etc.

15. The swallows by the rainbow are made with DAS modelling clay, available from most craft shops, and hooked on to nails in the wall.

16. You can pick up our little Victorian photo frames very cheaply from junk shops. Take out odd photos but keep mounts. Put in nice postcards and cartoons.

So there you are a lovely, cluttered pretty room that will always give you something to look at!

OUR COSY COLOURFUL COUNTRY ROOM

How to create a glamorous setting that'll make you feel like a film star!

1. Paint your walls smooth chocolate — doors, window frames, etc. trendy cream or white.
2. Get rid of curtains — have sleek blinds instead. Go to a shop specialising in roller blinds and buy a kit — this contains all the stuff that actually makes the roller snap up and down. Then buy your own material and put the two together — much cheaper than ready-made blinds! Sew fringing on them and add tassels for the authentic thirties look.
3. Make lots of cushions, in masses of different fabrics. Pick out a sizeable piece of material, then sew up three sides into a square or rectangular bag. Use Velcro, snap fasteners or a nylon zip for closing up the fourth side. Fill with Kapok or foam rubber, available from Woolworths or craft shops. Enclose the filling you choose in an old pillowcase and put it into the cover you've made.
4. Buy an old cane chair (scout round the junk shops) and paint it shiny black.
5. Paint a couple of sleek stripes around the edge of your carpet with Dylon Carpet dye.
6. Paint a simple thirties design on your mirror with mirror paint (available from most ironmongers). Or else use electricians' plastic tape which comes in lovely colours and different widths from electrical shops, would you believe!
7. Buy some decadent peacock or ostrich feathers (from the haberdashery departments of large department stores, craft shops, or you could always breed your own peacocks! Well, our Dorothy does, so there!)
8. "Frame" your favourite pics from magazines with silver or gold sellotape.
9. Make pomanders with oranges and cloves to give your room a lovely mysterious aroma.
10. Make super flower balls with artificial flowers on a polystyrene ball-shaped base (available from florists).
11. Start a collection of pictures made with dried flowers and grasses. You'll find masses of books in the library about this fascinating hobby.)

12. Acquire a long, low, display shelf by putting a plank on columns of bricks. (Planks are available in timber shops and try builders' yards for bricks.)
13. A poster looks instantly better if you stick it on to a large sheet of black card and screw it to the wall with bathroom screws (big, shiny, metallic tops, available from ironmongers.)
14. Arrange flashy mirror tiles on the wall behind your bed — they come in super shapes as well as in plain squares.
15. Make a display of beautiful soaps in a bowl.
16. Subtle lighting will make a terrific difference to your room — buy a nice lamp from British Home Stores to give you a soft bedside light.
17. Invest in a cane lampshade for you centre light or put long fringing round your own.
18. Buy fake leopardskin fabric by the yard and make a glamorous rug for your bed.
19. Cover cardboard boxes with leopardskin printed wrapping paper and use them as bedside tables.
20. Put up shelves in any available alcoves. If you happen to have a framed photo of Bryan Ferry lurking there, he won't spoil the mood!
21. Be impossibly extravagant with plants, the bigger and greener they are the better!
22. Some bath salts come in smart decanters — have one sitting around. When the salts are used up fill the decanter with cocktail coloured water.

And there you are — a luxurious retreat at a bargain price!

OUR SUPER SMOOTH 30's ROOM

BEAUTY QUERIES

Dear Beauty Ed — Although my usual cleanser takes off my eye make-up with no problem, I can't seem to get my mascara off — I always end up pulling it off with my fingers! Can you help?

Try putting a folded tissue under your lower lashes, closing your eye and gently stroking an eye make up remover pad down over your lashes. This should work effectively!

Dear Beauty Ed — Can you recommend a new perfume for me for summer? I'm still at school so can't afford to pay much, and I need one that's easy to carry, not a big aerosol or bottle. The perfume I'm using now just seems too heavy and wintery all of a sudden.

Max Factor's "Green Apple" is, as its name suggests, a deliciously cool, refreshing fragrance of apples. It comes in a beautiful glass apple bottle, too.

For easy carrying, however, you might like to try Miner's "Moods of Summer" wax perfumes, which come in beautiful little painted tins, are very cheap, and smell *exactly* right for summer! From most Boots branches.

Dear Beauty Ed — Is it harmful to your hair to use cheap shampoos? I can't really afford the more expensive ones, but since I started using a cheaper brand my hair seems to be a bit out of condition.

No, there's no reason why you shouldn't use the cheaper brands, as they're just as good as the more expensive ones. The one you tried probably wasn't right for your hair, that's all, but experiment with the Boots, Aronde, Kermval, etc. ranges until you find one which suits you.

Dear Beauty Ed — This may sound silly, but I can't decide what shape my face is. Sometimes it looks round, sometimes square, sometimes long! Is there any way I can find out, as I often read beauty advice for round faces, long faces etc. and don't know which to choose!

There is a fairly simple way of telling your face shape, actually — just look into a large mirror, and draw round the outline of your reflected face with a lipstick. A bit messy, of course, but quite reliable — just remember to clean the mirror afterwards!

Dear Beauty Ed — I know you can disguise ugly noses, small eyes etc., with clever make-up, but my problem is my mouth. The lips are very thin, but wide, too — my mouth seems to stretch from ear to ear!

Don't panic — the same rule applies to mouths as to eyes and noses! To "bring your mouth in" at the sides, simply stop your lipstick before you get to the corners. To counteract the thinness, use a light shade of lipstick, and always use a lip gloss or pearlised lip colour on top. It also helps to put a tiny touch of highlighter in the centre of your top lip — this will make your lips 'bigger' without being too wide.

jackie fashion

BUTTON

1. Yellow and blue long sleeved T-shirt, with coloured buttons along shoulder seams, from Irvine Sellars. Price: £4.95. Sizes: 1, 2, 3.
Bright red jump suit, with button-up front and tie belt, from Highlight. Price: £15.90. Sizes: Small, medium, large.

2. Turquoise/white striped top with short-sleeves and large buttons on neck, from C&A. Price: £2.25. Sizes: 10-16.
Denim skirt with bib, buttons on pockets, Price: £13.50. Sizes: 10-14.

3. White skirt with black patterned trim on pocket and hem and button-up side, from Louis Caring. Price: £7.99. Sizes: 10-14.

4. Strappy wedge shoe with button fastening, from Dolcis. Price: £8.99. Sizes: 3-8.

5. Black top from John Craig with red and white trimmings and buttons on shoulder seams. Price: £8. Sizes: Small, medium, large.

6. Peach-coloured short-sleeved cardigan with button fastenings, from Wolsey. Price: £4.55. Sizes: 34 in.- 40 in.

7. White short-sleeved top with buttons on shoulder flaps and side fastening, from John Craig. Price: £7. Sizes: Small, medium, large.

UP!

Fun buttons are appearing everywhere this summer – on skirts, shirts, trousers and even shoes. No more discreet zips and hooks – buttons are best – and the very latest are on show to everyone! So here's how to button up with some of the nicest clothes around!

9. Red/white stripy top, with white button loops at shoulders, from Shar Cleod. Price: £6.95. Sizes: Small, medium, large.
Super red straight skirt, with button tabs on slit sides, from Dorothy Perkins. Price: £6.99. Sizes: 10-14.

12. Blue top with red trim and large button on pocket, from Top Shop. Price: £4.99. Sizes: 10-14.

10. Red straight skirt with slit sides and buttons, comes from Top Shop. Price: £5.99. Sizes: 10-14.

8. Blue/cream stripy T-shirt with buttons on cap sleeves, from Shar Cleod. Price: £4.95. Sizes: Small, medium, large.
Denim dungarees with button down braces and large patch pockets, from Top Shop. Price: £13.50. Sizes: 10-14.

13. Red/white striped towelling top with buttons at shoulder seams, from John Craig. Price £2.30. Sizes: Small, medium, large.

11. Amazing red stiletto with double strap and button fastening for very special occasions, from Sacha. Price: £19.99. Sizes: 3-7.

14. Navy/white striped top with cross over button fastening, from C&A. Price: £2.30. Sizes: 10-16.

Further details and stockists on page 27.

what's your favourite outfit?

ON-THE-SPOT INTERVIEWS **where our roving reporters find out what *you* think**

Tina James, London SE13.
My brand new silver paper boiler suit. It's really the nicest thing I've ever bought. My friends all think I look like an astronaut in it, but that doesn't put me off.

Jeanette Findlay, London SE18.
Personally, I'm happiest when I'm wearing my jeans and T-shirt, but there is one outfit which, although I don't possess it, I'd like to one day.

I've seen it in a catalogue, and it's a three-piece rust coloured suit, consisting of trousers, jacket and a waistcoat. I haven't got the money but I'm hoping that my mum will lend me the money so that I can buy it!

Sharon Radley, Montrose, Grampian.
I like to look peasanty and my favourite outfit is fairly unusual. I wear a fantastic black apron with tiny pink roses on it, (which my mother used to wear for working in the kitchen!), with a black peasant blouse and near ankle length skirt, a blanket shawl and lovely flat tan crepe soled boots.

Not many people dress like that where I live, so they think I'm absolutely mad!

Kerry Anderson, Cardiff, S. Wales.
I like anything that's made in bright colours. I always feel happy in bright colours, but, if I'm wearing black or other dark colours, I feel sad and depressed. My favourite outfit is a very colourful knitted Peruvian outfit — jumper, gloves on strings, stripy scarf, socks and leg warmers, poncho shaped skirt, plus a red crocheted shawl. I hear black's going to be fashionable this winter . . . I suppose I'll just have to be out of date!

Rosemary Ward, Colchester, Essex.
A very flimsy looking party dress which I made from enormous flowery patterned, square scarves. I bought the scarves at a jumble sale for just 40 pence. I think it's much nicer than anything in the shops, and it's more original, too!

Julie Patterson, Newcastle.
I'm a great Queen fan so when I dress up I always wear black and white. Last time I went to a Queen concert, everyone was dressed in black and white too — it was almost like a uniform!

My favourite outfit is a tight skirt with slit sides, lace-up ankle boots, T-shirt, and a short jacket, all in black, with a white scarf. I wear black nail varnish, like Freddie Mercury, too!

Jennifer Blackley, Glasgow.
Ever since I saw a film on television which was set in Mexico, I've been fascinated by Mexican clothes. I have an enormous blanket poncho, which I wear belted at the waist, with my jeans tucked into cowboy boots. I also go for big baggy cotton shirts and ethnic Mexican style dresses. To top it all I have this really authentic tall Mexican hat which I bought on holiday which looks great, but I have to admit, I don't have the nerve to wear it very often.

Helen Doherty, Sydenham, Oxford.
A fantastic "Gatsby" suit. It's a black jacket and shirt which I bought from "Guys & Dolls" in London, for £30.00. That was an enormous amount of money at the time, but I managed to save up my pocket money until I was able to afford it — and it's definitely worth it!

Sandie Frampton, Northampton.
A super gipsy outfit with a frilly layered skirt and beautifully embroidered top. It's made in old, silky materials in bright, bright colours. I wear huge hooped earrings and a scarf tied round my head, to complete the effect!

Billy McIsaac, Slik.
My baseball gear, of course! We used to wear it every day, and then we decided that our own image would be the best stage image too! We bought our clothes in King's Road in London, at an amazingly cheap price, and we wear them all the time now — they're so comfortable.

Gay Kendall, Fareham, Hampshire.
I had this pair of long, baggy trousers, which were a bit out of date. So, I cut them off just below the knees, put a turn-up on them, and now I've got a great pair of culottes.

I made a purse bag out of the spare material, and I wear them with a waistcoat and wedgy wooden soled shoes.

Josephine Mattley, Molesey, Surrey.
A striped tube T-shirt dress. It makes me look slimmer and taller than any of the other clothes in my wardrobe. It does wonders for my ego. It was quite expensive, but worth every penny of the price considering the number of times I've worn it.

Ruby Backen, Manchester.
To me, what happens when I wear my clothes matters more than what they look like. My favourite outfit is a pair of tatty cord jeans and a track suit top, because that's what I wear when my boyfriend takes me out on his motorbike on Saturdays, and that's when I'm happiest!

Chris Lewis, Kew, Surrey.
It's a flimsy Victorian camisole nightdress with pintucking and lace on the front. It's much too pretty to just wear in bed, so I embroidered it, and now it makes a lovely shift dress.

I have a 1930's satin blouse with scalloped edging on the sleeves which I also love to wear.

Jill Bedford, Kirkcudbright, Kirkcudbrightshire.
Denim dungarees, a red checked shirt, red leather lace-up boots, and a visor make up my favourite outfit. The rest of my clothes are quite dull, so I really enjoy dressing like that for a change every now and then!

What's New... Hats

Jackie Fashion

Wrap up with a woolly hat and scarf! Hats come in all shapes and sizes . . . favourites are tight, pull-on cloche hats, berets, "Beanie" hats, and balaclavas. Take a look at our super selection!

1. Red tammy with pompom, trimmed with pink, yellow and navy, from Salisbury's. Price: Approx. £1.50. Fabric: 100% Acrylic. Colours: Red, navy, black, with trim. One size only. From branches of Salisbury's.

2. Blue woolly pull-on hat, with turn-back and pale blue trim, from Woolworth. Style No.: 549/6W. Price: £1.99. Fabric: Acrylic. Colours: Assorted. From branches of Woolworth. Enquiries to Mr L. Schaller, Etiquette Fashion Ltd., Radiant House, 28-30 Fowler Road, Hainault, Herefordshire (enclose an s.a.e.).

3. Grey knitted hat with zigzag print, from Hot Sox. Price: Approx. £4.50. Colours: Assorted. One size only. From Fenwicks, London W.1. and branches; Joseph, London S W 1. Enquiries to Hot Sox, Harcourt House, 27 Harcourt Street, London W 1 (enclose an s.a.e.).

4. Bright red tartan beret, from Kir. Style: WST Beret. Price: Approx. £2.50. Fabric: Woven Scottish Tartan. Colours: Red, green, blue tartans. One size only. From John Lewis, London W 1 and branches; Peter Jones, London S W 3. Enquiries to Mr H. S. Kirsch, Kirgloves Hitchin Ltd., Bury Mead Road, Hitchin, Herts (enclose an s.a.e.).

5. Cream beret with pompom and heather mixture stripes, from Littlewoods. Style No.: 97512. Colours: Assorted. Fabric: Bouclé. From a wide selection of hats at £1.99, at all branches of Littlewoods.

6. Pretty cream lacy-look hat with turn-back and pretty flower motif worn to one side, from British Home Stores. Style No.: 7069/8. Price: £1.15. Fabric: Acrylic. Colours: Assorted. From all branches of British Home Stores.

7. Red, head-hugging cloche hat with flower on side, from Littlewoods. Style No.: 972/3. Price: £1.25. Fabric: Acrylic. Colours: Assorted. From all branches of Littlewoods.

8. White knitted pull-on hat, with turn-back and red and navy stripes, from Woolworth. Style No.: 550/6W. Price: £1.99. Fabric: Acrylic. Colours: Assorted. Stockists as for 2.

LOOK OUT

LOOK Out looks at everything that's new . . . new things to buy, to make and to do to make yourself look really nice!

HAPPY BIRTHDAY

Freeman Hardy Willis have shoe shops in most towns, and 1976 is their 100th birthday, which is definitely something to celebrate! All through 1976 Freeman Hardy Willis will be having sales, genuine cuts in the prices of their shoes, so watch out for those at your nearest branch.

Just for fun, take a look at what fashionable ladies were wearing on their feet 100 years ago when Freeman Hardy Willis opened their first branch in Wandsworth, London. The buttoned boot is a reproduction of a 'Lady's Polish Gaiter Boot' dated about 1880, and the boot with the ribbons is an open front dress boot from 1878. Compare those with the equivalents of today . . . The wedgy shoe is for out of doors and the wedge sandal is a bit more dressy. Both from the Freeman Hardy Willis Spring collection coming into the shops soon.

SO FAR SEW GOOD Cheap and Cheerful Fashion Ideas

what a waist!

Make this quilted waistcoat in just an evening. It's a piece of fabric – ready quilted – 80cm. (31½") long and 28cm. (11") deep. Fold it in half, as shown, and cut out the shaded neck-section. Bind all the raw edges with bright bias binding, sew ribbon ties on the sides 10cm (4") and 20cm (8") up from the hem. Decorate it with appliqués or ric-rac!

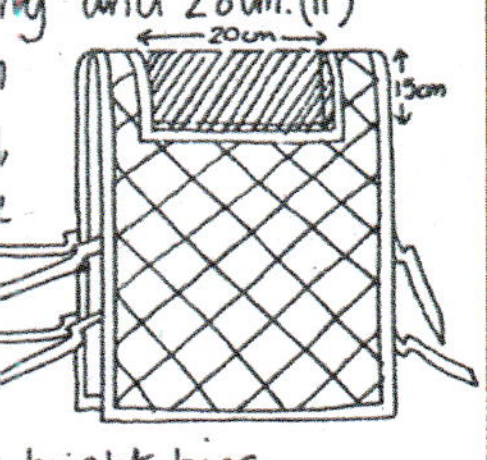

HENNA WITH EVERYTHING

The Henna plant must be one of the most useful plants around.

It's been used for hundreds of years by women to make their hair darker and shinier, and it also strengthens any red properties your hair might have. If it's slightly auburn already, you can use Henna to deepen the colour.

Now there's a new Henna Wax Treatment, from Henna Hair Health Ltd., which doesn't colour your hair, but it does condition it. They call it hair 'food' because it actually helps to swell the hair, feeding it with extra proteins and the special conditioning properties that Henna has.

Buy the wax treatment (it comes in a drum with enough for four to six treatments, depending on the length of your hair) from 80p from leading department stores and chemists, or write to Henna Hair Health Ltd., 5-7 Singer Street, London EC2A 4BQ for the address of your nearest stockist if you can't find one.

HENNA

BUDGET BITS

A pretty – and practical – long skirt in gingham check, with elasticated waist and frilled hem. Team it with T-shirts, blouses, jumpers – anything you like! And it's only a fiver.

Style No.: P64. Price: £5. Fabric: Cotton. Colours: Assorted. Size: One size, to fit 8 to 16. By post from Pixie Boutique, 329 Fulham Road, London S.W.10., plus 35p for postage and packing.

STARS AND STRIPES

Hold up your jeans with these braces and stretch belt complete with stars and stripes design, both from Trimfit. The braces cost £2.99 and the belt costs £1.99, both in stretchy elastic. Buy them from major department stores or direct from Trimfit, 34 to 35 Berwick Street, London W.1. No charge for postage and packing. The patches also come from Trimfit, price 50p each, from department stores, or from Trimfit at the above address.

ALL THE FUN OF THE FAIR

Miners have come up with some fun for Spring. In fact, they've gone plain crazy with four new crazy lipsticks, Crazy Spice, Crazy Wood, Crazy Dawn and Crazy Brick, 18p & 30p; four plain polishes to match the plain crazy lipsticks, 22p each. There are also six brand new Shadowmatic Eye Colours, Plain Sky, Plain Grass, Plain Hi-Lite, Plain Earth, Plain Haze and Plain Rain, price 29p each!

Look for the new Spring shades in larger Boots branches, chemists and department stores.

HAPPY HAIR

Greasy hair is a problem for lots of girls, and it can be really depressing. There are loads of shampoos on the market to help fight the problem, but it's always nice to hear of something new to try. We've been trying out Batiste, a new shampoo from Schwarzkopf, the makers of the Corimist range for dry hair, and so far we're very impressed.

The Batiste range is made up of Shampoo, Creme Rinse, Spray Set, Hair Spray and Dry Shampoo, all packed in yellow and green containers and perfumed with the clean smell of citrus fruits! The shampoo costs 27p for 5 to 7 applications, or 54p for 15 to 20 applications, creme rinse costs 48p, spray set 46p, hair spray 54p, and dry shampoo 62p.

The Batiste products should be on sale in most good chemists and department stores.

CHECK IT OUT!

1. Red zip-up jacket, with gingham trim on collar and pockets, and elasticated waist, from Top Shop. Price: £4.99. Sizes: 10-14.

2. Blue and white gingham collarless shirt, with long sleeves and white trim round neckline, by Ben Sherman for Grattan. Price: £5.99. Sizes: 34 in.-38 in.

3. Pretty red and white gingham sleeveless top with elasticated waist and frill round yoke, from Grattan. Price: £5.25. Sizes: 10-14.

4. Pretty white nightdress with pear motif, red and white gingham collar and frill round hem, from Dorothy Perkins. Price: £3.99. Sizes: Medium only.

5. Swirly full length green and white gingham pinafore with frill round the bottom and sleeves, from Pixie. Price: £7.50. Sizes: 10-16.

6. Super brief gingham bikini in pink and white, from Miss Ladybird. Price: £3.25. Sizes: 32 in.-36 in.

8. Navy and white gingham with two patch pockets trimmed with red, comes from Grattan. Price: £7.75. Sizes: 10-14.

10. Denim skirt with red and white gingham tie belt and red trim round pocket flaps, from Richard Shops. Price: £6.95. Sizes: 22 in.-28 in. (waist).

FRESH, GORGEOUS GINGHAM ISN'T JUST FOR COUNTRY GIRLS. IT LOOKS FANTASTIC ANYWHERE, ANYTIME — AND IT'S GREAT FOR SUMMER! SO CHOOSE CRISP COTTON SHIRTS, COOL SKIRTS OR LONG SWIRLY DRESSES FOR THE BEST SUMMER LOOKS . . .

jackie fashion

7. Blue and white small-brimmed gingham sun hat, from Charles Batten. Price: £3.25. Sizes: Small, medium, large.

12. Floaty long black dress with gingham bodice and frill and ties at the back, from Pixie. Price: £6.50. Sizes: 10-16.

14. Unusual red and white gingham skirt, with side buttons and smaller check trim round the edges and sleeves, from Stirling Cooper. Price: £8.95. Sizes: 1, 2, 3.

13. Cool purple and white gingham sundress with tie straps at shoulders and two patch pockets, from Marks & Spencer. Price: £6.99. Sizes: 10-16.

9. Red and white gingham skirt with buttons down the front, and on slit pockets, from Stirling Cooper. Price: £9.95. Sizes: 1, 2, 3.

15. Blue and white gingham top with short sleeves and tie belt from Dorothy Perkins. Price: £4.99. Sizes: 10-16.

11. Blue and white gingham skirt with double patch pockets at the front, comes from Stirling Cooper. Price: £9.95. Sizes: 1, 2, 3.

16. Red and white gingham shirt with short sleeves and collar, edged with smaller check, from Fergie at Tom Foolery. Price: £4.99. Sizes: 10-16.

HENNA is just about the oldest cosmetic in the world . . . and it's still one of the very best. Henna powder is usually thought of as a hair dye, because of the fantastic way in which it's used to redden the hair. That's not its only use by any means, though! It can be used for highlighting, conditioning, dyeing and even skin decoration! Read on and find out all about it!

dyeing for a change!

You may remember our model with the super hair from our Valentine cover. Now you can really see what a difference fantastic hair makes!

THE HENNA PLANT

Henna powder comes from the leaves of the Lawsonia inermis plant which are dried and then reduced to powder.

The flowers of the plant are small and delicately perfumed, but they give us a perfume called Cyprinum which is very sweet and heady, much stronger than the scent of the flowers when they're growing.

We know that Henna was used by the Egyptians and in other Eastern countries a very long time ago, not just on the hair but all over the body for decoration. It was also used on the palms of the hands and soles of the feet to prevent excessive perspiration — it was the earliest anti-perspirant! They used the leaves for this, rubbing them on to the skin . . . the odd thing was that the skin turned a reddish colour afterwards and remained stained in this way for a few weeks.

This gave people other ideas! We know that Moslem women in particular used Henna to paint intricate designs on their bodies. The Henna paste was painted on in the required design and, once dry, it would stay that way for many weeks, despite washing which would have removed all the usual paints and clay dyes.

To prevent flaking, a mixture of garlic, lemon juice and sugar was used, added continually until the henna was dry. When the paste was removed, the skin underneath was stained and stayed that way for quite a while!

HENNA AND YOUR HAIR

Nowadays, though, if you see people with healthy, shining hair and fantastic red highlights when their hair catches the light, you can be sure that they've used Henna.

Until quite recently the only safe way to have your hair treated with Henna was at the hairdresser. The powders for home use had to be boiled in saucepans, and the results weren't always quite as imagined! The powders now are much more refined. You just mix with boiling water and apply to your hair. You do have to leave the paste on for a long time, though, all night if you have really long hair and want a deep, rich colour.

The colours you get from the ordinary Henna powder with colouring properties, depend on the colour of your hair. There aren't any hard and fast rules because everyone's hair is different. If you already have red lights in your hair, the Henna will probably make it a distinct red, but if you use Henna on very dark brown or black hair without any natural red lights, it will just look richer.

With mid to dark brown hair you're fairly safe, there's no question of your hair turning *bright* red, but on light brown to blonde hair, the results can be very dramatic. Usually bright reddish ginger, especially if you leave the paste on for a long time. (Make sure you know exactly what you want, though, because once the Henna's on, you won't be able to wash it out. You'll have to wait for it to grow out.)

Here's a guide to the sort of colour you can expect with the use of natural Henna powder just leaving it on until it has dried:

Black hair . . . Henna will bring out any reddish/brown lights.

Dark brown hair . . . Henna will lighten it slightly, any red lights will be more noticeable.

Mid-brown hair . . . Henna will add red lights and the hair will be a richer, auburn colour.

Light brown/mousey hair . . . a marked difference with lots of auburn lights.

Blonde hair . . . Henna will make blonde hair very red, so be sure you want red hair before you start!

Red hair . . . Henna will strengthen the colour of red hair, making it richer and brighter.

The length of time you leave the Henna on makes all the difference, of course. If you just want to add a 'lift' to your hair, just leave the paste on until it's dry, (about four hours, but check your hair every so often to make sure), but if you want a greater depth of colour you must leave it on for longer.

HENNA FOR HAIR COLOURING

Henna powder is on sale practically everywhere now, look for Henna (Hair Health) Henna Powder, 82p a drum, which conditions, colours and puts health back into hair.

You can use it on tinted, permed or bleached hair with complete safety because it is a natural vegetable extract and doesn't contain anything synthetic that might harm the hair.

Spiritual Sky make Henné Naturel which is the normal, colouring Henna powder, available from craft shops, price about 35p.

There are other makes on sale, but you must make sure you read the instructions very carefully. Some require boiling before use.

HENNA FOR CONDITIONING

If you want to use Henna but don't want to change the colour of your hair, try using Henna Wax Treatment, made by Henna (Hair Health) Ltd., price 90p a drum, which is very easy to use because you just dampen the hair, apply the wax and leave for 15-30 minutes, then rinse out and shampoo as usual.

Spiritual Sky Henna Conditioning Powder (made in France) is also on sale in craft shops, but you must make sure you buy the right powder. The names are in French, so look for Henné Neutre which is Henna powder with the colouring properties taken out.

Henna Hair Health make a range of Henna shampoos which are non-colouring, but are excellent for healthy, shining hair. Choose from Henna Medic Shampoo to help arrest the production of dandruff and re-balance the hair, Henna Herbal Shampoo for normal or greasy hair, adds a natural shine and gloss, Henna Shampoo for Dry Hair which is super rich with protein and Henna extracts to help nourish dry hair. These cost 50p each for a 380 cc bottle.

Permed and bleached hair often looks slightly out of condition, so look for Henna Herbal Antioxidant Cream, a great conditioner to be used after shampooing, price 60p for a 380 cc bottle.

HOW TO USE HENNA

Once you've bought your Henna powder, you must read the instructions very carefully before use. The simple ones usually go like this:

STEP 1

It's usual to shampoo your hair before using Henna and, if your hair is very dry, it's a good idea to rub a little olive oil into the scalp because Henna could make it even drier!

STEP 2

Mixing the Henna into a smooth paste is a very important part of the process. Use rubber gloves to prevent staining and mix up the powder in a bowl (preferably china or earthenware) with boiling water. The consistency is important . . . the paste should be smooth, not lumpy or too runny. Add the water carefully, a little at a time, so that you don't make any mistakes.

STEP 3

Applying the paste is the trickiest part. You should start from the roots, making sure the hair is coated from root to tip. Some makes recommend using a brush for this — an old hair brush would be ideal! That way you can brush the paste on to large sections of hair and make sure that you're coating the length of each hair shaft.

STEP 4

Once you've applied the Henna, you should wrap your head in a towel, first making sure that you've removed all traces of the paste from forehead, ears, neck and anywhere else it might be. The hairline is the most important place, so do make sure that it's all gone.

Heat makes quite a difference during the drying process, so wrap your head up in a hot towel and sit quite near the fire or in a warm room while the Henna is drying. Don't set yourself on fire by burning the towel or sitting too close to the fire, though!

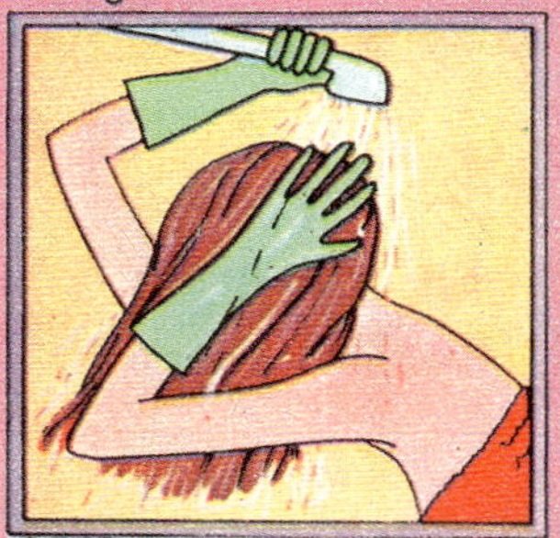

STEP 5

Deciding when to wash the Henna off is difficult, because there's no way of telling exactly what colour your hair will be until you've finished! We suggest that you leave the Henna on until it dries (about 3-4 hours) the first time, then wash it off.

You must rinse with warm water until the water runs clear and you've removed all trace of the dried Henna. When you've done this you can dry in the normal way into your usual style.

If you find that the result isn't strong enough, you can always repeat the process. Henna is a natural vegetable product, so you won't harm your hair with it, apart from making it dry, in which case you should use a cream shampoo and a conditioner until your hair returns to normal.

HENNA EXTRAS

Experimentation with Henna can produce all sorts of startling results . . . rich auburn shades of red from burgundy to Titian red (a sort of golden red), brown and even black. This depends entirely on the colour of your hair to start with, though, and you will need to spend a great deal of time experimenting if you want to achieve really dramatic results.

Henna Hair Health have just introduced a new product into the range, Henna Creme for golden highlights. It will produce golden lights in light brown/dark blonde hair and golden/red lights on mid-brown hair. It will have little effect on dark brown or black hair though, so stick to the powder if your hair is dark.

So, if your hair is dull, lifeless and needs a new lease of life, why not try Henna? It's harmless and great fun, as long as you read the instructions and follow them! The colour it gives is very natural . . . not synthetic and brassy, but it won't wash out . . . it just sort of wears off over the weeks! Have fun!

A JACKIE QUIZ

IS THIS THE YEAR FOR YOU?

Is 1976 going to be the start of something great for you? Answer the quiz below honestly, and on the vital evidence from last year, we'll tell you what sort of person you are and what the next twelve months is likely to hold in store.

1. How long do you usually keep your New Year Resolutions?
(a) Oh, at least a day or two.
(b) A few weeks or months.
(c) The whole year.

2. Are you starting off the New Year with plans for your future?
(b) Yes, lots of very elaborate plans.
(c) Just a few well-thought-out ones.
(a) Not many plans, really.

3. Which of these is likely to be nearest your main resolution?
(c) You'd aim for one specific goal to be fulfilled during the year.

(a) You'd resolve to be a better person than you were last year.
(b) You'd aim to be more organised about your life.

4. Looking back to the same time last year, do you think you have changed at all?
(a) I think I'm more or less the same.
(c) I've got new interests which I think have made me more aware and mature.
(b) I feel more confident now than I did then.

5. Do you think last year would have been better if . . .
(a) I'd had more opportunities to do things and prove myself,
(b) other people had been more considerate and encouraging,
(c) I'd take more control over myself?

6. When the New Year comes around, do you always think the year will be different, better in some way than the last one?
(b) Yes, I always have that exciting feeling that things are going to change.
(a) I'm usually too busy thinking about the next *week* let alone the next year, so I don't usually have any special feelings about it.
(c) I don't think anything will be different unless I *make* it different.

7. Which is the resolution you really *ought* to make, knowing it will be most difficult?
(b) To be better tempered.
(a) To work harder.
(c) To be more friendly and relaxed.

8. What, looking back, is the most memorable thing about last year?
(a) Meeting a smashing boy friend (or for that matter breaking up with someone you loved).
(b) Troubles and problems either at home, school or work, or socially.

(c) Passing an exam or a similar landmark in your life.

9. Generally, was last year a good year for you?
(b) It was a bit disappointing. I didn't do as much as I should have done.
(c) Quite good. No miracles happened, but I feel I progressed in various ways.
(a) In general I had a good time and enjoyed last year.

10. How do you feel about the difficulties and challenges which will face you in the next twelve months?
(a) I'll get along somehow — I always seem to manage to get by.
(b) I'm a bit apprehensive, but I'm trying to take myself in hand.
(c) I'm looking forward to the challenges and to seeing how I shall cope with them.

11. Are you still thinking and brooding about bad things which happened to you last year?
(c) I haven't forgotten them, but they don't seem so important now.
(a) Not in the least.
(b) Quite a bit.

12. What about the changes you would *like* to take place in the next year? Would they be concerned with —
(c) your ambitions (achievements and successes),
(b) yourself (changes in your character and attitudes),
(a) people (meeting them, getting on with them, falling in love with them)?

13. Unlucky thirteen. Are you superstitious? Do you think luck and fate will have a large part to play in your life in the year ahead?
(c) No, I don't believe in it. I mostly believe in the old saying that the more you put into life, the more you get out of it.

(b) Yes, I feel strongly that there are powers and influences outside my control, and I'm very aware of luck and fate in my life, both good and bad.
(a) Yes, I suppose so. A lot had to do with luck, although not everything. I feel quite a lucky sort of person mostly.

Now count your scores, mostly (a), (b) or (c), and read the conclusions on page 27.

QUIZ CONCLUSIONS

continued from page 22

Mostly (a) — You cope very well with life — even if mother/teacher/boss/boyfriend and granny are exasperated by you! You have a very optimistic, casual attitude to life, floating along without letting things get you down, and also without making any great efforts at self-improvement!

You're just naturally a happy-go-lucky kind of person and the extraordinary (and sometimes infuriating) thing about people like you is that you always seem to land on your feet whatever happens! Perhaps it's because you are basically so friendly and likeable, and quite free from any pretence or malice.

People might be irritated and envious of your ability to glide through good and bad things in life, but they also have to admire you and give you special treatment. In other words, your personality is the most important asset you have. You get by on your impulsive charm. However, a more serious approach to life would be worthwhile and help you to achieve more. While you're young you can afford to be a mad thing — but the future looms ahead, and you can't go on being mad and irresponsible when you're forty. So stop dismissing the things you don't want to know and face up to life more realistically.

The next year is bound to be fun for you, because you have a natural zest for life and enjoyment, and people find you great company. The danger is that another year will pass by and you'll think 'what have I done with it?'. The truth is that you will have frittered it away. We don't want to give you a boring old lecture (no doubt you've heard it all before), but come to your senses a bit more, won't you?

Mostly (b) — You are very reflective and romantic about life and often — dare we say it? — unrealistic. You live in your dreams a great deal, and you tend to make a meal of worrying about the future and brooding about the past. Try to snap out of it next year if you can. The trouble is you set yourself such impossible goals, and you tend to expect too much. You start off the year dreaming about all the fantastic and glorious things which will happen to you. So no wonder the harsh day to day reality of living is often uncomfortable and disappointing to you. You do think about yourself a lot, but you need a more down to earth approach to yourself. Don't try to do too much all at once, but sort yourself out little by little over the year, and then perhaps when next year comes along, you will feel more able to cope with life and less disappointed in yourself and your surroundings. It's great to have ideals and dreams as long as you sort them out a bit and modify them so there's at least a chance that you can make some of them come true.

You have a lot of valuable assets — sympathy, thoughtfulness, a very real awareness of yourself and people around you. People like you often have talents in art, music or literature, and other creative abilities. Make the very most of yourself because you have an awful lot of valuable qualities. The very fact that you tend to be moody and changeable means that there are a lot of deep feelings and unexplored abilities in your personality.

More living and less dreaming is what we advise to make next year as good as you want it to be

Mostly (c) — You have a lot of practical ability, a serious and realistic approach to life, and all the confidence you need. You seem to be planned and organised about your life. You are ambitious and you know what you want and how to go about achieving success in your chosen field. You are mature for your age. You have realised that in the main life is what you make it yourself, and that if you keep on working steadily and confidently towards what you want in life, you will succeed.

You have enough confidence not to be thrown by set-backs, and your single-minded determination must be the marvel and envy of many. It looks as though the future is bright for you, and next year will be a great step forward if you keep going as well as you did last year, or better. You seem almost a paragon of perfection, so what more is there to say? Only this.

Are you too concerned about your personal aims and ambitions and not enough about your relationships with people? This need not necessarily be so, and you are the best judge. Often single-minded people tend to miss out on the emotional things of life because they are always absorbed with the more outward successes and endeavours. Perhaps you need to relax a bit more and discover your heart as well as your head.

You are bound to have a good, successful year, but more contact with other people, more real feeling, will help you to lead a fuller life. You must admit that you tend to be self-centred, and might lose a lot by not joining in with the crowd a bit more, and letting yourself go sometimes.

Apart from that (which may or may not be true in your case) keep up the good work and the strength of character and mind, and 1976 should be a great year for you.

ARE YOU HEADING FOR THE BRIGHT LIGHTS?

SOMETIMES life at home seems unbearable, you walk out, slam the door and say to yourself that you're never going back. You hate your parents, nobody tries to understand *your* point of view and generally life is dreary, dull and not worth living!

Usually though, after a long walk or a visit to a friend you cool down, return home and find things aren't quite so bad after all!

But what would happen if you didn't do that? If, instead, you kept your silent vow and carried on walking? Well then, like some other girls, you'd probably make your way to the nearest station and get on a train to London.

You see, a lot of girls think that just by getting to London they'll solve all their problems. That somehow once they get to that golden place somebody will wave a magic wand — their life will be transformed into one long round of fun. They imagine that it's just like they see on TV, young people living in super flats, and rubbing shoulders with pop stars; after all that's where *they* all live isn't it?

In fact the truth is that wherever you go, your problems go with you. You don't automatically change yourself just by changing where you live and unless you're happy in your own mind, you won't be happy anywhere!

Running away to London then, doesn't solve any problems, it just brings new ones! Believe us, ending up in the great big city, penniless and homeless, isn't like being the heroine of a glossy comedy TV series at all.

You see, the first and most pressing problem is — *money*. When you leave home on an impulse, you don't usually have much money with you; sometimes just enough for the train fare, and sometimes nothing at all. So you're the natural prey for all kinds of unscrupulous people who hang around stations and bus terminals just looking for helpless, homeless girls like you!

If you manage to avoid these sharks, your next problem is where to stay. It's no fun trailing with a suitcase round London streets unable to afford to spend the night anywhere. In fact most runaways end up being picked up by the police — who will inform their parents — or in a charity hostel which can only be a very temporary measure!

SO what's the answer then if things go wrong at home? DON'T go running to London. Instead first go to someone locally for help. Try talking things over with the leader at your youth club or perhaps a sympathetic teacher at school.

Or if you're really desperate, try your local branch of the Samaritans (the number will be in the phone book) or a youth counselling service (most towns have them now; they're usually called things like Open Door or Grapevine).

If none of these are available try asking a relative to help you, or a friend's mum or even Cathy and Claire!

Once you've sorted out problems at home rather than trying to run away from them, you may still want to come to London to live and work. And this is where your attitude of mind really counts. You see, London can be fine as long as you don't look on it as an escape route. If instead you have a positive, planned outlook, then you'll get the very most out of it, providing of course that you're old enough to leave home in the first place!

So your first important step is to talk it all over with your mum and dad first and hopefully get their agreement. If you show that you're sensibly planning exactly how and where you're going to work and live in London, then they should start to believe that you're ready for such a big step!

The next step is to get a job. We contacted a London Youth Employment Officer.

"The facts are hard," she told us. "If you come to London there are NOT the jobs for the unskilled. And the jobs that there are for young people just don't pay enough for them to stay in bed-sits, share flats and do all the things they came to do in London anyway! In fact even the traditional employers of young, unskilled people like the London stores, are now mostly refusing to employ 16-19 year olds unless they live at home."

So what do you do? Well, the best answer is to consult your local Careers officer, and find out about the type of jobs available in London. Also the type of training you'd need first, which you should get locally.

There are a few firms which run training schemes in London and provide hostels, like some department stores or careers like Nursing, so ask your Careers officer to give you full details of all these too. Obviously there are age limits for most of these schemes.

Of course Shorthand/Typing, if you're fully qualified, is a skill that's always needed in London and it opens the door to lots of opportunities. So once you've trained, write to employment agencies *before* you come and find out whether the sort of job you need is available and at what time of the year it's best to come.

A *minimum* gross salary of £1,700 (£32.50 approx. weekly) is needed for living without hardship in a bed-sitter or flat-share. Net salary approx. £24.

It sounds a lot of money but you'll see from our breakdown where it all goes:

Basics	
Rent	£ 9.00
Electricity/ Heat	1.50
Travelling in London	2.50
Food (apart from lunch)	4.00
Lunches	1.57
per week	£18.57
Extras	
Chemist	.50
Clothes	1.50
Entertainment/ holidays (incl. visits home etc).	2.00
Launderette, cleaners, shoe repairs	.75
Miscellaneous (gifts, stationery etc.)	1.25
per week	£ 6.00
Total per week	£24.57

OF course a living-in job as a mother's help or au pair would cut down on some of these expenses so it's worth finding out about these from your Careers officer too.

Once you've got the job situation sorted out, you have to find *somewhere to live*. And facing facts again, this is no easy task. Miss Jean Whesson of the Y.W.C.A. Accommodation Bureau told us,

"Most landlords don't want young tenants, and with the accommodation situation the way it is, they can afford to pick and choose. In summer, London is filled with tourists and in September with students, so either way working people lose out!"

But again persistence and planning ahead pay off. The best idea is to book well in advance at a temporary hostel for at least two weeks while you're looking for a permanent flat-share or bed-sit.

A booklet STAYING IN LONDON lists over 100 hostels in the London area. It costs 40p, including postage, and you can get it by writing to the London YWCA Accommodation and Advisory Service, 16 Great Russell Street, London WC1B 3LR.

You will need to bring money to London with you, of course, and you should bring enough money to pay for your hostel and one month's rent in a flat (maybe £40-£45) plus another £20-£40 for a deposit (returnable on leaving the flat in good condition). If you're hoping to live in a bed-sitter, you will usually need at least one week's rent in advance. £6-£10 is the average weekly rate.

The London YWCA Accommodation and Advisory Service can help in finding a bed-sitting room or flat share. And it makes things easier if you have a couple of references to take with you to any future landlord or landlady. They also have a list of employment agencies that girls have already found friendly and helpful. (Same address as above).

But remember, before you get all set to go, that although London has lots to offer, it can be the loneliest place in the world, especially if you don't already have any friends or relatives living there. However dull or dreary you might think your small town or village is at times, at least when you walk down the street you recognise people; even the shopkeepers know you and to a certain extent are concerned about you. But in London you can walk down a street thronged with people and not know a single soul! That's when it hits you that you really are alone!

Also it's often hard enough to adjust to working life after school, and it's ten times harder if you have to adjust to "big city" life as well.

So first take a real good look at your own home town and make sure that you're really trying to get the most out of it. Really, consider all the advantages you have there before deciding to make a move.

Then if you're still determined to live in London, make all your arrangements well beforehand, go to a job that you're properly trained for and with the ability to pay your way, and we hope you have the super time you expect!

Please remember, if you *have* left home without telling anybody you were going, somebody will be worrying about you. Tell them you're alive and well by phoning 01-567 5339. Your message will be passed on to the person you want exactly as you've said it.

NINA'S NATTER

I'M sure everyone's got at least one craving they're desperately ashamed of. Something they normally wouldn't be seen dead in or with.

Take men, for example — haven't you ever found your very masculine, 'none of this romantic 'rubbish' boyfriend secretly poring over your copy of Jackie? Jumping as though you were the battle of Waterloo, he hastily puts it down, muttering something about 'Just wanted to see what sort of trash you wasted your time reading'.

He'll be biting his nails for the rest of the evening, too, if you caught him in the middle of a story. Better do him a favour and slip it quietly into his pocket before he goes home.

With one friend of mine, it was pink plastic boots. She noticed this dreadful craving emerging one year, crawling from its resting place in her hideous subconscious. She was in trouble.

What could she do about it? She couldn't stand pink plastic boots. She wouldn't be seen dead in them. But yet — there it was. She found herself having little fantasies about them, followed by nightmares of pairs of them always just out of reach.

Eventually she confided in me — she had to, it was driving her crazy. I listened sympathetically and suggested she looked for a pair. To my astonishment, she actually found some in a shop and bought them.

They were awful. Not just ordinary pink, but a sort of nasty, pucy, distemper-type pink, the kind of musty colour old aunts knit bed-jackets in. Once she had actually acquired the wretched things, the urge wore off. She was cured! I'm not even sure I actually ever saw her wear them. There they sit, to this day, in a dusty old wardrobe, all five quids worth. But, I think, cheap at the price!!

Another friend of mine had this thing about baby food. She couldn't resist those horrible sludgy tins of anaemic semolina that Britain's babyhood are reared on. She bought them surreptitiously by the dozen, slipping them furtively into her bag and planning a secret midnight snack or two. She was too sensitive to face the teasing her passion aroused, and is even too clever now to be caught at it.

Another went in for winklepickers (yes, you can still buy them); yet another had a thing about mock Tudor houses and Frank Sinatra. I even know one young lady who is an ardent follower of the Queen. Old ladies think it's wonderful in one so young, but she is thoroughly ashamed of herself.

She just can't seem to help herself poring over the newspaper for the odd paragraph or two, or peering off the top of her bus in the hope that *one* day Her Majesty will be strolling by the west wall of the Palace.

Of course, what you may be dreadfully ashamed of may seem perfectly natural to someone else. Most of my boyfriends' secret lusts have been for things which seem perfectly harmless to me, like Winnie the Pooh and Woman's Hour. If you find out about it, they will swear you to secrecy with a frightened look, and rarely dare to indulge in such a weakness in your presence.

And what about me? Well, I don't know that I'd really like to say. I mean, that kind of thing can be private, can't it?

Well . . . since I've got myself into this, I must confess a certain yearning for very early Beatles' records . . . Not too bad?

How about those stiff petticoats from the 1950's . . . Worst of all? Ah well I'd better confess — it's school stories. 'Top of the Fourth' 'Penny the Prefect' 'Three Thirds in a Pickle.' Oh I've read them all. But don't you laugh at me, that's all.

And since I've told mine, how about *you*???

WHAT'S YOUR FAVOURITE MEAL?

ON-THE-SPOT INTERVIEWS where our roving reporters find out what YOU think

Carol Downes, London, S.E.1.
Right now I've got a craze for a terrific sandwich my American pen-friend told me about: it's peanut-butter, banana, lettuce and mayonnaise! It sounds horrible, but just try it!

Susan Bradshaw, Leeds, Yorks.
Best of all, I like the traditional meal Mum makes for us on Sundays. It's the one time when all the family is together, and Mum makes Yorkshire pudding, roast beef, two or three vegetables, boiled and roast potatoes, and usually follows it with apple pie and cream. It's all delicious!

Norah McIlvar, Truro, Cornwall.
Shepherd's Pie. We learnt to cook it at school so I make it for the family about once a week, and I'm getting quite expert at it now. Sometimes I wonder if they're beginning to get fed up with it, but anyway it's still my favourite!

Mary Manson, Rothesay, Buteshire.
If I were a mouse I'd soon be trapped. I can make a meal of a nice piece of cheese!

Barbara Finlayson, Edinburgh.
The meat and potato dish better known as mince and tatties! Every day thousands of Scots sit down to dine on this, so it can't be bad!

Norma Hogg, London, N.1.
Fish and chips — but it has to be cooked at home! No chippy can do it like my mum!

Julie Heaton, Wakefield, Yorks.
My favourite meal is the scrambled eggs I make. I'm such an awful cook that it's quite exciting to find out whether I'll actually get scrambled eggs — or an omelette!

Lesley Hines, Warrington, Lancs.
It starts with scampi; then a luscious, gigantic steak, with lots of those crispy little chips and a salad; then strawberries and cream. Then you all fall down!

Janet Gardener, Croydon, Surrey.
Lobster salad. It's so expensive, though, I've only eaten it twice in my life — which is probably a good thing, as I'm not likely to get tired of it!

Gerard Earl, Corsham, Wilts.
Spaghetti Bolognaise plus fish and chips. Very exotic!

Chris Lacklison (Kenny)
I'm very partial to beefburgers and chips, and my second favourite is scampi. I don't like vegetables at all and I'm lucky that although my favourite food is pretty fattening, I don't seem to put on any weight.

Marjorie Crawford, Uddingston, Lanarkshire.
Cold meals are the kind I like best. For example really unusual salads, with everything in them from rice to raisins.

Betty Rowbottom, Badger's Mount, Kent.
My idea of heaven is six knickerbocker glories in a row — but I doubt if I'd actually make it if I had the chance. So I'll settle for my all-time weekly treat — bangers and cherryade.

Brenda Forester, Minehead, Somerset.
My mum moans that I don't appreciate decent meals. What I really enjoy are things out of tins or frozen foods. I love tomato soup and cold baked beans eaten straight from the tin, followed by a big dollop of ice-cream. I suppose you'd call me a nutritionist's nightmare!

Sharon Haydon, Salisbury, Wilts.
Anything Chinese. The dishes are so varied and never taste the same twice. There are so many flavours: sweet, sour, spicy, bland, etc. Eating Chinese is a real experience!

Lynn Rickards, Orpington, Kent.
My favourite meal is steak, egg, chips and mushrooms. I like steak because it's chewy and full of flavour, and as for chips, I'd eat them any time. In fact, I've even had them for breakfast!

PATCHWORK

WILL HE MARRY ME?

Do you ever wonder if you'll get married, and what your future husband will look like? Well, why not try to conjure up a vision of him with the aid of a little bit of magic?

In earlier times when marriage was the only future open to girls, they invented all sorts of strange rituals, hoping to discover if they would marry or not, or who the man would be. The ceremonies varied according to the district, but basically they were all meant to have the same result!

In Oxford, a girl carried hempseed into her garden at nightfall, then sprinkled it over her left shoulder as she sang:

Hempseed I sow,
Hempseed I hoe,
He that is my own true love,
Come after me and mow.

After repeating this verse nine times, she sat back and waited hopefully to see the figure of her future husband . . . . but if, instead, she heard a bell ringing, this meant she'd never marry.

In Scotland, a group of girls lined up facing a mirror and each girl in turn brushed her hair three times. If the vision of a man looking over her shoulder was reflected in the looking-glass, she would marry him within the year.

A Welsh girl preferred to scratch her boy's initials on a leaf, which she placed in her shoe and wore all day. If she could read the letters next morning the boy would marry her, but if they had faded the friendship would end.

One Devon custom was for a girl to tap on a henhouse door at night. If the hens cackled she would remain unwed, but if the cock crowed she would marry shortly.

A game which used to be very popular was for a girl to suspend a borrowed wedding ring by a hair from her head. If it moved round slowly, she would marry once, but if it spun round madly she would marry twice.

Yorkshire girls associated the ash tree with magic and love, and they often went to sleep with an ash leaf under their pillow, after reciting:

Even-ash, even-ash, I pluck thee,
This night my own true love to see,
Not in apparel strange or rare,
But in the clothes he everyday wear.

For centuries girls have linked the red rose with love and it's still believed that if you dream of a red rose your love life will be exciting, but if you dream of a white one you can expect a broken heart.

So there you are — take your pick and find your love!

Well, what are the problems of your everyday life? They're guaranteed to be reflected to an uncanny (or uncanine?) degree by that increasingly popular Beagle, Snoopy, and friends from the Peanuts gang. Would you believe they're 25 years old now, though they don't look a day over — well . . . they certainly don't look 25!

Hallmark have been busy extending their range of things featuring this soppy, puzzled, lovable group; as well as greeting cards, you'll now be able to get rulers (metric, too), scribbling pads, party invites, playing cards, handkerchiefs, greetings books and Decals — self-adhesive decorations to brighten up doors and desks.

Hallmark's Peanuts Gallery range is on sale now at leading Hallmark stockists and department stores.

WHAT A LAUGH!

If you're one of the thousands of people who've been cracked up laughing at The Pink Panther, you certainly mustn't miss the new Peter Sellers film, The Return of the Pink Panther.

Peter Sellers, of course, is the accident-prone but successful Inspector Clouseau, who actually helps a bank robbery by chatting to the look-out man, then proceeds to knock the bank manager unconscious. Herbert Lom is Chief Inspector Dreyfus, whose ambition it is to kill Clouseau, and Christopher Plummer and Catherine Schell are the "villains," Sir Charles and Lady Litton.

They all clown hilariously amidst the complicated series of events, which include robberies, insanities, obsessions and double-crossings. The film opens at London's Leicester Square Theatre on January 29.

POLDARK!

Been gripped by sheer exciting, romantic adventure on Sunday evenings for the past (very many past) weeks? Bet that lovely tall hunk, Ross Poldark, played by Robin Ellis, has had a lot to do with it. We think there's more to it than that, too — have *you* noticed the resemblance to Bryan Ferry??

When he's got some time for anything apart from work, Robin likes reading, listening to records, and playing squash; and he's been known to go to the occasional pop concert, too! Here he is for you to have another ogle at . . .

You can re-live Poldark's adventures now too, by reading the books of the series; they're by Winston Graham, published in paper back, and you can find them in most booksellers.

JACKIE RECIPE

SAY CHEESE!

This recipe couldn't be simpler — and it's very versatile! Try it as a healthy lunch, a snack supper or an interesting dessert!

BEING CRAFTY!

Knitting or candlemaking, toys and jewellery, macrame, tapestry, plaster-casting, batik, painting, origami — makes you wonder why you've been wasting your time these long, dark evenings when you think of all you *could* be doing, doesn't it? Well, if it does, and you're in the Home Counties, it's well worth a visit to the Craftsmith shops in Richmond and Hemel Hempstead to inspire you further!

Under one roof you'll find everything you need for a huge range of craft activities. These aren't just any ordinary handicraft shops, either. People are there to give informed, enthusiastic advice and information — not only to experienced craft workers, but to those who'd like to have a go but haven't got a clue where to start!

They've got all the basic kits to interest beginners and materials for advanced work to satisfy experts; you'll find it all, from patterns through raw materials to trimmings, dyes and finishing materials. Their information leaflets and samples are all part of the service.

At the moment Craftsmith shops are at 216-218 The Marlowes, Hemel Hempstead and 18 George Street, Richmond. Watch out for more though. They hope to open, eventually, in other parts of the country.

YOUR PATCH —

NEW HATS FOR OLD!

That's the idea from Susan Blanks of Harlow, Essex.

It'll do on any fairly plain type hat you've got tired of. Susan made a colourful bird — a strange sort of parrot with a great long, flowing tail — out of scraps of old material: you can use felt, satin, even old denim — anything bright and cheerful.

Then she just sewed it bang on the side of the hat, so the tail came hanging down. Adds quite a bit of interest, as you can see!

Got an idea for Your Patch, yourself? Send it in to Jackie, 185 Fleet Street, London EC4A 2HS, and you might win £1, as Susan did.

KNOW YOUR CENTIMETRES

Going silly over centimetres? It is confusing — not to mention frustrating — when you're confronted with a measurement that means nothing whatsoever to you. But we managed it with old pence into new pence. Now there's not too much you can do with inches, except learn to re-think them.

Remember all those little converter cards we thought we'd never be able to do without? Here they are again, so you can do a quick change till a 55.9 centimetre waist sounds more usual than a 22-inch one! Smiths Metric Converter is a handy size to carry around with you, and solves all sorts of problems of sizes in dresses, skirts, trousers — even carpets, if you happen to be buying one! It costs 40p from main branches of W. H. Smith & Sons.

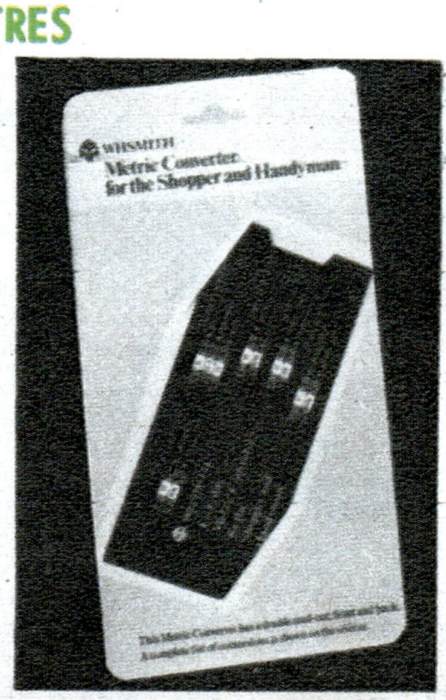

The foot/"centi-pede" ruler shows — wouldn't you guess? — measurements in inches on the foot-shaped side; turn it over and read the length in centimetres on the "centi-pede" side! It costs £1, and you can get it at Robert Jacksons of 171 Piccadilly, London, W.1. If you want to send away for it, enclose an extra 18p for postage and packing. Happy conversions!

ARE YOU A SHRINKING VIOLET?

A JACKIE QUIZ

WHAT kind of flower best matches your personality? Are you a blushing violet or an exotic hothouse bloom? Try our fun quiz and find out! The answers may surprise you!

1. Where would you most like to spend a day?
(c) An indoor jungle full of exotic plants.
(f) A park full of grass and flower beds.
(a) A fabulous Disneyland-type amusement arcade.
(b) A beautiful stately garden with fountains and statues.
(e) A nature reserve.
(d) A safari park.

2. How do you see yourself in five years' time?
(a) Very much a career girl.
(e) Just being happy.
(c) Trying to achieve all your ambitions, possibly abroad.
(f) Going out with loads of boys and having a great time.
(d) You've no idea.
(b) Settled down and married, with at least one child.

3. Which of these would you prefer to get from someone very special?
(b) A delicate spray of wild woodland flowers.
(d) Eidelweiss, the flower which only grows on the most inaccessible mountain peaks.
(a) A bunch of blue roses.
(f) A whole basket of assorted flowers.
(c) A single tropical orchid.
(e) Sprigs of lily of the valley.

4. Which of these would you prefer to have in your garden?
(d) A bird house.
(c) A monkey puzzle tree.
(a) A rock garden, complete with garden gnomes.
(e) A wishing well.
(b) A stone cupid.
(f) A highly original modern sculpture.

5. Which music would you choose to relax with after a long, hard day?
(e) Judy Collins.
(c) Alice Cooper.
(b) Nilsson's love songs.
(f) A big pile of the Top Twenty singles.
(d) The 1812 overture.
(a) Bryan Ferry.

6. Which of these smells holds special memories for you?
(b) That unmistakable scent of freshly cut grass.
(d) A bottle of cough medicine.
(a) A very special perfume.
(f) A bottle of sun tan lotion.
(c) The smell of brand new school exercise books.
(e) The scent of a real, old-fashioned Christmas tree.

7. Which of these would you like to visit your garden?
(c) Nightingales.
(e) Butterflies.
(a) Persian blue cats.

(f) Black panthers.
(b) Birds of paradise.
(d) Tame lion cubs.

8. Which spot would you choose for a picnic with your boyfriend?
(a) An empty Caribbean beach.
(d) A rugged mountaintop.
(e) A tranquil river bank.
(f) A field of golden corn.
(c) A planet somewhere in outer space.
(b) A meadow of buttercups.

9. Which of these would you choose for dinner?
(b) Flower-petal salad.
(d) Tropical stew.
(f) Plant pie.
(c) Herb nectar.
(a) Magnolia mousse.
(e) Lotus-flower soup.

10. You are modelling for a glamorous fashion photograph. Which background would suit you best?
(d) A mass of wild ferns and giant flowering grasses.
(b) An old-fashioned border of lupins and hollyhocks.
(e) Clusters of water lilies on a pond.
(a) A display of exotic hot-house plants.

(f) A thicket of enormous cactus plants.
(c) A display of strange flowering bushes from a temple garden.

11. Which of these films would you find most exciting to watch?
(b) A wildlife documentary.
(c) The story of a girl who's haunted by a ghost from the past.
(f) An adventure set in the deepest jungle.
(e) The fight for life by a young couple trapped in a burning building.
(a) An intriguing spy film set in Paris.
(c) Trick pilots performing daredevil flying stunts.

12. Which sounds most romantic to you?
(f) The Mountains of Eternity.
(c) The Garden of the Three Veils.
(d) The Sundown Desert.
(a) The Palace of Happiness.
(e) The Valley of the Half-Moon.
(b) The Midnight Grotto.

13. How would you react if your boyfriend called you by the wrong name?
(b) You'd start having suspicious doubts about him.
(a) You'd never speak to him again.
(f) It wouldn't worry you.
(d) You'd just call *him* the wrong name.
(c) You'd have a furious row with him
(e) You'd cry about it, but you wouldn't mention it to him.

Now count your score, mainly (a)'s (b)'s (c)'s etc., and turn to page 30.

ARE YOU A SHRINKING VIOLET?

CONCLUSIONS

Mostly (a) — You're the typical English rose type — cultivated rather than wild. You're a sophisticated person, who enjoys all the good things civilisation has to offer. You like comfort, luxury and glamorous situations, and you love to be the centre of attention, surrounded by admirers. You tend to be proud, and although you are undoubtedly one of the most beautiful flowers, it's also true that every rose has thorns. The prickly side of your nature displays itself in a short temper and intolerance of people who don't come up to your high standards.

You like people who are interesting and lively company, but tend to dismiss those who don't make an immediate impression on you. In your love life, you expect to be treated well, and you are quick to find fault with boyfriends. However, when you first fall in love, you tend to exaggerate your emotions and this sometimes leads to disappointment. You have greath strength of character and could be very popular indeed if you were just a little more tolerant of people!

Mostly (b) — You're a beautiful, sensitive flower, a lily. In fact, you have all the good qualities associated with lilies — gentleness, delicacy and romance. Everything in your garden should be lovely, as you have the gift of creating a good atmosphere around you. You are honest and sympathetic, aware of things around you, and you have a good understanding of other people. You are capable of deep friendships, and are a romantic at heart. Although you are a bit of a dreamer, you are able to see beauty around you, and even though you may sometimes go through periods of depression, you are basically a stable, happy person.

You have a vivid imagination, and it is likely that you would be good at anything artistic. When you fall in love, it'll probably be the real thing. Having a very appealing nature, you often float through difficult situations, using your special personal charm, without even realising the effect you have on others. Romance should follow you wherever you go!

Mostly (c) — You're that strange, mystical flower, the orchid. You live by your instincts, and you have a tendency to go for anything out of the ordinary — occult beliefs, supersititon and so on. These things fascinate you and satisfy your longing for difference and variety. In fact, you often go out of your way to be different just for the sake of it! You are very much an individual, with an inner life of your own, and you would *hate* to be thought of as typical or ordinary.

For this reason, you tend to dramatise yourself to extremes and to get carried away by weird, zany ideas which don't always fit in with the practical business of living from day to day! No wonder your family and friends sometimes accuse you of being a complete loony!

You're a very aware person and you'll certainly gain a rich experience of life, as you go along your original path through it! Trouble is, nothing is simple for you. You enjoy dramas, and tend to complicate situations and relationships out of all proportion. People don't always find you relaxing, but at least you're interesting and lively-minded and will give your friends a lot to think about! You tend to be moody, going from the heights of joy to the depths of misery and back again, but at least you'll never be bored with life!

Mostly (d) — You're that lovely wild flower, the bluebell. You're impulsive, adventurous and full of the joys of life. You have a very deep feeling for nature and for everything that is wild, free and unrestricted. You hate to be shut in, and need a lot of space and freedom to express yourself. You are extremely independent — you know your own mind, and you know what you want in life. You want to go your own way and live your own life, uninfluenced by others. You are inclined to be impatient, and although you dislike routine, you can be practical when you really have to be!

You're easy-going and extrovert, finding it easy to make friends, but you avoid relationships which tie you down, and you are often inclined to get bored with people after a while. Deep relationships are not easy for you, so you don't fall in love easily. It would take someone very special to sweep you off your feet, because although you can be romantic and flightly at times, you are basically quite a hard-hearted type. You are a free spirit, not hampered by doubts or dogged by fears. You are extremely active, and it's a good bet that you'll go far in life. You'll find success in your chosen way of life, and it's likely that with your spirit of adventure and your wander-lust, you'll cover quite a bit of the surface of the globe, too!

Mostly (e) — You are the violet — a gentle, shy flower. Although you tend to be very reserved, you genuinely love people and you bring peace and tranquillity to those around you. You have a quiet inner strength that others envy, and in a world of rush and panic, you manage to keep calm. You are a good listener, and a trustworthy friend. You don't need great dramas in your life, for you can see pleasure and interest in everything around you. You know how to relax, too, for however tense situations are, you have that special quality which enables you to cope. In many ways, you are a very cool person.

Although you may sometimes appear shy or easily led, you are in fact, very much your own person. There's no deceit or malice in you, and you have a deep self-confidence which enables you to trust your own judgment and be independent when you have to be. You fall in love easily and yet there is always part of you which can remain slightly detached, and this may often prove to be a saving grace. Don't ever get caught up in the mad whirl of life — you are like a haven of peace to your friends and family and can bring great happiness to them, and to yourself.

Mostly (f) — You're the sunflower brave, bold, cheerful and always wanting to be right where the action is. You're very sociable, great company, and the life and soul of any party. You're impulsive (even to the point of thoughtlessness sometimes), and you tend to go charging through life like a bull, full of go and energy, and the kind of vitality which oftens makes weaker mortals wilt under the strain! You can go anywhere, and do anything you set out to do. This is because, although you never plan anything in a logical way, and you're not necessarily more capable than others, you have that incredible enthusiasm which carries you along until success is in your reach.

You're a lively and stimulating friend (if they can keep up with you!) and you'd bring great interest and amusement into the life of any boy. You can be tremendously popular, if you want, for you have the knack of making people feel instantly at ease with you. Mind you, it's likely that you talk so much they can hardly get a word in edgewise! Even if people don't always like you, they certainly can't ignore you, so stay as dynamic as you are!

IF YOU GO DOWN TO THE BEACH TODAY...

1. Colourful pink floral print bikini with bow front and halter neck ties, by Triumph. Price: £2.50. Sizes: 30 in.-36 in.

2. Green swimsuit with gathered cups, ties at the front, and halter neck, from British Home Stores. Price: £3.99. Sizes. 34 in.-36 in.

3. Blue swimsuit with gathered cups and pretty, beaded halter neck ties, from Dorothy Perkins Price: £3.99. Sizes: 10-16.

4. Sunny yellow bikini with ring front, halter neck, and rings at brief sides. from Top Shop. Price: £3.99. Sizes: 10-16.

5. Bright stripy bikini in turquoise and white from Boots. Price: £2.99. Sizes: 10-14.

6. Striking red bikini with bra-clip front, adjustable cups and halter neck ties from Boots. Price: £2.25. Sizes: 10-14.

7. Red and white striped towelling bikini with ring front and halter neck, from Marks & Spencer. Price: £3.99. Sizes: 10-16.

8. Denim bikini with tie halter neck, rope ties at bra front and brief sides, from Sunarama. Price: £3.99. Sizes: 32 in.-38 in.

9. Bright orange bikini with adjustable cups and halter neck, and ties at brief sides, from Palmers. Price: £3.99. Sizes: 32 in.-36 in.

. . . You'd better take the very latest swimsuits and bikinis if you want to be in the swim! They come in all shapes and sizes in all sorts of colours, decorated with ties, beads, rings and embroidery. They're just perfect for sun-bathing, so choose your favourite from our selection and head for the sun!

11. Blue swimsuit with lace-up front, from Richard Shops. Price: £4.95. Sizes: 32 in. - 38 in.

12. Colourful red flowery swimsuit with cross straps at the back, and gathered front, from Marks & Spencer. Price: £4.99. Sizes: 10-14.

10. Multi-coloured bikini with continental style "house" print, from Marks & Spencer. Price: £3.99. Sizes: 10-14.

13. Unusual blue bikini with red stitching trim on bra and briefs, and red rope ties on bra, from Silhouette. Price: £5.50. Sizes: 32 in.-36 in.

17. Striking navy and white wide striped bikini, from Top Shop. Price: £3.99. Sizes: 10-14.

14. Beige bikini with pretty floral embroidery and adjustable cups, from Miss Ladybird. Price: £4.50. Sizes: 32 in.-36 in.

18. Lovely pink/blue checked bikini with halter neck ties, gathered cups and tiny briefs with ties at the sides, from C & A. Price: £2.95. Sizes: 10-16.

16. Green bikini with bra neck tie and gathered front, from Dorothy Perkins. Price: £3.99. Sizes: 10-14.

15. Royal velour bikini with halter neck ties, from Woolworth. Price: £3.29. Sizes: 10-14.

Further details and stockists on page 28.

Do you wanna DANCE?

Do you feel shy when you go to a party or disco because you think you can't dance? Well, worry no more! Your problems are solved with our step-by-step guide to disco dancing, demonstrated by Katie and Christine, two pupils at London's Dance Centre.

the JACKIE

1. Feet apart and you're ready to start!
2. Step to the right, touch left foot behind (with a bounce).
3. Feet apart, ready to –
4. Step to the left and touch right foot behind (with a bounce).
Repeat over and over again, turn around when you feel like it, do what you want with your arms, keep your elbows up like Katie or let your hands swing low! It looks great, it's simple and you can use it to dance to just about anything. Specially good to Black Soul, Stylistics.

O K? Now you've got a basic dance you can do anywhere, anytime. So let's be a little more adventurous and twist the night away!

the TWIST

1. Twist heels to the right, feet together.
2. Twist heels to the left, feet together.
3. Bring right foot out and move your hip to the right.
4. Twist on the left foot and lift the right leg.
5. Twist down. Twist up higher and higher gradually.
6. Arms up, twist on the spot.

Now you can twist! A few extra hints though if you're having trouble. To get your feet right, pretend you're crushing something (preferably not your partner's toes!) with your heels. And your arms should twist towards the hip that's out, just like rubbing a towel behind your back. Good twisting records are: Let's Twist Again — Chubby Checker, Twist and Shout — Best of the Beatles.

ANOTHER IN OUR "HOW DO YOU KNOW" SERIES

YOU KNOW HE LOVES YOU WHEN...

. . . you find it written up on a local oak!

. . . he puts a message in the paper, under "Public Announcements," and he gives a copy to each of his friends

. . . he doesn't mind missing his last bus home, just so that he can see *you* all the way home, safe and sound.

. . . he wears his hair the way you like it.

. . . he kisses you good-night — for two hours!

. . . you introduce him to your blonde, blue-eyed, fantastically-pretty girlfriend and he *still* prefers you!

. . . he stops buying fish 'n' chips — and buys a bottle of wine instead.

. . . he doesn't mind going shopping with you — on Cup Final Day!

. . . he wears the jersey you spent *weeks* knitting for him, even if you can only see his eyes above the polo-neck. *And* he wears all the other awful, lop-sided, mixed-up things you knit for him!

. . . he can't kick a ball straight if you're watching.

. . . he stops being complimentary and says your nose reminds him of a bit of putty.

. . . he'll let your smelly, hair-shedding old dog get into his new car.

. . . he gets personally invited to escort Princess Caroline of Monaco to a party in St Tropez, but he turns it down to take you to the pictures as arranged.

. . . he visits you every day when you're in bed with flu and doesn't bat an eye-lid when he sees you without make-up, hair unwashed, and your nose and eyes all red and streaming!

. . . *he* wears your Jackie love brooch and it spells "I love you" for all to see!

. . . he hires a plane to sky-write that you're the most beautiful! girl in the world.

. . . he queues all night for tickets for the Rollers' concert you wanted to go to, then doesn't shout at you when he finds out you've gone off them!

. . . he teaches you to play chess, then lets you win against him.

. . . he phones every night and never runs out of things to say to you.

. . . he'd rather spend a quiet evening with you than go for a night out with the boys.

. . . he floats heart-shaped paper darts across the classroom at you and doesn't even object when the teacher catches them instead.

. . . he wants to know if you can cook.

. . . he lets you read your "Jackie" uninterrupted.

. . . he tells you he does.

the L.A. STOMP

A good ice breaker at any party is a dance that everyone can do together in a long line. The L.A. Stomp is just such a dance. Practise it yourself at home first teach it to your friends then start doing it at the next party you go to.

1. Touch right foot to the back twice.
2. Touch right foot forward twice (with a bounce).
3. One touch back, one forward, one touch back and kick.
4. Step back with your right foot, step back with your left foot, step back on your right foot. Touch your left foot to the back.
5. Step forward on the left foot, step forward on the right foot, step forward on the left, touch right foot forward.
6. Step to the right with the left hip cut, join your feet together.
7. Step to the right again, touch the left foot to the right.
Repeat 6 and 7 only this time to the left.
8. Step to the right and touch, step to the left and touch, step to the right and touch, then click your heels together with a bounce. Dance to: Art for Art's Sake by 10 C.C.

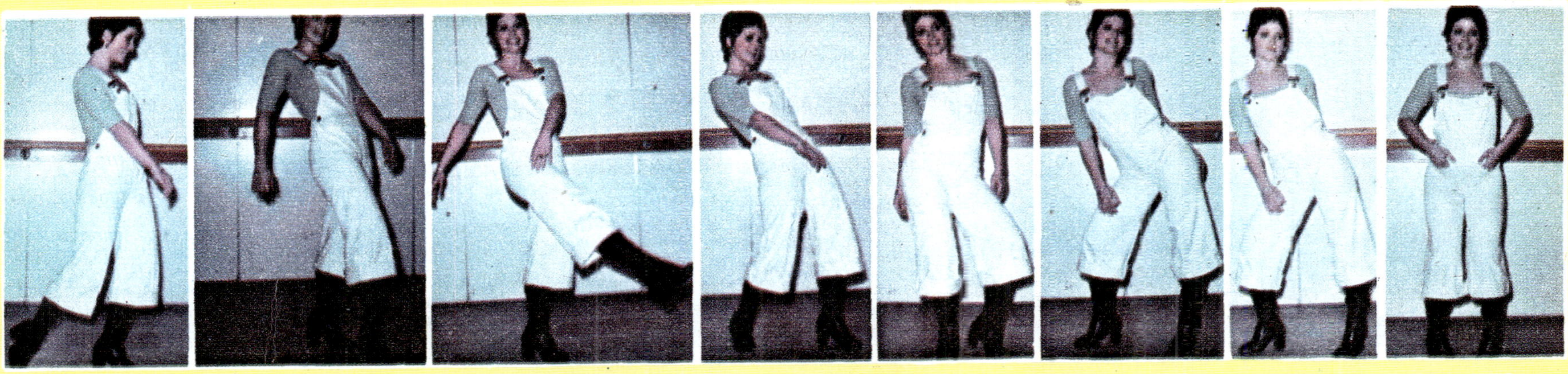

Finally, by this time you should be ready for the bump. One of the easiest dances, but also one of the most extrovert. So grab a partner and MOVE!

the BUMP

1. Face each other and bump right hips.
2. Lift left leg up and bump left knees.
3. Jump with feet apart and bump right shoulders.
4. Jump with feet together and bump bums!
Then repeat if you dare!
Dance to: any Kenny or Bay City Roller Records — and have fun!

By the way, if you live in London and would like to go to the disco dance classes at the Dance Centre, Floral Street, London W.C.2. then here's the info. The classes are run by Arlene Phillips (who's trained Sue and Mary of Pan's People!) and Christine Wickham. They're held every night of the week at five o'clock and on Saturday mornings at 11 a.m. There are classes to suit beginners and they go right up to the advanced classes. How long you take to move up classes is entirely up to you and how good you are! The fee is 90p per class and there is no enrolment fee but you should ask the Dance Centre first for details. (You'll find their number in the phone book).

They also have classes in tap, soul, rock/jazz ballet, yoga and classical ballet, so there's something to suit everyone. If you live outside London, don't despair, many ballet schools now hold disco dancing/rock ballet (Pan's People style dancing) classes, so check up with your local school, you'll probably be pleasantly surprised!

And now if a boy says "Do You Wanna Dance?" you'll be able to say Yes!

ON-THE-SPOT INTERVIEWS
where our roving reporters find out what YOU think.

WHAT NEW GADGET WOULD YOU LIKE TO INVENT?

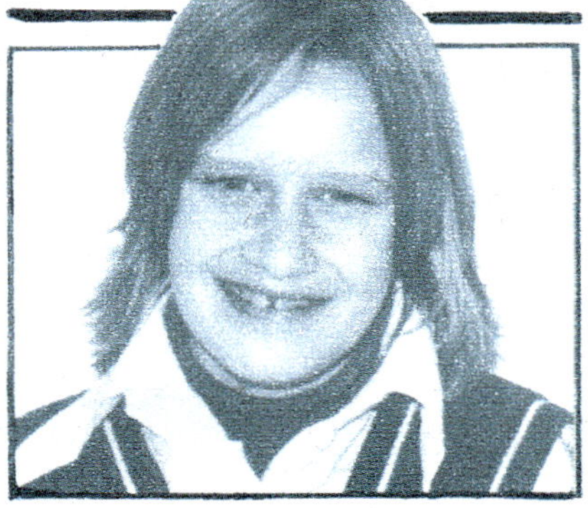

Dawn Saggers, Chelsea, London.
I'd like to invent a robot that looked exactly like me, something like the Six Million Dollar Man, and then she could go to school for me and do my homework and sit my exams, and I could spend my time doing exactly what I wanted!

Rowena Duthie, Glasgow, Scotland.
I'd like to invent a gadget which tells me who's at the other end of the phone, before I pick up the receiver. Then I could practise a spine-thrilling, sexy "Hello"; or pretend to be out, depending on who's calling.

Jill Hodges, Purley, Surrey.
Something to make lettuce, grated carrot and crispbread taste like fish and chips or ice cream.

Sheila Sutcliff, Leeds, West Yorkshire.
I'd like to invent a new super automatic cooker which not only cooked food without any attention, but also prepared it.

Belen Lewis, Salisbury, Wilts.
I'm hopeless at spelling so I'd like to invent something like a spelling-calculator; for instance, you would just say a word — Unitarian for example — into a microphone and the machine would spell it out for you. I can just imagine the surprise on my English teacher's face when I got full marks for spelling!

Alan Richmond, Alderbank, Ayr.
I'd invent something which can work out where all my money goes; that's more than I'm ever able to do. It just seems to disappear without trace.

WOODY (BCR)
My invention would go round after Eric tidying up!

Tracey Chambers, Birmingham.
I'd invent a computer that I could feed my homework into, then go out and leave it — a bit like my mum's automatic washing machine. When I came in at night, the homework would be all ready and correct to take to school next morning.

Mary Reilly, Lewisham, Kent.
I'd really go crazy for an automatic nail-varnisher! My hand always seems to shake and I just never get the stuff on smoothly; it would do toes too, of course!

Angela Jones, Accrington, Lancs.
I think I'd like to invent a gadget which flashed a little red light every time my dad was angry or in a bad mood. That way I'd know when not to ask him if I can stay out late — or for some extra pocket money!

Anna-Maria Guglielmucci, Milford, Wilts.
It'd be an automatic typewriter that didn't even need a typist anywhere near it! That would be popular and save everyone an awful lot of time!

Wendy Tailor, Frodsham, Surrey.
Something that would wash my hair for me! I'd just relax with my head back in the bowl and these little rubber fingers would take all the work out of it. I'm not just lazy; I have waist length hair and washing it is really a drag.

Susan Davies, Manchester.
I'd like to invent a real genie. So any time I wanted something I could rub my alarm clock or something and the genie would appear and get it for me!

Fran Lane, Bristol.
My gadget would tip me gently out of bed in the morning, wash and dress me and do my face and hair — and then drive me to work! Sort of a cross between my mum and a robot au pair girl!

Dorothy Potts, Kilwinning, Ayrshire.
An automatic bed maker would be a boon in the mornings. I'm sure my mum would appreciate it too — and there would be no more arguments about who makes my bed, with my great invention on the job.

Susan Burton, Birmingham.
It would beam me wherever I wanted to go, like they do on "Star Trek." I get sea-sick on ships, bored on trains and I'm terrified of flying so it's the only way I'll ever achieve my ambition to see the world!

Colin Hide, Huntingdon, Huntingdonshire.
It would polish all my shoes at the press of a button. I hate cleaning my shoes and try to hide them under extra long trousers when they need a good polish.

GUESS WHO?

So you think you know your pop stars? Well, here's Jackie's special fun quiz to find out whether you really do! All these eyes, lips and so on belong to your favourite pop people. So see if you know what belongs to who. Don't worry—the answers are on p25!

Whose Hats?

Whose Nose?

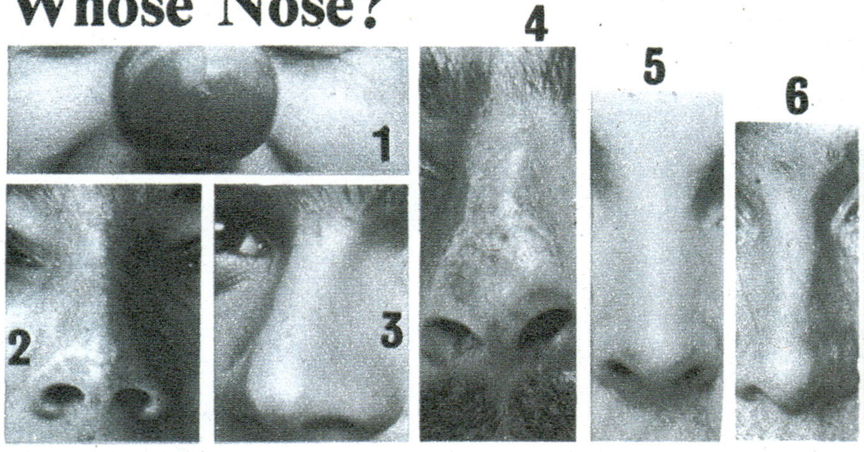

Whose Eyes?

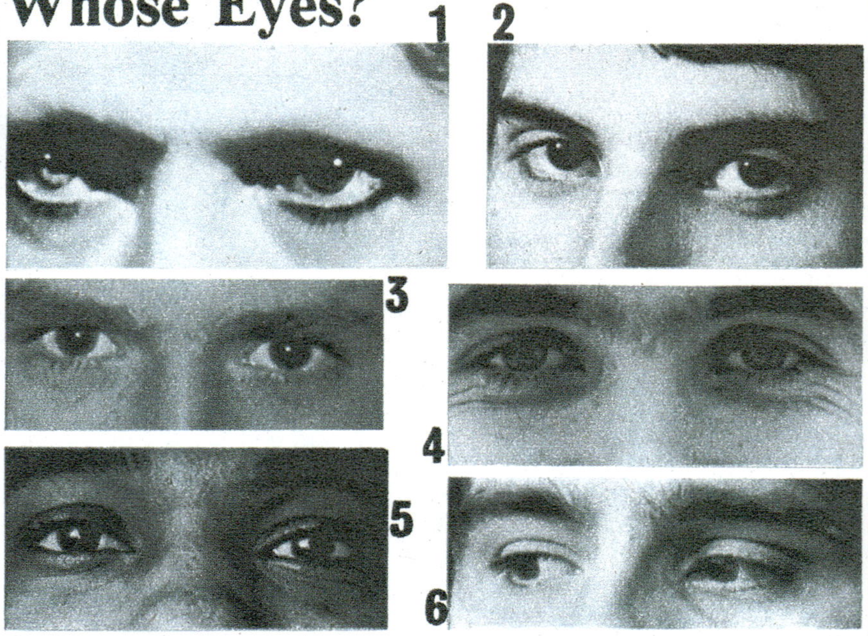

Whose Lips?

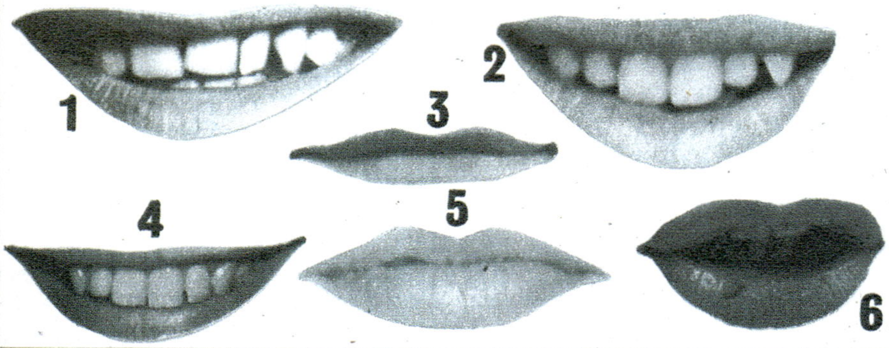

Whose Hair?

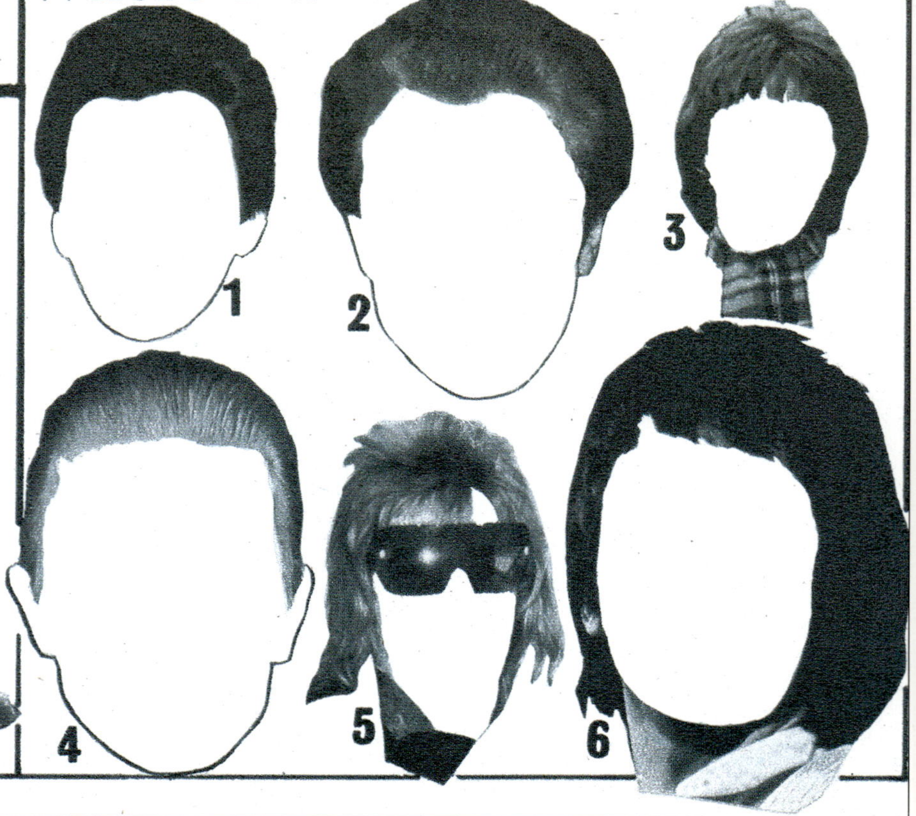

Whose Bits 'n' Pieces?

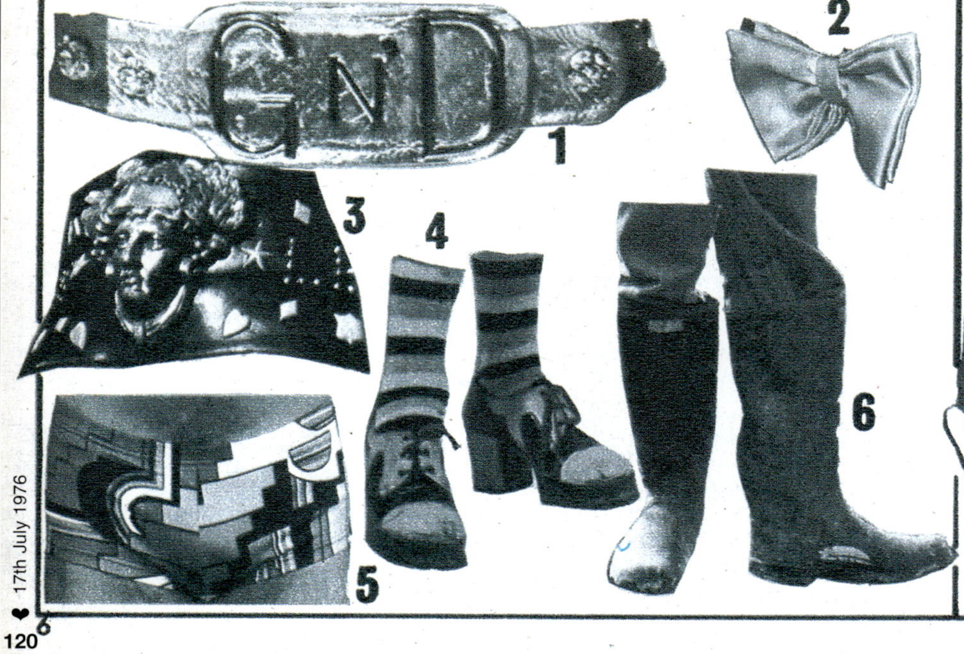

ALL SORTS OF GOODIES!

HERE'S OUR PICK OF THE GOODIES! A SUPER ASSORTED BAG OF ALL THE LOVELY THINGS WE LIKE. SOME INTERESTING, SOME USEFUL — OTHERS JUST DOWNRIGHT DELICIOUS! SO DIP INTO OUR GOODIES BAG AND HELP YOURSELF!

What about a jolly good sport? One of our favourites is swimming which is lucky because it's one of the best ways of exercising! It's just so relaxing, especially when you're feeling a bit tense. And it does have another big advantage — it can be as energetic or as lazy as you like!

Fred Astaire's got to be one of our favourite film goodies. What wouldn't we give to dance with him? The way his toes twinkled down flights of stairs or glided over ballroom floors, and those top hat and tails sequences. It leaves us feeling like breathless carthorses!

And jeans – we always come back to them – 'cos they look and feel good, all the time, everywhere! With floppy, silky blouses, T-shirts, a favourite baggy jumper – they're always a goodie!

We know the foods that are good for us and keep us healthy, but there is the occasional time when you want a "goodie" like a bag of chips, a sausage sandwich or our all-time favourite — a bacon roll!

Here are two recipes for "naughty goodies" that are irresistible . . .

COCONUT ICE

Mix together 4 tablespoonfuls condensed milk with 12 oz. sieved icing sugar. Stir in 6 oz. desiccated coconut. The mixture should be very stiff.

Divide into two parts and tint one half of the mixture pale pink with a drop of cochineal. Shape the mixture into two identical bars and press firmly together. Dust a tin or plate with icing sugar and leave the coconut ice on this until it's firm.

FUDGE

Put 1 lb. granulated sugar, ½ pint milk, 2 oz. margarine in a strong saucepan, and stir over a low heat until the sugar's dissolved. Boil steadily, stirring occasionally, until the mixture forms into a soft ball when a little is dropped into a cup of cold water. Remove from heat and beat till the mixture starts to thicken. Pour into a tin greased with butter. When nearly set, cut into neat pieces with a sharp knife.

You can flavour it as follows:

1. Chocolate

Blend 2 oz. cocoa or 6-8 oz. plain chocolate with the sugar mixture when the sugar has thoroughly dissolved.

2. Fruit

Add 6-8 oz. dried fruit (sultanas, raisins, etc) just before the fudge reaches the "soft ball" stage.

3. Nut

Add 6-8 oz. chopped nuts (almonds, walnuts, etc) just before the fudge reaches the "soft ball" stage.

4. Vanilla

Add 1-2 teaspoonfuls vanilla essence to the sugar mixture.

What could be better than the two dishiest policemen on television — those gorgeous goodies, Starsky and Hutch?

Do you want to be arrested by them? Well, Paul Michael Glaser, who plays Starsky, likes girls who are up to the minute, and David Soul, who plays Hutch, prefers the shy romantic type.

It would be worth being a baddie, just to get arrested by Starsky and Hutch!

And who could forget those recent goodies, Dustin Hoffman and Robert Redford, who tried to untangle good from bad in "All The President's Men." Of course, they are good-looking as well!

And in an assortment of goodies we couldn't leave out Tim Brooke-Taylor, Bill Oddie and Graeme Garden, the original Goodies!

You can keep your beauty treatments cheap and natural with these home made goodies.

Hair Conditioner.

Melt down two tablespoonfuls of honey, mix in a teaspoonful of olive oil, and then add wheatgerm (available from health food shops) until the mixture is a suitable consistency for applying.

Leave on for about ten minutes, then rinse off thoroughly.

Skin Freshener and Hair Rinse.

Add two heaped tablespoonfuls of dried peppermint leaves (available from health food shops or chemists) to one pint of water. Bring to the boil and simmer for two minutes. Mix with one pint of cider vinegar.

Leave for 48 hours before use.

Add half a cupful to your bath-water, or use as a hair rinse.

And we really dig earth shoes (sorry!). They're just so comfortable and good-looking. Give us lovely warm leg-warmers in stripes or spots, to go with them, too.

Be charming, with good luck charms on chains. Wear them round your neck, on your wrist, even round your ankle, and extra special good luck will be sure to dog your footsteps!

Horseshoes, four-leaf clovers, chimney sweeps, silver threepenny pieces, keys — all bring good luck.

Legend has it that if a girl wears a four-leaf clover in her right shoe, the first man she meets will be her future husband . . .

Of course there are some goodies other people might think are baddies. What about poor old King Kong – we've always had a soft spot for him. After all, it wasn't really his fault that buildings fell down when he touched them. And he can't be all bad or they wouldn't be making a new, bigger and better film about him. He's going to be 50 feet high, take fifteen-feet strides, and weigh the equivalent of 500 men!

For a good night out at the cinema we've plumped for "Gone With The Wind." With a large box of Kleenex on your knees and Rhett Butler in front of you, what could be better?

ALL GOOD THINGS . . . . . . strawberries and cream . . . Peter Pan . . . The Rollers . . . rose-coloured specs . . . jasmine tea . . . coloured wellies . . . faded blue jeans . . .

Guess Who? Answers

Hats–1–Noddy Holder; 2–Elton John; 3–Donny Osmond; 4–David Essex; 5–Mick Jagger; 6–Andy Walton.

Lips–1–Les McKeown; 2–Brian May; 3–Harpo; 4–David Essex; 5–Marie Osmond; 6–Mick Jagger

Bits 'n' Pieces–1–Dominic Grant; 2–Elton John; 3–Les Gray; 4–Woody; 5–Noddy Holder; 6–Roger Daltrey

Noses–1–Noddy Holder; 2–David Cassidy; 3–Donny Osmond; 4–Alice Cooper; 5–Paul McCartney; 6–Bryan Ferry

Eyes–1–David Bowie; 2–Freddie Mercury; 3–Les McKeown; 4–David Essex; 5–Errol Brown; 6–Steve Harley

Hair–1–Jim McGinlay; 2–John Miles; 3–Ian Mitchell; 4–David Bowie; 5–Rod Stewart; 6–Paul McCartney

FASHION GOES WEST FOR THE BEST NEW LOOKS AROUND! TRAILBLAZERS ARE WEARING DRAINPIPE JEANS, COWBOY BOOTS, CHECKS AND FRINGING. SO BE A BIT OF AN OUTLAW IN THE NEWEST AND WILDEST CLOTHES TO HIT TOWN YET!

The Best

1. Leather cowboy hat, with criss-cross decorative stitching, from Trading Post. Price: £5.50. One size only.
Green, orange and blue checked shirt, from British Home Stores. Price: £4.99. Sizes: 10-16.
Dark green prairie jacket, with horse motif, two slant pockets, stud fastening, hood and comfortable quilted lining, from Emperor of Wyoming. Price: £12. Sizes: Small, medium, large, extra large.
Tan zip-up saddle bag with two flap-over pockets, worn across the body, from Saxone. Price: £6.99.
Fantastic khaki gauchos, with button trim at front, from Gordon King. Price: £12.99. Sizes: 10-16.
Flat leather boots with string top stitching, from Dolcis. Price: £19.99. Sizes: 3-8.

2. Green sheriff's shirt with button fastening and pockets on sleeves, from City Swingers. Price: £6.99. Sizes: 10-14.
Bright blue, red, white and yellow big checked waistcoat, from Prêt à Porter. Price: £7.95. Sizes: 10-14.
Calf-length denim skirt, with button tabs on pockets, from Made In Heaven. Price: £14. Sizes: 8-14.
Green knee-high boots with flat crepe-look sole, from Dolcis. Price: £19.99. Sizes: 3-8.

3. Fawn outlaw's stetson hat, from Marida. Price: £2.60. One size only.
Green fringed neckerchief, from British Home Stores. Price: 60p.
Country style red checked collarless shirt, from Peter Robinson. Price: £6.95. Sizes: 10-14.
Country girl navy cord dungarees, from Peter Robinson. Price: £16.95. Sizes: 10-14.
Tucked into sturdy, low-heeled tan cowboy boots from Ravel. Price: £18.99. Sizes: 3-7.

4. Blue square scarf, tied round neck, from Boots. Price: 95p.
Denim shirt, with orange top stitching, from C&A. Price: £7.75. Sizes: 10-16.
Grey, blue and red swirly checked shirt, from Stirling Cooper. Price: £12.95. Sizes: 1-3.
Warm, red fluffy ankle socks, from Morley. Price: 90p. One size only.
Tan moccasin shoe with wooden wedge and plaiting detail on front, from Dolcis. Price: £10.99. Sizes 3-8.

of the West!

5. Very special denim collarless top, with unusual lace-up shoulders, orange embroidery on front and back, and two slant pockets, from Made In Heaven. Price: £16. Sizes: 8-14.
Red, grey and black checked shirt, from C&A. Price: £3.50. Sizes: 10-16.
Tight, straight-legged denims, with two slant pockets in front, and patch pockets in back, from Highlight. Price: £7.99. Sizes: 10-16.
Super, blue suede shoes, with orange top-stitching, from Saxone. Price: £8.99. Sizes: 3-8.

6. Cheerful red tartan collarless shirt, from Van Allan. Price: £5.99. Sizes: 10-16.
Navy sleeveless shirt, with red "cowboy" fringing on front and back, from Strawberry Studio. Price £7.95. Sizes: 10-14.
Dorothy Perkins denim straight-legged jeans, with red top-stitching and two slant pockets in front, worn turned up. Price: £9.99. Sizes: 10-14.
Bright red knee high socks, from Brettles. Price: Approx. 50p. Sizes: To fit most shoe sizes.
Sporty blue suede and leather lace-up ankle boots with flat sole, from Sacha. Price: £12.99. Sizes: 3-7.

7. Jaunty black felt stetson, from Baily of California. Price: Approx. £5.50. Hat sizes: 6-7½.
Special wild west white shirt, with contrasting red yoke, collar and cuffs, heart-shaped buttons and bootlace tie at neck, from Miss Mouse. Price: £12.50. Sizes: 10-16.
Straight-legged black jeans, with green top stitching, from Made In Heaven. Price: £14.99. Sizes: 24-36 in. waist (men's sizes).
Stunning red patent cowboy boots, with white top stitching, from Saxone. Price: £17.99. Sizes: 3-8.

8. Blue check cowgirl dress with elbow length sleeves, button fastening and "shirt tail" hem, from Prêt à Porter. Price: £11.95. Sizes: 10-14.
Red long-sleeved shirt with two patch pockets in front, from Richard Shops. Price: Approx. £3.95. Sizes: 12-16.
Thick ribbed navy tights, from Wolsey. Price: £2.45. Sizes: 8½-9½, 10-11.
Calf-length blue suede cowboy boot with white top stitching, from Sacha. Price: £14.99. Sizes: 3-7.

STOCKISTS ON PAGE 26.

WHICH POP STAR WOULD YOU LEAST LIKE TO MEET?

ON-THE-SPOT INTERVIEWS where our roving reporters find out what you think.

Lorraine Day, Carshalton, Surrey.
I wouldn't like to meet David Bowie. His records are okay, but he scares me a bit by the way he dresses and performs. He's definitely a bit weird and he gives me the creeps!

Elaine Parker, Great Durnford, Wilts.
Gary Glitter, because all that hair just *can't* be real. Personally, I think he's too old to be on the pop scene anyway.

Margaret Stone, Wilton, Wilts.
Telly Savalas. I wouldn't want to meet him because I just don't like bald-headed men!

Maria Catelli, Brentford, Essex.
Lynsey de Paul! I'd be devastated by jealousy as she seems to have everything!

Fiona Davidson, Glasgow, Scotland.
I don't think I'd like to meet Bryan Ferry. Not because I don't like him, it's just that he looks so smooth and sophisticated that I'd feel like a scruffy idiot.

Angela Dixon, Sheffield, South Yorkshire.
Dare I say it? I'd hate to meet the Rollers! It's not that I don't like them — in fact I think they're great — but I'd be scared to death of being trampled under foot by the thousands of other fans who were also trying to meet them.

Leo Sayer
Bob Dylan — because I've always been a great admirer of his, and if we ever met I'm sure I'd be completely tongue-tied.

Brian Lee, Enfield, Sussex.
I've always absolutely loathed Mick Jagger! He has a big head and not much talent nowadays; he used to be good — but that isn't good enough now!

Tim Cawley, Cambridge, Cambs.
I wouldn't like to meet Elvis Presley. Why? Because I've avidly collected his records since I first got interested in music and as far as I'm concerned he's the King, he's the greatest and I wouldn't like anything to spoil my idea of him. Meeting him could be brief and disappointing so I'd rather not meet him in the flesh as it might ruin the stage image I have of him.

Julia Williams, Reading, Berks.
Roger Daltrey. I once wrote him this soppy fan letter telling him he was my favourite member of the Who. The letter got more and more slushy and sentimental as it went on. I got carried away with my prose. So I wouldn't want to meet him in case he remembered my ghastly letter. Though I must admit this would be unlikely as he probably gets sacks full of fan mail.

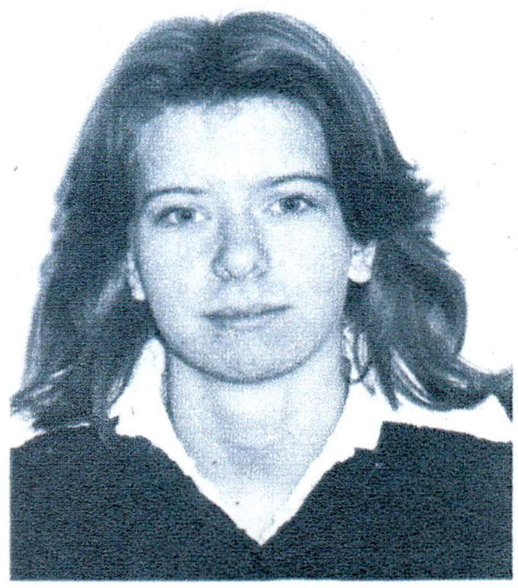

Susan Squirrell, London S.E.9.
I adore the Osmonds but I don't think I'd like to meet them because I'd go all tongue-tied and wouldn't know what to say. I mean, if Donny looked at me with those gorgeous dark eyes of his I'd go all weak at the knees. Mind you if I was given the opportunity to meet them — I'd go like a shot!

Angela Downie, Aylesbury, Bucks.
Any of the Bay City Rollers. I've seen them interviewed on television, and I can never understand a word they're saying!

Beth Whitaker, Leeds, West Yorkshire.
I wouldn't like to meet Rod Stewart. I'd be too tempted to give him some throat lozenges to see if they would improve his voice!

Maurice Keele, London, N.10.
Elton flaming John. I think he messes about too much. He should stick to music and not get sidetracked into football. And he should buy a wig!

Sarah Goodge, Exeter, Devon.
Alice Cooper. I can't help it but he gives me the creeps to be honest. He always looks sinister and foreboding. It's the clothes and weird stage make-up that does it of course. I've got nothing against him personally. He's probably very nice underneath it all.

Identipop

Here's an Identipop — a quick quiz to test your knowledge of pop. From the clues listed below, try to work out the identity of the mystery star. The answer's upside down at the foot of the column — but no looking until after you've had a go at the quiz!

* His first job was as an office clerk.
* His real name is Harold.
* He plays guitar and sings.

* His first public appearance was at Butlins Holiday Camp.
* He's one of Britain's longest-serving pop stars!
* He has three sisters, called Donella, Jacqueline and Joan.
* He used to have a backing group who shadowed him everywhere!
* He has dark brown eyes.
* He's often on TV.
* He's just over 5 ft. 10 ins. tall.
* He sometimes wears glasses.
* He's a very keen badminton player.

* His latest record is called "I'm Nearly Famous" — which is an understatement!
* He says he puts on weight easily — but he nearly always weighs 10 st. 2 lbs.
* He's a bachelor.
* He's appeared in several films.
* His favourite TV programme is "Star Trek"!
* One of his biggest early hits was called "Living Doll."
* He was born in India.
* His birthday is on October 14.

Did you get it? This week's mystery star is CLIFF RICHARD.

THE CATHY & CLAIRE PAGE

Don't bottle it all up and suffer in silence—tell us all about it and we'll do our best to sort it out. Our address is: Cathy & Claire, Jackie, 12 Fetter Lane, Fleet Street, London EC4A 1BL.

DEAR CATHY & CLAIRE — Last weekend I went to a party at a friend's house and had a really super time. Most of our crowd from school were there and the two boys from the sixth form that I knew by sight.

One of them, Mike, asked me to dance and spent the rest of the evening with me. When the party had finished he walked me home and said that he would phone me up later in the week and that he would see me at school on Monday.

Well, on Monday morning, I passed him in the corridor and he ignored me, completely. I put this down to the fact that he was with his friends and was maybe a bit embarrassed about speaking to me. I waited in, all week, hoping that he would phone but he didn't. I was really disappointed and I just can't understand his behaviour.

It's always very upsetting and disappointing when a boy behaves like this. It was a bit inconsiderate of him to say that he would phone and then not bother but there isn't really much you can do about it.

He probably enjoyed your company at the party. Perhaps he thought that he would like to see you again at the time but since he hasn't got in touch with you to date, we don't think he'll get round to it in the near future.

There's no accounting for a boy's feelings, but don't let this boy's behaviour bother you in any way. The best thing you can do is to forget about this incident.

There are lots of other boys on the scene and we can assure you they won't all behave as rudely as he has. So cheer up and put this incident to the back of your mind.

DEAR CATHY & CLAIRE — Sheila and I usually sit next to a couple of other girls in our class at school. Recently we've noticed that one of them, Jane, smells quite unpleasantly.

All the other girls in our class are laughing and speaking about her behind her back. We've tried dropping hints but she doesn't seem to be getting the message!

She's also a bit lazy about her appearance and doesn't bother about pressing her clothes or cleaning her shoes.

She's a nice person in other ways and good fun to be with. We want to help her but don't want to hurt her or lose her friendship. What should we do?

If you've tried dropping hints to this girl, and they haven't had any effect, the only thing you can really do is to tell her that you've noticed she seems to have a personal freshness problem.

Try and tell her when you're alone with her sometime — don't embarrass her by telling her in front of other people. Be gentle — explain that you couldn't help noticing it and you wanted to tell her because you're her friend.

Of course, no matter how nice you are about it, it's likely that Jane will be a bit hurt. All that you can do if that happens is to continue to be nice to her and hope she'll soon get over it.

DEAR CATHY & CLAIRE — When I left school my boyfriend, Simon stayed on to take his A-levels. Now he has no time for me. He's too busy swotting to go out except at weekends, and I'm not really welcome round at his place. I'm sure his mother thinks I only take his mind off his work. I tell him there's no point in us going on like this, yet I'm too crazy about him, when it comes to it, to make the break. I just don't know what to do.

We can appreciate how frustrating you find the present situation, yet shouldn't you be proud of Simon's ambition and single mindedness?

It can't be easy sticking to school when your girl is out and about in the world, AND pulling hard in the opposite direction! Studying is bound to be demanding, and if you can't give your boy your whole hearted support, he'd be better off without you, we reckon. Simon is thinking, quite properly of his future, and you should understand the importance of a fella's job to him.

In your heart you obviously don't want to finish with him. Instead of feeling resentful and neglected why not take a leaf out of his book? Enrol at evening classes so that you have another interest to occupy your time. Whether you're academically minded or not there's a wide range of subjects to choose from. We hope you'll both come out with flying colours!

DEAR CATHY & CLAIRE — The people at school are making my life a misery all because of the way I speak. They say it's very snooty and snobbish and some have even been unkind enough to say that it's all put on to impress people, especially the teachers. I can't help the way I speak. My family have just recently moved house, so it's bad enough having to get used to a new school without people ganging up on me because of my accent. It's come to the stage where I hate school so much, I'm thinking of leaving it and taking a job. I'm willing to be friends with the people at school but they just won't give me a chance.

Do you think I should leave school and forget the idea of trying for 'A'-levels next year or should I put up with all the nastiness for the sake of passing exams?

If we were in your shoes we'd go back to school determined to sort the whole problem out. A change in your attitude would help, be more confident in yourself and don't be ashamed now, or ever, of the way you speak and the accent you have. You can face up to the people at school, of course you can! After the holidays you can start afresh.

If the situation doesn't improve then you *must* speak to a teacher about the problem. But, we're sure that if you try to ignore comments, you'll find it easier to be accepted. Of course it's not something that is easy, but do try. If after a while you feel nothing is going to change, then you can consider leaving school and finding a job. OK?

DEAR CATHY & CLAIRE — My mum's always spoiling my fun. She says I need eight hours sleep every night so she makes me come home at around ten. This means I look really childish when I have to leave places like the youth club disco a lot earlier than any of my friends. Their parents don't seem to mind what time they come home at.

Mum won't listen to me when I explain that I don't need eight hours sleep every night. She also said that if I disobeyed her and stayed out longer than ten, that as a punishment, she'd stop me from going out with my friends for a fortnight. What can I do?

You don't really need us to answer this one for you. You know yourself that the obvious and most sensible thing to do is obey your mum.

We agree, not everyone needs eight hours' sleep but we don't really think that's the issue at stake.

Your mother trusts you to come home by ten and is therefore giving you responsibility. If you break that trust, you will ruin any chances you may have of being allowed to stay out later than ten, say when there's a special disco or party you want to go to.

So the best thing to do is have a chat with your mum and explain the situation. Point out that you don't mind coming home at ten if your mum would trust you to come in a little later, for example on a Friday night. If you show that you're being quite sensible about the whole thing we're sure your mum will respect the way you feel.

DEAR CATHY & CLAIRE — Life has become such a drag. I find I don't want to get up in the morning — there seems nothing to get up for. I can't understand what's happened to me. It's only since I left school and got a job that I've felt like this. At first I felt great, but the novelty of working soon wore off. I work in a bank, following in Dad's footsteps actually, and there's good prospects if I do well, but I feel I can't look that far forward. I don't like saying anything to my parents especially when I seem to have nothing to get really depressed about.

Sometimes depression is a very true and useful friend, because it shows up what our true selves need. Use it to learn about yourself, love. Yours might be an indication that your job is wrong for you. You don't seem to be getting anything out of it. Maybe you didn't shop around enough before you went into a bank. It occurs to us you might simply be doing your father's 'thing' not yours! We think you ought to face this possibility, and do talk it over with your parents and your local careers office. A job can be a bit like a new boyfriend — not quite what you thought when you get to know it. Chuck it and find one that makes you happy.

DEAR CATHY & CLAIRE — What can you do about yourself when you haven't even one redeeming feature? I've got frizzy hair, too-small eyes with glasses, a big nose, crooked teeth — *and* sticky-out ears. I could go on right down to my bent left toe, but I don't want to depress you!

It depresses me, though, looking like this. What can I do?

Almost anything that will stop you feeling so depressed! First of all, plan to spend a bit of money — and make the first 5p. of it an investment in a notebook and pencil.

Now make three columns and head them "Feature," "Fault" and "Cure." Starting at the top and working down, the first entry will read: "Hair. Too frizzy. Needs good cut and straightening treatment." Too-small eyes just need good make-up — look back at some old JACKIE beauty features, or write to our Beauty Editor for personal advice.

Glasses are a personal thing. Sometimes you can never see the face behind them — but some faces look all wrong without them! Spend some time in front of a mirror looking at yourself with and without, and decide which type you are. If you like yourself better without, go to every optician in town tomorrow and ask about contact lenses. Apart from all that walking doing you good, you'll find prices vary even in the same town, and some opticians will have credit facilities while others will want all the cash at once.

Complete your list right down to your toes, then do three things. *Don't try* to be Miss World by next Friday — but do get going on correcting one thing at a time. Accept that there will be some things you *won't* be able to do anything about, and learn to live with them — the rest of us rub along quite well with our little faults! Tell yourself that looks aren't everything, and even when you're gorgeous, you'll only be loved if you've got a nice nature too! Luckily, actually working at your problems instead of just moaning and moping about them gives you a feeling of confidence — and that's a sure blues-chaser.

Lastly, *don't* add up every single penny the New You is going to cost — or you could get *really* depressed, instead of enjoying your new image!

DEAR CATHY & CLAIRE — I know you've heard it all before but my problem is a typical holiday romance — and the inevitable broken heart. I went on holiday to the Lake District with my parents, and I met Geoff at the hotel we were staying at.

We made the most of the fortnight we had together and I was sure at the time he felt the same way about me — he was like no other boy I'd ever known. Even my parents liked him. He's a student and lives in a hostel. We exchanged addresses and phone numbers, but he said he'd contact me first. The problem is, he hasn't. All my friends are making comforting noises and assuring me it happens to everybody sometime. Trouble is, I don't just want to settle for memories.

Don't worry love, we won't make any further comforting noises!

Let's just suggest you set aside your pride, pick up the nearest phone or pen, and contact him — now. The poor bloke could have quite easily lost your address, and may right now be frantically nibbling his nails waiting by the phone. If you don't move now, love — you won't be the only one who's left with memories.

DEAR CATHY & CLAIRE — I was walking up the road with my friend when a group of boys on the other side of the road started whistling at us and shouting to us to come over and talk to them. My friend and I just ignored them. But later that evening when we were down at a friend's house one of the boys came into the house. He was really super but the thing is, he pretended he didn't know us and ignored us most of the time and only spoke to our friend's brother.

How can we get to know him and get him interested in us?

Easier said than done and quite frankly we don't know whether you'll think it's worth all the trouble. It could be that he was embarrassed at seeing you in his friend's house. Or it could be that the encounter you had with him earlier that evening was nothing more than a piece of bravado along with the other boys who all fancied the idea of chatting you two up.

Maybe they were interested in you, maybe they only intended to have a bit of a laugh with you. Anyway, you didn't rise to the bait so you've no need to be embarrassed when you meet him.

Give him a friendly smile and say 'hello.' If you get a friendly reaction you'll know you can try to get things on a friendly footing. If he doesn't show any interest, then the only thing to do is to forget him as a potential boyfriend.

Warm yourself up with some of the hottest clothes around. Wear red from top to toe and you'll positively glow! Red is sensational, so choose the brightest clothes from our stunning selection and you'll stop the traffic wherever you go!

TRAFFIC

1. Neat red towelling-look top with half sleeves and tie-belt at waist, from British Home Stores. Price: £4.99. Sizes: 12-16.
Stunning tight straight red skirt with slit in back, from Dorothy Perkins. Price: £6.99. Sizes: 10-14.

2. Bright, red slash neck top with half sleeves and pretty Fair Isle trim on neck and sleeves, from Woolworth. Price: £3.99. One size only. Skirt as for 1.

3. Crisp white, green and red striped shirt, from Mates at Irvine Sellars. Price: £6.95. Sizes: 10-14.
Worn under bright red cardigan with thick ribbed knit trim on sleeves and edges, and two patch pockets in front, from Richard Shops. Price: £8.95. Sizes: 34 in.-36 in.
Flared calf-length skirt with double frill at hem, from C & A. Price: £5.75. Sizes: 10-16.

4. Red knit jumper with slash neck and grey trim on cuffs and neckline, from Jonathan Miller. Price: £9. Sizes: 1-3.
Brutus jeans with two slant pockets in front, and two patch pockets in back. Price: £8.95. Sizes: Men's sizes: 26 in.-32 in. waist.

STOPPERS!

Jackie Fashion

5. Red T-shirt with unusual cartoon print, from Graffiti at Irvine Sellars. Price: £4.95. Sizes: Small, medium, large. Jeans as for 4.

6. Super red dress with mandarin collar and toggle at neck, gathered waist, colourful stripy trim at sleeves, neck and waist, from Woolworth. Price: £8.99. Sizes: 12-16.

7. Cheerful red top, with pretty floral appliquéd motif, tie-belt and navy striped trim round hem, from C & A. Price: £4.75. Sizes: 10-14.
Smart red skirt with front zip, from Woolworth. Price: £4.99. Sizes: 12-16.

8. Red slash neck top, with navy and white patterned trim, from Littlewoods. Price: £2.99. Sizes: 10-12, 14-16. Skirt as for 7.

FASHION STOCKISTS ON PAGE 28

Are You A New Year Nibbler?

A SLIMMING EXTRA

DESPITE all our warnings, some of you could be feeling a bit flabby by now, after all the goodies you've been eating lately. Now's the time to do something about it.

DON'T panic and cut down your food intake too drastically . . . your body still needs fuel to keep it going, especially in the cold weather.

DO avoid any boxes of chocolates left over from Christmas; try to cut out cakes, crisps, puddings, pastas, pastry, potatoes, thick soups, sausages, rice, honey, nuts, bananas and baked beans.

If you think that means there's nothing left for you to eat, don't worry, there *are* alternatives. You don't *have* to give up the sugar. For instance, if you really can't bear your tea or coffee without it, you could try Slimcea cubed or granulated sugar. It's twice as sweet as ordinary sugar so you only use half as much and therefore save half the calories. Try a low-calorie bread such as Slimcea as well, which only has 35 calories per slice instead of the 51 that normal bread has.

You can eat chicken (casseroled, roast or grilled), liver, kidneys, fish, fresh vegetables, salad, fresh fruit, eggs, natural yogurt, Cheddar, Edam, Camembert and Cottage cheese. Drink fresh fruit juices, soda or Perrier water, tea with lemon slices and not more than ½ a pint of milk everyday. Try Bovril, too, for a satisfying drink at bed time.

BREAKFASTS

Breakfast is probably the most important meal of the day. If you have a good one you won't be so tempted to nibble mid-morning.

Breakfasts to choose from are (only ONE of them!):

Orange segments mixed with natural yogurt.

½ grapefruit.

Kipper fillet with a tiny dot of butter.

Grilled Cheddar cheese on 1 slice of Slimcea bread topped with a slice of tomato.

1 egg scrambled with a slice of tomato or sliced mushroom.

You can have a slice of toast (low calorie of course) spread with a low calorie margarine such as Outline. Drink fruit juice and tea with a slice of lemon.

LUNCHES

Best to take food with you if you have to eat away from home at lunch-time.

Choose from (again only ONE!):

Cold chicken joint with slices of cucumber.

Cold lamb chop with tomatoes and an apple.

Two slices of lean ham with a coleslaw salad made with grated carrot and shredded white cabbage mixed with yogurt.

If you prefer to take sandwiches, use low-calorie bread with one of the following fillings:

Chopped hard-boiled egg.

Cottage cheese mixed with a little curry powder.

Drained tuna fish with sliced tomato.

Edam cheese with sliced tomato.

Lean meat with sliced cucumber.

Take fresh fruit or natural yogurt to eat afterwards.

Eating out at lunch-time you should go for omelettes with green vegetables, salads, grilled or roast meats, steamed or poached fish.

EVENING MEAL

Start with one of the following:

Clear soup

Tomato juice with Worcester sauce.

½ grapefruit.

Tomato stuffed with drained tuna, sprinkled with lemon juice.

Main Course:

Any white fish cooked in the oven in foil, topped with melted cheese to make a golden sauce, served with fresh vegetables.

Chicken portion glazed with 'made' mustard and baked in the oven, served with Brussels sprouts and a large baked onion topped with grated Cheddar cheese.

Lean roast meat served with cauliflower topped with melted Cheddar cheese.

Kebab . . . grill bite size pieces of lamb, mushrooms, onions, tomatoes, put them on a long skewer, serve with green vegetables.

Any lean meat casseroled with carrots, celery and onions, served with green vegetables.

DESSERTS

Choose one of the following:

Fresh fruit salad mixed with natural yogurt.

Sliced apple and Edam, Camembert or Cottage cheese.

Baked apple sweetened with Slimcea sugar.

Fresh pear with Slimcea granulated, topped with whipped egg white and crisped in a slow oven.

WILL IT BE

You can find out very simply — just by looking at his T-shirt! Did you know that there's a lot you can tell about a boy just by doing a few simple deductions from whatever it is he's got stretched across his chest? Although he may not know it, his T-shirt will give him away — every time! So read on — and find out exactly how to tell him — by his T-shirt!

THE MOTOR-BIKE KID

IF he's going around with a 1000 cc motorbike roaring across him, you can bet your bottom dollar he'll have a harmless little 50 cc Suki Yaki parked at the back of the Youth Club.

And he'll just adore that bike — mainly because he spent all summer heaving baked bean cans around the supermarket to afford it!

If you fancy this guy, be prepared for long discussions on the merits of the bike's one spark plug, its dear little carburettor, and its ability (or non-ability) to climb hills. A spare crash helmet tucked away in your wardrobe is sure to make him realise *your* merits as a prospective pillion-seat occupier. Add some oil-splattered jeans, carry a spanner in your handbag — and you can't fail.

You may feel like you're living in a goldfish bowl, but buy him half a gallon of petrol and he'll be yours for life!

THE ROCK FREAK

ANOTHER easy one — he'll be going around with two words emblazoned across his rib cage, like, Thin Lizzy or Deep Purple or, a dead cert, Status Quo.

The name he's sporting is very important, and an instant guide to his whole personality.

Someone with the words 'Mozart Rules' should be well and truly avoided, and left to the charms of the violin teacher down the road. (Okay, she may be sixty-five, but that's his problem.)

The true rock freak's T-shirt will have been to every concert within a 100-mile radius, and has probably never been washed since Francis Rossi's guitar lead touched it on the sleeve for a fraction of a second.

An intimate knowledge of his favourite group is essential here — nothing as elementary as just knowing the names of the group members will do. Impress him by talking knowledgeably about Fenders and fuzz-boxes. Know — and wear — the group's favourite make of jeans, and let him into the secret of what kind of pickle they take with their hamburgers.

It shouldn't take him long to realise that here is his ideal rock-mate, and you can be blissfully happy attending rock concerts together until your hair goes grey and you carry a walking stick instead of a guitar.

JACKIE FASHION

WHAT'S NEW . . . KNICKERS!

OUT with old and in with the new — treat yourself to a brand new pair of knickers to celebrate the new year!

1. Lacey, stretch knickers with long legs, by Wolsey. Style No.: M36C. Price: Approx. £1.70. Fabric: Stretch nylon lace. Colours: White, pink, navy. Sizes: Medium, large. From Rackhams, Birmingham; Trerons, Sauchiehall Street, Glasgow; D. H. Evans, Oxford Street, London W.1.; Draffens, Dundee; Frasers, Union Street, Aberdeen. Enquiries to Courtaulds Press Office, 22 Hanover Square, London W.1.

2. French knickers with slit sides and lace trim come from Miss Selfridge. No Style No. Price: £1.80. Fabric: Nylon. Colours: Black, white, peach, mint, blue. Sizes: One size. From selected branches of Miss Selfridge.

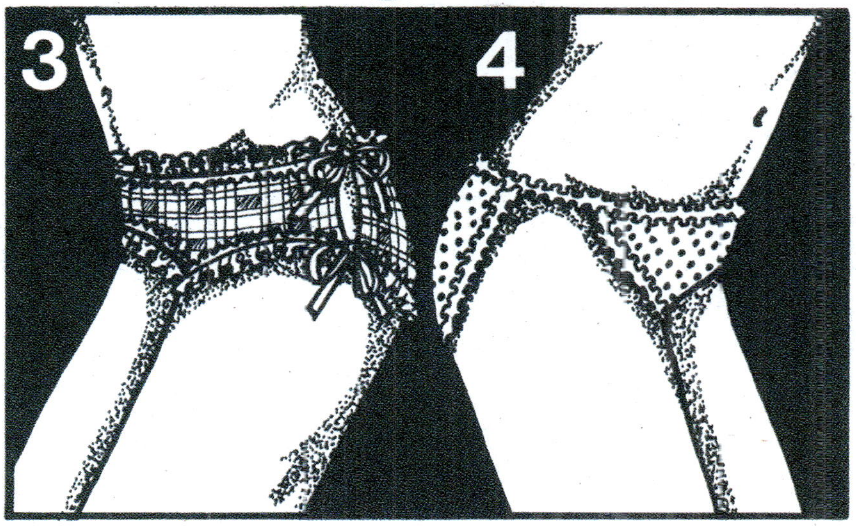

3. Checked knickers with white lace trim and ties at the sides, from Dorothy Perkins. Style No.: 5701. Price: 35p. Fabric: Terylene/nylon. Colours: Pink, white, blue, green. Sizes: One size. From all branches of Dorothy Perkins.

4. Red and white spotty knickers come from the Nylon Hosiery Company. No Style No. Price: 55p. Fabric: Nylon. Colours: White, black, navy, brown, red. Sizes: One size. From Peter Robinson, Oxford Circus, London W.1.; Enquiries to Nylon Hosiery Co., 214 Oxford Street, London W.1.

5. Denim-look briefs with zip and pocket print on front and back, from British Home Stores. Style No.: 2031. Price: 49p. Fabric: Polyester. Colours: Chocolate, blue. Sizes: One size. From most branches of British Home Stores.

6. Combed cotton knickers with long legs from Wolsey. Style No.: M14/CW. Price: Approx. £1.10. Fabric: Combed cotton. Colours: White. Sizes: Medium, large. Stockists as for No. 1.

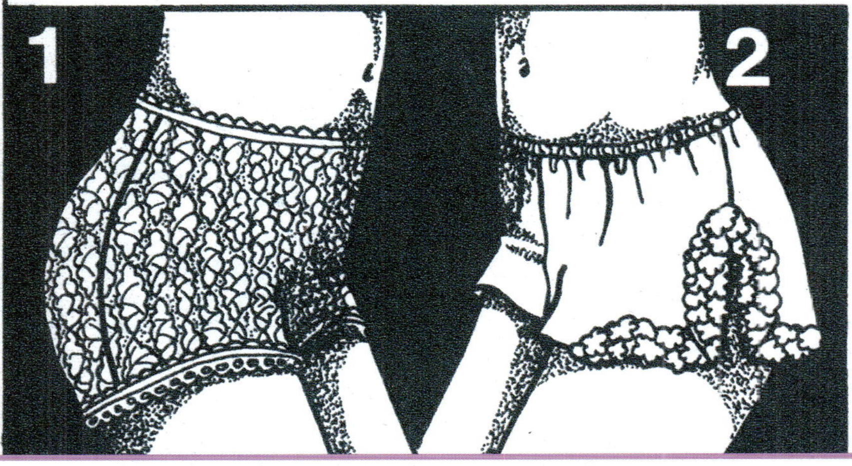

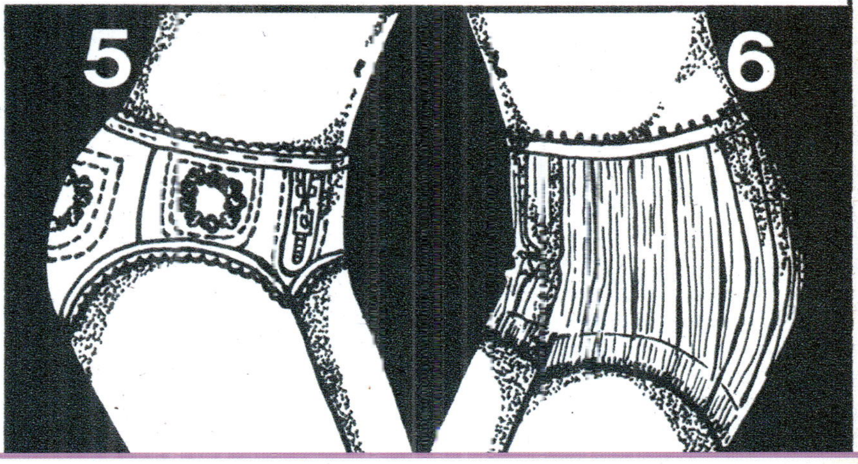

T FOR TWO?

A JACKIE FUN SPECIAL

THE PUNK

THE rock freak leads on to the punk. Again fairly easy to recognise, his T-shirt will be saying something straight-forward and simple like 'Spit In Your Eye' or 'The Punk Panther', or something slightly more basic like, 'I Never Wash Behind My Ears', which, incidentally, you'll need to start never doing too.

And of course, his T-shirt is unique in that it'll probably be in at least three different pieces and be held together by safety pins.

If he's the one for you, you'll need to be well up on New Wave music, to have bags of energy for all that energetic pogo-ing at the disco, and strong ears to combat the noise. Clothes will be no problem here — you'll just need a supply of bin liners and a rather large packet of safety pins.

Comply with his requests to dye your hair blue, and even safety pins couldn't make the pair of you any closer.

THE HIPPY

AFTER the punk comes the hippy, still going strong even though he was probably only five in the great flower-power era of 1967.

His T-shirt will carry an easy-to understand' one-word slogan, like, 'Peace' or 'Love', artistically entwined in flowers and daisies, and it's quite likely you'll find more of these draped about his person. He's the kind of guy whose soul-mate will already have appeared before him in a vision, but don't be put off. Everyone looks the same in a vision, so all you have to do is materialise before him with your long flowing hair and long flowing dress, reading poetry, softly playing acoustic guitar, and eating wholemeal bread and yoghurt.

You'll have to be patient though — time won't matter much to him, so be prepared to

sit around waiting till his vibes are right, or he feels you're both on the same wavelength. And if you can see beauty in a fifteen storey block of flats, and appreciate the cosmic wonders to be found in a stroll round Woolies, so much the better. Embroider him a headband to match his T-shirt and it won't be long till you're sharing the delights of peace and love together.

THE ECOLOGIST

THE ecologist (scientific type) is likely to sport a T-shirt telling you to save the whales or trees or support another such deserving cause, like the recycling of rubbish.

He'll be an earnest sort of bloke, generally more keen on the feathered type of bird than the variety you represent, but if he appeals to you, at least you'll have the consolation that your main competition is a short-eared owl rather than Farrah Fawcett-Majors.

He'll be full of facts about such interesting things as the world's wild life (not raving late night parties but things like how many varieties of antelope there are in deepest Africa).

Keep him happy by always having your Observer's Book Of Birds handy and look terribly interested when he starts telling you about the life-style of

the lesser-spotted humpbacked toad. A supply of jam-jars and butterfly nets will always be handy to help him add to his already ginormous collection of insects(creepy-crawlies to you). You never know, you might find that you *do* have a secret liking for earwigs, but if spiders bring you out in a rash and the thought of picking up a worm brings on hysterical fainting fits, then there's nothing else for it — forget him!

THE SHOW-OFF

LAST, but by no means least, is the extrovert, devil-may-care boy. (In other words, a big-headed twit who fancies himself without you even bothering.)

This guy will have a wardrobe-ful of T-shirts printed with every conceivable slogan, which will range from the very rude, which we won't go into, to the pretty harmless, which are too dull to bother with. In between those two extremes will be an assorted bunch, one for every day of the week, with specials for evening wear, most of which, if nothing else, will get him noticed. They'll probably also get him laughed at into the bargain, but being a show-off to begin with, this won't bother him one bit. In fact, he'll rather enjoy it.

The only slogan to watch out for when you're with him is that nice little number that says something not very complimentary like, 'I'm with this idiot' with a very definite finger pointing towards the person (you) on his right. If that's the case just be certain that you always walk on his left-hand side. The only way to get the better of the show-off who's got a snappy slogan for everything is to wear a T-shirt with a better slogan than his. Wear something like 'He Pays To Go Out With Me' or, 'My Mother Didn't Warn Me'.

But you can't say we didn't!

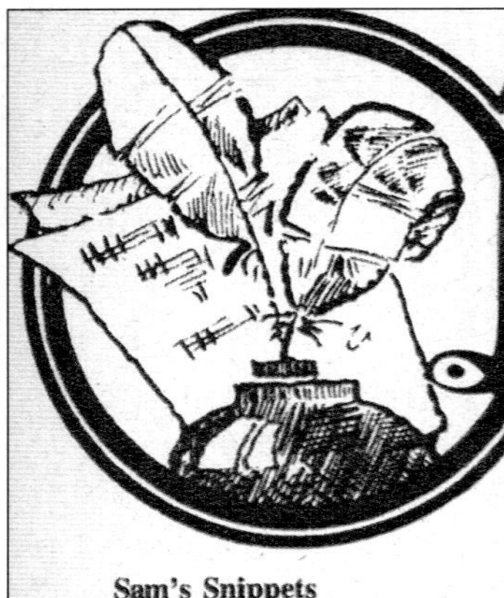

Letters

Have you ever wondered what it would be like to have your portrait painted? I've always wanted to see my face the centre of attraction in some famous Art Gallery — until recently, that is. Maggie's taken up painting and, like an idiot, I agreed to be the model for her first ever portrait. So, last weekend, I got all tarted up and sat for *hours* while Maggie threw bits of paint at the canvas. At least, I'm sure she *must* have thrown it — you couldn't explain the results any other way!

Cheer me up by sending your letters to me, Sam at Jackie, 185 Fleet Street, London EC4A 2HS. The writer of the Star Letter can choose between a Pifco Go-Girl Hairdyer, a transistor radio, a Boots 17 Make-Up Kit, or £4 in cash. Every other letter printed wins £2. Remember to tell me the three things you like best in Jackie (not counting my page, of course!). And keep those letters original!

PUNK RULES

Why are people always criticising Punk Rock groups? If they were called by their proper name, "New Wave", there wouldn't be so much criticism. The music they play is easy to listen to, and it isn't too rowdy or obscene.

It's their extreme followers who are the real "Punk Rockers," with safety-pins through their noses and cheeks. I've listened to many New Wave records and found them very enjoyable, so please don't judge Punk Rock on the extremist fans or by what other people say.

Listen, and hear for yourself.

Jackie Reader,
Halifax, Yorks.

This week's winner has chosen £4 cash as her Star Prize.

Sam's Snippets

. . . a tasty sandwich made with two slices of white bread with a lightbulb in between . . .
. . . lots of big iron birds scratching the sky . . .
. . . thought the poor washing machine looked tired, so I let it lie down for a while . . .
. . . lips are there to stop your mouth from fraying . . .

MAKES A CHANGE!

The other Saturday my friend and I were shopping in town and she dragged me into a new boutique to try some clothes on. As I was bored waiting for her I wandered away from the changing cubicles to the other side of the shop. Suddenly, I saw a hand appear from behind a curtain holding a pair of trousers and a cheese-cloth shirt.

A disembodied voice said, "Hang on to this a moment!" A bewildered man, waiting for his wife in the next door cubicle, took hold of the clothes and waited. A few minutes later the same hand came out with a blue dress saying, "I'll just have to lose weight, it won't fit over my bum."

My friend's face was very red when she discovered why I was rolling about on the floor!

S. Meyrick,
Cardiff.

A LONG, LONG WAY TO GO.

A few weeks ago, my little brother decided to leave home. It wasn't for a while till we noticed that he was missing. After a long search we eventually found him "camping" in the spare room.

His equipment comprised six eggs, a chair, and a bucket of water. Seeing our amused faces he announced he would stay there till he was sixteen and old enough to leave home. He's only six!

Brenda Ward,
Runcorn, Cheshire.

WRONG DOOR

As everyone knows, gentlemen are a dying breed. Nowadays, us girls just open doors, put on our coats and pay bills without thinking. But the other day my friend and I were about to get into my dad's car when he opened the door on the far side.

Neither of us realised we were supposed to get in separately — so we piled into the other side, causing severe injuries to the arm rest!

Boy, did we feel idiots when it dawned on us what we'd done!

Katherine Johnson,
Oxford.

(Maybe it's just as well chivalry's dead! – Sam.)

LIVING LESSONS

My dad's always on at me to speak properly and was very disappointed when I failed my English exam. I was disappointed, too, as he'd promised me two little ginger kittens if I passed.

However, he relented. I was thrilled, and said, "What shall we call them, as we won't know one from the other?"

"How about 'Shall' and 'Will'?" suggested Dad, with his face like a lemon. "You can't tell them apart either!"

That dampened my enthusiasm a little, believe me!

Mary White,
Falmouth, Cornwall.

STOP ME AND BUY ONE

Last Sunday we went to the sea for the day in our Dormobile, which is white, and we stopped to have our sandwiches in the van. Halfway through our lunch a lady stuck her head in my dad's window and asked what we got. Looking rather surprised, Dad said, "Jam sandwiches."

It wasn't until the woman had said "Huh!" and walked off that we realised she thought we were in an ice-cream van!

Kathleen Watson,
Batcombe, Somerset.

PANDERING TO HIM!

I've just got over yet another crisis, and once more my best friend listened to my troubles with much interest. He didn't butt in or laugh, but instead maintained a compassionate silence.

He often gets bashed to bits when I'm in a bad mood, or tossed around my bedroom. He's drowned in the washing machine and then pinned on the washing line by the ears. When his body has elongated to twice his normal size, he's then drowned in tears when I think how cruel I was to pin him up in the first place.

Even though he's stuffed to the eye-balls in fluff and leads a rotten life, my panda is the best friend I have!

Denise Whittington,
Harrogate, Yorks.

PLEA FOR RESPECT

When I recently visited an old, quaint church in the country I was shocked to see children walking on graves, playing in the pulpit, and rude and disgusting words written in the visitors' book.

It must be offending for visitors like me and especially for the local folk, to see this sort of thing going on. Has respect for other people's property gone out with good manners?

Mary Lutley,
Wallington, Surrey.

BRING BACK BEAUTIFUL BOPPERS!

I was looking through my old Jackies and I saw a letter which said how people didn't smile any more, especially on Top of the Pops or at discos. But what *I've* noticed is that, although we're one of the best pop nations in the world, we're certainly the worst dancers!

People at discos usually have to take at least an hour to pluck up courage even to get up, and when they do, everyone dances the same as each other. Even the people on Top of the Pops can only manage to shift from one foot to another, as if they are absolutely exhausted!

Sometimes, on T.V., you see clips from an American show called "Soul Train" and there the audience are *really* dancing and looking as though they are enjoying themselves. Anyone who dances originally over here is looked on as a show-off, even though their dancing is lots better than the "zombie shuffle."

So what about all of us trying to make our dancing as good as our music?

Jill Phillips,
Wirral, Merseyside.

LOST, STOLEN OR STRAYED?

Not long ago my cousin got married, but the wedding wasn't without its bad moments. The day before she was due at the church she went to collect her dress from the shop where it was being made. To her horror, the assistant, after a lengthy search through drawers, cupboards and order books, declared that she could find no trace of the dress.

My cousin let out a wail of despair and started to look round the shop herself. It was only then she realised she'd gone into the wrong shop in the first place!

Elizabeth Brittain,
Birmingham 20.

ROAST TEA?

Every day my mum asks my sister and me what we had for lunch at school. As neither of us are particularly fussy, she was surprised when my sister complained about the roast meat she'd had that day.

"It was horrible," she said. "It had green tea leaves all over it."

Yes — you've guessed — it was lamb and mint sauce!

C. Balls,
Norwich, Norfolk.

TEENSCOPE

For the week beginning Saturday August 20.

LEO (July 22-Aug. 21)
An unusual day is in store this weekend and you could end up with more than you bargained for as far as romance is concerned. You hear a totally amazing piece of news midweek — and only time will tell if it's true! You get cross with a friend who's inclined to be a bit of a stick-in-the-mud — and this spoils a foursome for you towards the end of the week.

VIRGO (Aug. 22-Sept. 21)
There's a strong chance of you coming into some extra money this weekend, and this will make all the difference to your enjoyment of it. You meet someone new and misjudge him rather badly. This will affect the progress of another relationship you've long had hopes about. You may have to be very diplomatic when bringing together two people who dislike each other.

LIBRA (Sept. 22-Oct. 22)
An important date on Saturday won't be all you predict it would be. It's a time for Librans to concentrate on the present and not get involved in future planning. Someone criticises your work and this could make you feel sorry for yourself. It's not until Friday that things begin to pick up and you'll find then that a friend makes an effort to help you enjoy yourself.

SCORPIO (Oct. 23-Nov. 21)
You may feel neglected at the weekend when two of your friends get on a little too well together and leave you out in the cold. Someone tells you about a boy you met recently and this news changes your whole attitude towards him. A letter will arrive mid-week from an old friend.

SAGITTARIUS (Nov. 22-Dec. 21)
A disappointing weekend for Sagittarians, as a trip you'd counted on fails to materialise. Next week will be more exciting, but you'll find that a lack of cash limits your activities. Romance is pretty boring just now but a meeting at the end of the week should be promising.

CAPRICORN (Dec. 22-Jan. 19)
You should feel on top of the world at the weekend when a long-awaited letter finally arrives. There's a chance you'll find someone special is very attentive and this will help you have a good time for the next few weeks. You'll grow further apart from a childhood friend unless you listen to her for a change.

AQUARIUS (Jan. 20-Feb. 18)
New friends will help you enjoy this weekend, provided you don't place too much hope on a compliment a boy pays you on Saturday. Another flirtation will get out of hand and may be an embarrassment to you. Midweek, you feel like being more independent, but someone will want to keep you securely tied down.

PISCES (Feb. 19-March 20)
At the weekend a friend seems to get all the attention from the admirer you thought was yours — but grit your teeth and say nothing, your turn will come! A holiday romance sweeps you off your feet — but don't pin your hopes on him. He'll be going home soon — and so will you! The letter P will be lucky for you in some way.

ARIES (March 21-April 20)
Someone says something embarrassing to a friend and this will make your love-life complicated for the next few days — but difficulties won't last. You'll probably meet up with an old friend — or at least get a letter from one — and this will mark the beginning of certain changes in your life.

TAURUS (April 21-May 20)
A meeting with a new boy at the weekend may not be very well-starred as far as romance is concerned — but he'll be great as a good friend. You could receive good news about a planned outing on Monday but there will be opposition from someone at home. Wear a lucky charm on Thursday.

GEMINI (May 21-June 20)
Try not to impose your will too much on a friend who's quieter than you — it could have nasty side effects at a party this weekend. You'll have to do a good deal of fast talking to get back in a boy's good books this weekend — but it should be worth it! Wear pink for luck on Friday.

CANCER (June 21-July 21)
News from abroad makes the weekend exciting — especially if it's from someone you've more than a passing romantic interest in! A problem about your holiday crops up yet again, but an older person may provide the solution. You meet a girl you once knew well and she makes quite an impact on your group of friends.

HOW DO YOU DOODLE?

Well, how did you doodle? Now's your chance to find out!

FILLED IN:
This doodle belongs to someone who probably feels depressed about his/her personality at the moment.

SEVERAL SQUARES TOGETHER:
The square is usually a male symbol and several together mean a practical, sensible person. Made by a girl it's a sign she's very down-to-earth. She's also very loyal and is looking for lasting love.

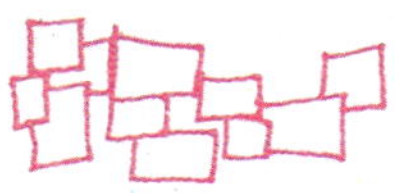

FLOWERS, HOME:
These are all feminine symbols and represent a girl's desire for home and children. Boys who draw houses are also showing their desire to settle down some day.

CARS, TRUCKS, MACHINERY, BUILDINGS:
These are male symbols and show that the person is very much involved in a man's working world.

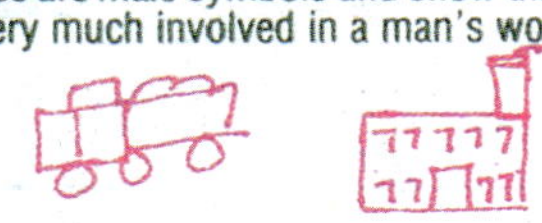

ARROWS, SHARP POINTS:
Arrows, sharp points or jagged edges mean keep off! Here's a hostile person with a chip on his/her shoulder. This person likes to fight and would be jealous, moody and bad-tempered in love unless constantly pampered.

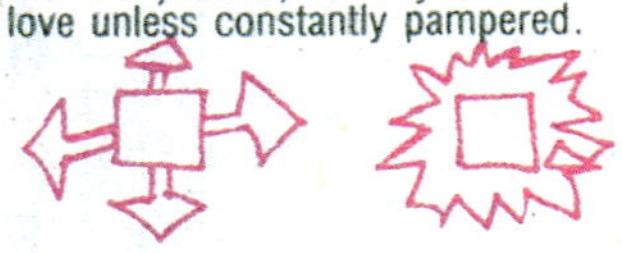

RADIATING STRAIGHT OR WAVY LINES:
When a sunburst of straight or wavy lines surrounds the square it could mean this person likes to be the centre of attention. He/she will sulk if neglected.

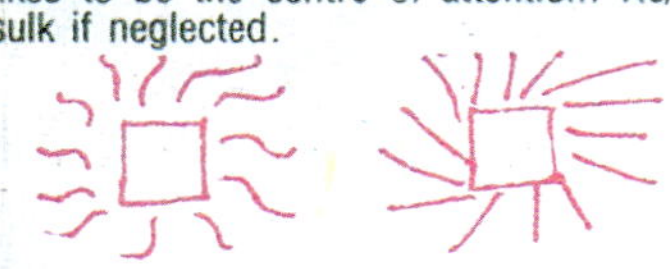

FRAMES, SQUARES ENCLOSING SQUARE:
This person is shy, reserved and may not like his/her personality. Such a person dreams of breaking out of their present life but feels trapped

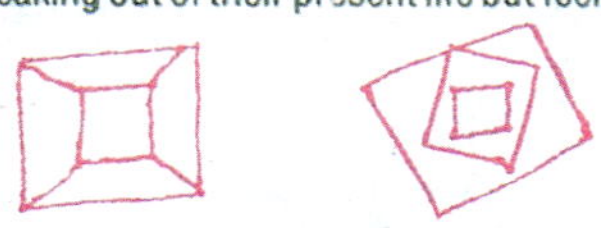

FRAME WITH LINES MOVING OUTWARDS:
This person is trying very hard to come to terms with shyness and emerge from their shell. He/she needs to be encouraged to express their true feelings.

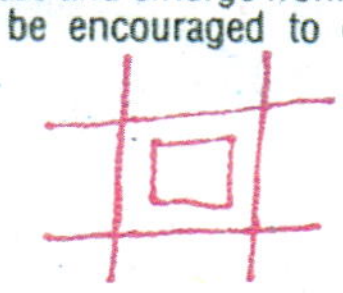

BARS, CIRCLES, PEOPLE, DOT, DIAGONAL LINES INSIDE SQUARE:
This type of doodle is often made by someone very concerned with themselves. They are insecure and afraid to move beyond the small circle of friends and family where they feel safe.

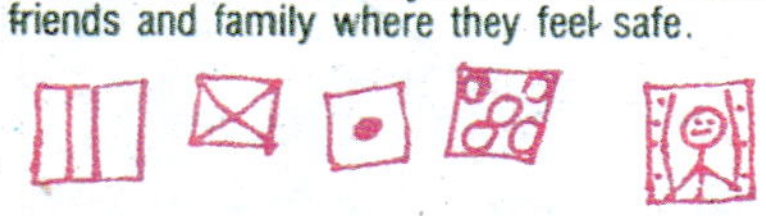

MAZE OR LOOPS:
A square enclosed by circles, a maze or a circle of loops is a sign of a very reserved person who is timid and wants to be protected by a stronger personality. A boy doing this doodle probably needs the sort of girl who will mother him.

FLOWERS, ANIMALS:
These are typically feminine symbols expressing a girl's interest in the home and hopes of marriage and children, someday.

EYES, FACES:
Eyes and faces are usually drawn by girls—girls who are preoccupied with looks. They feel they are being closely watched both by other girls and by boys. They may feel self-conscious about their looks, wishing they were as pretty as the girls they draw.

SUNBURST, ENLARGED DOT:
A sunburst of lines or enlarging of the dot reveals a show-off who likes to draw attention to himself/herself.

DOT SURROUNDED BY SQUARE, MAZE OR LOOPING CIRCLE:
When the dot is surrounded by such symbols it indicates a person who puts a wall around themselves for protection. Such people are often retiring and afraid of being hurt.

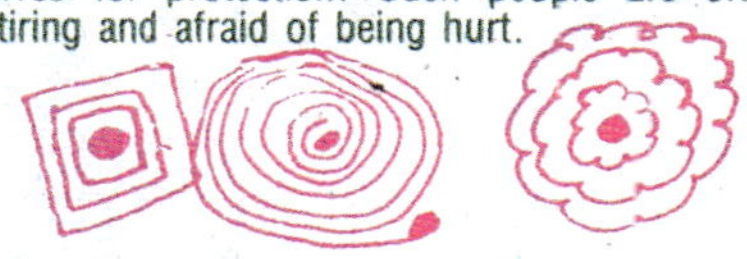

LINES, WEB, GRID OVER DOT:
This person is telling us they lack confidence. They're preoccupied with what other people think and are very emotionally dependent on others. He/she is probably easily hurt and needs understanding.

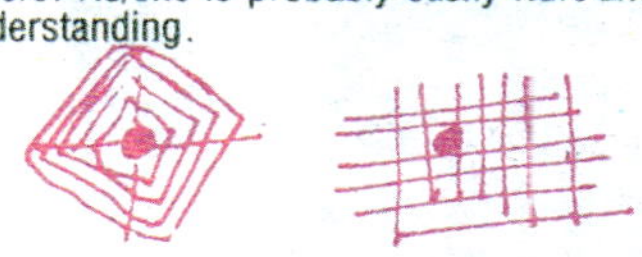

ARROWS, SHARP POINTS, JAGGED EDGES:
Here is a hostile, aggressive person with a sharp tongue and quick temper. Quick to take offence, they would be difficult to live with, and as a romantic partner they could be jealous and spiteful.

SURROUNDED BY DOTS, CIRCLES:
This doodler is very sociable, easy-going and happy to treat everyone as an equal.

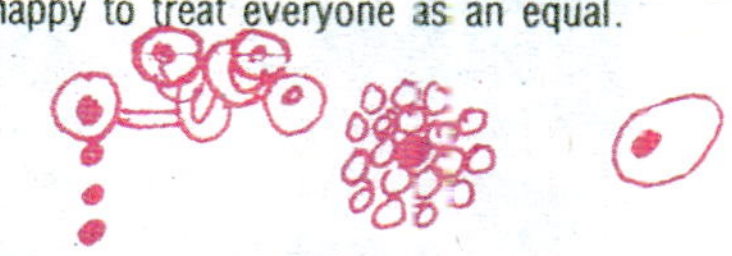

DOODLING YOUR NAME:
This is a sign of preoccupation with self and with the impressions the doodler creates on others. He/she is probably self-conscious and shy.

FILLED IN:
This doodler doesn't have much time for romance — they'll leave that to someone else. But they will always be level-headed and loyal in love.

VERY ROMANTIC HEARTS:
These kind of hearts are usually made by girls. They show that the doodler is a romantic dreamer who believes in a fairy-tale romance.

SURROUNDED BY SQUARE, CIRCLE, LARGER HEART:
When a person encloses the heart within another symbol it shows that they are very cautious in romance. Such people usually hide their feelings and appear to lack romance until they find someone they trust.

SURROUNDED BY LARGER HEARTS, RADIATING LINES:
These doodles show a dramatic and very emotional person who expects a lot of attention.

DIVIDED, BARRED HEARTS:
This type of doodle could be the sign of someone with mixed attitudes to love. It could be conflict between head and heart, or this person could be going out with two people at once.

BROKEN, BLEEDING HEART:
These doodlers are obviously unhappy. They've been hurt more than once.

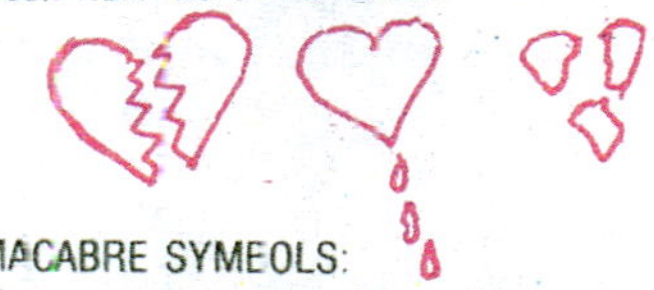

MACABRE SYMBOLS:
These strange, frightening doodles are sometimes made by people who have been hurt in the past and now want to get their own back. They can be cruel and unfeeling — so be warned!

FIGURES, FACES:
These doodles, usually made by boys, show that the doodler isn't the type to fall in love easily. When drawn by a girl they show she is very concerned with her appearance and the clothes she wears.

ARROWS, BARBS, POINTS:
When sharp arrows, barbs or points surround the heart it shows the doodler is on the defensive, has been hurt in the past and now has a hostile attitude toward romance. Getting involved with such a person could cause heart-ache.

WHORLS:
Elaborate curves and whorls inside the heart show a very sensitive, idealistic and emotional person who may be something of a mystery. He/she is also a romantic worrier, always analysing relationships and making mountains out of molehills.

SMALL STARS, HEARTS SURROUNDING HEART:
These are the doodles of a flirt with a sense of humour who sees romance as an enjoyable game.

MACHINE SYMBOLS:
This boy is definitely more interested in plumbing than romance!

IS HE THE BOY FOR YOU?

Knowing a few basic facts about doodles makes it possible for you to compare your doodles with those of the boy in your life to see if he really is the boy for you!

If your doodles are basically feminine with flowing, curved lines, circles, flowers, trees, animals, "S" shapes, houses or stars and his are basically masculine with squares, triangles, oblongs, machinery, cars or buildings then you would both fit into a fairly normal romance! But to find out how happy you would be we have to look closer.

If the doodles of both of you contain similar whorls, circles or mazes you're

HERS: *HIS:*

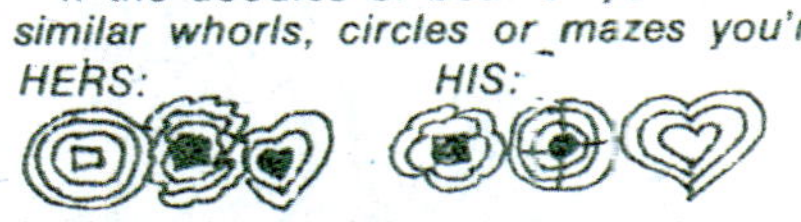

both seeking to be protected by your romantic partner. You're basically gentle, sensitive people who would look after each other.

If, however, one partner has the above traits while the other has sharp angles, the gentler partner may not be able to cope with the aggressive, forceful personality of the other person.

A girl whose doodles lack the feminine interest symbols would hardly be happy with a boy whose maze-like doodles or pictures of houses reveal he is looking for a motherly girl to shelter him.

HERS: *HIS:*

A girl whose doodles show her to be an extrovert and possibly a bit of a show-off may not be happy with a boy whose doodles reveal he is an introvert.

HERS: *HIS:*

A very romantic girl should be forewarned if the boy she is interested in fills in his hearts or encloses them. She definitely won't get the romantic love she wants.

HERS: *HIS:*

A girl with a very idealistic, sensitive view of love would be totally unsuitable for a boy whose doodles show he is more interested in a girl's looks than in her sensitive heart.

HERS: *HIS:*

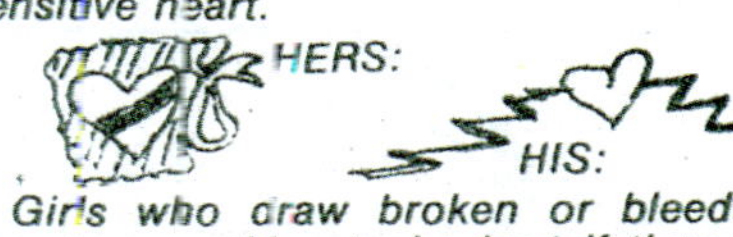

Girls who draw broken or bleeding hearts are asking to be hurt if they get involved with boys who draw sadistic symbols around their hearts or surround them with sharp points or barbs.

HERS: *HIS:*

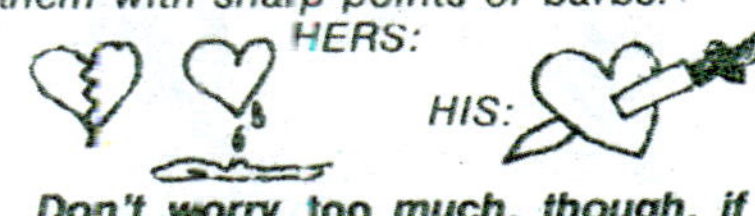

Don't worry too much, though, if he doesn't seem to be the one for you – if you know what goes on in that mind of his you'll understand him and be able to cope with him that much better! And remember – love conquers all – even doodles!

If You Were Santa Claus, Who Would You NOT Give A Pesent To?

On-The-Spot Interviews — where our roving reporters find out what *you* think.

Susan and Jennifer, twin models.
Susan: My sister — we never give each other presents!
Jennifer: My sister . . .!

Graham Pascoe, Truro, Cornwall.
Lord Longford. He really annoys me because he has such double standards. He condemns today's permissive society and then he turns round and supports the release of people who have been sent to prison for really horrific crimes, like child-murder. He just doesn't make sense.

Kid Jensen, Radio One.
I wouldn't give a present to big businessmen who think of Christmas as a way of earning lots of money. Every year, Christmas becomes less and less meaningful, and the spirit of goodwill disappears with it. I think it's a shame that we're forgetting what Christmas is really all about.

Alison Soutar, Douglas, Isle of Man.
I wouldn't give a present to anyone who doesn't like the Rolling Stones. I think they're great, and it really makes me mad when I turn on the radio and listen to all that rubbish called New Wave. How can anyone say the Stones are past it when there's no-one new to replace them?

Melody Gibson, Gravesend, Kent.
Edward Heath. He's the one person I can't stand. He's always trying to force his opinions on other people, and I think he was a bad P.M.

Elaine Smart, Johnstone Castle, Renfrewshire.
I'd find out all the people who have done cruel things, and make sure that they didn't get anything. Judging by all the unhappiness in the world, it would make my sack of presents a lot lighter!

Anne McMillan, Glasgow.
There's a boy at school who's been annoying me throughout the year. I'd make sure I "forgot" to visit his chimney, and that he knew why, too!

Pamela Baillie, Bath, Somerset.
I wouldn't give a present to the comedian Dave Allen, simply because I think that he tells duff jokes. My entire family fall about the place laughing when his show is on the screen, but I honestly can't see what's so funny about him.

Susie Smith, Padstow, Cornwall.
I wouldn't give a present to my French teacher — she gives us far too much homework!

Susan McLintock, Paisley, Renfrewshire.
I wouldn't give a present to any of the Sex Pistols. They haven't contributed anything to the music scene, and they probably don't believe in Christmas, anyway.

Liz Dearlove, Sheffield, South Yorkshire.
All the people who didn't believe in Santa last week — they don't deserve a present, and it would serve them right!

Kathryn Wilkinson, Bradford, West Yorkshire.
The thief who stole my bike from outside the supermarket while I was doing a favour for one of our neighbours!

Lee Brilleaux, Dr Feelgood.
I'll give you a clue — she's a real busybody. Yes, you've guessed it, it's Mary Whitehouse! It really annoys me that she thinks she knows what is best for all of us. If I want to see a film, I don't want to find that somebody else has decided it's no good. I want to make up my own mind, so Mary Whitehouse wouldn't get a present from me!

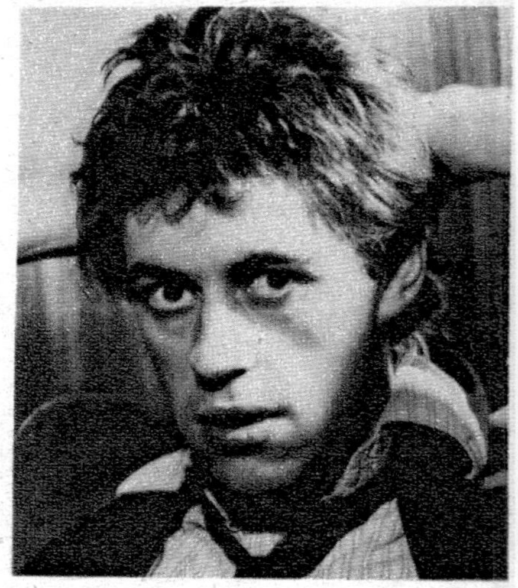

Bob Geldorf, Boomtown Rats.
Eugh! I wouldn't give a present to Hughie Green — I can't stand "Opportunity Knocks." He's so insincere that my toes curl up in disgust if I happen to see it. He definitely wouldn't get a present from me!

Jackie Thurgood, Barking, Essex.
My section leader — he's really miserable and he's always trying to find fault with everyone, especially me! I suppose that it's really because of our job — we both work in the accountancy department of an insurance company, and you've got to do everything perfectly. But all the same, he still gets on my nerves!

Linda Entwhistle, Berwick on Tweed, Northumberland.
I wouldn't give a present to David Soul. He always seems to be trying to steal the limelight from lovely Paul Michael Glaser. I think he's far better than silly David Soul, anyway.

20 ways to patch up a quarrel

ANOTHER IN OUR EMERGENCY KIT SERIES

1. Organise a Peace Treaty with the enemy. Well, it worked for Napoleon and Caesar!
2. Try a kiss and a hug . . . and an enormous box of chocolates, just to be on the safe side.
3. Do it gracefully — in coloured ink on floral notepaper (lavender-scented, of course!).
4. If it's your mum you quarrel with, say, "I expect we row so much because we're so close to each other."

5. Get out the old sewing machine, cut a patch from your old jeans . . . and repair the damage!

6. When you know you're at fault, a little tear can work wonders (especially if it's your boyfriend you're trying to make up to!).
7. With an obstinate, stubborn person, be first to apologise — it's not easy, but it's worth it (for the sake of a little peace, if nothing else!).
8. Don't patch it, settle it — try looking it up in the nearest dictionary or encyclopaedia. And if that doesn't work, hit him/her/them over the head with it instead . . .
9. With a policeman . . . in this case, don't wait to patch it up . . . turn on your heels and run for it!
10. Buy a blank cassette and record all the singles you can with an "I'm sorry" theme to them! Then send it to the person you quarrelled with.
11. If you quarrel at a party, ignore him and start talking to his mates. He may crawl on his knees and beg forgiveness; on the other hand, you could make things twice as bad!

12. Send a huge "Let's Be Friends" card — guaranteed to melt the hardest heart.
13. Be nostalgic . . . and start going on about the great times you had when you first knew each other. (It works, as long as it isn't a new friend.)
14. There's nothing like a nice cup of hot tea in bed to patch up a quarrel with your mum!
15. Next time you see whoever you're quarrelling with, just act normally and assume they've forgotten about it.
16. With a bribe! He won't be able to resist you when you give him that Cup Final ticket.
17. Tell your mum how much younger and prettier she is than everyone else's mums.
18. Send round a hatchet, complete with instructions for its burial.
19. Don't use the phone to patch up a quarrel — when he hears the sound of your voice, he's liable to hang up, in a temper!
20. Tidy your bedroom *and* clean the fluff from under your bed . . . then your parents might just forget the quarrel.

Look Out for extra special romantic and fun ideas in beauty and fashion.

LOOK OUT

IN THE BAG!

There are a lot of really fantastic bags around just now — to go with every look you can think of. "Sporties" are carrying enormous lightweight tote bags, made from parachute material, which fold up into tiny packs. "Tweedy country girls" like natural tan leather bags; while the really fashion conscious go for duffel bags — in gold and silver!

Among *everyone's* favourites, though, are the "fun" accessories. Bags which make you smile — like clear plastic bags with swimming gold fish printed on them, or this terrific small size duffel bag which looks like a Heinz beans tin! Attach it to your belt, wear it round your neck, tie it to a bigger bag, or just carry it! It's useful for holding make-up, change and tiny odd bits and pieces. This duffel bag comes from Bridgebags, it's made in polyester and costs £1.99. It also comes with Heineken, Pepsi, 7-Up or Campbell's Tomato Soup prints! Available from all branches of C & A and Chelsea Girl.

CLEAN UP!

One of your spring-cleaning jobs should be to tidy your make-up bag and throw out all that useless make-up. That way, you can keep your purse as light and slim as possible so that it fits neatly into all the latest purses and pouch bags! And, when you're doing a quick repair job, you don't want to have to scrabble through loads of old make-up to find what you need.

All you should carry are a few essentials . . . you can leave the rest at home, and take some of the strain off the zip or clasp.

The essentials should be:

1. Medicated spot and blemish coverer for emergencies.
2. Mirror. If you have one in an eyeshadow or powder compact, so much the better.
3. Lip salve.
4. Lipstick. (Just one — leave the others at home!)
5. Blusher.
6. Eyeshadow — just the ones you're going to use that day, not your entire collection!
7. Mascara.

Remember to keep all pencils sharpened to a fine point, ready for use. Make sure that all caps are screwed on tightly, before putting things in your bag — powder shadows especially are liable to make an awful mess.

If your make-up's in tip top condition, then so will you be!

BE A VALENTINE

SO FAR SEW GOOD
Cheap and cheerful fashion ideas.

Here are two super ideas for Valentine's party T-shirts. Bring your old T-shirts right up to date . . . with the help of lovely feathers, ribbons and sequins.

For the first, you'll need about 1¼ metres of each colour of ribbon. Pin the ribbons along the neck of your T-shirt and leave them loose at the front, cut them the length you require, unpin the ribbons, and then thread colourful wooden beads (the beads will need to have wide thread holes), on to each of the ribbons. Sew feathers firmly to the ends of the ribbons, keeping the feather "ends" together. Pull beads over the "ends" of the feathers, to keep them firmly attached. Neatly stitch the ribbons to the back of the neck, along to the shoulder seams, leaving them to hang down the front. Sew coloured ribbons round the edge of the sleeves, too.

Or, decorate a plain vest-shaped T-shirt by sewing ribbon bows to the shoulder seams, and a gold-sequined heart motif.

You'll find sequins and ribbons in the haberdashery departments of most large stores, and the feathers are available from fishermen's shops.

BUDGET BIT

These super belts are the most unusual we've seen yet! They look fantastic with clear plastic pouches attached to them, with the latest cotton drill straight-legged trousers, or belted round the middle of a jumpsuit! Whichever way you wear them, they're great!

The belts are made all in plastic, with Coca Cola, Union Jack and Kit Kat prints. As well as being such nice designs, the belts are specially cut to any size you want!

You can order your belt from Alan Homer, Runneymede Productions Ltd., 104 Straight Road, Old Windsor, Berks. Price is 95p, **including** postage and packing (remember to state your size).

SPECIAL TIPS

Valentine's Day is fast approaching . . . so be ready to make February 14 th extra special this year!

PINK, this season's favourite colour, is just perfect for Valentine's Day parties! Delicious strawberry pinks make you look good enough to eat — dress up in lovely shiny pink satins, with lots of pink feathers, ribbons and a fan, and you definitely won't be short of kisses!

JEWELLERY: don't just wear your heart on your sleeve, wear hearts everywhere!

Look out for Corocraft's lovely miniature earrings, with either pierced ear or clip-fastenings, not only in the shape of delicate hearts, but also love knots, and birds and bees. Price is 95p a pair, from most department stores.

Make-up and perfume should be perfect, too — so choose extra carefully!

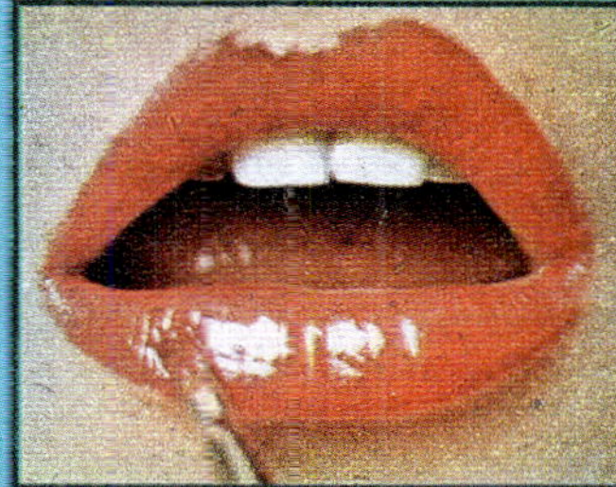

LIPSTICK should be bright and slightly shocking . . . no pale, sugary pinks. Look out for Max Factor Pink Chestnut in the Swedish Formula range, price 85p, Outdoor Girl Long Lasting Rose, 34p, or Perfect Pink and Pink Wisp in the Boots 17 Soft Lip Stix range, price 35p each.

FRAGRANCE is all a matter of personal choice: Sam in the office likes Fabergé's Babe, Wendy goes for Masumi by Coty, and Pete says he likes Aphrodisia by Fabergé (can't think why!). Other favourites are Jontue, by Revlon, a flowery fragrance that smells delicious, Chique by Yardley, Miners Butterfly Rose, and, just right for Valentine's Day, Love is Spray Mist from the Love is range!

SPRING SHAPES!

At last, winter must almost be over, because here's the newest shape for spring! The total look is very sporty. Emphasis is all on hips–tops are big, loose and baggy, drawn at the hips, worn with the tightest fitting drainpipe canvas trousers, and flat shoes. The colours are light and bright, top shades are cream and white and the favourite material is comfortable cotton Aertex.

Our spring shape tops come from Mary Quant. The first is a super loose baggy top, drawn at the hips and cuffs, with a hood and toggle fastening. It's made in comfortable Aertex, style: "Deauville," price: approx. £11.

The wide striped blouson jacket has short sleeves with tabs, button-fastening front pockets and drawstring bottom. It's also made in Aertex, price: approx. £11. Style is "Le Touquet."

Both come in sizes 10-18, and are available at selected large fashion and department stores.

NAILS NATURALLY!

Nails are often brittle and out of condition at this time of year and the skin around them is often broken and rough. Give your nails an early Spring Clean and get them into tip-top condition, the natural way.

First of all, there are some basic rules you should always follow if you want your nails to look nice. Be kind to them and wear rubber gloves when you do the washing up. Your hands may not appear to suffer, but the combination of hot water and detergents and soap powders can be very drying for hands, leaving them red and sore and making the nails dry, brittle and easily split.

Remove nail polish with a remover that has an added conditioner, those without it can be very harsh. Renew polish frequently, don't just paint over chips and cracks and leave it on for weeks. Manicure regularly using a wooden "orange" or manicure stick to clean under the nails with a little cotton wool wrapped around the end. Never probe around with sharp nail scissors as this can damage the skin under the nails and will be sore!

Always shape nails with an emery board and make them a rounded shape rather than a pointed one.

Strengthen your nails by soaking them regularly in warm olive oil in a small bowl for five minutes. Do it while you're watching television so you don't get bored!

Make a delicious conditioning cream for your nails with equal quantities of honey, olive oil and egg yolk. Apply this to your nails and leave it on for about 30 minutes, then rinse off.

Good nails show you care about yourself, so make sure you take good care of yours!

ARE YOU A FLOP?

Feel your hair's a complete flop? If *your* hair's always a mess, you'll know what we mean! Tatty hair ruins your whole image, no matter how much care you take with your clothes and make-up, so take steps now to make your hair into your crowning glory. It's simple enough, so hair goes . . .

IF you're as fed up as Lesley in our photo, you'll need to take instant action! Her hair's naturally wavy and a good colour, but right now she looks like most of us feel from time to time . . . fed up!

We rushed Lesley along to top stylist Sue at the Elida Gibbs salon in London, to ask her advice. Sue diagnosed the problem at once!

"Like lots of girls, Lesley's hair is inclined to be greasy and that often makes it hard to manage," she told us. "And not being cut in a definite style makes it look a bit frayed around the edges when it needs a wash.

"Anyone with greasy hair should use a mild shampoo for washing, one that helps to remove excess grease without disturbing the natural balance of basic oils which are necessary for keeping the hair healthy!

"It's important to wash gently, making sure that scalp and hair are clean and rinsing very thoroughly. The water should be warm, not hot."

While Sue was telling us this, Lesley's hair was being washed with Pears Shampoo for greasy hair, and she emerged with it wet and ready for trimming. Lesley shrank at the sight of the scissors, but Sue was very firm.

"The secret of a really successful hairstyle is a good, basic cut," she says, "only professional cutting will ensure that your hair looks good all the time. A trim once a month will get rid of split and damaged ends and keep the shape right."

After a thorough wash with a mild shampoo like Pears Shampoo for greasy hair, the hair's rinsed really well and cutting begins.

SOFT AND SHINY

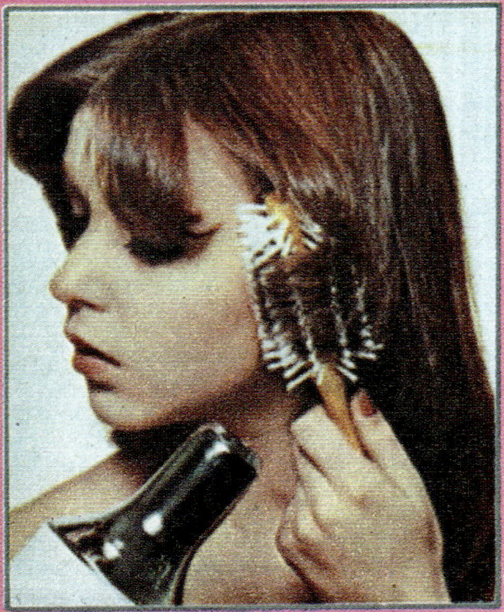

Blow-drying's a quick, simple way of keeping your hair natural and beautiful. All you need's a good cut, a drier and a circular brush!

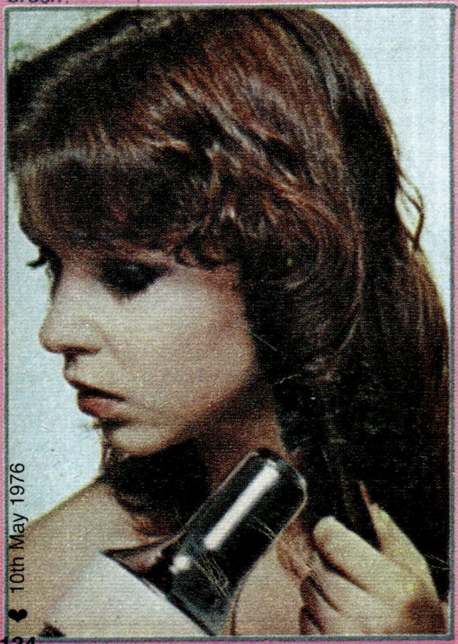

Success: A glossy, smooth style that's right for anytime. And you really can do it yourself at home, once you've been for the basic cut!

Blow-drying's best for easy, natural styles, and it's a very simple way of keeping hair nice, once you've got the basic style! All you need is a drier and a *round* brush for styling and shaping as you dry.

Sue showed Lesley how to blow-dry her hair herself after it had been trimmed and shaped, and gave us a few hints on blow-drying at home.

"Never hold the drier too close to the hair or you'll end up with a burnt, frizzy look. Don't use steel combs or spiky, wiry brushes either, as these can strip the outer layers of hair, leaving it in very bad condition."

Lesley's finished straight style was neatly turned under and very smooth and shiny, shaped down the sides to give an angular line. Sue stressed that the hair *must* be clean and shining for this style to look its best. And Lesley certainly looks at her very best now!

TOP TIPS

Your hair won't look right unless the basic cut is good. So don't moan if your hair looks terrible, go to a hairdresser and have something done about it!

Do use a shampoo that's right for your hair-type and do choose a mild shampoo if you have greasy hair. Pears Shampoo for greasy hair costs 29p, 44p or 75p for the economy size.

Always treat your hair gently—tugging with spiky brushes and combs will damage the hair and cause split ends.

Don't despair if your hair isn't in good condition, though. With correct cutting and conditioning it will be shining and healthy in just a few months!

ADD A BIT OF BOUNCE

Add some bounce for special occasions. Heated rollers are used to set the hair backwards from forehead, up at the back and the bottom.

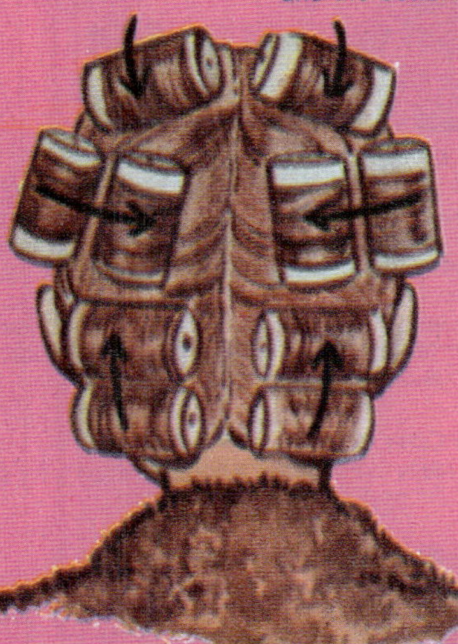

It's easy to get bored with a style, though, so we asked Sue to give Lesley a softer, curlier look for special occasions.

She used heated rollers for the evening style, showing Lesley how she can do exactly the same thing herself at home. The rollers are set back over the top and sides of the head, with the bottom hair rolled up at the back.

If you don't have heated rollers, you can achieve the same effect with ordinary rollers, setting the hair while it's still wet.

The final result's smooth on top, curly and bouncy at the sides . . . just right for any special occasion!

Great for evening . . . this style's pretty but very simple to do yourself with heated or ordinary rollers.

Another in our Emergency Kit Series

20 WAYS TO MAKE SURE YOU'RE NOT INVITED BACK!

1. Flirt with the hostess's boyfriend, and make sure she sees you doing it.

2. Make it quite clear that you're bored to tears by everyone in the room.

3. Talk to the boys all night, and completely ignore the girls — but only if you don't mind having no friends left at all.

4. Insult the other guests.

5. Find out what the hostess is wearing, and make a point of wearing exactly the same thing.

6. Drop something; anything from a trifle to your hostess's mother's most treasured family heirloom.

7. Praise the goulash, when you *know* it's meant to be a curry.

8. Get your boyfriend to park his motorbike in the hall, or better still, get him to bring his friends along and have them all park their motorbikes in the hall.

9. Arrive with 20 uninvited guests — just as she's trying to get rid of everyone else.

10. Take the hostess some chocolate mints — then eat them all yourself.

11. Shout to all and sundry that there are beetles in the sugar bowl.

12. Play that fine old British sport "bounce the glass" with her mother's fine crystal wine glasses.

13. Arrive with one guy and leave with another — preferably someone else's boyfriend.

14. Be sick over the cat.

15. Pour your drink all over her dad's 200 year old, highly polished pearl inlaid walnut harpsichord.

16. Crack nuts between your teeth — ugh!

17. Be prettier and wittier than any other girl there.

18. Start a fight.

19. Drop lemonade/sticky toffee/nail varnish/a pair of pointed scissors on her favourite Bay City Rollers' L.P. — and just leave it there.

20. Just go in and take over the entire party!

LEARNING YOUR LINES!

A Jackie Guide to Palm Reading

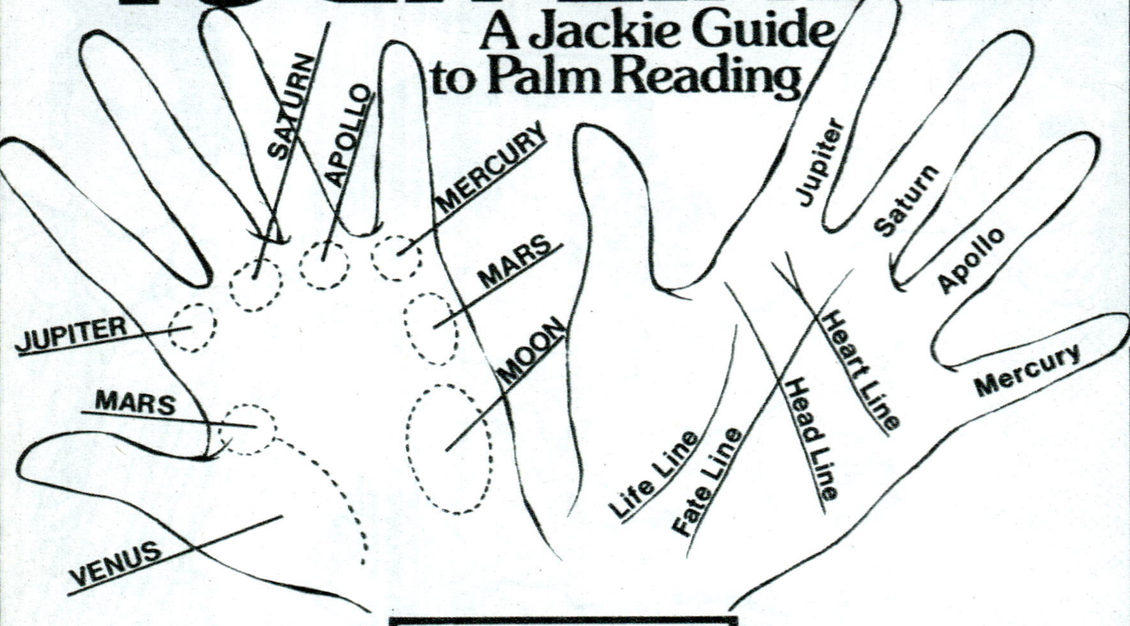

Take a look at your hands and what do you see? Not a lot, you might think. But — to the trained eye of the palmist, the lines on your hands can reveal all sorts of secrets about your personality and your future life. So here's our special Jackie guide to seeing the future in your hands!

IF they're doing a really detailed reading, palmistry experts look at everything from the shape, size and colour of the hand to the size and appearance of the fingers, the shape of the nails and the size of the finger joints!

But this sort of approach can take a long, long time, so in our special Jackie guide we'll be concentrating on the fingers and palms to find out what the future could hold for you!

So let's take a look at the fingers more closely, taking the left hand. There are certain characteristics associated with each finger, and the longer the finger, the more of the characteristic you'll have.

The first, or index finger, is called "the finger of Jupiter" and shows how ambitious, clever and faithful you are.

The second, or middle finger, "the finger of Saturn" shows how serious, thoughtful and how good at saving money you are!

Good health, beauty, success in life, optimism and sensitivity can all be measured by "the finger of Apollo," the third finger.

The fourth finger, "the finger of Mercury" shows how alert and quick you are — and how good at sports you are!

Your thumb, too, will tell you how much will-power, self-control, and logic you possess.

The degree to which you have the qualities related to each finger depends on the length of the finger, in relation to your other fingers. And the longer the finger, the more of that particular characteristic you have.

So for instance, if you have a long third finger, you're more than likely to be a cheerful, happy sort of person who will probably make a success of your life! If, though, your third finger is quite short, you could be a bit moody and tend to think the worst of people occasionally.

THE MOUNTS

(see diagram A)

AT the base of each finger is a pad of flesh, known in palmistry as a "mount," which takes the name of the finger to which it's related.

For instance, the mount at the base of the first finger, the finger of Jupiter, is known as "the mount of Jupiter" and so on.

The qualities related to these mounts are the same as those related to the particular fingers and like the fingers, the more pronounced the mount is, the more you possess its particular qualities.

As well as the mounts at the base of the fingers, there are four other mounts on the palm, making a total of eight in all.

These others are the two mounts of Mars, the mount of Venus, and the mount of the Moon.

The mounts of Mars show strength of character and courage. The mount of Venus shows how generous, sociable and sensitive you are; and the mount of the Moon shows how much imagination and "sixth sense" you have.

And again, the more pronounced these mounts are, the more you possess their particular qualities.

THE LINES

(see diagram B)

MOST people, when they think of palmistry, think of the lines of the palm. There are four principal lines: the lines of heart, head, life and fate.

The length and clearness of these lines give the expert palmist a picture of someone's past, present and future. But if you know where the lines are, and what to look for, you can build up a pretty accurate picture yourself!

The *heart line* is the one which runs from near the mount of Jupiter to the base of the mount of Mercury, and it shows just how you feel about love and romance.

If it runs past the mount of Mercury on to the back of the hand, it shows you're extremely faithful and steadfast in love. If the line is broken, it could be a sign of some emotional problem.

The *head line* starts midway between the thumb and first finger and runs straight across the palm to the top of the mount of the Moon.

If it's near the heart line, it means that your heart rules your head and that you're liable to act impulsively.

A strong (clear and deep) head line shows intelligence.

The *life line* runs round the mount of Venus, but a short life line doesn't necessarily mean a short life! Breaks in the line, though, can show serious illnesses and small lines crossing the life line can show minor ailments.

If your head line is joined to your life line, you're probably a bit self-conscious, shy and retiring. If it's not joined to the life line, the opposite will be true and you'll be very self-confident and extrovert.

The *line of fate*, sometimes called the line of fortune, or the line of Apollo, is the guide to success or failure.

It runs from near the wrist to the base of the mount of Apollo. It's often a difficult line to see, except in people who are destined to be extremely successful!

If, though, instead of ending on the mount of Apollo, it ends on the mount of Saturn, at the base of the middle finger, it shows a life of leisure and happiness.

As we said before, palmistry can be extremely complicated, and we've just concentrated on a few aspects. Still, next time a boy asks you out, you could ask for a quick look at his hand first — making it quite clear you're attempting a palm reading, not checking whether it's clean!

ON-THE-SPOT INTERVIEWS—WHERE OUR ROVING REPORTERS FIND OUT WHAT *YOU* THINK

IF YOU WERE THE ONLY GIRL IN THE WORLD,

who would you hate to be the only boy?

Bonny Tyler.
There isn't any particular boy I'd hate to be left alone with. But there is a certain type of guy that I don't really like. That's the kind who's very over-protective, plays the perfect gentleman all the time and never, ever, lets you lift a finger!

I couldn't stand that — I hate being molly-coddled!

Julie Sheaves, Bristol.
I don't think I'd mind being the only girl with anyone as long as it wasn't someone who played the bagpipes! Can you imagine being driven daft by hearing someone playing "Amazing Grace" all day?

Jane Macdonald, Dingwall, Ross-shire.
John-Boy Walton. He's so annoying, everything always works out the way he wants it to, and he can never do a thing wrong. Besides that, I can't stand his squeaky little rasping voice!

Karen, Dorset.
The guitarist in Mud who wears flashy earrings and long flowing outfits! I couldn't stand the competition!

Ellen Jones, Kent.
Paul Nicholas. Only because I'd die of shame if he didn't fancy me — when he didn't even have a choice!

Claire, Northumberland.
Horrible, grinning, frog-in-the-throat Rod Stewart! I can't see why anyone likes him. He likes himself enough for all of us.

Elizabeth Firth, Batley, W. Yorkshire.
My brother! I'd have to end it all within about five minutes of being alone with him.

Mary Gardiner, Kidderminster, Worcs.
Henry VIII would be my unfavourite choice! He looks so horrible, fat and cruel. And imagine following on after six wives!

Carey Allerton, London SW15.
I think I'd rather do without boys altogether, than have one I couldn't stand. But the worst fate I can think of would be to be alone with Demis Roussos!

Sue Mehennick (Legs & Co.)
Definitely Frank Spencer in "Some Mothers do 'Ave 'Em." Can you imagine the situation with nobody left on earth but Frank, doing his bit to complete the final destruction?

Julie, Dorset.
Definitely toothy old Donny Osmond 'cos he's such a big show-off!

Karen Waterman, Virginia Water, Surrey.
Prince Charles, because I'd probably end up marrying him and becoming a Queen. He's probably very nice, but I don't think I could ever feel at ease with someone like him who comes from such a totally different background to me.

Jane, Swansea.
Sacha Distel. I just think he's so slimy and it always sounds like he's putting on a French accent! He'd probably sing most of the day, too — ugh!

Sarah Aitchison, Norfolk.
One of the Tetley tea bag men. The way they go on about their wretched little perforations is enough to kill any conversation stone dead. And what's even worse, I really hate tea!

Julie Forsyth (Guys 'n' Dolls)
If there were only two of us left in the world, I think I'd really hate it if the other person were Idi Amin. Makes me shudder at the thought. Can you imagine it? It'd be bad enough trying to scrape together an existence anyway, but with Idi Amin, there would be a heap of trouble to start with!

Amanda Cater, Newcastle-on-Tyne.
Jim Callaghan, Edward Heath or Cyril Smith! In fact, any politician. Imagine having to listen to those party political broadcasts all the time!

Judy Goldsmith, Tenterden, Kent.
My boyfriend! That may sound odd, but although I like him a lot, we're always bickering and arguing about something. And I don't think I'd have a very enjoyable time if there was no-one else around to stick up for me.

Cherie Woods, Maidstone, Kent.
Someone famous in the pop world who is used to getting mobbed by loads of girls. I'd hate to end up with Donny Osmond, Rod Stewart or David Essex or one of the Rollers. I don't think they'd be able to get used to the idea that they'd lost all their female fans.

And just think how exhausting it would be rushing about all over the place pretending to be a big crowd of fans. Anyway I couldn't be bothered to keep on asking them for their autograph!

Jill, Aberdeen.
Definitely Ilie Nastase! Not only because I can't play tennis, but because he's so bad-tempered. I couldn't stand having to face him throwing his tennis racquet about and shouting and screaming.

But maybe if I told him I wasn't an umpire it would be all right?

These are very personal views. The more controversial ones are being kept anonymous for their own safety!

A LIFE ON THE OPEN ROAD!

THIS IS MY LIFE – another in our occasional series about girls whose lives are different. This week – what it's like to be a gipsy girl . . .

LIFE amongst the gipsies has a romantic ring, hasn't it? The gipsy life's a travelling one, and perhaps everyone's favourite gipsy image is one of colourful caravans with crooked chimneys wending their way along country lanes, or camped overnight in some peaceful field.

But, like all romantic ideas, this one's not exactly the real picture. True, there are still thousands of genuine gipsies in this country. But their lives are changing fast, and to find out exactly what it means to be a gipsy today, I went along to speak to 17-year-old Sherry Lee.

You may have seen Sherry on television last year, when she was specially chosen to read from a book of gipsy poetry.

Sherry comes from an old gipsy family, and although she was born on a piece of waste ground and spent the first fifteen years of her life continually on the move, she now lives on a permanent caravan site, in a modern motor-drawn trailer.

"People aren't so willing now to let you use their fields!" Sherry said ruefully. "There are lots of evictions and gipsies aren't really left alone in peace.

"So my family decided we'd have an easier life if we were camped somewhere we knew we could stay!"

I wondered whether Sherry's life had been a difficult one before her family settled, and how she felt about being constantly on the move. But she seemed very contented with her past life, probably, as she said, because, "I never knew anything else, really. We used to travel all over England and spend a week or so in each town. I must have been to most places in the country!"

Of course, Sherry couldn't go to school or get a regular job while she was moving around like that, and I asked her what she'd done to fill up her day and whether she ever got bored.

"No, I was never bored!" Sherry laughed.

"There was always too much to do, just keeping going! For a start, with a family of five there was the caravan to keep clean and tidy — it's washed and scrubbed down several times a day.

"Then I used to help my father — he collected scrap to sell, and we went round farms asking if they had any we could take away. That was known as 'scrapping'! As well as that, there was the 'hawking' — that's really the women's job. I'd go round with my mother selling things at people's doors."

Of course, we're all familiar with the lovely flowers that gipsies often bring round to sell, and lots of Sherry's time was taken up helping her mother make delicate elderwood flowers and clever baskets from willows.

"When I was very little, too, my mother had a wonderful gipsy way of carrying me, in a scarf like a sling, so I was held close to her front. It's so practical and cosy and keeps babies very warm and happy!

"Other things we'd do were collecting wood for the fire, for cooking out of doors; go hare-coursing, and rabbitting, and searching for berries and fruits to eat.

"There was quite enough to do making a living in our own way.

"Now we use ordinary shops to supplement our food — but a nice blackbird's still a great delicacy to us gipsies!"

IT'S obvious that the gipsy way of life is pretty far removed from the usual sort, and I wanted to find out whether Sherry thought the gipsies did anything else that made their lives different.

"Well," she pondered, "I think we're a bit more formal than other people. Gipsies tend to be very old-fashioned even in the way they talk to each other — they really look down on bad language

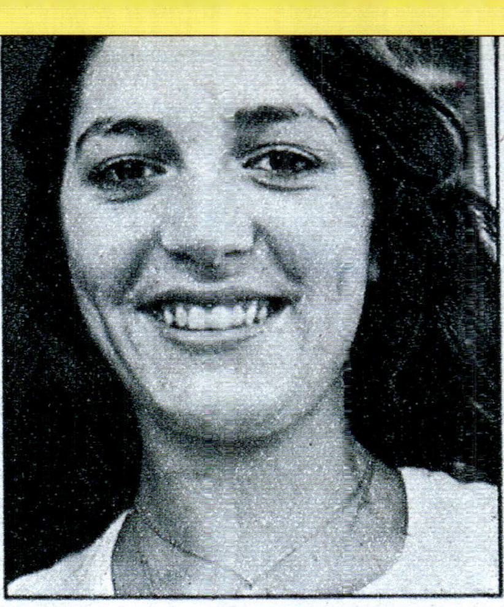

— and it certainly comes out when it comes to boyfriends.

"We're not really supposed to have boyfriends at all!"

It's pretty difficult to imagine getting married without having gone out with at least one or two boys beforehand, but gipsies have their own customs regarding arranging a wedding.

"It's called 'jumping the broomstick'," Sherry explained. "What that means, is a gipsy boy and girl decide they're going to get married to each other, and they just run off and spend a few days together.

"That proves to everyone that they're formally engaged!"

I asked Sherry what a gipsy wedding was like, because with their unconventional courting habits I wouldn't have thought they'd go in for the normal sort of wedding, either!

"Well, in fact, we tend to have more weddings in church now than we used to," Sherry said.

"Before, though, the couple were just accepted as being married once they'd spent some time together, and that was that!"

As well as marriage customs, gipsy families have very definite beliefs about death.

"If a travelling gipsy dies inside a caravan, for instance," Sherry told me, "then the whole caravan and all his things have to be burnt. If he dies outside, though, then only his clothes are burnt.

"And would you like to know about some more customs to do with the way we live? There are lots about quite simple things like doing the washing. We have quite a ritual about it!

"First the tea towels have to go in, then the tablecloths, then the underwear — all strictly separate!

"And when a gipsy woman's doing the cooking, she wouldn't dream of not having her hair tied back. If she's so much as got a sore on her hands, someone else has to take over the job.

"We aren't allowed any animals inside our caravans, either. So you see, these customs are all for quite practical, hygienic reasons!

"And we go in a lot for herbal cures when anything's wrong — the older gipsies are still very suspicious of doctors and your sort of remedies.

"When it comes to having their babies, the women tend to go off without the help of hospitals and midwives. My mother wouldn't have dreamed of anything else!"

MOST of Sherry's time, I could see, was taken up with the business of living. But gipsies have to have holidays like anybody else, and since Sherry's family travelled around so much anyway, I wondered where on earth they could go for a change!

"Oh, to the big fairs!" she told me. "They have them at Doncaster, Epsom, Newcastle — and though they aren't run by real gipsies, but by people we call 'showmen,' we all use them as a chance to get together!

"Of course some gipsies do work there, telling fortunes and doing things like that, but for most of us it's a great holiday! Even though we often move around the country in groups, a fair's a place where you can meet all your family and friends."

Since her family have stopped moving around now, Sherry's life's changed a bit, of course. One important thing is that she's now learnt to read and

write — which she couldn't do two years ago.

The site she's on has a special teacher for gipsies who didn't go to school. Sherry also does more of the things that interest other girls of her age — going to the pictures, discos, etc.

And she's got more chance to develop interests in the pop world — she's become a great Bay City Roller fan!

"I've got lots more friends outside the gipsy world now," she told me. "It's much nicer really, visiting houses and seeing how people live without caravans!"

Despite a more ordinary sort of life now, though, Sherry's gipsy roots still go deep. She's enjoying the comforts of a more permanent existence, but when I asked her what she'd like to do later on she answered without hesitating, "Oh, I'd like to go off travelling again!"

20 Ways to keep a secret

ANOTHER IN OUR EMERGENCY KIT SERIES

1. If you really *must* tell someone, send it in a letter to your great-aunt in Australia. For those who don't have a Great-Aunt in Australia, write it to yourself — have fun reading it when the postman brings it!

2. Try catching a bad cold and losing your voice!

3. Make up something which is twice as interesting and leak that instead (better not mention any names, though, or you'll end up in worse trouble!).

4. Learn an obscure foreign language, then you can shout it to as many people as you like and they won't understand a word!

5. Enjoy hogging it to yourself — keep your friends guessing. Be annoying, giggle a lot and look very knowing!

6. Keep it safe under your woolly hat, in your woolly head.

7. You could always hit yourself on the head, in an attempt to lose your memory (if it's worth forgetting everything else for one secret!).

8. If you can help it — don't listen to any secrets!

9. You can hint subtly, but don't go too far.

10. Faithfully — that way you'll keep your friends too!

11. Convince yourself that you're a secret agent, and that wild horses or even Chinese tortures couldn't drag it out of you!

12. Hire a Securicor man to escort you round and dissuade anyone from asking you questions.

13. Think about how much you'd hate people to know about it, if it was your secret!

14. Confide in the cat, if no one else.

15. When someone tells you a secret, exchange one of yours — that way you risk something if you tell!

16. Write it down, put it in a bottle and throw it into the sea — then you're rid of it without hurting anyone (imagine the fun they'll have when they get hold of it in Norway or America!).

17. When you see a gossipy friend on the horizon, put a paper bag over your head and make a run for it.

18. Develop a reputation for always telling stories . . . whoppers . . . so if you do tell anyone, they won't believe you!

19. Wear a balaclava over your mouth, then you can't be bothered to tell — it isn't worth a faceful of wet wool.

20. Shout it from the top of the nearest windy hill top!

STARSKY OR

It's no secret that Starsky and Hutch, alias Paul Michael Glaser and David Soul come out top of everyone's list of favourite men at the moment! But — imagine the lovely situation if you had to choose between them. Which one would you choose? And which one would be right for you? Are you and Starsky made for each other? Or are you the perfect girl for Hutch? To find out who's right for you — and to discover some secrets of your personality — try our special quiz. Everyone's bound to win a prize!

1. If you were lucky enough to get the star treatment, what sort of actress do you think you'd be?
(c) You'd only appear in really glamorous, feminine roles. If your career looked like ruining a big romance, you'd quite happily give it all up for love.
(a) You'd go after realistic parts in films, and you'd try to be very liberated in your outlook. In your private life, too, you'd make sure you had a few good, close friends.
(b) You'd like to be the sort of actress who could do really funny parts as well as the more serious ones — and you'd make sure you'd have lots of fun doing both!

2. If you wanted to get a boy really interested in you, would you try —
(a) the friendly approach — finding out about all the things you've got in common,
(b) the traditional method — letting him make the first move and generally do all the running,
(c) the vampire method — charm, sex appeal and looking fantastically beautiful all the time?

3. Which of these types of boy do you admire most?
(b) One who makes it to the top all by himself.
(c) One who has a really strong personality.
(a) One who has very high principles, especially about right and wrong.

4. To which of the following places would you take your dream boy?
(c) A lively youth club.
(a) A small, friendly restaurant.
(b) A disco.

HUTCH – WHO'S THE ONE FOR YOU?

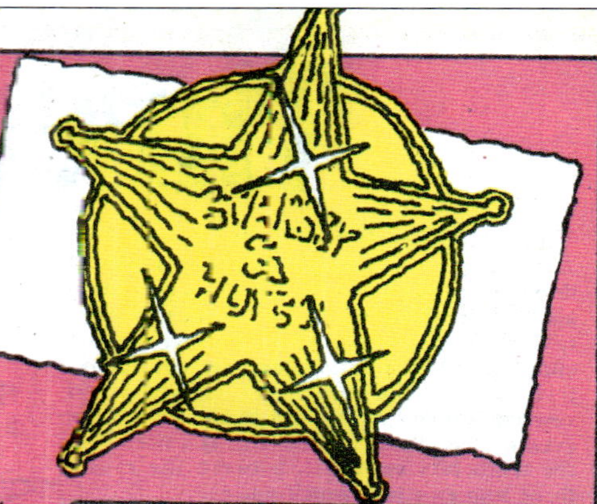

5. When would you feel happiest?
(a) Surrounded by people you care for, and with whom you feel totally at ease.
(b) Sitting with your feet up, relaxing completely, maybe just reading a book or generally pottering about.
(c) Doing something wild and free — like driving along in a fast car with the wind whipping your hair.

6. If you were to fall into a fortune and suddenly become a millionairess overnight, would you —
(c) enjoy your money and be carefree with it while it lasted, living only for the present,
(b) have a glorious spendthrift time, splashing out on minks, yachts, diamonds, champagne and generally spread some happiness around you,
(a) be really confused — you wouldn't really know what to do with it all?

7. If your boyfriend got into a fight, would you think —
(a) he's probably been forced into it,
(b) he's a fool,
(c) he knows how to stick up for himself when he has to?

8. How much do "sweet nothings" mean to you?
(a) Quite a bit — you want to be told how much he loves you.
(c) You don't need to talk about love all the time, as long as *you* know he cares deep down.
(b) You can take them or leave them — and anyway, it depends on how sincerely he says them.

9. If you had an hour to spare would you be most likely to spend the time —
(c) leaping round your room doing yoga or keep fit exercises,
(b) doing two or three things at once and, if you've been very good, maybe finish one of them!
(a) curled up with a book, or listening to music?

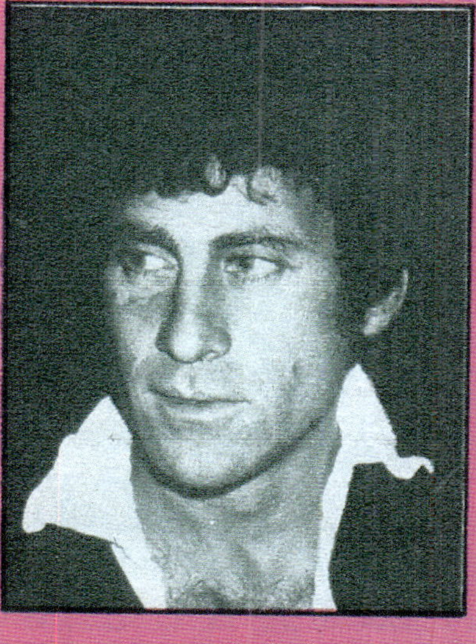

10. What do you think of family life and family get-togethers in general?
(b) It has its appealing side, but it can be a bit wearing at times!
(a) Smashing — all warm and cosy. There's nothing to beat a really close family.
(c) It's fine in moderation, as long as it doesn't tie you down too much.

11. Everyone has *some* faults. Which of the following are nearest your own?
(a) Moodiness and patches of depression.
(b) Defensiveness — it takes you ages to decide to treat someone as a friend.
(c) Restlessness — you get bored very easily.

12. What kind of romance would appeal to you most?
(b) The crazy, whirlwind kind — so strong that there can be no doubt about it lasting.
(a) Where you start off as just good friends and then gradually, with a slow sense of excitement, realise that you're falling in love.
(c) The instant attraction kind, where you find out you've got loads in common and your personalities are perfectly matched, too.

13. Which of the following heroines would you have most liked to be?
(a) Florence Nightingale.
(b) Joan of Arc.
(c) Queen Elizabeth I.

CONCLUSIONS

Mostly A
You and Hutch were made for each other! You're tender and romantic and only real, true love is good enough for you!

Because you are emotionally very honest and your feelings go very deep, you look for deep communication and understanding in relationships. You want a soul-mate, a true friend and a romantic lover all in the same person — that's why you go for the Hutch type!

And he'd love you too, because you've got everything he wants in a girl — gentleness, sensitivity of feeling, a brain as well as a pretty face and, most important of all you have your own thoughts and opinions. You also have the inner strength to do your own thing and even although you are independent, you're never aggressive, never boastful or pushy, but always quiet and understated.

You and Hutch would really hit it off perfectly. You have the same tastes and you like the same things. You'd enjoy quiet evenings with a few close friends instead of empty, superficial fun at a wild party.

Emotionally, you're great for each other — you'd help each other through moods and bad patches, and you'd bolster up each other's confidence because you're both inclined to be shy and to lose faith in yourselves sometimes.

Alone in your love nest, the trappings of success wouldn't bother you, and you'd be happy whether you were rich or poor, for neither of you holds much store by the money god.

Love, not money or success, would make your world go round together!

Mostly B
Maybe you were just born lucky, but in your case B stands for both Starsky AND Hutch's girl!

You've got such a likeable personality — you've got lots of charm and you're such fun to be with — that you're sure to be popular with just about everyone you meet. Laughter and enjoying life mean a lot to you, and you like to see everyone happy all of the time.

You're so easy-going that you can adapt to any situation that crops up — even the most difficult ones. You've got a thousand faces — you can change personality with the coat you're wearing and if you're with Hutch, you'll be everything he wants — fluent, witty, charming and generally nice to know. A quick change into a tracksuit and you're wild, free and fun-loving — everything Starsky could ask for, in fact!

You hate violent scenes and you can't stand argument or disagreement of any sort. You love the quiet life and would prefer to bow down and do what other people want, rather than stand up and be yourself.

Starsky and Hutch would both be very attracted to you. You've got a very fragile, feminine air of defencelessness about you that makes most boys fall under your spell sooner or later.

You should be yourself more, though, and not hide behind a mask. Then, once you've decided who you really are and what you really want out of life, you can take your pick — Starsky or Hutch (some people really ARE born lucky!).

Mostly C
Starsky's the one for you! You're just the type he goes for — fun and sociable, with lots of character and confidence.

Like him, you look for variety and adventure, and, although you are basically sensible, you're not afraid to take reasonable risks because of your great zest for life.

You need someone like Starsky, someone's who's great company, a bit of a tearaway at times and who's full of ideas, energy and enthusiasm to make you feel really alive and happy. You've got the verve to keep up with him and to share his love of nature and the great outdoors, and you also have the strength of character to put up with him when he's difficult.

He's the first to admit that he's not always the easiest person to get along with, but because you've got a great deal of patience and understanding, you'll be able to cope. You're emotionally strong, so that even if he seems to lead you a merry dance sometimes, you'll have the faith to sit it out until he calms down and comes to his senses.

Starsky will need and value the stability you give him, and the atmosphere of security you create for him. He'll love your unaffectedness and your lively, outgoing personality.

Perhaps he won't always be other people's idea of the romantic dream but you can be certain of one thing — underneath that rough, tough exterior, he's really very soft-hearted, tender and loving — and you're just the girl to bring it to the surface!

HOW WOULD YOU LIKE TO CELEBRATE THE SILVER JUBILEE?

ON-THE-SPOT INTERVIEWS —

where our roving reporters find out what *you* think

Aileen Mcilwaine, Bathgate, West Lothian.
I'd like to go down to London and have Leo Sayer take me out to dinner in a smart London restaurant to celebrate the Jubilee. But first I'd go to a top beauty salon and have my hair and face done. Then off to buy a new dress for the occasion!

Judy Sinclair, New Malden, Surrey.
By designing a Jubilee T-shirt. There are certainly a lot of Union Jack T-shirts around, so one with the Queen's head on would go down well.

Mandy Craig, Newcastle upon Tyne.
I'd like to go to London and see the Queen, like the pussy cat in the nursery rhyme! I really would though! I'd like to see the Queen in her coach and wearing the crown and all the robes like at the Coronation. I've seen films of it with all the soldiers in their shining uniforms — but I'd love to see it for real.

Brenda Dixon, Warrington, Cheshire.
I'd like to celebrate with a barbecue and a bonfire with a huge firework display with all silver coloured fireworks!

Maggie King, London N10.
It would be nice to get a bit of the feeling of what it was like twenty-five years ago. I expect we'll get a few old television programmes, anyway! But for instance, if shops took down all their modern adverts and put old-fashioned ones up just for Jubilee Week, that would be a nice way to celebrate.

Janet Parker, Windsor, Berks.
By giving the Queen a year's holiday! She has one of the most demanding jobs in the world, and it would be kinder to give her some time to herself, rather than make her attend hundreds of Jubilee celebrations.

Brian Rowe, London SE6.
If we're going to do it we mustn't be half-hearted. There should be lots of flags and decorations and bands playing and people getting together and having fun! Not just a few old mugs and tea-towels!

David Essex.
I'm really into street parties and it would be a great idea to have one in the East End of London. But it might be a bit difficult if it started to get mobbed. As it is I'll probably celebrate the Jubilee down on the beach at my secret holiday hideaway!

Paula Tremayne, Blandford, Dorset.
I'd like to buy myself a silver charm bracelet and a silver cross. That would make it a special year for me, as well as the Queen!

Ann Tennant, London E17.
I'd like everyone to really decorate the town, clean all the grotty buildings, get everyone to paint up their own houses — in other words, do something that will last.

Marion Oakley, Petersfield, Hampshire.
By buying one of those large Jubilee mugs and filling it with champagne and drinking the Queen's health!

Debbie Owens, Newcastle upon Tyne.
I'd like a street party. Actually, we had a festival last year in Newcastle and lots of streets had parties on the last day of it. It was great — there were sword dancers, everybody made cakes or sandwiches, and there was a fancy dress parade, a pram race, and a potato race. I hope it's like that for the Jubilee!

Tina Rainbow, Aylesbury, Bucks.
My mum said that at the Coronation there were street parties, and people put long trestle tables and chairs all down the middle of the street, and she had jelly and blancmange in the street. I think that sounds a nice idea, but I don't know how you could arrange it — you'd have to keep the cars out of the street for a start!

Jane Holmes, Chester.
I'd like to celebrate by taking a tour of the Commonwealth, the way the Queen did recently.

Paul Fanshawe, Portland, Dorset.
I'd buy two silver goblets each inscribed with the year of the accession to the throne and the present year. It'd be rather a nice memento of the Silver Jubilee Year and something you could hand down through the family.

Zoe Eton, Sheffield.
I suppose each city should club together and give the Queen something silver, but I expect she's got plenty of that. Perhaps we'll just wave our flags and look happy!

John Christie.
I'm not going to do one particular thing to celebrate the Jubilee but I am determined to pay more attention to the country's heritage in the way of works of art. I'm going to visit as many museums, art galleries, historical buildings etc. as I can here in London, and when I'm out of town, I hope to have the time to visit some of Britain's fabulous stately homes and castles.

Linda Clark, Ayrshire.
I'd really like to make a parachute jump for the Silver Jubilee!

Hazel Sneller, Hastings, Sussex.
I'd like to spend an evening out in style with Prince Michael of Kent. I think he's very good-looking and he always seems to be smiling in photographs, so he must be a nice person.

Karen Thompson, Newcastle upon Tyne.
Have a day off school! Sit in front of the telly and eat a large box of chocolates — all strawberry creams! I would like to see the celebrations in London, but I hate crowds. So I'll just sit at home with my little Union Jack and wave it at the telly!

Anne Roberts, Leeds, West Yorkshire.
I'd like to go to one of those parties in the middle of the street where everyone is invited, the way they used to do — and I'd like to be the centre of attraction by being dressed all in silver!

1. Be a reporter for a national Sunday newspaper!

2. Get involved in deep conversation with your best friend's boyfriend and ask him how he feels about you (but be prepared to lose your best friend!).

3. Be seen standing outside the Register Office with a piece of confetti in your hair.

4. As your friends arrive round for coffee late one evening, let them catch you hurriedly changing out of a long white satin evening gown.

5. Let it be known that you slapped Britt Ekland's face!

6. Dress differently — wear enveloping black coats, black wide-brimmed hats, and carry gold accessories. If you look weird, people are *bound* to start spreading scandal about you!

7. Go shopping with your cousin who's staying with you for a holiday (they're not to know that this tall, dark handsome stranger is only your cousin).

8. Be very elusive — flit about from place to place so that your friends can only guess what you're up to.

9. Never ever give anyone the full details of your private life. Instead, just hint at it mysteriously.

10. Ask the baddest bad boy in town to take you out (if he says "no", call him all the worst names under the sun — that should still cause a scandal).

11. Black rim your eyes with Kohl, and say you can't sleep because of all this dreadful scandal going on about you.

12. Get yourself a motor-bike and zoom home really late every night . . . loudly!

13. Don't tell people that you heard it from a friend who heard it from a friend who heard it from a friend who heard it from . . . !

14. Start a nudist colony in your back garden (maybe you'd better wait till the height of summer, though!).

15. Let a book on "Travelling by camel across Morocco" fall out of your handbag at an appropriate moment.

16. Start loud, violent arguments with your boyfriend, in public (watch out though — you'll start the scandal, but he'll finish with you!).

17. Burst into tears in front of as many people as possible, and swear you'll never speak to David Soul again.

18. Push your aunt's new baby through the town on a busy Saturday afternoon, and when you meet your friends, say, "Don't you think he/she has my big blue eyes?"

19. Chalk it up on the biggest wall you can find . . . and sign it!

20. Wear a plain gold ring on a ribbon round your neck and refuse to tell anyone where you got it!

HAVE YOU GOT STYLE?

Continued from page 5

ALL THE LATEST!

HERE are just some of the latest styles to come from top London stylists . . . you may not find exactly the right look for you, but they may give you — and your hairdresser! — some ideas to work from.

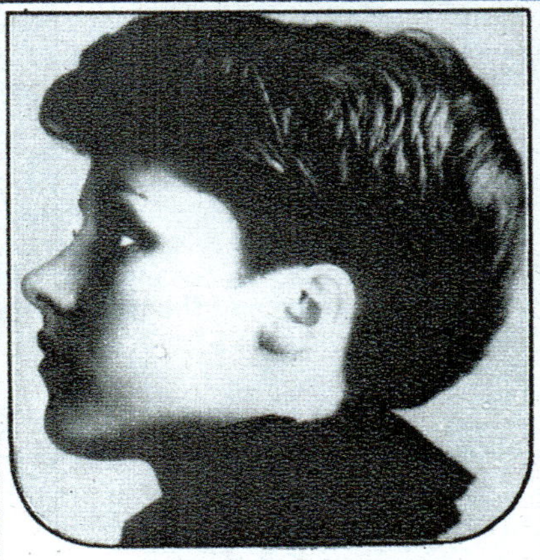

Short Cuts vary enormously and the type of short cut that's right for you may depend on your hair type and the thickness and condition of your hair.

1. This style is called 'The Elf', and was created by Leslye of Mane Line, Savile Row, London W1. She used a light perm to give the extra body necessary for this shape and highlighted the hair with Golden Bronze colour.

2. This is a softer short cut created by the Steiner Styling Team. The hair was geometrically cut to suit the model's features and then blow-waved to give a soft, feminine look. Extra body was added with a Steiner 'Swurl'. Steiner Glo-Ahead gives the hair a warm, shiny look.

Long Locks need careful attention, too, and there *are* lots of things a hairdresser can do, especially for evenings.

This style for longer hair was created by Jingles of Baker Street, using La Maur Apple Pectin shampoo and conditioner and a light Apple Pectin perm to add soft curls to fall to the shoulders.

Longer Hair needs to be beautifully cut and kept in tip-top condition if they're going to look great all the time.

1. The style on the left was created by Susie of Andre Bernard Hair International on very fine, straight hair, permed with Schwarzkopf Natural Styling *before* cutting. After neutralising, a Schwarzkopf Toning was applied and the hair was precision cut and brushed into the style without being blow-dried at any stage.

2. The style on the right, also by Susie, was created on hair that was naturally wavy at the front only. The back hair was precision permed then cut and brushed into shape for a fuller, softer effect. The natural and permed hair blend perfectly — so no-one can tell the difference.

Soft and Curly styles are very flattering and very right for the latest autumn looks.

1. Linda at Sissors, 69a Kings Road, Chelsea, came up with this softer variation of a geometric shape. She permed the fringe and the back for a soft, curly look, cutting the fringe quite far back to emphasise the model's cheek-bones.

2. Soft, natural curls are usually very flattering and this one's a perfectly balanced style created by the Steiner Styling Team. A Steiner Temperate Wave gives body and a soft, natural curl, leaving the top hair straight and shiny.

So there you are . . . ideas for all sorts of different styles for all lengths of hair. So be bold and make up your mind to have a style of your very own!

A Reader's True Experience

It can't always be as bad as this

HAVE you ever noticed when grown-ups want to blame or excuse you for something they come out smugly with the sure fire favourites—'Oh, it's only a phase—' or 'Don't worry you'll get over it—' etc. etc.

Unintentionally they even make it worse.

Well, how do they know? How do they know the blues and frustrations I'm going through right now? Because they've lived through it too? But not *my* blues, not *my* frustrations, they belong to me alone.

Monday morning, ugh. School and school dinners, the usual round of boring lessons taught by crab-apple teachers who taught my mother, or someone so groovy and cool it just isn't true.

It isn't fair either. Why should some of them look like that?

Making the difference between us more pointed, as if it weren't bad enough. We're lucky to get away with a trace of mascara—and then there's the gruesome dull grey uniform which makes us all look like convicts.

I didn't always feel like this. At first I thought it was wonderful to be urged to stay on at school, take 'A'-Levels, after I'd done well in my 'O'-Levels. I was swept along on my teacher's enthusiasm, the glittering prospect of all the opportunities that would be open to me dangling before me like so much bait.

And I was hooked. Hooked with all the noble phrases like a good education being an insurance policy for the future, how those who left at the earliest chance would regret it later etc. etc.

The bitterness hadn't crept into my life then. The resentment I felt at not being able to do what my friends were doing, the basic necessity of a few shillings in my pocket they all took for granted, and had to be budgeted carefully if I was to last out the week. It's funny how jealous you can get over a few midis and the odd maxi!

They tell me sometimes it isn't all honey, being at work. There are still crab-apple faces, and the boss's ulcer and the smart secretary who treats you like so much dust to be swept under the carpet . . .

And then they tell me how lucky I am, to have ten weeks' holiday every year, and all those half-terms and so on. They've already forgotten the homework, the pressures to pass the exam . . . or else you've been wasting time, your parents' money, the country's education system, your own life . . .

I sit and dream sometimes, of how it would be if I had a job, and could buy the clothes I wanted, instead of having to beg my mother for every little thing and wait for birthdays and Christmas.

I do have a week-end job but the 'A'-Level course is so exhausting, I'm afraid I don't have much enthusiasm for it by Saturday. All I want to do then is spend the morning in bed, and forget, let myself unwind.

But I know that isn't fair. My parents are paying in the long run for my extra two years at school, and what then? Suppose my results are good enough for me to be offered a place at college? They'll want me to take it, I know. They'll be willing to make more sacrifices to let me stay on.

Sometimes I almost wish I hadn't been born with brains and I could just have left school with a couple of exam passes to my credit, and that was that. Like lots of my friends. It sounds arrogant talking like that but I don't mean it to.

Unwillingly, I have to admit some of them envy me. Some have told me they wished they had stuck it out too. It's hard to see them changing from kids like me to self-confident, trendy girls and know that I'm still the same. Except inside.

Inside I'm as mixed-up as it's possible to be. I *know* I have to do my best, and one day I'll look back and thank them for not letting me give in when the blue moods take over.

Perhaps when the blue mood has passed I'll laugh at it all, but right now it seems as if the days when you're young go so fast, and mine are all being spent in studying and there's this big chunk of life whizzing past me.

GO WEAR

1. Head for the swimming pools and the tennis courts – because sportswear in light, cool fabrics is hot summer news!
Red swimming goggles, from Badges & Equipment. Price: £2.25.
Loose white string top, with hood, from Jonathan Miller. Price. £5.99. Sizes: Small, medium, large.
White shorts, with back patch pockets, from Marks & Spencer. Price: £2.99. Sizes: 12-18.
Green ankle socks, from Mary Quant. Price: 65p. One size.
Bright green training shoes, with white laces, from Dolcis. Price: £6.50-£6.99, depending on size. Sizes: 3-10.
Roomy, navy plastic satchel, with gold trim, from Way In at Harrods. Price: £6.15.
White cricket jumper, with striped trim, carried over arm, from Stirling Cooper. Price: £5.99. Sizes: Medium only.

2. Going to work? Cheer everyone up by wearing something pretty but smart!
Small-brimmed straw hat, with pretty flower trim, from Charles Batten. Price: £5.00. Sizes: Small, medium, large.
Cool, natural-coloured apron dress, with two patch pockets and "Emanuelle" print across one, from Emanuelle. Price: £13.95. Sizes: 10-14.
Natural woven espadrilles, with low wedge and ankle ties, from Saxone. Price: £3.99. Sizes: 3-8.
Brown "bucket" bag, with stripy trim, from Peter Robinson. Price: £4.95.

3. Shopping can be really tiring – especially if you're not dressed for it! Wear something that looks good, and feels good, too . . . like this year's version of the eternally fashionable shirt and jeans.
Shades of pink candy-striped collarless shirt, with matching tie belt at waist, from Simon. Price: £7.99. Sizes: Small, medium, large.
Pink straight-legged jeans, from Kobi. Price: £14. Sizes: 10-14.
Hessian sandals, with leather trim and woven wedge soles, from Trueform. Price: £6.99. Sizes: 3-8.
Circular wicker shopping bag, with big round handles, from Bridgebags. Price: £4.99.

STOCKISTS ON PAGE 28

YOU PLEASE!

Fashion's so much fun, and there are so many new looks around, that there's something to suit everyone – wherever they are! Go your own way, in your own favourite style. . . and be a fare lady!

4. For the bright, lively girl who's at college, and likes to look a little different, here's a cheerful outfit which is practical and suits her life style.
Bright red safari shorts suit, with button fastening and tie belt, from Eagle. Price: £12.95. Sizes 1, 2, 3.
Short-sleeved T-shirt with multi-coloured zig-zag print, from Jonathan Miller. Price: £5.50. Sizes: Small, medium, large.
Red lace-up boots, with rope soles, from Saxone. Price: £6.99. Sizes: 3-8.
Red visor, from Charles Batten. Price: £2.99. One size.
Round sunglasses, with fine metallic rims, from Corocraft. Price: £4.50.

6. Be beautiful for your boyfriend in a flouncy petticoat skirt with a camisole top – just the look he'll love!
Brilliant orange lace-up camisole top, from Mary Quant. Price: £9.45. Sizes: 10, 12.
Pretty, tiered petticoat skirt, with beaded tie belt and contrasting top-stitching, from Marks & Spencer. Price: £6.99. Sizes: 12-18.
Navy-blue high-heeled sandals, with peep toe and flower trim, from Dolcis. Price: £9.99. Sizes: 3-8.

5. When you visit your friends, you can wear your very latest fashion look. Be right in style, with the newest, shorter than short skirt lengths, in your favourite bright colours!
Skin-tight, white, V-necked sleeveless T-shirt, from Marks & Spencer. Price: £1.50. Sizes: 32/34, 36/38, 40/42 in.
Small leather pouch purse, from a selection at any large department store, or chain fashion shop.
Super red corduroy mini skirt, from Strawberry Studio. Price: £9.95. Sizes: 10-14.
Cool white espadrilles, with peep toes and string trim, from Littlewoods. Price: £4.99. Sizes: 3-8.

The Cathy and Claire Page

We can't promise the perfect solution, but we'll do our best. If you're stuck with a problem and you can't see the way out, write to us at this address: Cathy & Claire, Jackie, 12 Fetter Lane, Fleet Street, London EC4A 1BL.

DEAR CATHY AND CLAIRE — I went out with this boy Stephen a couple of times, but he was really draggy so I finished with him. Then I met this super bloke called Craig, and we hit it off right away. We've been going around for two months and last week I was invited to Sunday tea at his house.

His mum was very friendly and seemed to take to me. She said she was pleased Craig had found a nice girl, as her other son had had a hard time from a girl who had treated him very badly.

At teatime, Craig's brother came in and I could have died — it was Stephen! He looked a bit shocked at seeing me, but didn't say anything. But I'm sure he'll tell his mum who I am, and I won't be welcome there again.

The thing is, I never realised Stephen was really keen on me, and I never meant to hurt him. He just wasn't my type.

Then that's a point in your favour when you bring the subject up with Craig and Stephen's mother — as you're bound to do, because it's obviously bugging you, even though Stephen may not have said anything.

Now she's met you, Stephen's mother can obviously see that you're not hard and heartless — though Stephen may have felt you were because you didn't fancy him as much as he did you. Tell her this, stress that the romance was never serious, you'd only been out a couple of times; and you'd no idea Stephen had taken it so badly.

Craig's mum sounds a sensible person, and probably won't hold it against you — in fact, your honesty will probably convince her you're not a villainess — but as nice as Craig thinks you are!

DEAR CATHY & CLAIRE — I've been going out with Barry for nearly a year. Well, sort of, I mean, we go out for five or six weeks, then he breaks it off and says he doesn't want to see me again. A week later, he's ringing me up and saying can't we get back together again, and then it's all right — for another six weeks.

A couple of times *I* rang *him* and suggested we made it up, but he didn't want to know. Then a week later he seemed to come round. I do love him, but I'm fed up with this on-off state of affairs.

Could be you'll have to accept it, love — your Barry's showing the classic "I don't want to be tied down" symptoms, even though he keeps coming back to get re-tied!

Trouble with boys in this frame of mind, is that they have to feel they're running the show — if you start pushing them, they cool right off. (Look what happened when *you* suggested getting together again instead of waiting for him to suggest it.)

Next time he breaks it off, you could try finding yourself another boy in the interval. If Barry acts indignant, you can be equally indignant — why shouldn't you find someone else if it's all over with you and him? That might make him think twice before shooting off again. Or it *might* send him off for good!

That's what you've got to decide — whether you can love him the way he is, or whether you're willing to risk a permanent break-up in your effort to put an end to things as they are now.

Only you can tell which you'd rather be without . . .

DEAR CATHY & CLAIRE — Why are all boys so horrible? I must have been out with fifteen or so in the past year, and never with any of them more than twice. The reason is that they all want to go too far, and when I say no, they get all offended and that's the last I ever see of them.

I *want* a boyfriend, but I just don't believe any more that there's such a thing as a nice, decent boy.

Stand by to get lots of angry letters from our thousands of readers with nice, decent boyfriends!

Seriously, though, there obviously *is* something wrong with your love life. And it's not that there aren't any decent boys around — because there're plenty — it's just that you seem to attract the other sort!

If you're honest with yourself, can you pinpoint a reason for this? Boys ask you out, so you must be attractive. But do you act in a provocative way to get a boy to notice you? Do you dress fashionably, or do you exaggerate your clothes and make-up and maybe look slightly common?

Certainly there's something about you that gives boys the wrong impression — if you really can't work out what, ask a friend's opinion, and don't be offended at what you may hear!

Of course, even nice, decent boys try it on occasionally — it's just human nature. But if you spring back with loud shrieks of horror, they'll think they've mortally offended you — and won't ask you out again because they figure you won't go.

You don't have to abandon your principles, you simply have to use tact in applying them. It's possible to be gentle *and* firm. "I'm sorry, Danny, I like you a lot but I don't go in for that kind of messing around. Can't we just keep it friendly?"

Or make a joke of it. "If you're going to try the 'Me Tarzan, you Jane' bit, shouldn't you be up a tree?"

Of course, you *could* just stop going out with boys completely if you don't want this problem — but we don't think that's the best solution at all!

DEAR CATHY & CLAIRE — My boyfriend, Dave and I have been going out together for over a year now and we have a very good relationship apart from one problem.

My best friend, Margery lives next door to Dave and she is forever interfering in our affairs. Dave says that he has often seen her watching him through her bedroom window. And sometimes when he is trying to study for his exams she goes round to see him and prevents him from working for the rest of the evening.

Whenever I see Margery all she wants to talk about is Dave, Dave, Dave. I'm beginning to think that it's her who is going out with Dave rather than me!

What can we do to get her off our backs? Her behaviour is beginning to get on both our nerves.

Quite possibly, Margery doesn't realise how much her behaviour annoys you and Dave. She probably regards her interference in your affairs as her taking a friendly interest in two of her oldest and closest friends.

But it does sound very much as though Margery doesn't have a very large circle of friends or a boyfriend of her own at the moment and this could account for her almost obsessive interest in you and Dave.

One way of helping her and solving your own problem at the same time would be to go out in a crowd sometimes and include her, so that she has the chance to increase her circle of friends and meet some boys.

You'll probably find that once Margery has a boyfriend of her own to interest her, she'll pay a lot less attention to you and Dave. In fact you might begin to feel quite neglected!

DEAR CATHY & CLAIRE — Please help me, as I'm beginning to feel really depressed. My problem is quite a common one, I'm sure. I live in a small village and there's absolutely no entertainment. I do have some friends but there's nothing for us to do and we get really bored. I was wondering if it would be possible for you to give us any addresses so that we could write to people who live in foreign countries.

It would lift the monotony for us, and give us something to do in all our spare time.

We think that this is a really good idea as you'll get a lot of fun and enjoyment from hearing about life in other countries.

Here are a couple of addresses for you to write to:
Teenage Penpal Club, Falcon House, Burnley, Lancs.
International Friendship League, 3 Creswick Road, London W.3.

DEAR CATHY & CLAIRE — I know that I'm attractive, neat, tidy, slim, have good taste in clothes and keep up with the latest fashions.

The problem is, I've never been asked out by a boy in my life. I know lots of girls who aren't nearly as good-looking as me, but they're always being asked out by boys.

What's wrong with me?

Em . . . well . . . at a guess, we'd say that boys are probably put off by your high opinion of yourself. After all, they reckon, since you love yourself so much, there can't be much left over for anyone else!

So come down from your golden cloud, love, and start being a normal, friendly, warm, loving, ordinary girl — not someone who's so perfect you scare everyone off. Looks aren't everything, you know — as you're finding out to your cost . . .

DEAR CATHY & CLAIRE — A few weeks ago I found a stray kitten and brought it home. My parents weren't too keen, but they could see how I felt about Trixie, so they let her stay. Now they've decided she'll have to go. Mum says it isn't fair for her to be alone at home all day, but we can't let her out because she's too young and hasn't had any injections against disease. I know what's really bothering them is the fact that she's growing now and is getting up to a bit of mischief around the house. Mum says she feels embarrassed when people visit because there's always a "cat" smell. Can you tell me how to persuade my parents to let her stay?

No, love, we can't. Because we can see both sides of the argument. Your parents do have the kitten's interests at heart, or they could have got rid of her long ago. As we see it, you only have two alternatives, and whatever happens, your parents have the final say, because it's their house the cat's living in.

If you live in a block of flats, and have no garden of your own, it is unfair to the kitten, and in that case, we'd suggest you advertise locally to find a home for it, preferably *after* you've had her inoculated. Or perhaps you know of someone living alone, perhaps elderly, who would have the time to look after a pet. Again, it'll be easier to find a home for her, if you've already seen to the expense of her veterinary care.

If you do have a garden, you can let her out and teach her to find her own way home again. Having her neutered would mean she couldn't have any kittens herself, and therefore it would be quite safe to let her roam. That way, your house wouldn't smell quite so much, and she'd have the freedom that is her right. That's our advice, so talk it over with your folks. They may not agree, but we hope they do. Good luck.

She Won't Believe I Love Him

DEAR CATHY & CLAIRE — I've been going out with Dave for two years, since I was fourteen, so it's fairly obvious to me, at any rate, that we're serious about each other. Dave wants us to get engaged soon, but when I told my mother this she got very angry and said it's just teenage infatuation and we don't know what life's all about. She did say I can go on seeing Dave, but said she doesn't want to hear any more about an engagement.

But we *want* to get engaged. What can we do?

Quite frankly love, although you think your mother's being a bit harsh, we can understand how she must feel. You're not a little girl any more, but you're still her daughter and she'll always want what's best for you.

She wants you to get the most out of life, to enjoy yourself and have fun while you've still got the chance. She probably thinks that an engagement is as total a commitment as marriage and your fun will be restricted once you've taken this step.

It's up to you, love, to prove her wrong. You can show her that you'll still be enjoying yourself even though you're engaged. In fact, you should be happier, and having more fun, with your fiance there to share all the good times. She certainly doesn't seem to object to Dave, as she doesn't mind you going on seeing him.

Make her see that your life from now on is not going to be drastically changed, and that you're not going to be burdened for a long time yet by the financial and other problems which can often arise with young newlyweds.

In this way, your mother should realise that an engagement is all you really want and what will make you happiest.

Just one thing, though — remember that an engagement *is* a promise to marry — nothing more or less. Your mother realises this — but she's not too convinced that you do.

So before you do anything, have a good, long, think about the true meaning of, "an engagement". You might find your mother knows best, after all . . .